PELICAN BOOKS

A HISTORY OF SPAIN AND PORTUGAL

William C. Atkinson, who was born in Ireland in 1902, graduated through the universities of Belfast, Madrid, and Durham to the chair of Hispanic Studies in Glasgow from which, after a tenure of forty years, he retired in 1972. Having come, over the years, to know Spain and Portugal better than his homeland, he added Latin America to his parish and has six times over the past quarter of a century made the grand tour of that brave New World, visiting every one of its twenty countries and lecturing in almost every university of note there. In between he led a first Scottish cultural delegation to the U.S.S.R. and visited a score of universities throughout the United States. The war years saw him responsible for Spain and Portugal in what is now the Foreign Office Research Department. His first book was a history of Spain, long since out of print, and he translated for the Penguin Classics *The Lusiads* of Camoens, recently reissued. His recreations: his wife and four children, travel, tramping, and book reviewing.

A HISTORY OF
SPAIN & PORTUGAL

BY
WILLIAM C. ATKINSON

PENGUIN BOOKS

Penguin Books Ltd, Harmondsworth, Middlesex, England
Penguin Books Inc., 7110 Ambassador Road, Baltimore, Maryland 21207, U.S.A.
Penguin Books Australia Ltd, Ringwood, Victoria, Australia

—

First published 1960
Reprinted 1961, 1965, 1967, 1970, 1973

—

Copyright © William C. Atkinson, 1960

—

Made and printed in Great Britain
by C. Nicholls & Company Ltd
Set in Monotype Times

Contents

Editorial Foreword

IT is often urged that world history is best written without the limitations of frontiers, that, for example, a history of the development of Western Europe has more historical validity than 'nationalist' histories of France, Germany, the Low Countries, and Britain. Nevertheless it is national character, national development, and national power which incite the curiosity of most of us, and it is these things which seem to be behind most of the international problems with which we are faced today. Therefore, in preparing the plan of THE PELICAN HISTORY OF THE WORLD it was decided that the old and familiar emphasis upon national history has meant sufficient to justify its continuance in this series.

Each volume is written by a specialist, and the emphasis given to such matters as trade, religion, politics, foreign relations, intellectual and social life varies and must vary between volume and volume, but the interplay of nationalism is as much part of national history as internal events, and it is hoped that THE PELICAN HISTORY OF THE WORLD will be both a series of national histories and, in the true sense, a history of the modern world.

The following eight volumes have been published:

A History of the United States; Vol. 1: *Colonies to Nation;* Vol. 2: *Nation to World Power,* by J. E. Morpurgo and Russel B. Nye.

A History of Modern China, by Kenneth Scott Latourette.

A History of Modern France; Vol. 1: *Old Régime and Revolution 1715–1799;* Vol. 2: *From the First Empire to the Fourth Republic, 1799–1945,* by Alfred Cobban.*

A History of New Zealand, by Keith Sinclair.

A History of Spain and Portugal, by William C. Atkinson.

A History of Modern Japan, by Richard Storry.

J. E. MORPURGO

*Vol. 3: *France of the Republics, 1871-1962,* has since been published.

Introduction

'HAPPY the country that has no history.' Unhappy, the corollary would seem to say, those that have too much; though a distinction falls to be made between the active and rewarding experience of shaping one's destiny and the passive frustration of being shaped by it. The pages that follow attempt to deal selectively with the crowded, perhaps overcrowded, pageant of events, spanning two thousand years and more, in virtue of which Spain and Portugal, Spaniard and Portuguese, are today what they are. The story ranges widely, over Europe, Africa, the Americas, the Far East, even to Australasia. At times the action takes place too in the Peninsula, the actors Celts, Greeks, Carthaginians, Romans, Visigoths, Muslims, Flemings, Frenchmen, Germans, Englishmen. In the background, Spaniards and Portuguese; even, on occasion, in the foreground. When in the foreground their actions, to the curious onlooker, often take a lot of explaining, and can still seem inexplicable by any ordinary criteria of logic or self-interest.

For it is one of the paradoxes of their history that these two peoples have consistently seemed surer of themselves when engaged in imposing their will on others beyond their frontiers than when at the helm of their own affairs behind the Pyrenees. The incident is a hundred years old, and has lost none of its pertinence, of the Spaniard who, hearing the United States ambassador to his country expound the merits and the inevitable spread of democratic government, said sadly, 'Yes, I suppose it has got to come here too. The first five hundred years will be the worst.' Behind the remark lay more than an awareness that Spaniards and Portuguese are not as other Europeans, in terms of the complexity of ethnic strains in their blood-stream and of the long tale of invasions and occupations to which they have been subject. Even more have they been put upon, and done to, in the centuries since 1492, that *annus mirabilis* that, with the ending of the 'reconquest', saw them once again, after close on eight centuries, masters in their own house and free at last, or so it seemed, to do what they would do and be what they had it in them to be.

Instead, fate led them out of the promised land, tied them to the chariot wheels of alien dynasties, engaged them in war after war not of their choosing and infinitely destructive of their true interests, and, in denying them responsibility, sapped their will-power and their competence against the day when they should be called on to act for themselves. Hence the proneness in both countries over the past century and a half to civil war, and the despairing incompatibility, to which no solution is as yet in sight, between 'progress' in the liberal western European sense and the virtues of an ordered society. 'Anarchy or hierarchy' is a grim choice: just how grim, and why still the choice, the reader who has forgotten the course of the first Portuguese or the second Spanish republic will here be reminded.

These considerations may serve to forestall one criticism. The author, concerned to present an analytical account of the forma-tion and evolution of the two peoples, to trace the slow and much bedevilled growth of their society, does not present that account as a social history. Such could have been an easier book to write: it would not have made the contribution to under-standing that the non-peninsular reader needs. If the peninsular reader has his own difficulty in understanding why his society should be as it is, and falls prey only too easily to the pessimism of that definition of nationality advanced when the 1876 con-stitution was under discussion, 'All those are Spaniards who cannot be anything else,' one reason is that he has so often been ill-served by his own historians. For to the degree that Spaniards and Portuguese have been denied government by consent they have been expected to believe the version of their country's record that authority holds good for them: in the mid twentieth century they still may not read what they will, but only what they are allowed to.

The vicious circle follows, justifying dictatorship on grounds of political immaturity and making inevitable the collapse of any such exercise in self-government as chance or uprising may provide. To say this is not to upbraid the dictator or impugn his motives. He, more than anyone, wishes he knew the answer to the dilemma: he too is the product of his country's past. Far be it from the historian, still farther from the foreign historian, to suggest the way out. His function, if he be allowed one beyond the objective telling of the tale, is to point the dilemma, and to explain whence it arose.

W. C. A.

Bearsden, June 1959

1

The Setting

SPAIN and Portugal, which have become through the vagaries of history two nations, were but one land to Romans, Visigoths, and Muslims, and remain one geographically. The Iberia of the Greeks, the Hispania of the Romans was the Peninsula which received its cultural heritage in common, grew to nationhood under the influence of common pressures, and shaped a way of life at home and a destiny abroad whose communal traits the lapse of centuries has been powerless to obscure. Nationhood is a great incentive to the affirmation of personality, even without the play of different ethnic strains and a distinctive tongue; but if one may no longer fuse, or confuse, Spain with Portugal, their divergences are still but the enrichment of an underlying unity, and neither wider nor deeper than have existed between constituent parts of the present Spanish whole. On the historian's canvas the frontier and its implications must indeed appear, though not till late in the story; the true frontiers remain the enveloping ocean and the land barrier of the Pyrenees. It is they, and the setting in space, which have made of both countries what they are.

In Europe but, thanks to the Pyrenees, for long periods doubtfully of it; drawn gravitationally towards Africa, from which it is separated by a mere dozen miles of water; facing eastward to Rome and Greece whence, in the wake of trade and conquest, were to derive its dawning civilization and culture, and westward to the great unknown, a challenge the eventual acceptance of which was to open up new continents and to add new dimensions to that other awakening we call the Renaissance: the Peninsula's peninsularity on the fringe of the old world stands out as the first determinant of its destiny. In the successive heydays of Phoenician, Greek, and Roman maritime expansion it figured inevitably as the *ne plus ultra* of their drive to the west. Celts and Visigoths alike, though at a thousand years' remove in time, sweeping south-westward from northern Europe in their great nomadic surges, found their way over or round the Pyrenees, as the Arabs, in their westward sweep across north Africa, found its momentum carry them over the straits.

So far the Peninsula was at the receiving end, schooled to passivity. There followed the centuries of struggle against the Muslim for repossession of its soil and of its soul. Success brought, with the elation of power, the awareness of being at long last in control of its own fortunes, and the wheel of fate was strikingly reversed. The Peninsula so often invaded turned invader. It carried its armies and its flag to Athens and the Near East, holding sway there for close on a century; to Italy, where its writ ran for more than twice as long; across the Pyrenees to annex the Holy Roman Empire; across the straits to found not one empire but two in Africa; westward across the ocean to incorporate in Christendom a vast new world; and southward, rounding the dark continent, to hold for a century and a half the whole gorgeous east in fee. A bridge between Europe and Africa, between Mediterranean and Atlantic, the Peninsula stands at the confluence of the ways, its civilization as complex in its givings and receivings as any in Europe, its role in history often bedevilled by the very fact of its facing so many ways at once.

Internal geography also plays its part, a large part, in the unfolding picture. The map of the Peninsula, that reminded Strabo of a bull's hide outstretched, shows a relief of average altitude second only in Europe to that of Switzerland. With the exception of the Ebro valley to the east, the Tagus-Guadiana and Guadalquivir valleys to the west, and a narrow coastal belt, all is upland; of the upland half is mountain, the hills coming almost to the sea on the north and south coasts, and much of the rest is dotted with out-croppings of rock. Rivers, though numerous, are therefore in the main short and precipitous. Rainfall is erratic and ill-distributed, the climate tends to extremes – 'Nine months of winter and three of hell' is the popular description of that of New Castile – and agriculture over wide areas wrings but an indifferent subsistence from the soil. Difficulty of communication, nature's other chief impediment, has weighed heavily in fomenting that regional particularism, loyalty to the *patria chica* to 'little fatherland', which runs through, greatly complicating, the whole of Spanish history.

Of the primitive inhabitants of the Peninsula, whose relics place them in the early stone age, comparatively little can be inferred. The cave paintings of Cantabria, best exemplified in those of Altamira which have been variously dated as between fifteen and thirty thousand years old, are confined to animals – wild horse, bison, stag, hind, ibex, boar, ox – and have their affinities north of the Pyrenees. The same animals appear in the rock-shelter art of the eastern region (Albacete to Lérida), but combined with stylized human figures admitting relation to rock-drawings in north Africa. There is evidence here of two early societies, and possibly of two distinct stocks. The Basques, sitting astride the Pyrenees, were recognized by the earliest writers on the Peninsula as differing in important respects from the other inhabitants – their language is still an enigma to philologists – and may derive from a race of aboriginal Pyrenean cave-dwellers. The others, the 'Iberians' of the same writers, are held north-African, probably Hamitic, in origin and, though only documented from the sixth century B.C., may have reached the Peninsula as early as the thirtieth. By the third, and possibly much earlier, they had spread from east and south-east to the central tableland and on into what is now Portugal.

On to this basic stock, if it be allowed as such – for as there is no fixing the date of first arrival, so there is no telling whether they found the land uninhabited or, encountering other tribes, displaced or absorbed them – there was grafted over the centuries a succession of new racial elements. A distinction is to be made here between those who came to trade, founding at most coastal settlements, and those whose aim was conquest and colonization. The former made specific contributions to the civilization of the Peninsula, the latter altered its ethnic composition and in so doing modified its whole way of life and its potentialities for the future. First among the traders were the Phoenicians, who came the length of the Mediterranean in search of the mineral wealth of that Tartessos – the Biblical Tarshish – which is sited conjecturally, no trace having survived into modern times, at the mouth of the Guadalquivir. Twenty miles away they founded their first and greatest colony in the Peninsula, Agadir, the modern Cadiz, on what for a thousand years thereafter was still an island. The date, traditionally placed about 1100 B.C., modern research would make some three hundred years later. With time there were Phoenician settlements dotted along the coasts of the Peninsula and in the Balearics, and the civilizing process had begun. The newcomers brought with their language the use of script, with their trade the use of money, and with their thirst for metals techniques in the mining of silver, copper, lead, and iron far beyond what the natives had evolved for themselves.

The Greeks, rivals with the Phoenicians for the possession of Sicily from the eighth century, carried that rivalry to the Peninsula from the base they had established at Massilia (Marseilles) about the year 600. Phoenicia was by now a waning power, and its eclipse shortly after, with the fall of Tyre to Nebuchadnezzar of Babylon in 573, transferred to Carthage its residual interest in the western Mediterranean. For the Greeks too the lure of Iberia was its mineral wealth, the copper of Río Tinto, the gold of the Sierra Morena, the silver of Cartagena; and the eastern and southern coasts were thus again the chief beneficiaries of contact with a people that gave no less than it took. The bust of 'The Lady of Elche', belonging to the post-Greek era, is the most notable of the many surviving sculptures, bronzes, and pieces of pottery that bear witness to the enriching of native by Greek art; in agriculture, vine and olive proved still more lasting contributions to an evolving pattern of life.

'Iberian', a vague if convenient label, had never served to characterize all the racial elements found by the Greeks in possession of the Peninsula. From possibly as early as 900, waves of Celts from central Europe had been making their way south by first the eastern and then the western end of the Pyrenees. The last invasion in strength took place in the early sixth century, coinciding roughly with the founding of Greek settlements along the Mediterranean coast. Phoenician and Greek maritime traders were little concerned with penetration and conquest. The Celts, expelled from their former homes, came in search of a new one, and spread over the Peninsula to the extent that they were a match in arms, being doubtfully superior now in civilization, for the tribes already in possession. These held their own in the east and south, thanks chiefly, it may be presumed, to their earlier external contacts. In the west – Galicia and Portugal – the Celts came to predominate, and the temptation remains strong to label as Celtic the most distinctive traits of the Galician–Portuguese temperament, its gentle melancholy, the yearning (*saudades*) for what has been and is not, its impracticality, its pre-eminently lyric genius. The central tableland, more sparsely populated, proved able to accommodate both races; here, with time, they fused to give the Celtiberians of the early geographers, within a whole still known as Iberia.

The brief interlude – a mere two generations – of Greek dominion in the western Mediterranean came to an end with its overthrow at the hands of Carthaginians and Etruscans in Corsica in 535. Carthage, succeeding to the role, succeeded too to its predecessor's trading hold on southern Spain – though Greek settlements on the east coast persisted and some new ones were founded, probably by refugees from Corsica – and maintained its foothold for the next two centuries and more. Archaeology has documented, through sculpture, jewelry, and ceramics, the wealth of the Carthaginians' artistic contribution, while fish-curing and the manufacture of esparto grass, no less than mining, bore testimony to their industrial gifts.

But the importance of the Carthaginian interlude lies not in the addition of one more layer to the complex of extraneous influences that was slowly shaping the Peninsula; nor in the forging of new links between the Peninsula and the continent with which its destiny has so often been bound up that some have held applicable far beyond geography the geographers' dictum of an Africa beginning in the Pyrenees; nor in the fact that the Carthaginians, using the Iberians as mercenaries, first taught them to fight over strange lands and waters. The second Punic War, a war to the death between Carthage and the rising power of Rome, was not fought for control over the Peninsula, but it was largely fought out in the Peninsula – a portent of much that time still held in store – and the coming of the Romans, with intent soon to stay and to add no mere coastal fringe but the whole to their dominions, was to prove the most important single fact in its history.

By the end of the first Punic War of 264–241 the Carthaginians, driven out of Sicily and crippled by the indemnity exacted by their victors, also found their hold on southern Spain reduced by opportunist native attacks until little save Cadiz remained. Hamilcar, initiating from there in 237 a policy of conquest which aimed both at redressing Carthage's fortunes and at providing the sinews of a renewed war against Rome, occupied or reoccupied much of the south and east and some part of the central table-land. Hasdrubal, founder of Carthago Nova (Cartagena) as a strategic fulcrum of Punic power, carried its sway still farther north to the Ebro in 226, by which time Roman suspicions were definitely aroused. Hannibal, in command in the Peninsula from 221, penetrated northwestward as far as Salamanca, his object being to intimidate the tribes throughout the land before provoking a new collision with Rome.

The spark that set off the second war in 219 was his attack on Saguntum, a fortified town midway up the east coast which Rome claimed to be under her protection. By the following year, while Hannibal's army fought in Italy, a Roman army effectively backed by a Roman fleet fought in Spain, establishing itself first north of the Ebro, then, after many vicissitudes, in Carthago Nova itself, brilliantly assaulted by the younger Scipio in 209. By 206 Cadiz, the first and last Punic base in the Peninsula, had fallen and the African was back across the straits. The native inhabitants, seeing their country thus made a battlefield for two foreign powers, had fought indifferently on either side and often indeed changed sides as the fortunes of war affected the local prestige of this leader or of that. They could not know it was their own destiny that was at issue and that the victorious Romans, treating them as the vanquished, would forthwith set about romanizing them with a thoroughness which was to make their effective history appear thereafter to have begun at this point.

2

Roman Foundations

THE moment is opportune to consider the picture presented to the Romans as they took the full Peninsula into their ken. Strabo's description, written towards the end of the first century B.C., of a land he had not himself visited is based on accounts of three earlier Greeks who had, during the last third of the preceding century, when the extension of Roman sway was already opening up the land to travellers. Poor soil irregularly watered and a general uninhabitability were the first impressions, the fertile south contrasting strongly with the hills, forests, and arid tablelands of the rest. The valley of the Guadalquivir, the exception, ranked with the richest regions to be found anywhere in the Greek world. Wheat, wine, and olive oil (this last unsurpassed in quantity and quality) were among its exports; wax, honey, fish, cochineal, wool, and esparto grass were others. Animals both domestic and wild abounded, the whole land being sorely plagued with rabbits. Minerals, found throughout the Peninsula, were again richest in the south, the deposits of gold, silver, copper, and iron moving the foreigner to wonderment. Forty thousand workers toiled in the silver mines of Carthago Nova.

'Iberians', still to Strabo a generic name for the inhabitants, covered peoples with widely differing characteristics and ways of life. With the greater natural endowment of the 'Tartessians' and its consequences in trading relations with the outside world went a higher degree of culture, including writings – poems and laws in verse – of some antiquity. Tribes in other parts also knew writing, but their alphabets varied, like their languages. The Lusitanians, occupying the territory between the Tagus and the north coast, were held to be of all Iberians the most redoubtable and were the last to submit to Rome. Their lands too were rich in crops, flocks, and metals, but the tribes were much given to fighting among themselves and to raiding their neighbours. Agile and resourceful, they were skilled in ambushes and in pursuit, and sacrificed their prisoners, reading the entrails for omens.

Across the north stretched successively the territories of Galicians, Asturians, Cantabrians, Basques, and the Pyrenean tribes, whose isolation in hilly country ill-served by communications and with a harsh climate was part cause of their inhospitable and savage nature. They too sacrificed goats, horses, captives; parricides they stoned, other criminals they hurled over cliffs. They ate goat's flesh and bread made of acorn-flour, wheat being unknown to them; they drank beer; and they used lard instead of oil as the olive did not grow so far north. Among the Cantabrians society was largely matriarchal, their customs in this respect 'if not properly civilized being not those of savages either'. Celtiberia corresponded roughly to the central uplands, where nature was generally unkind and life austere. The inhabitants were mostly forest-dwellers and preyed on settled communities within their reach, their god a moon-deity whose name was taboo.

The Iberians as a whole were warlike in disposition. They fought lightly armed, 'after the fashion of bandits', with javelin, sword, and sling. As horses were plentiful, foot and horse commonly fought together. Their bravery and ferocity in battle were proverbial, and so was their devotion to their leader, for whom they gladly laid down their lives. In adversity they would commit suicide, carrying with them for this purpose the leaves of a poisonous plant. 'Their bodies inured to abstinence and toil, their minds composed against death, all practise a stern and constant moderation,' was how Pompeius Trogus described them about the same time; 'they prefer war to ease and, should they lack foes without, seek them within. Rather than betray a secret they will often die under torment, setting a silent reserve before life itself. Active of body, restless of spirit, they commonly set more store by their horses and fighting accoutrement than by the blood of their kin.'

The collapse of Greece Strabo attributed to its division into small states and to a local pride which prevented their forming links strong enough to allow the presenting of a united front to external aggression. Pride, raised to a much higher degree and allied to a 'versatile and complex' character, was, too, the undoing of the Iberians. The fierce independence of the individual tribes, making their relationship one of continuous alarm and assault; great personal daring and hardihood, to the point of contemning death, with as its reverse the inability to make common cause against a common threat; lack of that social cohesion, fusing the many *patrias chicas* into the one *patria grande*, on which alone great enterprises can be carried through: on these rocks, says Strabo, that same independence foundered. 'Then came the Romans, conquering the tribes one by one, and although it took a long time, two hundred years or more, they at length had the country wholly under their feet.'

The process was relatively rapid in the east and south, where long experience of invasion had conditioned the natives both to the idea of alien overlordship and to respect for the civilization this had commonly connoted. There too lay the wealth which was the immediate reward, if not the immediate objective, of Rome's victory over Carthage. It was the consolidation of that victory, driving the Romans inland, which revealed the true dimensions of their undertaking. The tribes may have lacked the cohesion necessary for a big war, but *guerrilla*, 'little war', is a peninsular term for a strategy, then evolved for the first time in the Peninsula in the peculiarly favourable terrain of the central tableland, which was to prove infinitely disconcerting and costly to the orthodox commander.

In 197 B.C., nine years after the overthrow of the Carthaginians, it having become clear that the newcomers were there with the intention of staying, a first wave of revolt swept through the occupied areas, from Tartessus to the north-east coast, of a ferocity that augured ill for Roman prospects in all the territory still unsubdued. With the arrival of further legions the situation was restored two years later, though not before it had seemed possible that all might in fact be lost. Guerilla warfare continued, and became more serious as renewed attempts at penetration brought contact with the untamed and redoubtable Lusitanians and Celtiberians. By 179, when these tribes too had to all appearances been subjected, over 150,000 troops had been drafted to the conquest of this *horrida et bellicosa provincia*, whose fighting spirit had imposed on Rome the necessity for permanent military service. The peace was soon rudely shattered. In 154 a renewed confederation of the Lusitanians launched a general rising which inflicted defeat after defeat on strong Roman armies. Twice the commanders of these had to sue for peace. Rome refusing to ratify such humiliating treaties, her generals were driven to humiliations greater still, resorting to perjury, treachery, and massacre to bring low an enemy strong in his refusal to recognize when he was beaten.

No name on the Roman side in these twenty years of warfare admits comparison with that of Viriatus, the first great figure in the peninsular scroll of fame. Though born a mere Lusitanian shepherd, he was a born leader of men, and his daring sallies at the head of a small band in the mountains of Estremadura attracted others to his banner from far and wide. Surviving where most of his tribesmen perished, in a particularly ruthless massacre perpetrated by Galba under promise of peace, he became the recognized head of Lusitanians and Celtiberians and for eight years proved himself more than equal to the best armies Rome could put in the field. Honourable and chivalrous, he threw into relief equally the bad faith and the barbarity which repeatedly sullied the repute of a foe driven at last in 139, since it was no match for him in battle, to compass his assassination by bribery.

The campaigns of Viriatus had their contemporary counterpart in the defence of Numantia, the symbol of a no lesser greatness in defeat. Numantia, on the Douro near modern Soria, was a natural stronghold which for some fourteen years defied Rome and humbled its every effort at capture, until veterans and recruits alike came to dread the name and to rebel at such an assignment. In 134 it sent its greatest general, Scipio Aemilianus, with a force of 60,000 men to invest the town that even he did not feel strong enough to take by assault: its defenders numbered some 4,000. Building fortifications all around and denying it supplies, he was able after sixteen months to enter a shambles where the last survivors, having fired their homes, committed suicide rather than live to grace his triumph. The memory was to burn itself deep into the heroic consciousness of later ages. Cervantes made of it a moving play which in the War of Independence, nearly two thousand years after, inspired the defenders of Saragossa to comparable extremes of valour against Napoleon.

But for the mountainous north-west, native resistance had now, after three-quarters of a century, spent itself. It was still not the end of fighting, for once more the Peninsula was to become the battle-ground for issues not its own. The evils that eventually undermined the Roman republic can be traced back to the second Punic War, and the civil wars that accompanied its eclipse and the transition to empire were largely fought out on the same territory.

Sertorius, proscribed by Sulla, crossed to the Peninsula in 81 in answer to an invitation received either from the still restless Lusitanians or from the now numerous mixed population, offspring like himself of Roman fathers and Iberian mothers, who chafed at being denied the full status of Roman citizens and saw in the dissensions in Rome their opportunity for redress. Lusitania and the upper valley of the Guadalquivir adhered straightway to his banner. Soon he was joined by the Celtiberians of the centre and the Iberians of the north-east and, fixing his headquarters at Osca (Huesca), was able for close on two years to flout the power of Rome. Hailed as an Iberian patriot, in the succession of Viriatus, he met his end in 72 in the same way, by assassination. In fact his acceptance by the native tribes is eloquent of the extent to which they were already romanized. That clock there was no putting back, and under him the process, far from being reversed, was quickened.

A generation later, in 49 and again in 45, the grim struggle between Caesar and Pompey, who had led the final campaigns against Sertorius and, when consul, had received the Peninsula as his province, brought Caesar on to the scene, with objectives that soon outstripped the immediate personal issue. The territory between Tagus and Douro, lying still on the fringe of Rome's effective sway, Caesar was now able to subdue, and an expedition which he despatched by sea from Cadiz against the north-west coast preluded the reduction by Augustus of the last nuclei of resistance in Asturia and Cantabria. The campaign which Augustus as emperor initiated in person in 26 triumphed at length in 19. The defeated tribes were forcibly removed from their mountain fastnesses to new settlements in the plains, where Roman legionaries were settled among them, and the conquest was over. At long last the Peninsula was incorporated in fact as well as in name in the great Roman empire, and knew the Roman peace. Two centuries it had taken, and in the process not the Peninsula alone but Rome too had changed out of recognition.

Scipio, in leaving behind him in 205 one general in charge of
'nearer' and another of 'farther' Hispania, had paved the way for
the formal division of the new territories in 197 B.C. into the two
provinces of Hispania Citerior and Ulterior. Hence the frequent
reference hereafter to *Hispaniae*, a pointer to that marked plurality
which was to continue to characterize Spain for long after the
achievement of nominal unity. The two were still then essentially
coastal strips, especially Citerior, which stretched from the
Pyrenees to a little beyond Carthago Nova with a substantial
indentation up the Ebro valley. Ulterior continued along the
coast to the mouth of the Baetis (Guadalquivir); inland, this river
provided a natural dividing-line to well beyond Cordoba. By
mid-century, Rome had occupied approximately half the Peninsula, the line running through what are now Seville, Toledo,
Sigüenza, Calahorra, and Jaca to the centre of the Pyrenees.
With the Lusitanian collapse after the death of Viriatus the north-
west frontier of Ulterior was gradually advanced from the
Guadalquivir to beyond the Guadiana, to reach eventually, in
Caesar's day, the Tagus.

Not until 27, the year that marked, with the beginning of
the empire, Augustus's great administrative reform of its far-
flung provinces, was the territorial division of the Peninsula
overhauled. By then, on the eve of the final overthrow of
Asturians and Cantabrians, it had become clear that while the
empire lasted the Peninsula's future was destined to be a Roman
future; and for this Augustus's recasting of the two existing provinces as three, embracing the entire territory, served to lay the
administrative basis. The boundary of Ulterior was carried back
from the Tagus to the Guadiana, its north-eastern limits remaining as before. Renamed Baetica, the province once more centred
on the valley of the Baetis, home of the early Tartessian civilization. All that lay beyond the Guadiana, stretching north of the
Douro to include Callaecia (Galicia) and Asturia, was constituted a new province, Lusitania. In this western third of the
Peninsula lies the historic kernel of modern Portugal. The remaining province of Citerior, enlarged with the addition of Cantabria, was rechristened Tarraconensis, from Tarraco (Tarragona), seat from the beginning of Roman power in the Peninsula.
Twenty-five years later Callaecia and Asturia were withdrawn

from Lusitania and attached to Tarraconensis, so that responsibility for these still restless areas might be vested in the same command responsible for Cantabria. Lusitania's northern boundary thus receded to the Douro. It remained, like Tarraconensis, an imperial or 'armed' province, the long-since peaceful and more highly civilized Baetica being an 'unarmed' or senatorial province. Tarraconensis, covering now some two-thirds of the whole and lacking the cultural unity of the other two, was to be twice subdivided in the third century A.D., the emperor Caracalla raising Callaecia with Asturia to the rank of fourth province, called after the former of the two, and Diocletian making of the southern half of what remained a fifth, Carthaginensis. In attaching to the government of the Peninsula, as two additional provinces, the Balearic Islands and Morocco (Mauretania Tingitana), Diocletian laid the foundation of the Peninsula's later claims to sovereignty over these territories. Within the province the *conventus* was a centre of civil administration serving the surrounding district. Normally set in the largest town, its institution denoted a peaceful and stable society. It is found first in Baetica, where four were defined by Augustus, and last in Tarraconensis, Augustus's new settlement of Caesaraugusta (Saragossa) on the upper Ebro making there a third to Tarraco and Carthago Nova.

Administration in the Peninsula evolved initially by trial and error. The new territories were declared on conquest to pertain to the state, and compensation for the cost of their acquisition was sought both in the exploitation of their economic resources – mines being either worked by the state or leased on a royalty basis – and in the tribute exacted from all save the most privileged communities as rent for their lands, this being payable at once in money, in kind, and in compulsory military service. Not until the fall of Numantia did the process of romanization, as distinct from exploitation, get formally under way.

Here Sertorius, paradoxically, was a major influence in the liberalizing of policy. Fighting against Rome, he set himself to win over and hold the tribes by the recognition that they too had rights, including the right to such benefits of a superior civilization as Rome could give. Eloquent of this attitude was his founding at Osca of a school where the sons of chiefs received training in Latin, Greek, and what we should now call civics. Caesar learnt the lesson and, having vanquished Pompey and his cause, addressed himself to the creation of townships endowed with charters which, in the measure of their approximation to the status and privileges of Roman citizenship, rewarded the loyal, attracted the waverers, and set before the tribes a specific goal of social achievement.

This was to prove the chief means thereafter whereby the country would be gradually, and in the end wholly, won to the Roman way of life. The new townships fell into two main categories, 'colonies' and 'municipalities', the former for Romans or Italians, the latter for natives. Ex-soldier communities in frontier or lately pacified areas served a semi-military purpose at the same time as they exemplified the gains to be derived from acquiescence in the new order. Civilian colonies, peopled by the overspill of the population at home, irradiated the habits and the standards the newcomers had brought with them throughout regions the more easily permeated after long experience of Roman rule.

Varied inducements – reductions in tribute, grants of land, more efficient justice, ocular evidence of the benefits that flowed from life lived as the Romans lived it – made membership of a *municipium* a high privilege for the native and gradually won the tribes to that collective, settled conception of society which constituted the prerequisite for effective government. Caesar's concern was, too, to implant through local self-government a sense of civic responsibility as the concomitant of civic privilege, and the tale of his settlements is correspondingly long. By the time of Augustus there were in Baetica nine colonies and ten *municipia* with Roman rights and twenty-seven townships with Latin rights. Tarraconensis had twelve colonies, thirteen *municipia*, and a score of towns with Latin rights. For Lusitania the figures were five, one, and three. The total of one hundred privileged communities dotted throughout the Peninsula represented perhaps one in four of the full number of sizable centres of population.

With Augustus a shift in emphasis is apparent. Standing at the apex of a highly centralized empire, he used the grant of citizenship less as an incentive to the assumption of civic responsibility than as reward for complete conformity with Rome's requirements, and the individual so conformable and so rewarded tended now to find his future in Rome rather than in his home province. Instead of a policy of political education for self-government, Augustus thus offered to the Peninsula the economic and social benefits of a benevolent dictatorship.

This was the great age of road-building: initially military in intention, the 12,000 miles of highways with which the Romans honeycombed the Peninsula – the greatest of them the Via Augusta which hugged the coast from Cadiz to the Pyrenees – served no less its economic development and long remained the most visible monument of Rome's material achievement. Amphitheatres and aqueducts, of which notable examples survive, likewise testify to the rising standard of living and of culture in a land now made over to the arts of peace. And no contribution to this end proved more effective or more acceptable than Augustus's determined attack, even before he became emperor, on administrative abuses and corruption. By making the provincial governors salaried officials he attacked the evil at its source and opened the way for far-reaching fiscal reforms. One such, the introduction of a new general tax, with the measures of social reorganization its levying entailed, was held to be of such moment that the date, 38 B.C., was taken to mark the beginning of a new era. By this 'Spanish era' peninsular scribes and historians were to continue to reckon down to the late Middle Ages.

Of Pliny's 520 towns in the Peninsula perhaps one-third had already achieved some measure of civic emancipation before the advent of the emperor Vespasian, whose decree of A.D. 74 enfranchised the remainder at a stroke, conferring on all the status of *municipia*. With this each received a charter granting full Latin citizenship to the annually elected chief magistrates and their families, together with control over local revenues and the dispensing of justice. Augustus's garrison of three, later two, legions was reduced to a nominal one, and recruits were enrolled in increasing numbers – the condition being possession of citizenship – to serve in legions stationed elsewhere throughout the empire. In the following century some would help man the Roman Wall in the north of England.

That wall was built by Hadrian, a Spaniard, mention of whose name invites consideration, in terms of individuals, of the transformation that had been coming over the Peninsula ever since 206. Alongside romanization as a policy, and independently of it, more subtle factors had been at work. Not only were Roman colonists settling and Roman colonies being settled: within two generations the mingling of Roman and Iberian blood had already become an element in the situation of an importance well exemplified in the revolt of Sertorius. Already in 171 a colony had been founded at Carteia (El Rocadillo, near Algeciras) specifically for individuals of mixed parentage, and slowly there was taking shape a new racial stratification of the Peninsula closely akin in nature to that which fifteen hundred years later would result from the peninsular conquest of the New World. The Roman born in Rome, the Roman born in Spain (the *criollo* of America), the offspring of Roman father and native mother (the *mestizo*), and the native Iberian: each had in the beginning his own interests and grievances. But gradually the dividing lines grew blurred – there entered here, fortunately, no complication of colour – and, just as earlier Iberian and Celt had given Celtiberian, so before the Roman chapter ended the peoples of Rome and Hispania had merged and will enter upon the next phase as Hispano-Romans.

Latin, the speech of the conquerors, of garrison and settlement, of administration and education, became with time the speech of the population as a whole. In Baetica, Strabo noted, the native tongue had by his day been forgotten. It was vulgar, not classical, Latin, coloured with local peculiarities of idiom and pronunciation that provoked a smile in Rome, but it was still Latin, out of which a thousand years of growth and adaptation were to produce modern Castilian Catalan, and Portuguese. Current throughout the Peninsula – only in the mountainous Basque country, the last to be subdued, did the earlier language subsist alongside – it became another factor making powerfully for the unification of hitherto disparate societies and for the acceptance by these of all the social values of which it was the channel and exponent. It afforded the passport no less to Rome, whither the eyes of the provincial graduated into citizenship were inevitably drawn.

From the time of Augustus, this deliberate objective of policy, the denying to the native of any share in the higher direction of his own country's affairs, caused Iberian talent to seek its outlet on the larger Roman stage; and there, during the early empire, it played indeed a notable part. Cordoba, founded as a Roman colony in 151 had early become the focus of the Peninsula's intellectual life; a century later its poets were winning high praise from Cicero himself, who found to criticize only, in their language, a something rich and rare (*pingue quiddam adunque peregrinum*) that has been the mark of Andalusian poetry, as contrasted with the austerity of that of Castile to the north, ever since.

A little later and the silver age of Latin literature was dominated by peninsular names. Among them were the two Senecas and Lucan, all three born in Cordoba, Pomponius Mela the geographer, Columella the writer on agriculture, Quintilian the prince of rhetoricians, Martial the satirist. All, with the exception of Mela, lived and achieved fame in Rome, bearing witness there both to the cultural life of their mother country and to certain intellectual trends in that life which by their recurrence down the centuries have come to suggest constants in the national character. The stoicism of the younger Seneca has seemed to some to be the very philosophy of the Spaniard; Martial's pungent satire exemplifies the complementary capacity for pricking the bubble of pretence; while Lucan and Quintilian initiated two of the most persistent flaws of Spanish letters – a deliberate obscurity and the over-stressing of formal artifice.

There emerged too men of action – soldiers, administrators, emperors. Trajan, born in Italica near Seville, *c.* A.D. 56, his father being governor of Baetica, saw peace and prosperity in the Peninsula at their height; its people, raising in due course memorials to the benefits his own reign conferred, saw too in him how high it was now open to each of themselves to aspire and found therein the final touchstone of what the coming of Rome had meant. Hadrian and Marcus Aurelius sprang likewise from Hispano-Roman families.

The provinces were nonetheless still provinces, and written prominently into their relationship with the central power remained the obligation to help finance the empire. Stateownership of mines and control by Roman capitalists of numerous industrial enterprises transferred much of the Peninsula's natural wealth to Rome, there to minister to the growing indulgence in luxury that contributed to the eventual collapse of the whole mighty structure. By the third century A.D. the empire was already in decline, one measuring-rod being the increasing absolutism and rapacity of its emperors.

Under them the *municipium*, from being a school of training in citizenship, became a convenient instrument of extortion. Members of the municipal council were made personally responsible for the collection of taxes, and found escape from the millstone impeded by a ban on residence outside the town. The degree of exaction grew such that men abandoned their estates from inability to pay, and large areas gradually became derelict, while free men sold themselves into slavery. Election to the council being now a thing to be avoided, candidates were not to be found and office was made hereditary. In the fourth century craftsmen's guilds, hitherto voluntary, were declared compulsory, and membership of a craft likewise became hereditary.

With an imperial policy thus in process of debasement the teachings of Christianity came necessarily into conflict, and the persecution of the new religion by successive emperors proved as inevitable as the response this awakened wherever, as in the Peninsula, the native tradition was one of fierce individualism. Belief in one God and one standard of justice for all men gave hope of a new dispensation in strong contrast to the Roman cult not merely of many pagan deities but of the emperor himself, symbol of an authoritarian society in which slavery figured as part of the natural order. Tradition associates St Paul and St James with the earliest preaching of Christianity in the Peninsula. The second and third centuries witnessed the rise of numerous Christian communities, which suffered cruel repression and many martyrdoms before the conversion of the emperor Constantine and his promulgation of the edict of Milan in A.D. 306 announced a new policy of toleration. Religious liberty was henceforth assured to all Roman citizens throughout the empire, and communities of the new faith were confirmed in the right to hold property. The Spaniard Theodosius, the last emperor to rule over the whole Roman world (378–95), made of Christianity its official religion and sought himself to follow its dictates. In his intolerance now of 'heresy' he revealed the conception of the

Church as an instrument of state policy, and of compulsory orthodoxy as a basis for political unity, that after another thousand years and more was to prove the peculiar mark of peninsular Catholicism.

With recognition, the organization of the Church proceeded rapidly. Each provincial capital throughout the empire became the seat of a bishopric, the bishop of Rome being accepted as titular head or Pope. Among the early councils that met to deliberate and legislate on Church matters, three were held in Spain, at Illiberis (Elvira, near Granada) in 313, at Saragossa in 380, and at Toledo in 400. The first of these is remembered for the principles there enunciated of the celibacy of the clergy and of the prohibition of marriage with non-Christians; the second for its condemnation and violent persecution of the heresy, much influenced by native religious beliefs, of Priscillian bishop of Avila concerning the nature of the Trinity, resurrection, and the transmigration of souls; the third for its endorsement, for the Peninsula, of the Nicene Creed adopted at the first oecumenical council of the Church held in Nicaea in Asia Minor in 325. That council, whence derived the Church's new name of Catholic, was convened by one Spaniard, the emperor Constantine, and presided over by another, bishop Hosius; and in its concern with the definition of orthodoxy and its rejection of Arianism something can be seen in kernel of Spain's subsequent readiness, under rulers invested with the proud title of 'Catholic Majesty', to assume the charge of upholding the inviolability of the faith everywhere.

Among the earliest Popes was the Spaniard St Damasus (366–84), whose compatriot and contemporary Prudentius is counted the first truly great Christian poet. Religious fervour found another outlet in asceticism. The council of Illiberis told of its spread in the Peninsula, as did that of Saragossa of the growth of monastic communities on a scale, the record suggests, already such as to cause disquiet to the regular clergy. Priscillianism was here a complication, from the appeal of the ascetic side of its founder's teaching to many who cared nothing for theological profundities: while Priscillian was put to death, monks and nuns were by some held close kin to heretics. In the peninsular Church there would be no room for dissidence, and successive councils were at pains to reassert the duty no less than the nature of strict conformity.

But Christianity was not only a new religious faith. It taught also a new social doctrine of human rights and relations. Inevitably, in consequence, as the evidence of decay throughout the whole fabric of empire could no longer be gainsaid, it came to win acceptance and to wield influence in the secular sphere too. By the time the empire disintegrated the Church was playing a recognized part in the administration of justice, in municipal affairs, and generally in defending the commoner against abuses of power. Amid increasing chaos it stood for order, amid corruption and extortion for ethical values resting on a divine sanction. In the discrediting of an empire which had lost its *raison d'être*, and which, when the final assault came from without, very few within had any cause to defend, the Church thus found itself heir to an ever expanding sphere at once of opportunity and of responsibility.

3

Visigothic Overlay

THE gains from centuries of close association with Rome were permanent, and laid the foundations on which peninsular civilization would develop. In language, literature, law, administration, and religion Spain and Portugal are the product of Rome, just as the nations of Latin America are of Spain and Portugal. But the privilege of that association in the days of Rome's greatness also carried with it involvement in the process, and not merely in the consequences, of its decline. With a frontier extending across Europe from Greece to Britain, an empire in decay within could no longer contain at all points the 'barbarians' now constantly probing its outer defences, and during the third and fourth centuries it knew the repeated humiliation of having to come to terms with the enemy and even of accepting him as ally in the holding of exposed territories against other enemies still more barbarous and redoubtable. In the end it was due to the invoking of such dubious foreign aid not against foreigners but in a civil conflict that the floodgates opened and the might of imperial Rome collapsed – a portent of what was to happen in the Peninsula itself just three centuries later.

Theodosius had already, on his deathbed in 395, divided the empire into east (Byzantium) and west (Rome) under his two sons. Honorius, aged eleven when he succeeded to the western inheritance, soon saw his authority challenged by one Constantine, nominee of the legionaries in Britain. This was the threat he sought to counter in 406 by the desperate measure of allowing three Germanic peoples, the Alans, Suevi, and Vandals, to cross the Rhine and stream over Gaul. Constantine, not seriously impeded thereby, was able to march his legions south, unseat his rival, and overrun the Peninsula. The road to Rome he found barred by the fact that the Goths had already swarmed over northern Italy. But it mattered little thereafter who ruled in Rome. Roman Spain, defenceless, lay at the mercy of the invading hordes, now invited across the Pyrenees by Constantine's own general in a personal bid for power.

The year was 409. It marked the end of an age, for the Roman edifice in the Peninsula crumbled without the striking of any concerted blow in its defence. The cultural heritage was secure enough, but the social structure so patiently nurtured now revealed the shallowness of its roots in a soil ever impatient of centralization, while the draining of Iberian manpower for service throughout the empire had of itself prepared the way for the invader. Famine and disease were added to the terrors of invasion, and general chaos ensued when the newcomers fell to fighting among themselves over the division of their conquests. The Suevi were driven westward into Galicia; to the Vandals fell the rich lands of the south, where they were to leave their name in Andalusia; the Alans found themselves deflected partly to the east coast, partly to the south-west. Substantial areas remaining initially unabsorbed kept alive the memory but not the reality of Rome: the spell of six centuries was broken.

Thus disunited, the barbarians in their turn fell easy prey to another race of nomads. The Visigoths or western half of the Gothic people had for some three centuries been drifting diagonally across Europe from Scandinavia to the Danube, there to come into contact and inevitable conflict with the empire. Pressure of the Huns from behind drove them in the late fourth century across this river frontier and compelled an understanding with Byzantium, to which they stood thenceforth in the relation of uncertain allies for the ward of the northern marches. Already converted to Christianity, a condition of this understanding was their further acceptance of Arianism, that eastern heresy denying the Trinity which we have seen condemned at the council of Nicaea. This was to have its sequel in the Peninsula, and to prove the first chapter in the long entwining there of politics and religion.

Soon the Visigoths, sensing the growing weakness of the imperial power, were making war on their own account, first against the eastern empire, then, moving westward, against Rome itself, which they entered in 410 before passing on to Gaul. Here they carved themselves out a kingdom with Toulouse as capital and, bartering recognition of this by Rome against a renewal of the alliance, engaged themselves to regain the Peninsula for the empire from the tribes in possession. Already they had made one independent incursion south of the Pyrenees, occupying Barcelona in 414. A campaign against the Alans in 418 reduced these to impotence, the Vandals crossed the straits to Africa *en masse* in 429, and the Suevi, having enjoyed a brief period of expansion as the others were worsted, themselves suffered a resounding defeat in 456.

This was not the end of the Suevi, but with that date the barbarian interlude may be considered closed and a new chapter begun in the history of the Peninsula, the second in the trio of major alien occupations whose combined imprints have made of Spain and Portugal what they are. Though it proved the shortest of the three – it was to last less than three centuries – it had far-reaching consequences. That same year had seen a new and decisive break with Rome, over another disputed succession to what remained of the western empire, and the adoption by the Visigoths of a policy of independent conquest. The empire maintained a shadow existence for another twenty years: only in 475, the year before its demise, did it formally recognize Visigothic sovereignty.

By then the Visigoths had achieved substantial control over the Peninsula, though Galicia was for long denied them. This mattered little while the Peninsula still represented but a southward extension of their kingdom north of the Pyrenees; but pressure there from the Franks acted as pressure elsewhere from the Huns had earlier, and the fixing by Athanagild of his capital in Toledo about the year 554 finally sealed recognition of the fact that his dwindling territories in Gaul had become but an apanage of the Peninsula. Where the Romans had come in pursuit of an enemy who threatened their homeland, the Visigoths sought living space and, having at long last found a land they hoped to be able to hold, made that their homeland. Hence the feeling long after, when the Peninsula had to be won back for Christendom in a struggle of centuries against the Muslim, that it was as descendants of the Visigoths and for the recovery of the Visigothic, not the Roman, heritage that men fought; and when another thousand years had passed and Spanish America fought for its independence against the mother country, the term of opprobrium with which feeling was stirred up against the enemy would be not 'Spaniard' but 'Goth'.

'Barbarians' themselves originally to the empire, the Visigoths had lost much of their barbarism, thanks to long and intimate contact with that same empire, before establishing themselves in their new home. They possessed the Bible in their own speech, and codes of law which testified to their respect for an ordered society. That the imprint of Rome was to survive intact in so many spheres in the Peninsula bore witness to their esteem for and continued readiness to learn from a civilization admittedly superior in the arts of peace. Where the Celtiberians had learnt Latin the Hispano-Romans did not now learn Gothic: instead the Visigoths too came to speak a Latin to which they contributed terms, a mere two hundred or so, from their own speech, indicative mostly of war and dress. This cultural absorption of victor by vanquished is thrown into stronger relief by the consideration that the Visigoths arrived not as armies but as communities, with their womenfolk and their own social sufficiency, and, settling on the land, made at first but scanty contact with the predominantly urban society of the Hispano-Romans, whom they were content to leave largely unmolested in return for due payment of tribute.

Two factors were destined soon to bring the races together. Working from opposite directions and curiously complementary, their fusion may be seen in retrospect to have laid the basis of society and the state as these were to develop down to our own day. They were, from the Visigothic side, the institution of monarchy, and from the Hispano-Roman, the Catholic Church. The Peninsula, schooled by Rome to the principle of hierarchy and a head, had never had its own head. The Church, organized on the same principle, accepted allegiance to a foreign Pope. Under the Visigoths the land was to become one again and be ruled from within, a kingdom in its own right where it had previously ranked merely as provinces of an alien empire; and with full acquiescence in the new dispensation the people came to find in the crown, its focal point, a symbol to command their loyalties as these had never before been commanded.

The elective nature of the Visigothic monarchy, the king being but a noble chosen by his peers, did not make, it is true, for social peace or stability; in the end it would lead to the ignominious collapse of the regime and the overrunning of the land anew, this time from Africa: but the symbol had come to stay. Meanwhile that full acquiescence depended on two things: the effective consolidation of Visigothic sway throughout the Peninsula and a settlement of the religious cleavage that more than anything else divided Arian conquerors from Catholic conquered. Both developments proved tardy.

The Franks had continued to harass the Visigoths even south of the Pyrenees. In 533 they seized Pamplona and laid siege to Saragossa; but a resounding defeat here put an end to threats from Gaul for another two centuries. Twenty years later the Athanagild already mentioned created another threat to the south-east on a pattern that was to persist down the ages. A noble ambitious to wear the crown, he invited the emperor of Byzantium to his aid. Justinian, who had done so much to reintegrate the Roman empire of old, having won back Italy, north Africa, Sicily, Corsica, and Sardinia, proved only too ready to accede, and sent an army which helped the usurper indeed to the throne, in 554, but remained to conquer and hold for the emperor large parts of Baetica and Carthaginensis. Soon Athanagild was at war with his allies as they sought to occupy more and more, and had the ageing Justinian applied all his earlier drive and resolution he might have won back the whole, for Hispano-Roman sympathies were still understandably on his side.

Athanagild's successor at one brief remove, his brother Leovigild (568–86), took up the double challenge to his dominion, the Suevi having by now recovered from their earlier discomfiture, and both for the energy he displayed and the measure of success he attained merits the title of greatest among the Visigothic rulers. He was the first to invest the monarchy with its full dignity and splendour, wearing a crown and sitting on a throne; the first too to strike an independent national coinage, marking thereby an epoch in the numismatic history of the west, for his predecessors and contemporaries had been content with anonymous imitations of coins of the empire. With Justinian's forces he contemporized initially, marrying the daughter of the Byzantine governor of Carthaginensis and basing his court ceremonial on the usage of Byzantium. Thus able to concentrate his efforts against the Suevi, he finally destroyed them in 585. His triumph over the imperial forces was less complete, but by the time of his death only two small areas in the Peninsula remained beyond his sway, the last surviving until 624.

The political aspect of Leovigild's reign was no less important. The constitutional problem he confronted squarely. Athanagild had died a natural death, but his four predecessors on the throne had all been assassinated by rivals. Monarchy by election, tolerable in the nomad state when of the leader there was required only that he led his warriors to victory or paid the penalty, revealed now its incompatibility with an ordered, stable society. The alternative, hereditary succession, posed its own problems: one the difficulty of ensuring in the heir the qualities necessary to his high charge – a dilemma this, soon complicated by the theory of divine right, placing absolute power in his hands, that was to prove insoluble for over a thousand years; another the more immediate and very acute question of persuading the nobility to sanction the change-over, with renunciation on their part of all hope of one day ascending the throne themselves. The principle being so much easier of acceptance than the consequences, centuries were to elapse before it could be considered firmly established; but Leovigild did succeed in obtaining from his nobles token concurrence in the experiment.

Hermenigild, his elder son, brought the religious problem to a head while his father still reigned. Married to a Catholic, he embraced her religion and was persuaded, being governor of Baetica, to raise the province in revolt against the Arian rule of Toledo. Only after five years of fighting did he submit; put to death a year later, in 585, he was venerated as the first Visigothic martyr for the faith and achieved canonization on the thousandth anniversary of his martyrdom. The full consequences of the rising were drawn by his brother Reccared on his accession in 586. The Hispano-Roman population held to Catholicism with an unshakable conviction. The Visigoths had accepted conversion to Arianism two hundred years earlier on grounds of political expediency: it was now demonstrably no less expedient, if they were to establish themselves permanently and acceptably in the Peninsula, that they should let themselves be converted back to orthodoxy.

In 587 Reccared announced his personal conversion, and Toledo cathedral was formally reconsecrated. Two years later he summoned Catholic and Arian bishops alike to a third council of Toledo to debate the issue, and it is significant that though the matter on which the crown thus called the Church into conclave concerned religion, the fundamental issue at stake was one of high state policy. The council resulted in the adoption of Catholicism as the official faith for the whole kingdom. Attempts to reinstate Arianism served as plausible cover thereafter for a number of revolts against the crown. Personal ambition still rankled at the hereditary succession, and with the assassination of the next two rulers this innovation collapsed. Kings were elected, or seized power, as before; but Catholicism remained the state religion.

Out of the alliance which had thus developed between crown and Church, and of the common interest of both in peace and stability, the secular power of the Church was born. And, the Church standing for the well-being of the common people who were as serfs to the Visigothic landed nobility, there can be seen here in embryo a new social alignment linking monarch with commoner against the aristocracy, which explains much in the later pattern of the Middle Ages and is a recurrent theme in Spanish sixteenth- and seventeenth-century drama.

The council of 589 had included civil as well as Church officers; that of 633, the fourth council of Toledo, would associate the bishops with the nobles in future elections to the crown, thus formally recognizing them as constituting a second estate in the realm. Reccared had already brought them into his consultative royal council, and with the creation of a new legislative council their influence grew apace. The king's power was increased, not diminished, thereby: in the same way as he claimed the right to bestow and annul nobility, he now constituted himself lay head of the Church and appointed and dismissed bishops, creating incidentally in this way a singularly long-lived bone of contention with Rome.

Two other measures played their part in the fusion of the two peoples. The first, carried out by Leovigild, was the rescinding of the earlier ban, Roman rather than Visigothic in origin, on intermarriage. The second belonged to the sphere of law. From the beginning Hispano-Romans and Visigoths had been subject each to their own laws, though those of the latter were influenced progressively by Roman procedure. Reccared had marked the official adoption of Catholicism by promulgating a number of edicts applicable to the whole nation, and the tendency grew stronger as clerical counsels weighed more and more at court. Finally the two codes were recast as one, drafted in Latin, and promulgated *c.* 654, the so-called *Liber judiciorum*, more famous from the thirteenth century, when it was translated into Castilian, as the *Forum judicum* or *Fuero Juzgo*. The hand of the Church is writ large across its enactments; yet the Visigoths, for all their receptivity, clung to their own conception of society, and it is this, with its aristocratic structure of serf and overlord, its delegation to the individual of the avenging of wrongs suffered, its communal ownership of hills and woods, its intolerance towards the Jews, which is here mirrored predominantly.

Eleven general councils of the Church are recorded between 589 and 694. They met regularly in Toledo, this being the primatial see as well as the capital, under a bishop whose prerogatives extended to the consecration, not merely of new bishops nominated by the king, but of the king himself on each new election to the throne. Cultural, and in particular literary, activity became another ecclesiastical domain. The Visigoths had brought their own script, called after the bishop Ulfilas who in the mid fourth century had translated the Bible to their tongue; but Reccared's burning on his conversion of every Arian, and hence now heretical, book on which he could lay hands effectively destroyed any possibility of literary developments therefrom, and no trace of its use in the Peninsula survives. The so-called 'Visigothic' script peculiar to this territory until the eleventh century, when monks from Cluny introduced that of France, is entirely Latin in origin. And it is from Latin, and specifically from the Christian-Latin tradition, that the literature of this age derives, its great exemplar St Isidore, who on his death in 636 had been bishop of Seville for close on forty years. His *Etymologiae*, a vast encyclopedia of human and divine learning, is but one work among the many he composed on history, philosophy, theology, language. A great educator in his lifetime, he continued to be much studied in the later Middle Ages.

The eighth council of Toledo of 653 witnessed a formal reversion to the principle of election to the throne. If this but confirmed what was once again the practice, it altered somewhat the position of the Church. The Church might side with the king, once crowned, against his turbulent rivals; the consideration that among these was to be found the next king constituted a powerful reason for not overstressing the alliance. And the alliance became the shakier as the lust for power at length made its way into the Church itself. The rebellion of an archbishop of Toledo in 693 provided one pointer to the general weakening of the social fabric which marked the close of the seventh century. Twenty years earlier the treachery of a general who, sent to subdue a revolt in southern Gaul, himself revolted and proclaimed himself king had revealed that full reliance could no longer be placed on the army. The Jews, implicated in the uprising, were discovered shortly after to be in intelligence too with others of their faith who had taken refuge across the straits, and slowly the shadow of invasion from Africa began to fall across the Peninsula.

Successive kings now vacillated between ruthless persecution and excess of clemency in their policy towards so many dissident elements. Neither availed them anything, for with the basic failure to remove power and the principle of authority from the arena of personal ambition the Visigoths never succeeded in building up a common loyalty to the crown as something greater than its wearer. That rebellion still succeeded rebellion, the abettors standing to gain little from success, the mass of the people nothing, underlines the fatal flaw in a state which omitted to provide itself with a theory of statehood and to educate public opinion in its defence.

The collapse came with the death of Wittiza in 710. Wittiza had inherited the crown thanks to his father's having shared the throne with him during the last years of his reign, a device already several times invoked by his predecessors as a step towards making the monarchy again hereditary, and was preparing the way when he died for his son Achila to follow him. This proved too much for the nobles, who promptly elected one Roderic, and again civil war broke out, provoked by Achila and his uncle Oppa, archbishop of Seville.

In this now so repetitive situation there was but one new factor, but it was decisive. Across the straits the fortress of Ceuta was held, as it seems for the Visigoths, by a count Julian, who had so far succeeded in holding off the Arabs then overrunning Morocco. Siding in this issue with Achila, and doubtless at his and Oppa's instigation, he came to terms with Muza, the Arab leader, and engaged his interest and support in overthrowing Roderic. In that same year 710 a first Arab reconnaissance was made on the south coast at Tarifa. The following year an army 12,000 strong, predominantly Berber but under an Arab leader Tarik, landed at the spot called thereafter the Rock of Tarik (Gebel-Tarik, Gibraltar).

Roderic, engaged in putting down yet another of the unending Basque revolts in the far north, hurried south, and in a seven-day encounter traditionally placed on the banks of the Guadalete, near Jerez de la Frontera, during which Roderic's two wings went over to the enemy, he and the Visigothic kingdom were lost. Oppa's treachery – he had commanded one wing – clearly implicated the Church in this betrayal of the Peninsula to the infidel, a crime not mitigated by the belief that the infidel, having received his share of the booty, would be content to return to Africa forthwith. Close on eight centuries were to pass before its final expiation.

It may be allowed nonetheless that the Muslim invasion and occupation would have come to pass even without this guilty collusion. A realm so divided against itself lay wide open to external attack, and the coincidence that brought the Arabs at the height of their expansive crusading fervour to the southern shores of the straits just when the Visigothic power to the north was at its weakest did the rest. The Peninsula's destiny thus far had been compounded of a succession of just such alien occupations, each contributing to the enrichment of its experience and to the complicating of its racial and cultural heritage: had this last incursion not come to pass, that heritage would today be much the poorer, and with it the significance of the Peninsula's role in history. The true differential of Spain in Europe is the Muslim chapter that began with the inscribing of a new name, Gibraltar, on its map.

4

Irruption from Africa

THE Arabs came to the Peninsula as fanatical worshippers of Allah and of Mohammed his prophet, at whose bidding and under whose spell they found themselves embarked on a career of conquest aimed at winning all mankind for Islam: peacefully if possible, the prophet had taught, by the sword if necessary. At once a social and a religious code, the Koran had made powerful appeal to a backward people still wedded to a primitive polytheism, and proved similarly acceptable to others. Mohammed died in 632. During the lifetime of the first caliph or successor, Palestine, Egypt, and Persia had already been overrun and added to the faith. Less than a century would suffice to carry it east to the borders of India and west over the extent of north Africa until it confronted Christian Europe across a narrow twelve miles of sea.

The Peninsula proved an easier prey than the invaders had had any reason to hope. Once again, apart from those who had sold the pass and admitted the infidel, and from the Jews, who had every reason for wishing the Visigoths ill, the mass of the people, unorganized for effective defence, uninformed of the real issues at stake, and possibly unpersuaded that it had much to lose, accepted the situation with comparative equanimity. Tarik and his Berbers were joined in 712 by Muza, governor of Mauretania, with a strong force of Arabs. Some cities were only taken after prolonged siege. In the north-east large numbers fled into Gaul, whence that region was later recaptured and resettled, a factor of much importance in the subsequent differentiation of Catalonia from the rest of Spain. In the north the Cantabrian mountains served as a bulwark behind which a nucleus of resistance prevented the total eclipse of the Visigothic Christian tradition, and from the spark there kept alive was fired the ideal of the reconquest of the Peninsula for Christendom.

But for the rest the victory was, by 718, complete, and Muza and Tarik were summoned back to Damascus to report to the

caliph on these surprising accretions to the territory of the faithful. Had their successors been alive to the danger of leaving even
one area, however apparently insignificant, unsubdued, the
Peninsula might still today be an Arab-speaking Mohammedan
country. Instead the invaders, their impetus not yet spent,
crossed the Pyrenees. In fourteen years they streamed as far
north as Poitiers, there to suffer in 732, in one of the decisive
battles of history, a crushing reverse at the hands of Charles
'the Hammerer' which saved Gaul for Europe. The Peninsula
was never wholly lost to Europe in the centuries that followed,
but it was a profoundly altered Peninsula that would one day
re-emerge to play its full part anew in that context.

Demoted thus suddenly from citizenship of a Christian
monarchy to the status of a subject race in an emirate or province
of the distant caliphate of Damascus, no less removed in space
than in creed and way of life, the population took stock of its
position. The newcomers were Arabs, Syrians, Moors, Berbers,
not to be spoken of collectively as any one of these races. The
only common denominator was religious: all were Muslims. So
too their opponents were not now to be reckoned Hispano-
Romans or Goths but Christians. The struggle that was to ensue
had many facets, and many remote and unforeseen consequences:
its rallying-cry on both sides would be to the faith.

Among the invaders the Arabs supplied the brains and direction, alike in war and in government, and the new official
language. Later their language would serve as vehicle for a civilization far in advance of that of medieval Christendom, and as a
channel through which were to flow into Europe the wisdom and
lore of the east and also, in virtue of the capture of Alexandria
by the Arabs in 600, the surviving inheritance of ancient Greece.
Meantime the plains of Andalusia offered a life of ease and plenty
after the arid deserts of north Africa; and the Arabs, sending the
Berbers north to hold the central uplands, made of Cordoba,
the ancient capital of the Romans, the centre of a territory
organized to a new and exotic pattern of living. That territory,
fluctuating constantly in extent with the vicissitudes of the reconquest, was always to them 'al-Andalus', the land of Andalusia.
'Hispania' remained the Christian term for the Peninsula as a
whole.

The prophet's charge to his followers to proselytize all peoples allowed, with time, of distinctions. Moors and Berbers were pagans and had to be converted. Christians were close kin in creed – much closer than was ever allowed from the Christian side – to a religion which included the Psalms and the sayings of Jesus among its sacred books and drew many of its prophets from the Old and New Testaments; and the Arabs, while requiring submission, left their new subjects in the free enjoyment and practice of their faith. Any Christian was free to embrace Islam, and many did, beginning with Roderic's widow, whom Muza's son and successor in command took to wife. Gaining thereby the full status of the Mohammedan-born, they were exempted from the poll-tax and other obligations laid on the Christian population.

The Arab rulers had thus a direct fiscal interest in not encouraging mass apostasy; and although later and specifically African waves of invaders were to prove much less tolerant, many Christian communities survived unmolested until, with the passage of centuries, the tide of conquest from the north reincorporated them in Christendom. In Cordoba half of the largest church was taken as a mosque; when later the whole was taken the Christians were allowed, exceptionally, to build themselves new places of worship. Toledo, which for more than two hundred years after 711 succeeded in maintaining a semi-independent existence, still enjoyed until very shortly before its liberation in 1085 its full ecclesiastical organization headed by an archbishop. But these *mozárabes* ('almost Arabs'), as Christians living in al-Andalus were called, were soon outnumbered by the *muladies* or converts, and within a few generations there was little to distinguish Muslims of peninsular from those of extra-peninsular origin. Among Mozarabs, and among women generally in the home, there persisted alongside Arabic the incipient Romance speech which at the time of the irruption had been slowly evolving from vulgar Latin; snatches of popular song in this have survived in Arabic and Hebrew compositions of the tenth century.

The first half-century of Muslim sway revealed weaknesses different in kind but not dissimilar in their effect to those which had brought low the Visigothic régime. Berbers and Arabs, Arabs and Syrians, disputing among themselves the spoils of conquest and fighting for power, reflected growing inability on the part of distant authority to make effective a control so very remote. Dissensions in Arabia itself had accompanied the gradual transformation of the caliphate from a religious to a secular power, and in 750 the reigning family were there violently overthrown by a rival and, with one exception, exterminated in wholesale massacre. The survivor, a youth of nineteen born of a Berber slave-woman, after an adventurous five years made his way to al-Andalus, was there welcomed by the many partisans of his house, and after some fighting entered Cordoba in triumph in 756.

The link with Damascus thus severed, Abd al-Rahman I reigned till 788 over an independent emirate. His territories were bounded by a line running from Coimbra in the west through Coria, Talavera, Toledo, Guadalajara, and Tudela to Pamplona in the east. North of this lay a no-man's land which a disastrous five-year famine at the mid-century had caused the Berber occupiers to abandon, thousands of them crossing back to Africa, never to return. To the north-east lay the Muslim government of Saragossa, controlling the middle reaches of the Ebro, which in 750 had become virtually independent of Cordoba.

For over twenty years Abd al-Rahman was confronted by an unending series of revolts, incited at times by his eastern enemies. Already convinced of the need of a standing army, he now recruited for it not merely among Berbers but, to the number of over forty thousand, among Slavs from various parts of southern Europe. Risings continued against his successors, memorable among them being those in Toledo in 797 and in Cordoba itself in 818. Both were suppressed by the army with savage ruthlessness, and the régime was maintained at the cost of becoming a military despotism. Also to be counted in the cost were the long breathing-spaces, as much as twenty years at a time, which these internal troubles afforded to the Christians in the north, enabling them steadily to consolidate and expand their scant residual territories.

It was during the rule of al-Haquem I (796–822) that the first signs appeared of that intellectual activity – the fruit of a renewal of contacts with the civilization of an eastern caliphate now resigned to the loss of its dominion over al-Andalus – which was to constitute the great distinction and the historic significance of the Muslim occupation of the Peninsula. Enjoying the favour of successive emirs who not infrequently, like al-Haquem, were themselves men of learning and letters, it encountered bitter opposition as often as it left the path of strictest orthodoxy from the class of *alfaquies* or theologian-jurists which wielded power or instigated revolts according to the greater or lesser piety of each ruler.

To the harsh repression of al-Haquem his successor Abd al-Rahman II owed the unity and tranquillity of an even longer reign, from 822 to 852. Some credit was due also to the avoidance by successive emirs of the great stumbling-block of the Visigothic elective monarchy: since the advent of Abd al-Rahman I a son – not always the eldest, for each emir had claimed the right to choose the one most fitted to govern – had regularly succeeded to his father. It was not, as time would prove, the perfect solution to the problem, since a son so passed over became inevitably a focus of discontent and knew strong temptation to fight for the inheritance; but it served as an intelligent safeguard against the falling of power into unworthy hands.

Under Abd al-Rahman II, whose concern for peace extended even to a ten-year truce with the Christians in the north, al-Andalus made notable strides in economic prosperity and cultural advance. The initiation in 840 of diplomatic relations by the emperor of Byzantium, in search of allies against the eastern caliphate, was one token of its growing strength and prestige. The army, furnished by compulsory military service and by mercenaries, was now much expanded; as for the navy, in 848 a fleet of 300 vessels was sent to quell disturbances in the Balearic Islands which, though likewise overrun at the beginning of the previous century, had been less effectively islamized.

Abd al-Rahman showed himself too a great builder, and did much in particular to enhance the beauty and grandeur of Cordoba and its great mosque. With a treasury full to overflowing he could indulge a taste for luxury which attracted the rare and the beautiful from the most distant markets of the east, such objects serving in their turn to stimulate native art and manufacture. Music and poetry were but two among the many interests in the realm of culture of this most cultured of all the emirs of al-Andalus. Religion, philosophy, medicine, astronomy, astrology, and the occult he both studied and caused to be studied, procuring from the east for the purpose copies of the most authoritative treatises there available.

His namesake Abd al-Rahman III (912–61), came to power at the age of twenty-one and proved the greatest ruler Muslim Spain was to produce. No other reigned so long, or invested his reign with such distinction, and when we speak of the splendours of Arabic civilization in the Peninsula, contrasting its enlightenment with the benighted 'Dark Ages' of western Europe as a whole, it is to the Cordoba of this Abd al-Rahman and to its inheritance that we refer.

The first task confronting him, and the pre-condition of everything else, was the re-establishment of a central authority that had been much weakened over the preceding half-century. In this the new ruler soon showed himself born to rule. One by one, in a series of carefully planned annual campaigns, he reduced the centres of resistance. By 928 the pacification of al-Andalus was complete, and Abd al-Rahman marked the occasion with his most decisive step, the repudiation of the nominal links still binding the emirate to the eastern caliphate and the proclamation of himself as sovereign caliph over his dominions. Badajoz, Toledo, and Saragossa still eluded him, these three centres drawing a line across the Peninsula that marked the effective northern boundary of his sway; but between 932 and 937 they too capitulated.

It had cost the new caliph exactly a quarter of a century to make himself master in his own house. Now at last he was free to think in terms of foreign policy, which meant firstly the containing within bounds of the no longer negligible Christian communities to the north. Established since 914 south of the Cantabrians with their capital in León, these had for long maintained a close intelligence, even at times a military alliance, with the Mozarabs of Toledo and the *muladies* of Saragossa, and had raided as far south as Evora, from which, after slaughtering the garrison, they had carried off captive 4,000 women and children.

Expansion southward was the dynamic of their existence, and the Muslims for their part had never had the manpower to settle and hold effectively the middle reaches of the Peninsula. The challenge was therefore in clear process of definition, with the roles of two centuries earlier reversed. Then the Visigoths – as previously against them the Hispano-Romans – had been concerned to defend a sedentary civilization against warrior tribes intent only on conquest. Now the Christians were the warriors bent on conquest and on the uprooting of a civilization whose religious foundations made it to them anathema; and Abd al-Rahman's preoccupation was at once to further the flowering of that civilization and to prevent it at all costs from becoming sedentary.

The caliph had already found time to lead two expeditions, one against León, the other against Navarre, inflicting on both occasions calamitous losses on his enemies. Pamplona, the capital of Navarre, he sacked, and destroyed its cathedral by fire. Once again, it seemed, the entire Peninsula might be reduced by the infidel and 711 be repeated. In 939, with peace and obedience reigning throughout his own territories, he launched what was intended to be the decisive blow. The 'omnipotent campaign' he baptized it, tempting providence as would the later launcher of an 'invincible armada'; and providence took his army of 100,000 men and, against the Christian forces before Simancas, broke it utterly. Abd al-Rahman fled, leaving on the field a priceless Koran that had accompanied him everywhere, and, back in Cordoba, crucified for cowardice 300 of his officers. He never thereafter led his armies in person.

The defeat was real, though not yet conclusive. The unity which the caliph had achieved in the south was as yet sorely lacking in the north, where to León and Navarre was added now the county, soon to be a kingdom, of Castile, with its own capital at Burgos, while to the east the county of Barcelona went its independent way. Between harrying expeditions, dynastic mischances and disputes, and diplomacy Abd al-Rahman soon retrieved the Simancas disaster, and before his death three, if not all four, of the Christian states were paying him annual tribute as the price of peace.

For the time being Muslim power was supreme once again in the Peninsula, in the ascendant in Morocco, where the caliph was simultaneously pursuing a policy of expansion designed to cover his southern flank against the eastern caliphate, and respected from the North Sea to the eastern Mediterranean, as the embassies which from Provence, Italy, Germany, and Byzantium visited his court bore witness. In the new city of pleasaunce which he built outside Cordoba, Medina Azzahra (the name a tribute to a favourite wife), artistic innovations in stucco and marquetry betray the hand of Greek artificers, and reports speak of gifts of precious Greek and Latin manuscripts and of the sending at his request of Greek scholars with the object of establishing in Cordoba, in collaboration with learned Jews, a school of translation. Abd al-Rahman left Muslim prestige in Europe at its highest point, Muslim sway in al-Andalus consolidated as never before, and in Cordoba a capital comparable for its wealth and culture with Byzantium itself. In his half-century of rule he had known, by his own reckoning, fourteen days free from care.

For the remainder of the century the caliphate retained the lustre with which Abd al-Rahman had invested it, and the Christian states of the Peninsula, far from uniting in a common cause, turned to Cordoba for support in their own petty quarrels. If no later caliph would prove of the stature of the first, the succession of a minor in 976 led to the rise of the greatest minister and warrior the caliphate was to know, the al-Mansur ('victorious') whose repeated raids into Christian territory over more than twenty years struck terror throughout the north. From 981 till his death ('and burial in hell', added a Christian chronicler) in 1002 his power over caliph and caliphate was supreme and his prowess in the field seemingly invincible. Zamora, Simancas, Barcelona in the far north-east, Coimbra, León, Santiago in the far north-west, and Burgos were among the many cities he seized and sacked. The outrage done in 997 to Santiago, whose cathedral he destroyed utterly, carrying off its bells and doors to Cordoba, scandalized Christendom, for its shrine of St James was a holy place. An indication of the intricate and constantly shifting relationships between north and south may be seen in the fact that among the wives of al-Mansur were daughters of the kings of Navarre and León.

This had been a great period for al-Andalus, but there was nonetheless a price to be paid. The sequestration of a caliph had sufficed to raise a dictator to the summit of power; but further drastic measures – the neutralization of the Arab aristocracy, the bringing over from Africa of large numbers of Berber troops, the honeycombing of palace, administration, and society with a spy system – were necessary to keep him there. And although his hope of creating a hereditary dictatorship was fulfilled first in one son, over a period of six years, and then for a few months in another, the damage done to the fabric of Muslim loyalties was beyond repair. Al-Mansur had perceived clearly enough how delicate that fabric was, and could never have over-reached himself, as did his second son, to the extent of asking from the caliph a decree appointing him his heir. This was the crowning folly in an ambitious weakling who lacked all his father's gifts.

The violence of the popular reaction that brought about his downfall would have been a matter of small moment had power and responsibility still rested where they belonged, in the hands of an able and resolute caliph. Here lay the real hurt in al-Mansur's climb to eminence, that he had sapped in Hixem II (976–1013) a will already enfeebled and destroyed a situation there was no retrieving. The beginning of the retribution visited on his son's final imprudence was civil war, and the end, after the most tumultuous twenty years in the history of Muslim Spain, the utter collapse of the caliphate. Those years witnessed in Cordoba, itself sacked in a revolt in 1013, a rapid succession of upstart rulers, most of whom soon met a violent death, and throughout al-Andalus the appearance of numerous local potentates able to snap their fingers at the capital. They saw perhaps no stranger sight than the recruiting from Africa by one briefly successful adventurer of a negro bodyguard. In 1031 a riot of the populace in the capital, fomented from above, ousted the last caliph from his throne. The caliphate, so resplendent but a generation earlier, had become an empty shell, and now it was no more. The reality was an al-Andalus in disruption, unable to impose its will, since a collective will it no longer had, either to the north or to the south. For Christian Spain a new day was dawning; and if its hopes were premature that al-Andalus could never again be united or a menace, sporadic Muslim resurgence proved only possible thereafter through the humiliation of successive new invasions from Africa which reduced the once proud kingdom to the rank of a dependent province.

Meantime there remained, over the next half-century, a mosaic of splinter states or *taifas*, some twenty-six in number, centring on the chief towns and often at war among themselves; often again, especially on the northern frontier, reduced in the whirligigs of fortune to vassalage to Castile. The Christian capture of Toledo in 1085 would be reckoned the most significant event in the Peninsula since 711; now it was the turn of Cordoba, Seville, and Granada to be raided from the north. Left to themselves the *taifas* were doomed, and knew it. The *alfaquíes* read the hand of Allah in this turn of events: irreligion in high places must bring its nemesis, and only a return to fervour could stave it off.

Across the straits, as it happened, the recent acceptance of Islam by some Berber tribes of the Sahara had created the conditions for a new crusade. These *almorávides* ('vowed to God') were filled with the fanaticism of the newly converted and, knowing nothing of the civilized values of the Arab way of life, cared nothing for them. It was therefore a hard decision that the leading *taifa* rulers were called on to make when the *alfaquíes* urged an appeal in this direction for help; but after Toledo the alternative loomed grimmer still. The appeal went out, and was answered.

In 1086 an army under one Yusuf crossed from Africa and, together with such effective forces as al-Andalus could muster, marched on Toledo. At Sagrajas, near Badajoz, it met and dealt a crushing blow to the Christian army, but failed to exploit the victory and returned to Africa. In 1090 the situation was as before and Yusuf returned, this time to conquer for himself, to the aggrandizement of his own African empire. His seizure of Granada opened the eyes of the remaining *taifa* rulers, and in panic they sought alliance now with Castile. The move resulted only in their denunciation by the *alfaquíes*, who called on Yusuf to depose them too. This, one by one, he did, Seville and Cordoba both falling to him in 1091, Saragossa not till 1110.

Al-Andalus was again one, but there could be no returning to the earlier greatness. It was one in subjection to the Almorávide empire of Morocco, in subjection more immediately to the Almorávides Yusuf had left behind, whose authority, especially under his son Ali (1106–43), reigned supreme. The Jews were able to buy off persecution; the Mozarabs could not, and large numbers suffered exile to Africa while all who could fled to the

north. Soon, however, the newcomers' crusading fervour succumbed to the enervating effect of an environment far superior
in the amenities to anything they had known in Africa. Toledo
they had never succeeded in recapturing, Saragossa they lost
again in 1118. Before long their star too went down in another
confusion of local rebellions, to be engulfed by yet another wave
of invasion from across the water.

The weakness under test of the Almorávides in the Peninsula
was in part explained by events in Morocco, where their sway
had been undermined by the rising of a still more primitive, and
correspondingly more fanatical, people, the *almohades* ('uni-
tarians') of the Atlas mountains. By 1146 these had swept down
to the coast and in that year, the pattern still repeating itself,
were invited to cross over by elements in al-Andalus who thought
to resolve thereby an increasingly intolerable situation, as others
were ready this time to risk invoking the assistance even of
the Christians. They found a territory again broken into fragments, and as before an easy prey. By 1150 most of it was theirs –
resistance proved strongest in the east, where Murcia only
capitulated in 1172 – and Muslim Spain was yet again one, ruled
by a governor appointed from Africa.

The Almohades likewise had nothing to contribute to the
civilization built up by their remote Arab predecessors. Religious
tolerance was long since become but a memory, and now, while
Mozarabs flocked northward in ever-increasing numbers to join
and reinforce their co-religionaries, the Arabs too were persecuted until they sought to conceal the very blood that had earlier
been their proud title to aristocracy. To the extent – a very considerable extent – that the social and intellectual values of
al-Andalus retained for centuries still to come their importance
in the unfolding of western civilization they would still be Arabic,
and Jewish, values, but with this latest admixture of Berber blood
the racial composition at last substantially justifies the common
styling of peninsular Muslims as Moors.

To the Christian north such renewed dependence on Morocco
clearly lessened the right of the Moors to be in the Peninsula at
all, and the urge to drive them back across the straits for good,
steeled by the growing conviction that their star was now
definitely waning, found expression in the formal challenge

delivered in 1194 by Alfonso VIII of Castile to the emperor Yacub in Africa. Yacub accepted, and on the field of Alarcos, near Badajoz, in 1195 the two met in what Alfonso hoped to make the decisive encounter. It resulted instead in one more disastrous reverse for the Christians, who were rolled back with the loss of strongholds as far north as Madrid and Guadalajara, though Toledo held firm, and in a lively fear that the knell had sounded anew. But Yacub's chief interests and problems still lay in Africa, and thither he returned in 1198, content with having taught the Christians a lesson.

This in truth the Christians had finally learnt, to the effect that their division was the enemy's strength; and where Castile alone had failed disastrously in 1195, Castile, León, Navarre, and Aragon in 1212 inflicted on a once again disunited al-Andalus at Las Navas de Tolosa, in the province of Jaén, what could be seen in retrospect as the *coup de grâce*. Disputes over the succession in Africa were the signal for repeated secessions from Almohade authority in the Peninsula. Soon the re-emergent *taifas* had renewed the strife among themselves, and their ability to withstand a resumption of the Christian advance was over. The loss of Cordoba in 1236, of Valencia and the Balearics by 1238, of Jaén in 1246, and of Seville in 1248, Muslim forces significantly helping Castile reduce the last-named, marked the stages in the collapse, from which this time there would be no recovery.

One *taifa* leader, who had raised his standard at Arjona in 1230, extended his rule to Granada and fixed there in 1238 the capital of a kingdom – to be known by the same name – which reached to the south coast from Almería to Gibraltar. This kingdom alone, of an al-Andalus that had once embraced most of the Peninsula, was to survive, paradoxically, for another two and a half centuries, incapable of serious offence and indebted to this fact, and to the larger preoccupations weighing henceforth on the Christian states of the north, for the anachronism of its continued existence. By the mid thirteenth century, therefore, the reconquest could be counted for all practical purposes at an end, and one may pause to consider what the long flowering of Islam on peninsular soil had meant to the Christian civilization which saw in it, in theory, its mortal enemy.

That enmity, the holy war, had been enjoined on the faithful too by the Koran. But the mark of the Koran, alongside the simplicity of a creed to which, to quote Gibbon, a philosophic atheist might have subscribed without overstraining his conscience, was the generous measure of its recognition of human frailty. 'War is prescribed to you; but to this ye have a repugnance.' And the already-mentioned consideration that the Koran was at once a religious and juridical code, while possibly contributing to the social weaknesses which underlay the fall of the caliphate and ultimately of al-Andalus, helps also to explain its influence on the cast of that society. Islam's conception of a life to come, and the requirements for its attainment, were not such as to weigh on the enjoyment of the here and now, which it described indeed as 'no other than a pastime and a disport'. The sensuous picture of a heaven of 'gardens with lofty apartments, beneath which the rivers flow', of eating and drinking and dark-eyed damsels waiting to wed the faithful, was in fact but a transcript of that good life on earth of which Cordoba in the great days of the caliphate was the epitome.

Arab writers of the time outdo hyperbole in their accounts of the city's magnificence and delights, its palaces and gardens and fountains, its 50,000 mansions of the aristocracy and governing classes, its 700 mosques and 900 public baths. The Muslim passion for ablution made cleanliness suspect in Christian eyes, and while the palaces, ransacked and plundered by Berber invaders, were destined to crumble into ruins, the mosques and baths fell victim in due course to the scruples of the reconquerors. One survival, the Mezquita or principal mosque, which had originated in a Christian church and was rededicated as a cathedral on the retaking of the city in 1236, suffices, in comparison with the Gothic cathedrals of northern Spain, to point how different were the values informing life and religion in the south. The largest mosque in western Islam, on which successive rulers had vied with one another in lavishing wealth and beauty, it is still, though only a vestige of its former self, a dream of light, grace, and colour with its low roof supported by many hundreds of slender columns, its maze of horseshoe arches, its porphyry, jasper, and marble, and its mosaics.

Religion, far from conveying to the worshipper a sense of his

own insignificance in the presence of the infinite or a view of
this world as but a dusty pilgrimage to the next, reinforced the
acceptance of life as something to be enjoyed in all its facets.
But a teaching implicit in Islam from the beginning is clearly not
the explanation, or at least not the full explanation, of the
development in al-Andalus, among a people who but two centuries before were nomadic tribes come over from Africa in
search of conquest, of a stable civilization which materially and
intellectually was centuries in advance of anything else to be
found in Europe outside Byzantium.

That achievement rested in the first place on a basis of economic
prosperity. In soil and climate nature has been kind to southern
Spain, and an industrious and enterprising people, entering upon
a heritage that had brought wealth successively to Phoenicians,
Greeks, and Romans, soon raised agriculture through a system
of small holdings to a new high level of efficiency. Irrigation
works, of which traces survive today, made fertile wide areas of
irregular or inadequate rainfall; rice, the sugar-cane, and other
exotic crops were introduced; and, although the Koran forbade
the drinking of wine, the vine was cultivated on a large scale.

Industry enjoyed a parallel prosperity, that ranged through
gold- and silver-mining, the weaving of wool and silk, the manufacture of paper, introduced into Europe by the Arabs, and of
glass, invented in Cordoba in the ninth century, metalwork,
ceramics, and leatherware. The fame of these products travelled
far, and to handle the flourishing commerce that resulted there
grew up a great trading fleet based chiefly on Seville, Malaga,
and Almería. Much went south to Africa, more east to Egypt
and Byzantium, whence the products of al-Andalus became
known in central Asia and India. With Mecca, Bagdad, and
Damascus relations were closer still. In return came all the products of the orient. Export and import dues constituted the
largest single source of state revenue under Abd al-Rahman III,
in whose day al-Andalus was one of the richest and most densely
populated areas in Europe.

This commercial reciprocity underlines the second great con-
tributory factor, the readiness and capacity of al-Andalus to
assimilate whatever others had to give. From the Mozarabs
derived most of their agricultural skill. The Jews, bitterly perse-

cuted under the Visigoths, they encouraged in the professions and employed in the highest offices of state, according them such favour that many came from the east to settle and the Talmudic school of Cordoba ranked among the greatest centres of Hebrew learning. Al-Haquem II (961–76) commissioned scholars from the east to teach in Cordoba. He was the scholar-king who lived in the company of the learned and built up a library credited by tradition with some 400,000 volumes. Other notable collections abounded throughout al-Andalus, the fruit not merely of a general love of letters and study but of a flourishing profession of copyists, aided by the rapid cursive of Arabic script and the relative cheapness of paper when compared with parchment or papyrus.

In 949 the emperor of Byzantium sent to Abd al-Rahman III an embassy bearing among other gifts a copy of Dioscorides' work on medicinal herbs. There being no one at that time in Cordoba who knew Greek, the caliph asked the emperor to send him further a scholar competent to expound it, and in 951 a monk arrived for the purpose. The event contributed notably to the development of botany and medicine, two fields in which al-Andalus was to achieve a particular repute; yet even more significant is the spirit of intellectual curiosity the incident reflects. It was a spirit which long survived the caliphate: the great age of Arabic medicine, science, and philosophy in the Peninsula was in fact the twelfth century and, philosophy still embracing the natural as well as the moral, these various disciplines often met and achieved distinction in the same person. In the most notable scholar and thinker of them all, the philosopher Averroes (1126–98), may be seen the ultimate fruit of the arrival of the monk from Byzantium two centuries earlier. For Averroes, finding in Aristotle the greatest and wisest of mankind, wrote commentaries on almost all his works, and it was largely through Latin and vernacular translations of these that knowledge of Aristotle spread through medieval Europe.

Al-Andalus, seemingly the negation of European values, thus played a vital role in conserving, developing, and transmitting to medieval Christendom that earlier Greek heritage that Roman Spain had already largely forgotten. Arabic provided the channel no less for much of the lore and learning of the farther east,

Persia and India, which through the apologue in particular strongly influenced early Spanish literature. And on these rich and varied foundations the intellectual aristocracy of peninsular Islam, often at variance with, often actively persecuted by, the narrow fanaticism of the *alfaquíes*, elaborated a culture, literary and scientific, which threw into ever darker shadow the rudimentary learning kept alive by the monasteries of the north.

Mathematics and astronomy figure prominently among the sciences on which lustre was shed. Arabic numerals, algebra, and alchemy recall some of the west's specific indebtednesses, as does the famous lament of Alvaro of Cordoba the impression already made on contemporary Mozarabs in the ninth century: 'Alas, all the Christian youths who become famous for their talent know only the language and the literature of the Arabs: they read and study zealously Arabic books, of which by dint of great expenditure they form extensive libraries, and proclaim aloud on all sides that this literature is worthy of admiration.'

Christian Spain grew early aware of the so strikingly different society to the south. It is customary but profoundly misleading to speak of the reconquest as an eight-centuries' religious war; the true picture was one rather of intermittent spasms of crusading or merely martial fervour alternating with long periods of acceptance of the situation and much crossing of lines of interest. Christian kings married Muslim princesses and gave their own daughters in marriage to Islam. They sent embassies to Cordoba, took refuge in al-Andalus when worsted in their own civil wars, and formed alliances with the infidel against fellow-Christians. The day came when they too formally recognized how much they stood to learn by organizing official schools of translators; but the process of assimilation, not so much of a literary culture as of an outlook on life, had been under way, unconsciously, since long before.

The large Mozarab population in the south was here a prime factor. Become Arabs over the centuries in all the material aspects of living, large numbers of them returned north at different periods to influence Christian communities, either in the wake of returning armies or fleeing from the persecution of Almorávide and Almohade. Those who remained were still in effect Mozarabs even after the final recovery for Christendom of the territory where they lived. When the last bastion of Islam, the kingdom of Granada, fell as the Middle Ages closed, and its Muslim citizens were given the choice of conversion or expulsion, most opted for conversion and remained to permeate Christian society for another century and a quarter.

The character of the Christian peoples of the Peninsula was forged therefore over these centuries not so much in opposition to the Arabs as in constant and subtle interaction with them; and the differences of temperament and outlook that today distinguish Andalusian from Castilian deviate less in kind than in degree from those that characterize Spain and Portugal as a whole in contradistinction to France or other countries north of the Pyrenees. The keeping of time in its place, the conception of this life as worth living for its own sake and of living as a matter not of work, wealth, and possessions but of sensuous response to all the stimuli of nature, a banishing of care to tomorrow with a fatalistic acceptance of what cannot be controlled or seems not worth the effort of controlling, a sense of personal dignity that finds itself notably ill at ease with impersonal authority, the rejection of rational criteria and especially of the cult of progress: such are some of the imponderables resulting from this long and subtle infiltration of peninsular Christendom by the enemy within the gates.

5

The Reconquest

THE Christian side of this centuries-long story of a Peninsula divided against itself goes back to a handful of Visigoths – as such, at least, they and their descendants proudly regarded themselves – who, having fled before the Muslim avalanche, found refuge and the courage to resist behind the defence-line of the Cantabrian mountains. The invaders' will to conquest had largely spent itself over the vast and uninviting expanse of the northern tableland. A small Muslim force did, however, cross the range and at Covadonga, in 718, fought and suffered defeat. This first Christian victory ranked in military terms as but a skirmish: its symbolic significance was immense, and from it history dates the beginning of the reconquest. No other nucleus of resistance having yet made itself felt, here, in the Asturias, modern Spain was born.

Pelayo, the leader, who appears to have been a high dignitary from Roderic's court at Toledo, was elected king and sought to resurrect as much of the atmosphere and usage of Toledo as circumstances allowed. Nobility and high clergy had accompanied him northward in sufficient numbers to ensure the survival of one feature of the first importance, a monarchy still torn between the elective and the hereditary principle. Six hundred years later the crown would still be enunciating, and the nobles still rejecting, the hereditary ideal. On that too hinges the fact that the seven-years' conquest by the Muslims should take over seven centuries to undo.

For the first of those centuries events moved slowly. The enemy accepted his repulse, thinking the issue of no consequence, and withdrew not merely south of the mountains but away from the bleak, wind-swept plateau. South of a line running roughly from Coimbra to Madrid and Guadalajara they found life good and felt at home. North of it stretched the extensive no-man's land across which Muslims made routine forays in terms of booty and the holy war rather than of conquest and settlement, and Christians probed south, taking the measure of the enemy and hoping less to return with spoil than with fellow-Christians from among the great majority who had not fled the invader. For the first, and over centuries the most acute, problem of the reconquest was man-power. The Muslim could beckon armies out of Africa to hold all he had a mind to. The Christian, tied to nature's slow increase, would soon range at will over almost half the Peninsula, but in planning to settle and hold he had perforce to school himself to the lapse of generations.

Help from north of the Pyrenees, where too the Muslim threat had for over a decade been so real, might reasonably have been invoked. Yet Charlemagne's incursion into Spain in 778 was at best equivocal, for it was as ally not of the Asturians but of the caliph of Bagdad against Abd al-Rahman I that he led an army to Saragossa and, foiled there in his expectation of a friendly reception, sacked the Christian town of Pamplona, centre of what was then gradually taking shape as the kingdom of Navarre, on his withdrawal northward. For this the Basques, readily allying themselves in their turn with the Muslims, visited on his rearguard memorable retribution at the Pass of Roncesvalles. The *Chanson de Roland* is thus a first monument to that xenophobia of the Spanish people re-emergent to which time was to add so many more. When in 797 Alfonso II of Asturias (791–842), who now had a capital in Oviedo and a sway extending west to Galicia and east to Santander, sought a formal pact with Charlemagne which would allow him to consolidate his hold on further territories within his grasp, he was constrained – tradition says compelled by his nobles, who would have none of foreign help – to renounce the project.

Help of another kind did come to Alfonso unasked, for in his reign the miraculous discovery was reported from Galicia of the body of the apostle James, buried in a field over which a star had hovered. Spain now had a patron saint, and – since he was a warrior saint, credited thereafter with appearing in battle on a white charger to turn the day for the Christians – a battle-cry, *¡ Santiago y cierra España!* ('St James and close in, Spain!'). Around the field of the star (*campus stellae*) there arose a city, Santiago de Compostela, and a mighty cathedral to house so sacred a relic, and as report spread of miracle and shrine this became the most famous place of pilgrimage in western Europe. The pilgrim route from France grew into an international highway, its successive plottings from Roncesvalles, first through Alava and Asturias, eventually, by the late eleventh century, through Belorado and Burgos, illustrating the progressive expansion south of the mountains of securely held territory. Along it new cultural influences would reach Spain and knowledge of Spain was carried to the outside world by many a good wife of Bath returned from 'Galice at seint Jame'.

Charlemagne returned to the Peninsula, but this time to the north-east. That region, the first to receive the impact of Roman civilization as it had earlier received that of Greece, continued under the Visigoths to be their window on the European world through the persisting interest, right up to the time of their collapse, in the Septimania – modern Roussillon – whence they had originally extended their empire south of the Pyrenees. There was found there, in consequence, nothing of the hostility towards France that existed farther west. A substantial part of the population had in fact crossed into southern Gaul as the Muslims overran their territory, and towards the end of the century the descendants of these engaged the emperor's interest in its recovery.

Charlemagne himself reconquered Gerona in 785. His son Louis took Barcelona in 801, and the whole of what later came to be known as Old Catalonia, stretching from the Pyrenees to the Llobregat, was free from the infidel. These two considerations, the centuries-old link, to persist for many centuries to come, between Catalonia and Roussillon, long implying territorial unity and still reflected in the linguistic proximity of Provençal to Catalan, and the fact that the Muslim occupation lasted here for less than a hundred years, explain much in the divergent character and interests of Catalonia *vis-à-vis* the rest of Spain.

Once liberated, the territory suffered incorporation with Septimania in the Frankish empire as the marquisate of Gotia. The peninsular part was organized as a series of counties, among which that of Barcelona soon emerged to the pre-eminence it would never afterwards lose. The first count of Barcelona was also marquis of Gotia, as were several of his successors, but all held the former the prouder title, and Barcelona, speaking in due course for Greater Catalonia as a whole, never renounced it to vie with the petty kingships it saw multiply to west and south. In 865 Charles the Bald detached the Catalan counties from the northern territory: as the Marca Hispanica or Spanish March they still formed a province of the empire.

The possibility of ending this subject relationship came at the close of that century with dynastic disputes among the Franks, and the Catalan refusal to recognize the succession of Hugo Capet in 987 at length set the seal on what was already a substantial *de facto* independence. Catalonia was launched on a career that, thanks to the Muslim kingdom of Saragossa to its south-west, would have strangely little contact with the rest of Christian Spain for several centuries to come. With growing strength it embarked in time on its own reconquest to the south; but it was in that other challenge of the sea to the east that it discovered in the end the key to a highly individual greatness.

The reigns of the immediate successors of Alfonso II of Asturias read like an appendix to the Visigothic régime. With the southern caliphate still at the summit of its power, Christian Spain remained perforce on the defensive, its rulers being at times little removed from vassalage to Cordoba. Within that Spain the old familiar pattern repeated itself: revolts of the nobles against the throne, violent despatches, repudiated elections, alliances with the enemy without, civil war. Alfonso III (866–910) had to make good by the sword his title to Galicia before carrying his banners southward, over territory the enemy were little concerned to dispute, as far as Coimbra on the Mondego.

His reign ended with an abdication forced upon him by his own sons, who between them divided up the kingdom into its constituent parts, León, being the extension of Asturias south of the Cantabrians, Galicia and its new extension southward into Lusitania, and the original Asturias. This pattern too was often to be repeated, the monarch himself not infrequently undoing on his deathbed a lifetime's achievement in the unification of his territories, leaving sometimes thereby as part of the inheritance a fratricidal civil war for repossession of the whole, and even where this did not follow halting the process and progress of reconquest.

Implicit in such an act was the continuing conception of the kingdom as the monarch's personal and disposable estate, a conception that as late as 1700 could still plunge the nation into war, international this time as well as civil. It should be added that the ease with which the medieval kingdom disintegrated bore witness to that same reluctance of the local to merge in the larger patriotism which has ever been a mark of the Spaniard. Ordoño II (914–23), who, receiving Galicia in the share-out, succeeded in reuniting it with León, is remembered for the transference of his capital in 914 to the city of that name. The new confidence implied in the ability of the Christians to hold their own without the protective barrier of the Cantabrians makes of the transfer a landmark. Progress of necessity was southward: the kingdom henceforward was the kingdom of León, until such time as the hegemony should pass to yet another offshoot which, continuing the advance, would relegate León, as León now relegated Asturias and Galicia, to the peaceful existence of the backwater.

That offshoot was Castile. The name denotes the many fortresses (*castella*) with which this exposed territory lying southeastward of León was of necessity dotted for its holding against the Muslim. Having come into existence as a county subject to León, it continued to exist not by grace of León but by the strength of its own right arm and its valiant acceptance of hazards which, in the second half of the tenth century, included exposure to the repeated dread incursions of the invincible and indefatigable al-Mansur. The fact has something to do with the distinctive character Castile forged for itself from the beginning. León stood heir to the Visigothic monarchy, by whose code, the *Fuero Juzgo*, it still sought to regulate its society. Its population was much reinforced by returning Mozarabs, their Christian culture, like their Romance speech, wearing a curiously retarded, anachronistic garb, the result of centuries of residence among Muslims. Its capital, seat of that Roman seventh legion from which the name derived, had been an important centre of romanization of the northern tableland. It represented tradition, respect for past standards.

Castile was born of danger, cradled in perils, schooled to evolve its own criteria *ambulando*. Its population derived from the mountainous north; its capital, Burgos, was one of its own *castella*, founded in 882, unhampered by a past of some one else's making, with only a present and a future of its own. The *Fuero Juzgo* had not foreseen and could not cover the conditions in which this new society was destined to evolve; its men repudiated it – tradition tells of a bonfire in the streets of Burgos in which perished ceremonially all known copies – and out of custom, precedent, and *ad hoc* solutions built up their own corpus of consuetudinary law, naming judges for the interpretation and administration thereof.

The speech of Castile bears out this independent, innovating character. Against a background of features common to the Romance of the whole Christian north, from Galician through Leonese, Navarrese, and Aragonese to Catalan, features common even to the Mozarabic of the south, Castilian breaks in like a wedge, evolving new tendencies or, where these were general, shaping them earlier and carrying them further. Today Castilian is Spanish, and the traits which characterize it in the family of the Romance languages are those which were already moulding the speech of this nascent pioneer community in the tenth century.

Tension between León and Castile was inevitable. In León the nobility were constantly at issue with the crown on grounds of personal ambition; the counts of Castile fought for independence from that crown in rebuttal of a distant and irksome authority. The struggle, later given epic expression in literature, was largely won by the greatest of their line, Fernán González (*d*. 970), a doughty warrior, as the times demanded, who by his prowess against both al-Andalus and León achieved such a loyalty and solidarity among his followers as León had never known, enlarged his territory, and – succeeding through personal prestige, where again León had so signally failed, in vesting the succession in his own heirs – formally repudiated León's right to administer it. Many vicissitudes were still to befall the new state, even after its promotion in 1035 to the rank and title of kingdom; but the foundations of greatness had been laid, and it faced south.

The immediate vicissitudes derived from Navarre, a territory which, comprising Basque lands on both sides of the western Pyrenees, was destined thereby to a somewhat uncertain role in the history now of Spain, now of France. Fierce independence had been the hallmark of the Basques since their first emergence in recorded history. Rome had never wholly subdued them, nor the Visigoths, and Islam still less. With the birth in Asturias and the consolidation in León of the effort to re-establish Christian authority over a reunited Peninsula, the Basques once more served notice that they sufficed to themselves, and by the late ninth or early tenth century at latest they too were firmly constituted a kingdom and were engaging in conquest to the south on their own account.

Under Sancho 'the Great' (970–1035) a combination of political accident and matrimonial alliance conferred on Navarre a brief supremacy among the Christian states. García, last count of Castile and Sancho's brother-in-law, was murdered at Leonese instigation in 1029, but it was into the lap of Navarre, not of León, that Castile fell. Sancho then overran León, detaching from it a large portion of territory which he added to Castile to form a kingdom for his second son Ferdinand. The rest he incorporated in his own dominions, these now stretching from the borders of Galicia to those of Catalonia. King of 'the Spains' he was bold to entitle himself; but already before his death in 1035 he too, having four sons, had undone his achievement.

The emergence of Castile as a monarchy under Ferdinand I (1035–65) proved in the long run the most important of the arrangements resulting; in the short run too, for Ferdinand, having slain in battle in 1037 the exiled ruler of León, added León and Galicia too to his rule and for the first time, if as yet only momentarily, it was the turn of Castile to predominate. The logic of peninsular history was already foreshadowing the ultimate design. Sancho's provision for his third son Ramiro had too its importance. East of Navarre, running along the foothills of the Pyrenees to make contact with Catalonia and hemmed in to the south by Muslim Saragossa, lay the three counties of Aragon, Sobrarbe, and Ribagorza, all in suzerainty to Navarre. Ramiro received Aragon with likewise the title of king and shortly after, his younger brother dying, added to the new kingdom the other two counties. From the beginning therefore Aragon looked east and south, as Castile did west and south. Saragossa became its field for expansion against the infidel, Catalonia its natural rival, then ally, in the expanding, and within a century and a half the two were to merge their destinies.

The last years of Sancho of Navarre thus mark the birth, from a common source, of the two new kingdoms, Castile and Aragon, which eventually were to share all of Spain between them, and trace too the watershed which kept their courses so long apart. Their eventual fusion would reconstitute in great part the territorial unity which the coming of the Muslims had disrupted. Sancho's reign proved memorable also for a second reason. Both as straddling the Pyrenees and because the pilgrim route or *camino francés* to Santiago passed through it, Navarre lay wide open to French influences, political and cultural.

The former would in time bring the kingdom, permanently weakened by the consequences of 1035, under the governance of a long line of French kings who from 1234 to 1512 virtually removed it from the peninsular sphere. The latter found expression in the entry into Navarre at Sancho's invitation, and thence into Castile, of monks of the order of Cluny, whose reforming zeal in the Church and in education and culture generally, these being – in so striking contrast with the position in al-Andalus – essentially Church preserves, was to prove far-reaching. Cluny's reports to Rome on the progress of the Christian cause in Spain led the Pope in 1063 to commend the reconquest throughout western Europe as a holy crusade, and in the following year contingents from France and Italy, forerunners of the many which would share in later campaigns, entered Spain a generation before the first crusade to the Holy Land.

By then the situation in the Peninsula had changed radically with the fall of the caliphate in 1031 and the disruption of al-Andalus into more than a score of *taifas* constantly at issue among themselves. Ferdinand of Castile, having weathered the legacy of nearly twenty years of civil war made inevitable by his father's dispersal of his realms, leapt to the opportunity, and for the remainder of his reign proved himself a very Christian al-Mansur, indefatigable in his hammer-blows east, west, and centre against a now hopelessly divided enemy. His aim, however, went beyond humiliation and plunder to conquest, his fixed goal the recovery of the fatherland; and although his strength in man-power was still inadequate for effective reoccupation on a large scale, with the taking of Coimbra he restored the Mondego frontier and, laying waste the northern part of the kingdom of Toledo, carried devastation even to Seville. In the end the *taifas* of Saragossa, Toledo, Badajoz, and Seville were alike his tributaries, not merely innocuous henceforth to the Christian north but helping build up its resources against their own ultimate destruction.

Ferdinand died in 1065. Like his father, he too had towered over his nobles to the extent of identifying the succession with his own family. Like his father, he made the costly mistake of throwing away that inestimable advantage and jeopardizing his lifework by himself ensuring that his demise would loose a new round of civil wars. Leaving three sons, he would have them all kings, of Castile, León, and Galicia, three vertical territories rising from the line Coimbra-Sigüenza to the north coast. With this the map of Christian Spain, with its five kingdoms and the cluster of eastern counties still in process of fusion into Catalonia, resembled from afar the *taifas* of the south, and the fate of the Peninsula became again precariously contingent on which side would achieve, or reachieve, unity first. Sancho, Ferdinand's first-born, dissatisfied with Castile alone, at once sought aggrandizement against Navarre, failing in which he warred against his two brothers, stripped them of their inheritance, and in 1072 was assassinated as he laid siege to Zamora, held as her personal estate by a sister.

Alfonso, the second son, who had been driven to take refuge with the Muslim king of Toledo, was the beneficiary of this costly reuniting of his father's patrimony. As Alfonso VI of León and I of Castile (1072–1109) he enjoyed a long reign made memorable on several counts. Himself a warrior of renown like his father, his incursions into the south, made first against Cordoba and Seville, carried him in 1082 to Tarifa on the coast where the Muslims had made their original landing, and culminated in the capture of Toledo in 1085, after the death of the king who had befriended him there in exile.

This was the most notable achievement yet. Strategically, the taking of the mighty bastion allowed the effective settlement of the many towns to the immediate north on which, in Muslim hands, it had cast too threatening a shadow. Geographically, it brought the Christians down from the high plateau across the no-man's-land into the very heart of the country, adding what was thereafter to be known as New Castile to the Old and laying the plains of al-Andalus at their mercy. Symbolically, Alfonso's fixing now of his capital in what had been the capital of Visigothic Spain spelt, in the long and arduous course of the reconquest, the end of the beginning and the beginning of the end.

Casting back to Covadonga and 718 there could be no doubting that the uphill half of the journey lay behind; and if what remained, until the fall of Granada in 1492, was in fact to take even longer, the disparity has its explanation in terms other than the difficulty of the enterprise. Al-Andalus itself harboured no doubt of this. *Taifa* after *taifa* hastened to come to terms with Alfonso, buying peace with tribute. Saragossa was invested, Valencia occupied, nominally on behalf of the dispossessed ruler of Toledo as part of the terms of cession. Alfonso took to himself the title 'king of the two religions'. The days of the Muslim occupation seemed numbered.

But Islam had still one card to play and, as has already been told, played it. In 1086 there arrived from Africa the new invading army of the Almorávides. Hastening to the encounter, Alfonso suffered a series of reverses that continued till the battle of Uclés in 1108, where his son and heir Sancho was slain, and that deprived him alike of Saragossa and Valencia. In the following year he died, a broken man. If the new Toledo front stood firm it was from the enemy's failure to press home his advantages.

The career of Alfonso's great vassal and Spain's outstanding epic hero, Ruy Díaz de Bivar, known to fame as the Cid (Arabic *sidi*, lord), is bound up with these two key-cities, and casts a vivid light on the shifting nature of the reconquest as still understood at the close of the eleventh century. A Castilian from Burgos who typified the reluctance with which Alfonso, held a Leonese, was accepted in place of his murdered brother, Ruy Díaz was exiled by Alfonso in 1081 on charges arising out of a mission to Seville to collect tribute. Offering his services to the Muslim king of Saragossa, he fought on his behalf against the count of Barcelona, whom he twice took prisoner, then began campaigning on his own in the direction of Valencia, reduced this city by siege in 1094, and reigned in lordly independence over the extensive kingdom it commanded till his death five years later. Had he left a son instead of daughters he might have founded an additional Christian monarchy; his daughters' marriages, to a count of Barcelona, son of his erstwhile adversary, and a prince of Aragon, showed the rank and esteem he had won for himself.

The *Poema de mio Cid* of *c.* 1150 is Spain's outstanding epic. Though largely imaginative in theme, hingeing on the hero's final restoration to the royal favour, it is realistic in the detail of his military achievement in stemming the Almorávide flood at its most dangerous, where Alfonso had failed. From the epic he passed through chronicle, ballad, and the drama to become the accepted embodiment of Castilian individualism and prowess against the foe. If his death gave Valencia back to the enemy, the memory remained of what one man, cast in the heroic mould, could achieve.

Alfonso had had six wives, one of them a Muslim princess, but he too left only daughters. The marriage of the younger in 1095 made history, for from it derived, in the fulness of time, the independence of Portugal. Teresa's husband was a count Henry of Burgundy, one of a number of French knights who won Alfonso's gratitude by their help in the taking of Toledo; as dowry she received the lands south of the river Minho, accepted as the frontier of Galicia, to form a new county of Portugal – the name coming from its chief town Oporto ('the port') – in strict suzerainty to Castile. But Alfonso had reckoned without the ambition of his son-in-law, and the still stronger ambition of his daughter and of her son Afonso Henriques, who, profiting from turbulence in Castile and waging his own reconquest southward over territories the Muslim had never held in strength, eventually forced recognition of an independent kingship from his cousin Alfonso VII in 1143. Spain, thereafter, no longer meant the Peninsula. Four years later he seized Lisbon with the help of English crusaders bound for the Holy Land, some of whom went no further: one, Stephen of Hastings, became first bishop of the city on the Tagus. Portugal was thus established much farther south than Castile at a much earlier period in her independent history, and with correspondingly less left to conquer. Another century would pass before the winning of the last remnant of this, the Algarve, by joint Castilian-Portuguese enterprise, and with the cession of all Castilian claim to it in 1267 the national territory was complete.

The fact is important: the reconquest, a preoccupation to Spain of close on eight centuries, was to Portugal a matter of a century and a half. Its conclusion endowed the young kingdom with full nationhood and unity, and allowed it thereby to set itself to the defining and working out of a national purpose and destiny, more than two hundred years before Spain. A second determining factor derives from geography. Portugal emerged as essentially a seafaring country, poised on the very edge of Europe, its gaze fixed on the riddle of ocean, while Castile, land-locked, thought of expansion and power in terms necessarily of land and armies. A third and more tentative consideration, already hinted at, would explain differences in national temperament by divergences in the intensity and permanence of the various racial infusions, from Celtic down to Arab and Berber, in the west as compared with the rest of the Peninsula.

The importance of Celtic settlements is borne out by place-names, and this element we may believe to have been less over-laid here than elsewhere by Roman, Visigoth, and Muslim, all of whom, arriving respectively from east, north, and south, administered the country from centres remote from the western fringe. The kinship of Portugal, well attested in language and literature, is with the Galicia of which it began as a southward expansion; and we have seen how early, in its relations with León and Castile, Galicia was relegated to a life of its own. Castile did not take kindly to the severance of Portugal from the body politic. Repeatedly down the centuries it tried, by diplomacy or arms, to implement in this direction too what it came to conceive as its unifying mission in the Peninsula: for the space of two generations, under the Habsburgs, the dream would come true. The reasons why, alone of all the medieval kingdoms, Portugal, the last to come into existence, should have maintained its independence will emerge in due course.

While these events were imposing in the west a new pattern of state frontiers, to the frustrating of the ambition of León-Castile in the centre to uphold the ideal of peninsular integrity, a not dissimilar development was shaping in the east. Aragon and Catalonia too, sharing in the general stimulus born of the fall of Toledo, were driving south, each at first on its own, against the considerable Muslim territory of Saragossa which barred their way. Catalonia was initially the slower, having so many interests north of the Pyrenees, where its sovereignty extended over half a dozen counties reaching from Toulouse to Nice; but the capture of Tarragona in 1091 substantially increased its coastline and made possible in the decades following a series of incursions into the kingdom of Valencia.

Aragon, under its fourth king Alfonso I (1104–34), crowned the achievements of his immediate predecessors by taking the city of Saragossa in 1118. There followed the crumbling of other fortresses throughout the kingdom that over centuries had been such a bulwark of Islam and impediment to Christian unity. Bursting its constricting frontiers, Aragon soon doubled its territory, sweeping a hundred miles south of the Ebro to Teruel; and in 1126 Alfonso, like his namesake of Castile fifty years earlier, raided farther and farther, through Valencia, Murcia, and Andalusia, until at Motril he too stood on the south coast and saw the day coming when the last infidel should have been driven back across the sea to Africa. From that raid he led back north some 14,000 Mozarabs to the resettling of Aragon.

Such incursions were spectacular. They did not bring dominion over the areas in question, as those of al-Mansur had not when he raided far north to the sacking of Barcelona and Santiago. Al-Andalus, reunited first under the Almorávides and from 1146 under the Almohades, was being deeply bitten into, but for another century it would continue to hold sway over perhaps a third of the Peninsula, stretching with a very irregular and fluctuating land frontier from Cape St Vincent and the Algarve to just south of the mouth of the Ebro. What they did make clear was Aragon's growing need to reach an accommodation with Catalonia to its right and, to its left, with Castile, with which the elimination of the kingdom of Saragossa had brought now for the first time intimate contact.

A marriage alliance disposed felicitously of the first issue. In 1137 Ramon Berenguer IV of Barcelona was betrothed to the infant Petronella, heir of Ramiro II ('the Monk') of Aragon. Ramiro, who on the death of his brother, without issue, had been fetched from his monastery to assume the throne and secure the succession, now returned there, satisfied that he had fulfilled his duty, and although the marriage did not take place till 1151 Ramon Berenguer acted throughout as regent of Aragon. When he died in 1162 his ten-year-old son by Petronella succeeded as Alfonso II (1162–96) to a kingdom which thereafter embraced both territories and could address Castile-León on terms of equality.

The new joint state was to advance to some extent on two legs, for the character and interests of the partners were very different. The prestige of the monarchy gave the title to Aragon and made of Saragossa, now its capital, the nominal seat of authority. Barcelona, a thriving town and seaport and for over three centuries now a hub of Christian activity, moved in a very different world of ideas from a city so lately rewon from the Muslim. The only capital in Christian Spain that had been a capital from the beginning, its horizons had never been dominated by the infidel. Aragonese, moreover, could only look south. Catalans looked north and east as well, and felt instinctively that destiny pulled rather in those directions. Down to the end of the Middle Ages they would still be the only true Europeans in the Peninsula. Union with Aragon gave them the necessary security against Castile and the necessary backing for the prosecution of their enterprises: there would never be any doubt which was the directing partner.

The desirable understanding with Castile concerned the delimiting of spheres of conquest to the south. Alfonso VI, it will be remembered, had included both Saragossa and, still more directly, Valencia in his programme, the full realization of which would have made Castile supreme among the Christian states. Each of these states had an interest in expelling the invader, but not to the extent of overriding more immediate objectives, a principle which has been seen to lead already on occasion to the allying of Christian with Muslim against Christian. With Castile now claiming the right to drive east while Aragon drove south, the risk of violent collision was real, and more than once was barely averted. At length diplomacy prevailed, and in 1179 the treaty of Cazorla drew a line, running roughly south-south-east from Logroño in the far north till it struck the east coast near Alicante, beyond which Aragon would not go.

Not for another 150 years would its writ in effect run so far, but already the triple and curiously symmetrical pattern of the reconquered Peninsula was taking definitive form, its central feature the three vertical bands of Portugal, Castile, and Aragon. The centre of gravity of the first-named lay in the south, and the fact that its territory did not reach to the north coast mattered the less because its gaze was fixed south and west. The last-named had its fulcrum in the north and cared little that its territory should stop short of the south coast since its gaze looked north and east. The middle band, territorially the colossus with its extensions to the north-west and south-east, lay poised about its geographical centre, introspective, self-sufficing. A line drawn through the three capitals Lisbon, Toledo, Barcelona gives the true axis of the Peninsula.

Alfonso VII, crowned king of León and Castile in 1126 after a long, unpleasant interlude associated with his Aragonese step-father's aspirations in these states, and foiled in an attempt to turn the tables on Aragon on the latter's death, concerned himself instead with the traditional enemy. By now the Almorávides' grip on al-Andalus had weakened and, the old tendency to disintegration reasserting itself, he too made some notable penetrations into the far south. The measure of Islam's present weakness was his taking of Cordoba in 1144, the capital city that stood to the Muslim as Toledo had to the Christian, symbol and epitome of all his former greatness. Granada and Seville he put to the sack, and in 1147 he in his turn reached the south coast, there to capture with the naval cooperation of Catalans and Genoese Almeria, which he succeeded in holding till his death in 1157. But once again, and in the same way as before, the doom of Islam was averted. The onward sweep of the Almohades, after their landing in 1146, was slow in comparison with that of the Almorávides of sixty years earlier, but Cordoba duly changed hands once more.

In his assumption of the title of emperor in 1135 Alfonso had shown an awareness of larger problems. His crowning as such in León brought homage from the king of Navarre, the count of Barcelona, and several others from north of the Pyrenees, together with various tributary Muslims. There was doubtless little real submission in the act, and the mood did not long remain; but Alfonso's intention, clear and significant in the Peninsula, went beyond it too. The imperial title, resurrected by Charlemagne and held from 962 by successive kings of Germany, was recognized by Rome and claimed by them to imply over-lordship throughout Christendom in general. When, later, it became identified with a real territorial empire, Spain's destiny was to be intimately mixed up with it; meantime Spain gave Europe formal intimation that the Peninsula belonged, and would continue to belong, to itself.

Determined also that what Islam had to offer to Europe should not be lost, whatever the fate of al-Andalus, it was Alfonso who, building again on his grandfather's foundations, made of Toledo a centre of intense literary activity where, with the aid of his own churchmen and of the many Jewish scholars now seeking refuge from Berber obscurantism in the south, the masters of Arab, Hebrew, and classical Greek thought were translated into Latin and Castilian, to percolate thence through-out western Europe. This was a first renaissance, its distinguish-ing marks the predilection for science and the oriental cast given to the Greeks by their Arab commentators. Toledo became a place of resort for students from France, Germany, and England, a new pilgrim route to rival that to Santiago de Compostela.

Santiago too commanded Alfonso's interest, for he had been brought up in Galicia and styled himself king thereof before coming into his full patrimony, and from the Pope he obtained the elevation of its diocese into an archbishopric. One con-sequence of the enhanced prestige resulting may be seen in the new French settlements which in the twelfth century begin to dot the pilgrim way, another in a series of disputes with the primatial see of Toledo, whose primacy Santiago made bold to challenge, though never successfully.

One lesson even the 'emperor' had failed to learn. Al-Andalus in the days of its strength had rarely needed to divide to rule; its enemies did the dividing themselves. Leaving two sons, Alfonso on his death dealt the reconquest yet another gratuitous blow, the full gravity of which would only appear forty years later, by bequeathing Castile to one, León to the other. Castile was the greater sufferer: its new ruler, having begun with a triple war against León, Navarre, and Aragon, lived to reign but a year, and the crown passed to an infant son during whose long minority the turbulence of the nobles again rent the kingdom with strife.

Alfonso VIII (1158–1214) ascended the throne in 1170 at the age of fourteen, married in that same year an English princess, Eleanor daughter of Henry II, and proved himself for close on half a century a great and tireless warrior. War with León continued intermittently till 1180, but already he was battling with the infidel and pushing steadily southward until the day came when, from Algeciras, he hurled his personal defiance across the straits at the Almohade emperor. The latter's reaction we know, as also how Alfonso, forsaken at the last moment by León and Navarre, both having promised help, suffered at Alarcos in 1195 one of the most calamitous reverses to befall the Christians in the whole history of the reconquest.

Alfonso's next move was very much in character. Signing a truce with the Almohades, he promptly went to war again with his defaulting cousin of León, then, after three years of fighting, gave him his daughter in marriage and engaged him anew to do his duty in the common cause. Navarre he proceeded to chastise more severely, depriving it of the province of Guipúzcoa and of part of that of Alava. Free now to turn to the avenging of Alarcos, Alfonso persuaded the Pope to sound once more the call to a crusade – many came, though few remained to fight – and again bade to the fray his fellow-monarchs in the Peninsula. León defaulted a second time, but with the others he met the Almohades at Las Navas de Tolosa in 1212 and this time won the day.

The encounter belongs to the category of decisive battles. Al-Andalus never recovered from the blow: to the renewal of its internal discords there would be no further effective answer from Africa. The Christians, picking their objectives at leisure, annexed them thereafter one by one. Between 1229 and 1284 Badajoz fell to León, Cordoba, Murcia, and Seville to Castile, and Valencia to Aragon. The fall of Seville, compassed with the aid of vessels from the north coast, signified the birth of the Castilian navy, and the building forthwith of shipyards for its development was to prepare the ground for enterprises as yet undreamt of. Had Castile gone on to reduce Granada, the reconquest could have been counted at an end, as it was now for Aragon and, within another few years, for Portugal.

It was some compensation for the failure to close the long chapter that in 1230, through a succession of dynastic vicissitudes, León was again reunited with Castile, this time for good, under Ferdinand III (1217–52). This monarch, reaping for Castile the rich harvest of Las Navas de Tolosa, was single-minded in his conception of the struggle as a crusade for the faith, and had his posthumous reward in canonization as a saint. The great mosque of Cordoba he reconsecrated as a cathedral, and Muslim captives restored to Compostela the bells that al-Mansur had carried off from there two hundred and fifty years before. He sent forces across the straits to Morocco, to raise the standard of the faith in the very home of the infidel, and was planning to follow up this bold gesture with a large army when he died. To his death the kingdom of Granada owed its survival, for with him died much of the crusading spirit.

6

Patterns of Society

WITH the chequered progress of the reconquest social development was of necessity linked, in a connexion so close that the mid thirteenth century is a dividing line here too. From now on each state will continue to have its share of wars, civil and external, but relatively fixed frontiers allow at once a measure of stability not known before, a concentration on the exploiting of native resources and potentialities, and the weaving above all of a fabric of government and administration which will define the functions and interrelationships of the divers estates in the realm. The stamp will still remain of the long earlier process of adaptation to constantly changing horizons. Two aspects in particular of the reconquest have left their mark on society down to today.

The monarch, as has been seen, enjoyed from the beginning a very relative authority over his nobles, who continued to regard themselves as his peers long after the hereditary principle had been conceded. 'We who are as good as you swear to you, who are no better than we, to accept you as our king and sovereign lord provided you observe all our statutes and laws; and if not, no': so ran the Aragonese oath of fealty to a new ruler. In the Marca Hispanica Charlemagne had implanted the feudal system as it was known north of the Pyrenees. The resulting sense of hierarchy, equating privilege with obligation, was never achieved elsewhere in the Peninsula to the same degree, and some have seen the consequences down to modern times in a proneness to social indiscipline. The power of the nobility was territorial: on their estates, lords over their vassals, they were sovereign. Castile and Portugal alike showed in their origin how it was open to a count, by independent conquest from the infidel and the increase in power and prestige resulting, to make of his county a kingdom. The Cid showed how a lesser noble, renouncing his fealty, might carve himself a kingdom out of the lands of al-Andalus.

This process no monarchy could long contemplate with equanimity: the need to keep control in his own hands of itself turned the monarch into a crusader. Against the still distant day, however, of the standing army his strength in the field was but the man-power of his own royal estates, save to the extent that the nobility answered his call to arms with theirs. Had his own resources been adequate to campaigning without such help, he still dared not go to war and leave his nobles at home to exploit the situation. The price of the nobles' support, on the other hand, was a share in the spoils, specifically in the territorial spoils, of victory, with the paradoxical result that the seizing of lands from the enemy often meant the strengthening not of the royal authority but, to its detriment, of individual nobles.

The founding in the late twelfth century of the military orders, after the pattern of the Knights Templar, increased the tendency. That of Calatrava originated in 1158 in the defence of the town of that name against the Almohades. The order of Santiago, founded shortly after, was concerned initially with the protection of the pilgrim route against robber barons such as the Galician count Garcia Peres who in 1130 despoiled English and French merchants of some 22,000 silver marks. Alcántara, the third, arose in 1166, again in connexion with the reconquest. These associations of the church militant with the landed aristocracy drew their authority not from the king but from the Pope, to whom they were pledged to obedience and with whom lay nomination to the powerful grandmasterships.

Such division of allegiance, and the loss to the crown of territories and revenues accruing to the orders as they reconquered for themselves, presented a new problem to an already sufficiently harassed monarchy. As regards the orders, there was to be no solution until the completion of the reconquest robbed their existence of further military justification. As regards the Pope, this footing for intervention in the material sphere in Spain foreshadowed a friction destined to increase with the growing concern of the crown to be master in its own house; it can be seen still embittering relations six, seven, and eight centuries after. In Portugal, whose first king had in 1143 formally accepted vassalage to Rome and bound the crown to an annual payment of tribute in respect thereof, to the end of avoiding subservience to Spain, the elements existed, and persisted, of a similar struggle for supremacy.

Once the ascendancy of al-Andalus had been broken, the no-man's-land over which marauding forces had swept to and fro, condemning the scattered Christian settlements to a hand-to-mouth existence, gave way to a frontier rolling steadily if irregularly southward and to the incorporation in the Christian states of new regions which had to be settled, held, and administered. This responsibility, often beyond the immediate resources of the crown, was apt to devolve on the great nobles by grant of the lands in question. Such reward for services rendered had, it will be remembered, been the origin of Portugal.

It was the origin likewise of the great estates or *latifundios* of the southern half of the Peninsula which have persisted down to modern times, in contrast with the diminutive peasant holdings or *minimifundios* of the north, as the most striking feature of its agricultural and social structure. As late as the mid seventeenth century a descendant of one such grantee could attempt, in emulation of the first count of Portugal, to erect his vast holdings in Andalusia into an independent kingdom. The economic and social consequences have lain ever since at the root of some of the Peninsula's most intractable problems.

At the time the immediate concern was less the overlordship than the effective holding of newly acquired territories. Earlier we have seen Mozarabs being attracted north to help settle sparsely held areas. Now it was necessary instead to attract Christians south, not only to build and man fortresses but to plant townships, raise families, and dig roots; and this process too had its far-reaching social and political implications. For hazards were involved, and incentives were needed to counterbalance them. These incentives took the form of a *fuero* or charter of the rights and privileges assured to settlers and their descendants in a new or recaptured township, enshrining too the obligations expected of them in war and peace. The major incentive was freedom, a greater personal freedom than the individual had previously enjoyed elsewhere, in virtue of which these new communities represent the emergence of a new social element, an embryonic middle class empowered to carve out its own way of life and both bold and strong to defend it.

The fuero, defining the relationship of the citizen individually and of the community collectively to its overlord, who might be monarch, noble, Church, or military order, thus became, and remained for long after the conditions governing the original grant had passed away, the rallying-ground for the defence of popular liberties. Wide variations in those conditions were of necessity reflected in the fueros, which thus became too with time an obstacle to the unifying of law and administration: in the main they provide a coherent and detailed picture of life in an exposed frontier community liable to be thrown entirely on its own resources and to have to solve each new day's problems as they arose. Unforeseeable contingencies were frequently remitted to the judgement of 'good men', citizens of standing, and the reinforcing follows of the trend already noted in emergent Castile towards consuetudinary law.

The rhythm of the reconquest may be seen mirrored in the granting of fueros. Excluding those of unknown date or origin, the list falls thus: 1 in the eighth century, 4 in the ninth, 7 in the tenth, 45 in the eleventh, 280 in the twelfth, 310 in the thirteenth, 140 in the fourteenth, 5 in the fifteenth, and 1, in the Canary Islands, in the sixteenth. The mid thirteenth century brings the spate, and it is noteworthy too that from then on the charters, previously in Latin, are drafted in the vernacular. The change reflects a new outlook and a new pride of nationality following on the collapse of Islam.

These hundreds of new townships soon became a factor of importance in the political balance. The Visigothic monarch had been early forced to lean on the Church for support against a nobility always under temptation to unseat him. Six hundred years had passed, but the independent spirit of the nobility was still a thorn in the side of the crown, and in the incrementing of their power through vast territorial holdings the nobles now found their interests curiously allied to those of the Church, the military orders providing a common field of action. A disputed succession to the crown still commonly meant civil war. Henceforth the monarch would turn increasingly to the towns, posing as the fount of law and justice, as the court of appeal against exactions of the immediate overlord, as guarantor of the political status already accruing to the third estate, and looking to them for buttressing against the others.

Their status had a further bearing on the progress of the reconquest. The consultative body known down the centuries in both Spain and Portugal as *Cortes*, which was to evolve eventually into the parliament of the nineteenth century, had its distant origin in the *curia regis* or royal council of the Visigoths, comprising the greater nobles and Church prelates. Among the privileges of these was exemption from tribute, this weighing only upon the ignoble and constituting the mark of their rank. Payable in kind or in services to their lord, who might or might not be the king, it corresponded only remotely to the modern conception of state revenue. But the state's concern with revenue was also then very different, and so long as al-Andalus was there for the spoiling the monarch's need for resources beyond those of the crown estates could always be met by conquest, or even by successful raiding.

The exhaustion of this possibility induced fundamental changes in the nature of the monarchy, as of the state; and alongside the royal council, still charged with administrative and judicial functions, there took shape the larger Cortes to deal with economic questions, and specifically now with the raising of revenue. Only from the townships could new revenue come, and these, possessed in their fueros of a bulwark against arbitrary exactions, had to be wooed. The result was a victory for the principle of no taxation without representation: the towns gained admission to the Cortes.

In León the innovation is attested from 1188, in Catalonia – which maintained its Cortes distinct from those of Aragon– from 1218, in Castile from 1250, in Portugal from 1254. Once the towns had been admitted certain incipiently democratic consequences followed, and in 1188 no other country in Europe knew such representation of the commons. But León was among the least democratic, being perhaps the most conservative, of peninsular states, and the reason underlying the departure of that year – a new king's desire to have the towns too swear fealty to a crown lately separated from and threatened anew by Castile – was innocent of devotion to a new political principle. In Catalonia the motive was a young king's need of allies against a turbulent nobility. Castile took the step once the fall of Seville spelt the necessity of ordering and financing the state on a new basis; Portugal as a royal move, made possible by the same virtual ending of the reconquest, to destroy the political power of the Church.

The people, in a word, were brought into the balance of forces by the crown for its own purposes, and the chequered history of the Cortes in the several kingdoms is an exact reflection, not of the growth of political capacity and power in the people, but of the fluctuating fortunes, now political, now financial, of the crown. Down to the beginning of the nineteenth century, while the conception persisted of a personal, absolute monarchy, the Cortes would be convened so often as the monarch had need of it, and left unconvened – sometimes for generations at a time – when he had not.

If the Cortes thus provided only an intermittent schooling in political responsibility and government, none other was available, and when convoked the towns turned it to good account. Their presence soon came to have one dominant significance, the crown's need for money: this only they, who were to pay it, could vote, and their price for voting it became the prior remedying by the crown of their grievances. The Cortes remained a consultative, not a legislative, body, the diversity of fueros and of jurisdictions still making it difficult for the king himself to promulgate laws of general application; in the sphere of high policy, including questions of peace and war, it had no say. It marked for the towns nonetheless a dawning political consciousness: the voting of taxes gave them a direct concern in the country's welfare, and the contact on this new footing with the representatives of Church and nobility brought home to these that their privileges were exposed to scrutiny and, if abused, to challenge from a new quarter. To the monarchy, whose major problem for the remainder of the Middle Ages was the recovery from Church and nobility of powers and resources improperly alienated from the crown, this fortuitous emergence of a new ally was an event of the first importance.

For Catalonia the early thirteenth century was coloured by territorial contractions and expansions not limited, as elsewhere, to al-Andalus. Alfonso II (1162–96) had been known as 'emperor of the Pyrenees' from a sway extending, by inheritance, conquest, or alliance, across the whole of southern France. He too at death committed the folly of dividing his kingdoms, and Provence was lost thereafter to Aragon. Peter II (1196–1213), inheriting the latter, completed the dispersal of his northern patrimony by his defeat and death at the disastrous battle of Muret, which spelt eclipse to Catalan rule beyond the Pyrenees and made possible the eventual unification of France. This marked the end of one greatness but the beginning too of another, for even before the taking of Valencia in 1238 concluded Catalonia's interest in the reconquest James I 'the Conqueror' (1213–76) had opened up for his country a more fruitful field of enterprise by his seizure of the Balearic Islands in 1229–35.

The ultimate fruits of this achievement none then could have foreseen, and James himself for the rest of his long reign kept to the mainland; but it remains of note that Catalonia had thus taken to the sea and discovered what was to prove its true line of destiny almost a century before Portugal followed, to the same effect, the same course. Castile, hemmed in by Granada, had to await its fall two and a half centuries later before it too could adventure beyond the Peninsula and show its prowess in overseas conquest. And those centuries conditioned it the more firmly to acceptance of its role as essentially a land power. When in due course empire came, in Europe and in the New World, it would be a land empire of the traditional type, in strong contrast to those fashioned by the other two on a basis of sea-power, coastal footholds, and trade.

For a moment it seemed that Castile too might be drawn out of its peninsular orbit. Alfonso X 'the Learned' (1252–84) was a monarch in the line of the sixth and seventh of his name who set himself to explore, harmonize, and make generally available the triple heritage, Christian, Hebrew, and Arabic, of peninsular culture. Himself scholar as well as patron of scholarship, to this he gave the energy and the resources now released from crusading, admirably seconding the work of the early universities whose founding (Palencia *c.* 1212, Salamanca *c.* 1243) was another symbol of the new age.

Alfonso's adoption of Castilian as the official tongue in place of Latin and the series of collective literary enterprises he launched in the vernacular, notably the great *Estoria de Espanna* or *Primera Crónica General*, contributed notably to the development alike of a national consciousness and of a national litera-

ture; while in the *Siete Partidas* he produced a vast legal encyclopedia, based chiefly on Roman law, which recognized far in
advance of its day – only in 1348 was it promulgated as the law
of the land – the need to standardize the administration of justice
throughout the kingdom as a first step to the building of at once
a strong monarchy and a strong and close-knit society.

The marriage of Alfonso's father, Ferdinand III, to the
daughter of the emperor of Germany had been one token of
Castile's growing prestige abroad with recovery of the national
territory. The connexion underlay Alfonso's nomination in 1256
as a candidate to the imperial succession. Fighting the election
with resolve against an English rival, he won and was duly proclaimed emperor in the following year, only to be thwarted of
such accretion of dignity and responsibilities by the combined
opposition of his own nobility and the Pope. The former were
incensed at a squandering of moneys to achieve it so reckless that
it involved a depreciation of the coinage, and were apprehensive
no less of the consequences to Castile of commitment in central
Europe; the latter was pursuing his own political and territorial
interests. Between them Alfonso was constrained eventually to
renounce the title in 1275, persuaded that his country was not
yet ready to play a part on the larger stage.

The decisive factor in this, if not peculiar to his reign, came
home the more acutely to one who had been at pains to enshrine
in law for the first time the principle of the hereditary monarchy
and the supremacy of the crown. The struggle for power between
crown and nobility had come to the fore again with the defeat of
the Muslim, and there was no shirking it. For centuries fighting
had been the nobles' profession, and the calling was the harder
to unlearn now that the crown could no longer reward subservience with lands. This was to be the dominant issue for the
remainder of the Middle Ages: its eventual solution in favour of
the crown the indication that states had achieved a social pattern
and a maturity adequate to just such a challenge and opportunity
from abroad as Alfonso now had to lay down.

Various rebellions had already punctuated his reign when the
death of his eldest son in the very year of his withdrawal from the
imperial scene precipitated a dynastic crisis, his second son
Sancho refusing to stand aside and see proclaimed, as the *Siete*

Partidas had laid down, his dead brother's infant heir. From the ensuing civil war Sancho emerged victorious, and Alfonso, erstwhile emperor-elect, suffered the indignity of deposition by the Cortes in 1282. His death two years later ended a reign as unfortunate politically as it was outstanding in cultural achievements, and left the throne a prey anew to violence and ambition. The rule of law had suffered a grave setback, though this but provided an early example of the truism, so often to be repeated in peninsular history, that legislation divorced as this was from social reality is foredoomed to failure. Had the cause of his infant grandson triumphed, the turmoil consequent on the inevitably renewed struggle for power during a long minority could have been still more disastrous.

Sancho IV (1284–95) is remembered for his treaty of 1291 with Aragon partitioning north Africa into respective spheres of interest, with the river Moulou as dividing line. This assigning of Morocco to Castile headed the latter's external interests back in a direction more logical and more congenial to public opinion. A step to the ultimate effective prosecution of the ambition implied was the taking in 1292 of the key fortress of Tarifa from the Benimerines, a new tribe of invaders from across the straits who in alliance with Granada were threatening a revival of trouble for Castile.

With the accession of Sancho's nine-year-old son Ferdinand IV (1295–1312) the kingdom lapsed anew into chaos, complicated by the intervention of the kings of Portugal, Aragon, and France, all fishing for themselves in waters muddied by the continuing legacy of Sancho's usurpation of the throne. The regent, driven to the verge of seeking alliance with Granada, brought back memories of Roderic and 711. The nobles took thought only for what each could wrest from the royal patrimony, while even the towns stood aligned against the crown. That the nation did not break wholly asunder was due to the astuteness in diplomacy of the queen-mother, María de Molina, one of the great women of Spanish history.

Ferdinand, come of age in 1302, bought off his rivals, reached an accommodation with his fellow-monarchs, and, in alliance now with Aragon, turned his country's attention to campaigning once again against the Muslim. His triple objectives, Almería,

Gibraltar, and Algeciras, showed a concern directed not at Granada but, like his father's, across the straits. Only Gibraltar was taken, in 1310, and the fuero granted it by Ferdinand in that year, with its promise of asylum to all who should proceed thereto and dwell therein, whether swindlers, thieves, murderers, or other evildoers whatsoever, or women escaped from their husbands, spoke at once of the importance and the difficulty of manning the fortress and foreshadowed the role it was destined to play, as a haven for Spanish political dissidents, long after it had passed from Spanish hands. In fact it was lost again to the enemy in 1333 and, resisting repeated sieges, remained in Muslim hands until 1462.

This reign and the next seemed likely to bring into irretrievable disrepute the prestige of the crown, for Alfonso XI (1312–50) was but one year old on his father's death and the earlier chaos was re-enacted, much intensified. María de Molina again had a hand in saving the prince his throne until he too, declared of age at fourteen, succeeded at length in laying discord under shadow of a renewed threat from without. The spectacle of a Castile so divided against itself had bred in Granada new hopes that the greatness of al-Andalus might yet be restored, and the Beni-merines were now again invited to cross over in strength. This they did, routing the Castilian fleet twice and retaking Gibraltar. Alfonso, unable to recover the lost ground alone, was eventually succoured by Portugal and Aragon and on the banks of the Salado in 1340 won a resounding and this time conclusive victory; artillery, it is said, was used here for the first time in Europe. Algeciras he captured in 1344, after a prolonged siege at which Chaucer's 'verray parfit gentil knight' was one of a goodly company drawn from abroad. Plague carried Alfonso off as he was investing Gibraltar, and once more chaos was his legacy.

The circumstances this time were different. Peter I (1350–69), known to history as 'the Cruel', inherited at the age of fifteen a difficult family situation which showed the state still at the mercy of personal considerations. Tension between him and his five illegitimate brothers, all raised by their father to high estate, was less initially than that between the queen-mother and her rival in the late king's affections, but the result was the same. The assassination of the rival drove her sons into open rebellion, and soon Peter was fighting for his crown with a ruthlessness that drenched the country in blood; half-brothers, cousins, an archbishop of Santiago, even, his enemies alleged, his French queen, were alike put to death without compunction.

Henry of Trastamar, eldest of the half-brothers, found allies in Aragon and in France, whence came on his behalf, under a knight of great renown, Bertrand du Guesclin, the 'White Companies' of adventurers whom king and Pope were only too eager to see depart from French soil. Peter sought help from Navarre and England, and Edward the Black Prince, then governing the English territories in south-west France, crossed over in 1367, less concerned with the issue in debate than with the prospect of adventure, the promise of townships, and the desire to measure himself against du Guesclin. Closer knowledge of Peter caused him to withdraw after one notable victory at Nájera when du Guesclin himself fell into his hands. The great ruby presented to him by Peter, who had butchered for it a friendly king of Granada, was to become the chief jewel in the English crown. In 1369 Peter fell to Henry's dagger in a hand-to-hand scuffle.

Henry's accession as the second of his name (1369–79) meant more than the giving of yet another twist to the dynasty. Peter's other epithet, 'the Dealer of Justice', is evidence that, whatever his vices, his people saw in him a monarch bent on keeping the nobles in check. With his failure that battle would have to be fought all over again, and on worse terms, for Henry rewarded those who had helped raise him to the throne on a scale not merely ruinous to the national patrimony but which, as it increased their power, lessened his. For the time being foreign complications overlaid this issue, Peter's brief alliance with the Black Prince having left a continuing English interest with far-reaching consequences in its train.

Edward's brothers, John of Gaunt and Edmund of York, had married two of Peter's bastard daughters – his indiscretions showed how little he had learnt from his father's – and Gaunt, proclaiming himself king of Castile on his wife's behalf, now declared war on the usurper. Henry proved able to hold his own against this threat, as against his other enemy, Portugal, whose monarch too laid title to the succession. The war with Portugal allowed the Muslims in the south, always quick to exploit Christian dissensions, to win back Algeciras and other lost ground. More important was the drawing together of England and Portugal on the basis of their common hostility to the line of Trastamar.

Portugal, having enjoyed full sovereignty now for some two centuries, had been working out her own solution to not wholly dissimilar problems. The same social unbalance already noted in Castile between the dense population and consequent small holdings of the north and the vast and much more sparsely settled estates of the south sprang from the same source. The dividing line here ran along the Mondego, as far as which the Muslims had already been overrun and to some extent dispossessed by León. It was the onward sweep to the Tagus, and beyond into the rolling plains of the Alemtejo, that had given to Afonso Henriques the royal title, assumed after his victory at Ourique in 1139, and the substance of power, including the wherewithal to create his new landed nobility.

His son Sancho I (1185–1211), driven back to the line of the Tagus by the Almohades in 1191, four years before Alarcos, was content to leave the reconquering, as he had already assigned the possession, of the lost territories to the military orders – two famed throughout Europe, the Templars and the Hospitallers, two come from Spain, Santiago and Calatrava – and to devote himself, insofar as repeated involvement in disputes with León, Castile, and Rome allowed, to the better ordering of the rest of his domains.

Among his objectives, that of subordinating the Church to civil authority brought the inevitable papal protests. Quarrelling deliberately with the more powerful bishops and seizing ecclesiastical estates and revenues, he bequeathed to his son Alfonso II (1211–23) as the corner-stone of policy the defence of the royal patrimony, which Alfonso accepted and carried even to a refusal, at the cost of prolonged civil war, to alienate from the crown the estates left by Sancho to his other children. He also made violent assaults on Church property and privilege, driving the primate-archbishop of Braga into exile and dying excommunicate in consequence. In 1220 he instituted an inquiry by royal commission into the validity of the titles of Church and nobility to their holdings, uncovering a mass of abuses and arousing in both estates such hostility as brought about, on his death soon after, a first serious threat to the stability of the throne. This culminated in the eventual deposition of his son Sancho II (1223–46) who, succeeding as a minor, never matched in statesmanship his outstanding personal prowess in the repeated campaigns he waged for the recovery of the Alemtejo, once more a crown concern.

Alfonso III (1248–79), who had headed the revolt – directly instigated by the Pope – against his brother, came to the throne in the year already signalized as marking, with Castile's recapture of Seville, the nadir of Muslim dominion. Moving his capital from Coimbra, where his three predecesssors had held court to Lisbon, he led an army southward and recovered without difficulty the lands lying beyond the Tagus. Frontier delimitation with Castile was here involved and led several times to hostilities, but in 1267, as has already been noted, Castile conceded recognition of Portugal's title to the Algarve, and the nation's boundaries were settled substantially as they remain today. For Portugal the reconquest was over.

Internal problems remained, and the need for constant vigilance against a neighbour never wholly resigned to Portuguese independence. Renewing the investigations into property titles, Alfonso soon found himself engaged in the same struggle against the Church and Rome that had cost his brother the throne, and only escaped deposition himself by capitulating, on the eve of his death in 1279, to demands fundamentally incompatible with the sovereignty of the state. His reign witnessed notwithstanding notable advances in the emancipation of serfs, in the growth and power of the municipalities, represented for the first time in the Cortes of Leiria in 1254, and in trade.

His son, Denis 'the Farmer' (1279–1325), is remembered for the stimulus he gave to agriculture, encouraging the nobles to cultivate their estates as the true source of wealth, and for his effective curtailing of the Church's holdings in land and of its right to acquire more. Following in the footsteps of his grandfather Alfonso X of Castile, with whom he had been brought up, Denis became too a Maecenas of learning and the arts, like him enhanced the dignity of the vernacular by making Portuguese the language of law and administration, gave to literature the similar impulse of royal example, and in 1290 founded the university of Lisbon which, after some centuries of peripatetic existence between the new capital and the old, was transferred finally to Coimbra in 1537. Portuguese literature may be said to begin in this reign.

Denis nationalized the Portuguese branch of the order of Santiago, and on the dissolution of the Templars in 1312 endowed a new native 'Order of Christ' with their estates. He founded a navy, crowned a hundred years of trading relations with England by signing in 1294 a commercial treaty with Edward I, and – again like his grandfather – knew in his last years the bitterness of civil war loosed by a rebellious son. The full price for this was paid in due course by the son, in the continuing unrest, extending beyond the frontier and involving still another war with Castile, that marked the first half of his own reign as Alfonso IV (1325–57). A new threat from Africa restored perspective, and Portugal shared with Castile the honours of the great victory of the Salado in 1340.

Over the remaining years of this reign there still hangs today, to the exclusion in popular memory of other aspects, the tragic story of Inês de Castro, a Galician lady and the great love of Peter, Alfonso's heir. Her diplomatic murder in 1355 reflected fear not alone of the threat through her children to the direct line of succession, but once again of Castilian interference through her brothers in Portuguese affairs. Peter's reaction was to raise at once the standard of revolt, plunging the country anew into civil war. His father dying soon after, he marked his ten years on the throne as Peter I (1357–67) by taking into his own hands the administration of justice, and even the meting out of penalties, throughout the realm, so that he too, like his namesake and contemporary in Castile, became known as 'the Dealer of Justice'.

The two Peters at first were friends and allies. In the ensuing dynastic struggle in Castile Portuguese sympathies veered to the side of the usurping Trastamar, then – under Ferdinand I (1367–83) – back again; and after the assassination of 1369 Ferdinand presumed to claim the Castilian throne for himself. Shifty in his foreign relations and in character a weakling, this one legitimate son of Peter I endangered instead the credit of his own throne and the independence of his country. Yielding as had his father to an unworthy passion, he married another man's wife who, bearing him a daughter, schemed thereafter to secure her the succession at any price. Affianced five times before she was twelve, Beatrice eventually married John I of Castile in 1383, and the price became apparent to all as the imminent loss of Portuguese sovereignty.

On Ferdinand's death John had himself proclaimed not consort but king of Portugal, with Church and nobility largely on his side. The commoners felt differently: rising indignantly against such betrayal, they acclaimed as their champion John, master of Aviz, as the order of Calatrava had come to be known in Portugal, a bastard son of Peter. In the event not merely was the dynasty changed, and its character, with profound repercussions on the social structure, and the threat from Castile laid for another two hundred years: the struggle necessary to success brought England into the picture, and the achievement of it allowed the guiding of a reinvigorated people into new and epoch-making paths of adventure.

Those paths Aragon was already treading, having greatness thrust upon it by association with Catalonia. The conquest of the Balearic Islands by James I was, as has been seen, a wholly Catalan enterprise; and though James ended his sixty-three-year reign with the now so familiar mistake of dividing among his children the territories he had laboured to unite, leaving the Balearics to the younger son, his people's gaze had by then been withdrawn from north and south, that were formerly regarded as its twin spheres of influence, and directed firmly to eastward.

James had a clearer vision of his country's needs and potentialities than most medieval rulers. His reign saw the beginning of full Cortes with representation of all three estates and notable developments in municipal administration. These played their part in promoting the rise of a middle class, its fortunes linked to a rapidly expanding commerce, and helped equip Barcelona for its new role of entrepôt of Mediterranean trade. The *Llibre del Consolat de Mar* or maritime trade code of its port tribunals achieved an international authority, backed by the consuls James sent abroad to protect Catalan commercial interests.

Politically the Aragonese scene, as distinct from that in Catalonia, continued to be dominated by the struggle between the crown and a nobility fighting for its feudal privileges and ready in their defence even to side with the king's foreign enemies. In 1287 it exacted from the weak Alfonso III (1285–91) a charter, the 'Privilege of the Union', which secured to its members virtual immunity from crown action save after joint indictment by *Justicia* – the supreme officer of justice, who in theory mediated between king and nobles – and Cortes and created, as Alfonso put it, 'as many kings in Aragon as there were great nobles'. James II (1291–1327) recovered some of the ground lost; but not until 1348, after a bitter contest both in Aragon and in Valencia, and against the towns as well as the barons, did Peter IV succeed in revoking the 'Privilege' and restoring a position which still left the fundamental issue unsettled. As Catalonia sided consistently with the crown in the conflict, its leaders came to play an increasingly prominent part in the royal counsels and administration.

From the marriage much earlier of Peter III (1276–85) to the only child of King Manfred of Sicily, a match consonant with James I's whole Mediterranean policy, there was to unfold a long trail of consequences. Manfred's sovereignty, extending to the mainland of Naples, raised wider issues than the mere succession to the island throne, for the Pope had long been disputing the possession of these combined territories, and now offered the title to them to Charles of Anjou in return for a promise of fealty. Manfred's death in battle led to the occupation of Sicily by Charles, until the tyrannical behaviour of his forces provoked in 1282 the rising famous as the Sicilian Vespers and an appeal from the islanders to Peter.

Finding himself very conveniently in Tunis, recently seized and held as an Aragonese protectorate, Peter crossed over with an army and was soon master both of Sicily and of a substantial foothold in southern Italy, and at war in consequence with France and the Pope. His deathbed resolve to restore Sicily to the Pope went unfulfilled, and the new kingdom passed, not to his firstborn Alfonso III, but – as with Majorca on his father's death – to his second son James.

James, succeeding unexpectedly to the throne of Aragon on his brother's death without issue, left Sicily to another brother

Frederick, then in 1295, as a peace gesture to his enemies, renounced his rights to the island in favour of the Pope, receiving in exchange a title to Corsica and Sardinia, which was to be made effective by conquest. At this cavalier treatment the Sicilians took matters into their own hands, elected Frederick as their king, and succeeded in holding their own against all comers until in 1302 a general peace was signed, leaving Frederick in possession.

From that peace sprang the great adventure that was to carry Catalan arms and prestige to an eminence none had foreseen. For like the White Companies whom Henry of Trastamar was later to draw from France, the large numbers of mercenaries, mostly Catalans, now unemployed and unwanted on the island cried out for a new field of activity. In answer came an appeal for help from the emperor of Constantinople, then hard pressed by the Turks, and some 6,500 troops under one Roger de Flor sailed east, to acquit themselves with such prowess in Asia Minor that the emperor bestowed on them in reward the whole of Anatolia. Strengthened by two further expeditionary forces of Catalan and Aragonese adventurers, and fighting soon alike against the Genoese, incensed to see the Mediterranean become a Catalan lake and the Balkans a Catalan preserve, and against such treachery on the part of the Greeks as threw them on their own resources, they seized the duchy of Athens and there maintained themselves as a sovereign state from 1322 to 1386.

Nothing in all this had derived from royal policy at home – the venture was born in fact as indirect consequence of a successful challenge to that policy – and no lasting consequences followed. It was still Catalonia's finest hour, and the finer precisely in that it sprang from individual initiative and showed the Catalans a people in every way deserving of the pride so freely expressed in them by their monarchs. The pride was reciprocal, and found literary expression – this was too the supreme age of Catalan prose – in the four great chronicles of James I, Desclot, Muntaner, and Peter IV, collectively a worthy and more individual counterpart to Castile's *Primera Crónica General*.

Before the duchy of Athens had run its course Aragon too, like Portugal, had become involved in the bitter struggle being waged for the throne of Castile between Peter the Cruel and his

half-brother. Peter IV – there were then Peters on all three peninsular thrones – had been at war with Castile almost continuously
since 1356, the Castilian having supported a pretender's claim to
the Aragonese crown. Aragon's logical retort was to support the
Trastamaran claim to that of Castile, and eventually a domestic
Castilian embroilment arising out of one man's evil character
became not merely a peninsular but a European issue, Aragon
and France being ranged with the pretender, Portugal and
England with the monarch. The immediate upshot for Castile
has been seen, as too the further implications for the Peninsula
deriving from the matrimonial alliances, its by-products, that
allowed Gaunt a title to the Castilian throne and John I of Castile
one to the Portuguese.

Both rested nominally on claims of legitimacy, but the principle had long since become too sullied to serve as more than
cover for ambition. Gaunt's wife was born out of wedlock;
John's was commonly held no better, while he was himself the
bastard son of a usurper. In 1380 Portugal had strengthened its
personal understanding with Gaunt into one with the English
crown, and shortly afterwards a first English army appeared in
Portugal to wage common cause against Castile, presaging the
more resounding events of 1385. In that year John of Aviz, the
people's nominee in their refusal to see their country pass under
alien rule, was formally proclaimed king by the Cortes, and John
of Castile invaded Portugal in defence of his wife's inheritance.
The decisive encounter took place at Aljubarrota, where English
archers played their part in humbling the intruder and confirming
beyond further question the new dynasty of Aviz.

Out of that victory, and of that change of dynasty, came in
1386 the formal alliance – 'for ever' – with England. Reaffirmed
down the centuries as a sheet anchor in the policies of both
countries, and today the oldest alliance in existence, it bound
alike the two thrones and the two peoples to the defence of each
other's interests and territories 'wherever they may be'. None
could then have conceived the full import of these last words, or
how the destinies first of Portugal, then of England, were soon to
lie along the ocean highways of the world, crossing, inter-
twining, threatening collision on occasion, yet working all the
time to the fuller realization of their interdependence.

A further consequence of Aljubarrota, in the defeat of the many Portuguese nobles who had sided with Beatrice and her husband, was the forging of close links between the new royal line and the towns, from which John had drawn the bulk of his support and out of which he now proceeded to raise up a new aristocracy rooted not in blood and landed estates but in commercial enterprise. Gaunt's return to the Peninsula in 1386 to prosecute his wife's claim to Castile proved militarily a failure but bore other fruits, for with him and his army had gone two daughters, one of whom, Philippa of Lancaster, he married to John and the other, Constance, to Henry, heir to the throne of Castile. With the latter marriage, uniting the grand-daughter of Peter I with the grandson of his half-brother of Trastamar, the dynastic question there was at last peacefully settled, and on the model of England's Prince of Wales the title of Prince of Asturias was created for Henry and borne thereafter by successive heirs to the throne.

In Portugal a new chapter of history began with John I (1385–1433) and his English queen, who with their five sons and one daughter were to go down to fame as the most illustrious royal family in eight centuries of monarchy. John supplied the strength of character and the driving power to identify the national will with his, Philippa the austerity and moral purpose to ensure the harnessing of that will to worthy objectives, their children the urge to keep alive the crusading temper that with the expulsion of the Muslim appeared in danger of eclipse. To them it had seemed that their country's heroic age was over; in fact it was only beginning. It began with the expedition to Ceuta of 1415, Portugal's first overseas enterprise, planned by John at their insistence and evidence that reconquest and conquest were at bottom one, a holy war.

Four sons accompanied their father. Philippa blessed the undertaking from her deathbed, presiding to that extent over the birth of Portuguese empire. The taking of Ceuta proved in itself of little more than token importance: not until 1437 with an expedition to Tangier, as disastrous as the other had been successful, was any attempt made to exploit it. What mattered more was that Henry, the third son, returned from Ceuta with a vision and a purpose to which he would remain faithful till his death.

As 'the Navigator' history recognizes in him the pioneer in a long process of exploration of the till then unknown world whereby it fell to the Peninsula to vitalize and enrich beyond recognition the dawning Renaissance, that had otherwise borne a predominantly literary character, and to lay the foundations of the world hegemony enjoyed for centuries thereafter by the nations of western Europe.

At Sagres on the south coast Henry established a school of navigation where he gathered around him pilots, cartographers, scientists, and shipbuilders, and addressed himself in yearly expeditions, each charged to penetrate a little further than its predecessor into the unknown, to the resolving of the great enigma presented by the west coast of Africa. The desire to discover new lands, for purposes of trade, conquest, or proselytization as opportunity might offer, to take the measure of the infidel by learning how far his sway extended, and to seek out possible allies against him, a hope fortified by the mysterious legend of Prester John, that ruler of a Christian empire located somewhere in central Africa or Asia where was to be found the earthly paradise: all this was in his mind and, presiding over the whole, the fundamental desire just to know.

Portugal, planted on the outer fringe of the continent, beyond the pillars of Hercules that to the Romans had seemed to set a term to the discoverable world, in facing the ocean accepted the challenge of ocean. Not until now had the two pre-conditions been fulfilled; but supreme at last in its own house and secure behind its frontiers, the nation sought in the unknown the greatness denied it in Europe by its insignificance as a land power. Madeira, the Canaries, and the Azores were already familiar, if vaguely, from Portuguese and Catalan voyages of around 1335–42, and their settlement now found a place – the Canaries, despite a Spanish interest dating back to 1402, from 1424, the Azores from 1445 – in Henry's comprehensive activities.

His true interest lay, however, south, not west. The belief that Africa must end somewhere, and could therefore be rounded, was later to open up the possibility of access by sea to the fabled wealth of the orient – spices, sugar, precious stones – that till then reached Venice, the distributing centre for the west, only through Muslim middlemen and at a price commensurate with the complexities of the Arab route. Out of that possibility, triumphantly realized, would evolve a far-flung empire, stretching from Brazil across Africa and Asia to the China Sea, with consequences for the world at large far outstripping the immediate fruits of achievement in the new flow of spices to Europe and of riches to Portugal.

Eighty years of patient exploration still lay ahead, years of gradual perfecting of the mariner's art and, with the invention notably of astrolabe and compass, of his resources. By the time of Henry's death in 1460 his men had reached to the Gulf of Guinea and added the Cape Verdes to the crown. Conquest on the mainland did not go beyond the establishment of forts and trading stations, stepping-stones to the still remote and uncertain objective and the source already of a considerable influx of negro slaves into Portugal in assuagement of the drain on manpower that was to weigh increasingly on the nation as the imperial adventure unfolded.

The death of John in 1433, after a reign of close on half a century, likewise weighed heavily, for in his son Edward I (1433–8) there succeeded to the man of action a scholar temperamentally unfitted for rule and remembered as king only for his revision and codification of the nation's laws and for his own 'lei mental' – so-called because it was averred to have been in his father's mind – declaring all Crown grants indivisible and inalienable and the property anew of the Crown in default of a male heir. This measure, born of the mischief done by John's over-generous rewarding of his supporters in his fight for the succession, would remain in force until 1832. But its benefits were of necessity long-term, and it came too late to bolster the authority of the throne when, after five years, Edward died leaving in Alfonso V (1438–81) a minor six years old.

Again a disputed regency led to civil strife, with again an illegitimate pretender as focus of all, especially noble, discontents. Another Alfonso, born to John before his marriage to Philippa, could claim to be Portuguese where his half-brothers were half-English, and as duke of Braganza he founded a line that two centuries later would in fact achieve the kingship, not against the house of Aviz, by then extinct, but against Spain. For long meantime it was to prove an irritant in the affairs of state, by reason both of its ambitions and of its immoderate accumulation of lands and wealth. The immediate struggle for control of the boy-king ended with a Braganza victory on the field of Alfarrobeira, in 1449, where perished Peter, second son of John and Philippa, famed for his early travels throughout Europe and the best fitted of them all for the responsibilities of government.

Braganza was not the king's only evil star. Alfonso's Aragonese mother and Castilian wife, and the marriage of his sister to Henry IV of Castile, were soon to underline once again not merely the proverb, already so dearly learnt, that 'From Spain there blows neither good wind nor good marriage', but the fatal attraction of each half for the other in what nature seemed so clearly to have designed as a peninsular whole. By then the interests of Aragon were likewise becoming intertwined with those of Castile, and for the same reasons of dynastic mischance and matrimonial alliance.

Peter IV (1336–87) proved the last notable monarch of the house of Barcelona, which from the early tenth century had supplied the county of that name and from 1134 the kingdom of Aragon with a succession of rulers outstanding in character and enterprise. Early in his reign he had reincorporated the Balearics in the crown of Aragon, and his intervention to the same end in Sicily towards its close, though he was forced to content himself with the title and to leave the rule to his second son, led the Catalans in Athens to offer him their dukedom in 1381 in return for a support that it could no longer rely on from Sicily. The year after his death that support proved insufficient. Athens fell to an attack from the Florentine lord of Corinth, and by 1394 was in possession of the Turks.

Thus ended a brilliant chapter in the history of Catalan expansion. The dispersion of effort and resources over the islands and coasts of the Mediterranean, and the international rivalries resulting, were imposing a strain beyond the capacity of a kingdom still subject to internal and peninsular embroilments. Neither of Peter's two sons, who reigned in succession after him, was of the calibre demanded by the situation, and when the second died in 1410, again leaving no heir, there remained a political vacuum of the kind that traditionally had invited solution by civil war.

The settling of the issue instead by judicial process, famous as the Compromise of Caspe of 1412, is commonly advanced in proof of the high degree of political maturity, and of the attachment to democratic principle, already in evidence in the northeastern kingdom; and in truth neither Castile nor Portugal would have been capable of so acting then or for long after. In it was seen the fruit both of the closer integration of crown and people and of the resolute and in the end largely successful campaign of the crown against the claim of the greater nobles, in Aragon as elsewhere, to be a law unto themselves.

The separate Cortes of Catalonia, Aragon, and Valencia agreed, at the instance of the first-named, that rival claims should be heard before a joint tribunal, which weighed them in the light of the principles governing the succession laid down by Alfonso X in his *Siete Partidas* and pronounced in favour of Ferdinand of Antequera, grandson both of Peter IV and of Henry of Trastamar, who was then acting as regent for his nephew, the eight-year-old John II of Castile (1406–54). Catalonia had strongly favoured a Catalan candidate, but it accepted the decision loyally.

Ferdinand had added to his better claim in law a greater general body of support. While this last could be explained in terms of a reasonable preference for peace rather than for the customary intermittent war with Castile, and of the potential benefit accruing from the enlisting of Castilian support for Catalan policies abroad, it is perhaps excessive to see in the election the beginning of the end of Aragonese sovereignty and independence. For the four years of his reign he continued to be regent of Castile, and his new country – in particular the Cortes of Catalonia – had to teach him some severe lessons regarding the respect due to its institutions and temper. Yet these, as the son of a Catalan mother, he took in good part. In the difficult situation caused by his double responsibility the affairs of both countries inevitably threatened to become somewhat mixed. As much was clearly present to the minds of the electors at Caspe, who must likewise have been prepared to find their new ruler tending instinctively to rule after the tradition and fashion grown familiar to him in Castile.

With Ferdinand's death in 1416 Aragon was free as ever to

follow its own interests, and under his son Alfonso V (1416–58) policy reverted straightway from this brief westerly interlude to its now established field, the Mediterranean. Here there awaited one of the most significant developments in Aragonese history, with the offer of the queen of Naples to Alfonso in 1420 to declare him her adoptive son and heir in return for present help against the duke of Anjou. That help rendered, the queen changed her mind and sided with her late enemy. Alfonso proceeded to make war on her too in defence of what he now held to be his legitimate title; and after her death in 1434 and many vicissitudes, including two years' captivity in the wake of a crushing defeat at the hands of the Genoese in the following year, he made it good in 1443 and, in possession now of the kingdom, with a brief prospect of inheriting too the duchy of Milan, compelled recognition even from the Pope of himself as king. In Naples Alfonso from then fixed his court, never more to return to Aragon, for the early Renaissance atmosphere of Italy captivated and won him to the way of life he now adopted, as a patron of the arts surrounded by men of letters and learning. Under him Naples became one of the most brilliant courts in Europe, and there was thrown over to Spain a cultural bridge across which flowed a traffic of ideas and influences of fundamental importance in the cultural development of the Peninsula as a whole.

Politically the pattern of the new enterprise followed that of the duchy of Athens a century earlier. While it redounded to the prestige of Aragon, it represented rather a personal adventure than direct aggrandizement of her territories. Alfonso had entrusted to his queen the conduct of affairs at home, and by leaving Naples to an illegitimate son he effected a detachment of the two kingdoms destined to last for half a century.

At home the queen meantime had had an uneasy reign, complicated by the temptation assailing Aragon to fish in the infinitely turbulent Castilian waters of the reign of John II (1406–54). This infant of months on his accession, declared of age at fourteen, had grown up with the spectacle of a nobility fighting first for power about his person during the minority, then for their own interests against an all-powerful favourite, Alvaro de Luna, who supplied the will-power lacking in the king and on his behalf fought over decades the battle for supremacy of the crown that in Aragon and Portugal had now been definitely won.

Ferdinand of Aragon, his uncle and late regent, had so involved the two royal families, already close kin, marrying John and his two sisters to a daughter and two sons of his own, that Aragon was now governed, in Alfonso's long absence in Naples, by a queen who was sister to the king of Castile and whose two brothers-in-law, princes of Aragon but Castilian nobles in their own right, were among the most rebellious opponents of Alvaro de Luna. The cleavage reached to open civil war, and at the battle of Olmedo in 1445 the nobles suffered decisive defeat. John, still unable to appreciate the real issue at stake, gave them their *revanche* some years later by abandoning his favourite at the instance of a second wife. Alvaro's execution in 1453 was followed a year later by the death of the king, who knew nothing of the business of ruling and had allowed a woman's whim to put back the clock by fifty years.

His son Henry IV (1454–74) thus had the battle to fight all over again, and though he saw Gibraltar won back from the Muslim in 1462 he was no fighter in the sense that mattered. His reign saw royal authority finally dragged through the mire, to the crowning humiliation of his despoiling in effigy and symbolical deposition by nobles and higher ecclesiastics assembled at Avila in 1465. The conflict turned ostensibly on the paternity of his Portuguese queen's one child Joanna, accepted and proclaimed by him as his heir, contemptuously dubbed by his enemies La Beltraneja after the court favourite Beltrán de la Cueva, and repudiated by the nobles in favour of Alfonso, the king's youthful half-brother.

Alfonso's untimely death in 1468 changed anew the course of peninsular history. His claim devolving on his sister Isabella, she refused to contemplate ascending the throne while Henry lived, and it became evident both that the succession would only be resolved by war and that, the two contenders being women, far-reaching consequences must attach to the victor's choice of husband. Isabella, likewise daughter of a Portuguese mother, had already made the momentous decision, rejecting the widowed and much older Alfonso V of Portugal whom Henry would have had her wed in favour of the youthful Ferdinand, heir to the throne of

Aragon, whom she married in 1469. On Henry's death in 1474 Joanna's supporters offered her hand and the throne to the flouted Portuguese monarch, who led his troops into Castile forthwith.

The issue was clear-cut. For centuries the Peninsula had been divided into three kingdoms. The events now set in train gave promise of a reduction to two. With the victory of Joanna those two would be Castile-Portugal and Aragon; with that of Isabella, Castile-Aragon and Portugal. Five years of fighting ensued until, with a treaty of 1479, Alfonso retired defeated to Portugal and Joanna to a convent; and Isabella knew the throne securely hers. The die was cast for union with Aragon. It could in fact have been cast the other way without Joanna, had Isabella accepted her other suitor, and none could then have laid the eventual fate of Aragonese sovereignty at the door of the electors of Caspe.

7

The End of the Middle Ages

ISABELLA'S personal preference had reflected, nonetheless, an instinctive Castilian policy. Hemmed in to east and west, restricted thereby to a southward gaze – and that still blocked by Granada – while its neighbours were achieving conquest and greatness one on the inland, one on the ocean sea, Castile had lost its place in the van and was become a backwater where degenerate rulers and rebellious nobles played out their discords, to the ruin of the common weal, as though a thousand years of history had passed over their heads in vain. John II 'the Ailing', Henry IV 'the Impotent', characterized the nation too in their sobriquets.

In its need for fresh blood, some new sense of purpose, and more open windows on the outside world, Castile found salvation at once in the accession of a woman, an event commonly fraught with untoward consequences either for the nation or for the dynasty, and in the resulting matrimonial alliance with a power that had always been European, in a sense in which Castile and Portugal were not, and was now riding the crest of a new prominence and prestige in the continent's affairs. Portugal lay on the outer confines of the old world, into whose ken the new had not yet swum, and stood committed ever more deeply to the pursuit of distant and still shadowy ideals. Aragon represented reality, and such accretion of strength and influence as would make of the two conjoined a force to be reckoned with among the nations.

Ferdinand for his part, in spite of his Catalan upbringing, was a Castilian on both sides, who found himself heir to Aragon through a series of hazards not dissimilar to those which had opened to Isabella the way to the throne of Castile. The death without legitimate issue of the absentee Alfonso V had transmitted the succession to his brother John II (1458–79), ruler by marriage of Navarre but born and bred, like his father, in Castile. John's embittered relations with his son and heir Charles of

Viana were further aggravated by a second marriage and the birth of a son whose mother schemed for him without cease or scruple. The quarrel eventually spread to John's new kingdom, where it fused with long latent discontents to provoke not civil war alone and the lively threat of disruption, Catalonia seceding from Aragon and recognizing as sovereign for over two years a Portuguese prince, but invasion both from Castile and from France.

In 1461 Charles died, poisoned – rumour immediately asserted – by the queen; and though the fighting did not end for another eleven years and John reigned on, long blindness notwithstanding, till 1479, there was neither rival now nor opposition to the accession of Ferdinand, in spite of his marriage ten years earlier, and subsequent continuous residence, in Castile. Aragon too had come to accept its destiny. Three and a half centuries earlier it had merged its fortunes with Catalonia, thereafter the dominant partner. Now its ways were to merge with those of Castile, also destined to predominate in the new union that would be called neither Castile nor Aragon nor Catalonia, but Spain.

Complete fusion still needed time, and lay still exposed, as the history of the Peninsula had so repeatedly been in the past, to dynastic vicissitude and the whims of inheritance. Both at her marriage and on her accession Isabella had in fact been at pains to define her husband's constitutional position. Their heir might look to succeed in due course with full and equal right to both kingdoms; meantime Isabella I (1474–1504) and Ferdinand II (1479–1516), sovereign each in his own country, would rank but as consort in the other. In practice, the lines were often blurred, and from the beginning it was clear that the pull would be all one way.

Ferdinand, bound early and closely to Castile, which he might not leave without his wife's consent, was as much at home there and as imbued with its traditions and outlook as Isabella was a stranger in Aragon; and the rapid castilianization of his kingdom – through the appointment of Castilians to high office, the introduction of Castilian institutions, and the creation of a supreme royal council for Aragonese, Catalan, and Valencian affairs with its seat not in those territories but at court, 'wheresoever we may be' – spoke of active rather than passive compliance in an obviously Castlian policy of centralization.

Isabella was from the first the stronger character; but Ferdinand likewise knew where he was going, and for his purposes as for hers concentration of power was the prime requisite. Their agreement on this was patently at variance with any thought the two peoples might have harboured that their countries could continue as before. And yet, by concentrating each on his special sphere of interest, which as it happened conformed closely to that of his respective kingdom, they succeeded in carrying their peoples along with them. Castile looked inward, crying aloud in the first place for drastic social reconstruction; Aragon looked outward, its triple goal a strengthened hold on its island possessions, the reincorporation in the crown of territories previously held and alienated, and the continued enhancing of its prestige in the councils of Europe. Isabella took to herself therefore home affairs, Ferdinand foreign, and the working partnership worked.

A queen at twenty-three, in the fullness of her powers, Isabella was to prove the greatest ruler Castile had known simply because she perceived so clearly and willed so unflinchingly her country's needs. No sooner was she secured on her throne by the final eclipse of La Beltraneja in 1479 – the same year in which Ferdinand mounted his – than she took up the task of imposing unquestioning respect for its authority. Sending out judicial commissions with military backing wherever feudal anarchy still reared its head – Galicia and Andalusia were especially notorious for the despotic abuses of turbulent overlords – she dealt out exile, confiscation of lands, and death as the crime demanded, without compunction or respect of persons; all castles and fortresses deemed superfluous to the nation's defence she razed. Resuscitating and reinvigorating an earlier institution, the 'Santa Hermandad' or Holy Brotherhood, she endowed it with powers of summary justice as a rural police force to secure the traveller and the unprotected. Within a few years the royal writ ran unchallenged throughout the land.

Symbolic of such realms within the realm were the three military orders, which had long outlived their crusading purpose, and were become vast concentrations of power and wealth capable of putting their own armies into the field and quick in the defence of their interests. Their dissensions could divide the country: contested elections to a grandmastership had been known to loose civil war. As each mastership fell vacant Isabella prevailed on the Pope to vest administration of the order, and eventually the mastership itself, in Ferdinand, and thus secured also for the crown their enormous revenues and patronage. A necessary concomitant of these measures was the attraction of the nobles from their estates, where they had ruled as petty kinglets, to positions of honour about the court. Later, in 1512, Ferdinand's creation of a palace guard open to sons of the great families would lay the basis for a standing army.

The cumulative effect of these and similar steps was to alter fundamentally the pattern of society, and even more the structure and functions of government, for the crown now had to control and administer from the centre on a scale unknown before. This brought into being what was in effect a civil service, manned by *letrados* or men of law trained in the universities which, encouraged by the queen's profound esteem for learning, were to play from now on an ever greater part in the nation's life. From 1480 the Consejo Real or royal council consisted chiefly of *letrados* – the greatest nobles still had the right to attend but were deprived of their vote – and other 'supreme councils' were added as new departments of administration came into the foreground.

Through the office of 'corregidor', appointed to sit with the *regidores* or town councillors, the crown already intervened in municipal government. That intervention was now intensified systematically in countless directions all tending to the same end, the strengthening of the royal authority; and though the third estate stood to gain in the resultant strengthening of the nation as a whole, it paid the price meantime in the undermining of municipal autonomy and with it of the old system of differential fueros. A profound respect and support for the religious function of the Church led Isabella to undertake a vigorous campaign of reform, the need for which may be gauged from the 400 friars who crossed to Africa and embraced Mohammedanism rather than mend their ways; but with this went hand in hand the no less rigorous repression of its manifold abuses and constant impingement on spheres outwith the ecclesiastical. The papal claim to appoint bishops was successfully challenged, and with the crown become in consequence the fount of preferment, the Church too could be made to subserve crown policies.

The Cortes of the three estates fared meantime no better than each had separately. Isabella's conception of kingship allowed no room for the ideas we now call democratic, and the summoning of Cortes for other than formal occasions was to her the recognition merely that her power was still inadequate to her absolute responsibility. In the twenty-eight years from 1475 to 1503 they met nine times, not at all in the years from 1482 to 1498 which witnessed some of the most resounding events and decisions in all Spanish history.

One measure of profound significance was to attract a lasting notoriety far beyond the bounds of the Peninsula. The Inquisition as a purely ecclesiastical tribunal concerned with the defence of orthodoxy had existed in Aragon since the thirteenth century. Isabella's 'New Inquisition', the so-called Holy Office, instituted in 1478 on a basis of virtual independence of Rome, developed into a major instrument for the welding of the nation into a united whole closely identified with the throne. This was not obscurantism, a wilful attempt to turn back the clock and to deny elementary freedoms. Isabella looked forward, and her proclaimed objective of 'one king, one law, one faith' rested on a shrewd analysis of political realities.

The reconquest had long ceased to give a sense of national mission; its progress latterly had in fact contributed to the weakening of social cohesion with the absorption of large numbers of Muslims and Jews, the former more industrious, the latter more skilled, than the mass of their fellow-citizens and both, alike in their economic prosperity and in their religious dissidence, an irritant in a self-conscious Christian community. Miscreants in the vital sense of the word, their loyalties were always suspect; and the odium attaching to the Jews in particular, in their most characteristic role of money-lenders and tax-collectors, was not allayed by the wholesale conversions which had followed such explosions of mob fury as the notorious massacres of 1391.

It was against this latter class, the *conversos*, that the Holy Office began its operations in 1480. The orthodox Catholic, in theory, had nothing to fear. In practice the opportunities that Inquisition procedure allowed for covert delation, combined with the impossibility even for the professional theologian of securing one's every religious opinion against accusations of deviationism, placed everyone at the mercy of the heresy-hunters, and for some three hundred years their activities can now be seen to have hung like a blight over Spanish society. In the sixteenth century they counted a professor of theology at Salamanca and even an archbishop of Toledo and primate of Spain among their victims; in the eighteenth their shafts could still be aimed at a prime minister.

Yet the defence of the faith did not seem then to be too dearly bought. As long as men were deeply in earnest, Froude has remarked, they were not tolerant: 'we only tolerate what we think unimportant.' And from the earnestness, and the pride, with which Spaniards took on their new role of champions of Catholic orthodoxy on the threshold of an era of dissolving beliefs it may be accepted that Isabella had judged her subjects aright and had in fact found what she sought, a unifying principle capable of inspiring them anew with something of the old religious zeal.

In all this Castile had been girding up its loins against the demands of a destiny that lay as yet unrevealed. Down the fifteenth century its course has been seen diverging more and more from that of its neighbours to east and west, in that they knew where their interests lay and conducted their affairs accordingly, while Castile merely drifted. In one direction indeed the path had been clear enough, and both John II and Henry IV had canalized some of the nation's energies along it. But with the lack of success that the sorry story of their reigns made inevitable Granada remained, an independent Muslim kingdom set within a Christian Spain, a challenge and an insult to faith and state alike and a constant impediment to freedom of action elsewhere.

With a coastline of some 300 miles stretching from a little north of Gibraltar to a little south-west of Cartagena, and reaching inland to a depth varying between 30 and 90 miles, it was still possessed of considerable defensive power, and ten years were to elapse between Isabella's capture of Alhama in 1482 and final victory. This, if greatly eased by a dynastic crisis among the Muslims, still required of Castile a concerted national effort, all Ferdinand's military skill and diplomatic astuteness, and the infinite resolve and resource of a queen who herself organized the supply and hospital services. When the Christian encampment on the hillside facing the enemy capital was destroyed by fire in 1491, Isabella's reaction was to build on its site a city-fortress of stone, christened Santa Fe, from where the siege was intensified until, early in 1492, Granada capitulated.

The reconquest, begun at Covadonga in 718, had ended; and Spain was sovereign at last in her own house after an experience unique in western Europe and which had moulded her more profoundly than she knew. To the immediate feeling of relief from a nightmare of centuries was added a glow of righteous satisfaction at the thought that the nation had done great things for Europe and for the faith in keeping the infidel at bay. Europe might forget, Spain never, and devotion to the faith entered still closer into the fibre of a people that, after so long looking south, could now look north again as a full member of the European community.

Meanwhile there were internal decisions to be taken. The expulsion from Castile and Aragon alike of all Jews, decreed in the same year 1492, had long been meditated; it had indeed been promulgated though not enforced nine years earlier. Its enforcement now betokened the conviction, growing after success at Granada, that God was on Spain's side and that religion constituted in consequence the very *raison d'être* of the nation's policies. To this principle successive monarchs were to hold fast over the next two centuries and more, however powerful the temptation or convincing the evidence to the contrary. In the event it might appear either that God's will had been misread or that God in these matters is neutral; but that lesson would not be learnt for a long time yet, and though the Jews represented the country's financial brains they were still held a blot and a menace to a Christian state, and the decree went forth.

A minority accepted the alternative of abjuring their beliefs and, joining the earlier *conversos*, became as 'new Christians' of immediate interest to the Inquisition. The rest, variously estimated to number from 165,000 to 800,000, emigrated mostly to north Africa, some to Italy, some to Portugal whence, under Spanish pressure, a similar measure of expulsion followed in 1496. Large numbers eventually drifted eastward to Salonica, where their descendants have continued down the centuries to form compact communities still mindful, in language and much else, of the land that treated their forefathers so ill.

The Muslims of Granada had been promised on capitulation full religious freedom, a promise that was progressively violated until, in 1502, they too were offered the choice between exile and conversion. Unlike the Jews, most held to their homes as the greater loyalty, and a new class of converts, known henceforth as *moriscos*, was added to society, exposed in due course to the same suspicions and the same inquisitorial persecution for backsliding as their fellow-apostates the *conversos*. Thereafter, again in theory, there remained throughout the length and breadth of Castile no single subject who was not a Christian and a Catholic. The 'Catholic Monarchs' were justifying the title the Spanish Pope Alexander VI had conferred on them in 1494.

Spain's *annus mirabilis* was marked by another event more epoch-making by far in its repercussions and implications than even the taking of Granada. The coincidence that Columbus's landfall in the Caribbean should have launched the nation on a career of discovery and conquest on a continental scale in the very year in which it achieved full stature and control of its destinies at home can suggest the providential. For this, it might appear in retrospect, Isabella's every act since her accession had unconsciously been preparing. Thanks to her the nation stood prepared, its energies at the leash, in the nick of time. And much in the unfolding picture of this brave new world across the Atlantic would have been very different had not the crown carried there too its new conception of a divine mission to spread the faith, and the individual Spaniard his new-found national pride and sense of purpose, whence he drew the faith in himself that was to underlie the all but incredible achievements of the *conquistadores*.

Yet nothing in the logic of Spain's past had pointed to this falling into her lap of an unsuspected continent lying across three thousand miles of ocean. For just such a destiny, on the other hand, Portugal had been consciously preparing since 1415, and it was in fact to Lisbon that Columbus first took his project for discovering a way to the wealth of the east by sailing west, 'the king of Portugal having a better understanding of the discovery of unknown lands than any other prince'. Rejected there, a measure of Portugal's commitments in other directions, he next submitted it, with the same result, to Henry VII of England. Isabella and Ferdinand, third in the list, likewise received the plan with scant enthusiasm, and only after six years of badgering and bargaining did Columbus secure their reluctant support.

His four voyages between 1492 and 1504 – not until the third, in 1498, did he set foot on the mainland, in what is now Venezuela – brought him only disillusion; and though he, and Isabella, died in the belief that he had truly reached his goal, as the terms 'West Indies' and 'Indians' imply, of the treasure and the reward that he had looked for there was no sign. When in the next reign the potentialities for Spain and Europe began to reveal themselves, they were still to prove very different from what had been envisaged. Accident thus presiding over the American adventure from the beginning, improvisation in the exploiting of it was for long its keynote. In time wealth did begin to flow home from El Dorado in quantities undreamt of, and the same unprepared-ness to deal with the situation produced at length the strange spectacle of a nation impoverished by excess of riches and foundering eventually in open bankruptcy.

Meanwhile, if alliance with Aragon had helped in the resolving of Castile's internal problems, it meant involvement equally in the external interests of its partner: specifically, it entailed de-parture from a now established tradition of peaceful relations with France. For France and Aragon had been enemies ever since their ambitions had first clashed over Sicily and Naples. The two centuries now to ensue of endemic war with France were not necessarily implicit in Isabella's choice of husband, the future holding its own causes of friction; but only by disowning all that Aragon stood for in Europe could Castile have continued now to shelter in peace behind the Pyrenees.

Naples, separated as has been seen from the Aragonese crown by Alfonso V, was still coveted by France, which assumed too lightly that Ferdinand and Aragon were not interested in its fate. The story of how Ferdinand exploited that assumption to win back first Cerdagne and Roussillon, territories north of the Pyrenees long since ceded to France, then half of Naples, then in 1504 the whole, covering the southern half of Italy, illustrates well how he came by his reputation for Machiavellianism.

Ferdinand is not to be dismissed as a mere opportunist; but, holding all fair in diplomacy and war, he missed no opportunity.

Accepting Isabella's role for Spain as bulwark of the faith, he accepted too that the first quality in a bulwark is strength, and set himself to make Spain strong without as she had done within. Fortunate in the fighting quality of his troops – it was then, in Italy, under the 'Great Captain' Gonzalo Fernández de Córdoba, that the Spanish infantry laid the foundations of the reputation for invincibility it was to uphold throughout Europe for the next century and a half – he still attached the greater importance to diplomacy, and by his creation of a secretaryship for foreign affairs and the personal schooling of his ambassadors to foreign courts he far outdistanced his opponents in the art. Only when diplomacy had failed did he choose recourse to arms, as with Navarre south of the Pyrenees, which he won back definitively for Spain, after close on three centuries, in 1512.

The great weapon of diplomacy was still matrimonial alliance, and the marriages arranged by Ferdinand and Isabella for their one son and four daughters were a clear indication, and an essential part, of the international future they planned for their country. The union of Castile with Aragon, in preference to Portugal, had not left Portugal out of the reckoning. Peninsular unity remained the goal, and provisions to that end figured in the very treaty of 1479. Two daughters were accordingly married into Portugal; a third, and the son, to the Habsburgs; and the fourth, the unhappy Catherine, to England.

The diplomatic encirclement of France was one important result. More important still were the consequences for the succession, and here death played a curiously persistent hand. John, in whose person the thrones of Castile and Aragon were to have merged, died in 1497 aged nineteen; his posthumous child died at birth. Isabella, wife of Manuel of Portugal, was next in line, and her infant son, whose birth in 1498 cost his mother her life, died at the age of two. With him faded still greater hopes, for he had been formally accepted by the respective Cortes as heir to all three crowns.

It would in truth have been a dazzling inheritance. John II of Portugal (1481–95) had learnt his lesson from his father Alfonso's costly meddling in Castilian affairs and, a much stronger and more far-sighted monarch, concerned himself instead with his country's own two problems. The first, the restoring of the crown patrimony and the humbling of the nobles, was very similar to that which had awaited Isabella on her accession; the second, the furthering of his country's developing interests overseas, to that confronting Ferdinand. Alfonso had dispensed new titles and grants of lands with a prodigality that seemed to his son to have left him 'only the royal highways' as his inheritance: the estates of his brother-in-law the duke of Braganza covered one-third of the kingdom.

John had his own touch of Machiavellianism. Proposing such measures as provoked the nobility to violent retort, he acted. Braganza he arrested and executed; the duke of Viseu, another brother-in-law, he slew with his own hand; a further eighty leading nobles were put to death with or without trial. Having broken their power and confiscated their wealth, John was king in fact as well as in name, and proved himself to his subjects an efficient and benevolent dictator, free now to devote himself to the great enterprise of maritime discovery.

By 1482 Diogo Cão had reached to the Congo. Five years later Bartolomeu Dias set out on the famous expedition which at long last resolved the riddle of Africa and rounded the 'stormy Cape', John showing his appreciation of its true significance by re-christening it straightway the Cape of Good Hope. Another mission penetrated into the heart of Africa, reaching to Timbuktu; a third located in Ethiopia the mysterious Prester John, who proved a disappointment to those who had hoped to find in him a powerful ally against the infidel. But it was the south-east passage on which John's hopes were pinned, to the extent shown in his rejection of Columbus's proposals, that might have given to Portugal priority too in the west. Death found him busily engaged on preparations for the final expedition which, exploiting Dias's discovery, should finally carry the Portuguese across the Indian Ocean to the goal of their long endeavour.

Before then Columbus, sailing under the Spanish flag, had reached his more dimly apprehended journey's end across the Atlantic; and, the ultimate objective of both countries being the same, access to the wealth of the east, an accommodation de-limiting their spheres of activity became necessary. Portugal's first proposal was a horizontal line through the Canaries, all lands and islands still to be discovered north of this to fall to Spain and all to the south to Portugal; which if accepted and made effective would have divided the Americas not into Anglo-Saxon and Hispanic, as today, but into Spanish and Portuguese. After some one-sided intervention by the Pope and a threat of war by Portugal, the two powers agreed in the treaty of Tordesillas of 1494 on a dividing line to run from pole to pole 370 leagues west of the Cape Verde Islands, conquests to the west to be Spanish, to the east Portuguese. What lay to the west was still largely guesswork, and to the east, for Columbus had still not set foot on the mainland of his new world nor da Gama sailed the Indian Ocean; nor, geographical knowledge apart, could science then in fact have drawn the line.

It is the magnificence of the gesture that impresses, the self-confidence with which two small nations, one but two years re-established in full possession of its homeland, the other boasting a population of perhaps a million and a quarter, should presume to parcel out between them oceans and continents yet unexplored, the whole of the unknown world. Well might Francis I of France later protest his curiosity to see the clause in Adam's will that denied him his share of the inheritance.

Another four years and, in 1498, Vasco da Gama reached India; Portugal too had achieved her goal, that straightway proved to be but the threshold to a still vaster *plus ultra*. It was a landmark for Europe too, for now at last east and west had met without intermediary, and the new chapter of Europe's long and deep engagement in the Orient had begun. Columbus and da Gama between them signify the true end of the Middle Ages, the dawn of a modern world in which Europe will still be for centuries the centre but no longer the whole, and its horizon of knowledge and ideas will be subject to constant enlargement as ever new realms of experience swim into its ken.

8

Literature and the Arts – I

THE disintegration of Latin over the centuries, in response to local ways of living and to the peculiar circumstances of the reconquest, gave rise to not one but half a dozen incipient Romance tongues whose distinctive traits may be seen emerging in notarial documents of the tenth century. Political vicissitude caused three – Castilian, Catalan, Portuguese – to achieve full independent status, and from the late fifteenth century gave to the first of these such hegemony as allowed of its equating to 'Spanish'. Galician retains the distinction of having fathered Portuguese, to which it continues much closer than to Castilian, and it has been at times the vehicle of a considerable body of writing.

The other regional speeches, Leonese, Navarrese, Aragonese, and Valencian, have long since dwindled to the dialectal. Mozarabic, the curiously retarded Romance kept alive in Christian communities overrun by but never fully absorbed into al-Andalus, is a thing of memory, though modern Andalusian retains its imprint of that distant experience of life lived at close quarters with an alien race, tongue, and mentality. Basque, the native non-Latin speech, threw up its first literary document in 1545 – and a translation of *Hamlet*, in Buenos Aires, in 1952 – but it has never established itself as a literary language and as a spoken one is rapidly losing ground under pressure of modern conditions.

Literature in the Peninsula thus means in effect literature in the three first mentioned; and the characteristics of these three – the clipped consonantal precision of Catalan, the equipoise and sonority of Castilian, the rich vocalism and musicality of Portuguese – will be found reflected in the works of their great authors.

Rome's heritage was not evenly spread, and curious consequences derive from the fact. The choice of Cordoba as centre of power and seat of culture indicated her preference for the smiling plains and easier life of the fertile south. The bleak table-

land of Castile, the barren mountain ranges of the north, had
no attraction. They had even less attraction for the Muslim,
under whose caliphs Cordoba continued to be the focus of a
now greatly enriched and diversified cultural tradition from which
the north was even more cut off than before, through religious
and racial antagonisms. Literature and its commerce with things
of the mind are growths therefore later by a thousand years in
Castile than their first flowering in the south.

And they are independent growths. After that notable monopoly of the silver age of Roman letters by the satirists and
moralists of Baetica there is no continuity of literary record.
The entire Visigothic chapter produced but the one name still
remembered today, Isidore: archbishop of Seville, he too was of
the south and set four-square in the Roman tradition. But the
formative factors persisted, and in the fifteenth century, in the
sixteenth, in the seventeenth, as still today, the writers of
Andalusia are marked by that same 'something rich and rare' of
Lucan and the Senecas, the intoxication of language, the lure
of the grandiloquent, the predominance of form over content and,
within the latter, of the senses over the mind.

Nothing of all this was known or felt in the north. Life there
was, as it still is, harder and grimmer, to be wrested from a much
more churlish nature. And in the absence of an imported literary
tradition, a cultural atmosphere of long standing, literature,
when it did come to birth in the eleventh and twelfth centuries,
sprang from the soil, instinct with experience, void of the graces.
It was a communal literature, written not for reading in the study
but to be recited in the market-place and held common property,
its listeners free to reshape it to their whim.

This first phase, of the anonymous heroic epic, is peculiarly
the creation of one region. It belongs to a period when Castile
not merely bore the brunt of the reconquest, with ultimate
success still veiled in futurity, but struggled for predominance
over the other Christian kingdoms; and though the infidel comes
into it, the central issues lie nearer home. Half a dozen poems are
known from prosifications embedded in the chronicles of a later
age: the *Poem of the Cid* constitutes the one major relic. Fidelity
of characters and setting keep this tale of a mere half-century
earlier notably close to earth and to reality: it still shows a

striking power of imaginative conception, idealizing the character of the greatest Castilian of his age and doing much thereby to shape the character too of Castile.

The stabilizing of the war against Islam, with the shrinking of al-Andalus to the kingdom of Granada, encouraged the development from the mid thirteenth century of a more settled and urbane Christian society, that could afford now to draw on the greater cultural riches of the enemy. Alfonso the Learned turned his chancellery into one great literary workshop out of which came translations from the Arabic, a vast, unfinished history of mankind from the creation, and – most important of all – his *General Chronicle* of the Spanish people that remains the greatest single monument of Spanish historiography. A repertoire of the whole peninsular past, fact and fable, it laid down the norm for chroniclers for another three hundred years and provided an inexhaustible quarry for writing in other veins. Itself reworked again and again, the *Chronicle* kept alive the epic themes that were soon to nourish the *romancero* or popular balladry, its great creative period the fifteenth and sixteenth centuries, which is one of the richest facets of Castilian letters and was destined in its turn to feed so much of Golden Age drama.

Remote beginnings for the lyric have been traced in Mozarabic snatches incorporated into Hebrew and Arabic compositions of the tenth century, but the first considerable body of lyric poetry comes from Alfonso himself, who, brought up in Galicia, chose its softer speech for his 417 *Songs of the Virgin Mary*. This conception of Castilian as proper vehicle for prose and epic, and of Galician as that indicated for subjective, emotional expression, persisted as a convention for long after.

Another type of verse composition was, however, established in Castilian from earlier in the same thirteenth century. French in inspiration and known as the *mester de clerecía* or school of the clerics, it waxed as the native heroic school of the *jongleurs* or *mester de juglaría* waned and boasted over this a more conscious artistry, particularly in the monotonous regularity of its single form, a monorhyme four-line stanza in Alexandrines. Its authors were men of book-learning, working in monasteries on written sources, their themes saints and heroes of Christian or classical tradition. Prominent among them was Gonzalo de Berceo, who spanned the first half of the century and is the first Spanish poet known to us by name, as well as one of the most voluminous. The most interesting product of the school, the *Poem of Fernán González*, is, oddly enough, an anonymous reworking of a lost epic, telling the story of the tenth-century count of Castile who won his country's independence from León.

Three names are writ large over the following century. Juan Manuel, nephew and kindred spirit of Alfonso the Learned, is remembered less for his serious works on law and society than for the *Count Lucanor*, a collection of fifty didactic tales told with much charm and a landmark in the development, out of the oriental apologue, of the art of imaginative prose. Juan Ruiz, archpriest of Hita, looked at life with sardonic gaze and filtered all he saw, as well as all he had read, into his irreverent *Book of Good Love*, by far the liveliest product of the medieval clerical mind. Cast in autobiographical form, it is of the earth earthy, and some of its characters and much of its spirit have lived on in Castilian literature. The chancellor Pero López de Ayala at the end of the century gave a new turn to historical writing with his personal chronicles of the four monarchs under whom he had served. The essence of long and often bitter experience he too distilled into the verse-form of the clerics, of which his *Poem of Palace Life* is the last monument.

Contact with Rome came at last as new winds began to blow from Italy in the early fifteenth century. A Genoese settled in Seville, one Francisco Imperial, was the pioneer in throwing a bridge over which knowledge of Dante, and in due course of Petrarch and Boccaccio, reached to the Peninsula. Soon, and for generations thereafter, Spaniards were to flock back along that bridge to school in Italy. Juan de Mena's elaborate allegory *The Labyrinth of Fortune* (*c.* 1444) represents a first sustained if lumbering attempt to write intellectual poetry after the new fashion.

The experiment brought home the relative poverty of the vernacular in the terminology of thought, and led to the whole-sale introduction from Latin of abstract terms and to a considerable re-latinizing of syntax, a movement that culminates in the 'hermetic' poetry of Góngora nearly two centuries later. Mena wrote in an accentual dodecasyllable of native tradition. His fellow-allegorist the marquis of Santillana made a gallant effort to naturalize from Italy the sonnet and the hendecasyllable. Success did not come here for another fifty years and more: it will be the first mark, and a clue to the achievement, of the poetry of the early sixteenth century. Meanwhile, in the famous *Stanzas on the Death of his Father* of Jorge Manrique, Santillana's nephew, depth and sincerity of emotion and a universal theme showed the common octosyllable to be still capable of sustaining a masterpiece.

The Middle Ages close with two works in prose, one backward-looking, one forward, that, differing greatly in intrinsic merit, were alike in the profound influence they were to exert. The chivalresque novel of fantastic adventure, in a setting of idealized sentiment and knightly derring-do, had a long if ill-documented history behind it before Juan de Montalvo, refurbishing and continuing in 1508 the most famous in the kind, *Amadís of Gaul*, captured the new reading public called into being by the printing-press and not yet won to higher things. From it sprang a monstrous progeny of Palmerins, Primaleons, and others that down the century fed an insatiable public demand among all classes and achieved its greatest triumph in provoking at length one Miguel de Cervantes into writing, as counterblast, his *Don Quixote*.

There was nothing escapist about the *Celestina* (1499) of Fernando de Rojas. This unactable *Tragicomedy of Calisto and Melibea*, to give it its proper title, unfolds over many acts a tale of passion uncontrolled and inexorable tragedy. Such is the purpose; but the author's depicting of the go-between with a realism not to be matched in Spanish letters resulted in her dominating the whole, until now the work is known only by her name. Sprung from Juan Ruiz's Trotaconventos, she too left a long descent, and contributed powerfully to keeping the theatre in its beginnings close to the soil.

For historical reasons already seen, early Catalan literature reveals the same close connexion with Provence as does the language. For a hundred years and more, from the late twelfth century, there flourished a school of troubadour poetry that numbered kings and counts among its practitioners. Like the

Castilian poets writing in Galician, they served a first apprentice-
ship in Provençal. Ramon Llull (1233–1315), perhaps the greatest
of all Catalan writers, ushered in the great age. With the *Book of
Contemplation*, an encyclopedia at once of religion and of medieval life in general, the *Blanquerna*, a vast utopian novel, and
numerous other writings, including poetry of deep emotional and
mystical appeal, he did for his native tongue what Alfonso the
Learned had done for his, making of it an instrument worthy to
reflect the mature achievements of the Catalan people.

These achievements are enshrined in the four great chronicles
of James the Conqueror, Desclot, Muntaner, and Peter the
Ceremonious, that span the late thirteenth and fourteenth centuries and record with a wealth of intimate and often eye-witness
detail the most stirring pages in the nation's growth and expansion. If Desclot is the best historian in the modern sense, it is
Muntaner, relating as a participant the stirring adventure that
led to the Catalan duchy of Athens, who most compels the
reader's mind and affection. Catalan was now become the
lingua franca of the Mediterranean.

By the late fourteenth century Italian influences were already
strong in the north-east, and a so-called 'classical age' is dated
from the Petrarchan tale *Walter and Griselda* (1388) of Bernat
Metge, first of Catalan humanists, whose philosophical allegory
The Dream is held the high-water mark of Catalan prose. Fiction
developed with an anonymous sentimental novel, *Curial and
Guelfa*, and, of more curious interest, the *Tirant the White* of
Joanot Martorell, who gave realism to the novel of chivalry by
basing it on the doings of Muntaner's stalwarts in the Near East.
The poetry of the age began with a backward look, under the
stimulus of floral games held annually in Barcelona from 1395,
on the model of Toulouse; but it was the spirit of Dante and
Petrarch that presided over the fifteenth century as a whole,
raising Auziàs March (1397–1459) to heights of philosophical
poetry as yet unscaled in the Peninsula.

In Portugal the lyrical note dominated from the beginning.
Indigenous love poems, known as *cossantes*, express from the
twelfth century that quality of *saudade* or yearning for an irre-
coverable past that is held a fundamental trait in the national
character. The Provençal imprint came early here too, and may

be seen reflected in a number of medieval *cancioneiros* or song-books, the work of some 200 poets: while they still sing chiefly of love, another category, of 'poems of scorning', gives vent to a strange capacity for scandalous invective. King Denis, grandson of Alfonso the Learned, at whose court he had been educated, shared his grandfather's devotion to the arts of peace and marked the heyday of this activity. Prose evolved more slowly, in obedience, like the marked absence of the epic, to the later achievement in the west of full heroic stature. Neither internally, as in Castile with the reconquest, nor externally, as in the Mediterranean expansion of Catalonia, was the national consciousness stirred on the grand scale until, with the early fifteenth century, Ceuta opened up vistas of unlimited challenge oversea.

By then the outlet was to be found, as Catalonia had already found it, not in the epos but in historical writing. The ground was prepared by John I, founder of the house of Aviz, and his son and successor Edward, who themselves figure among the outstanding artificers of Portuguese prose, alike in their stimulating of much translation of foreign works and in their own writings. John is remembered particularly for his *Treatise on the Chase*, and Edward for one on moral philosophy, *The Loyal Counsellor*. It was Edward who appointed as first royal chronicler Fernam Lopes (*c.* 1380–*c.* 1460), whom good critics have ranked in this branch of letters above his every European contemporary. Of the ten reigns he covered, the original text survives for only three: in these, vividness and spontaneity are most happily allied to the soberer parts of the true historian, and the language in his hands reveals itself capable of the whole range of effect and emotion. To Lopes one still turns today to discover the early likeness of the Portuguese people. His successor, Zurara, a lesser but still outstanding writer, dealt particularly with the early voyages of exploration.

In the arts Christian Spain had lagged far behind al-Andalus, being content at times to hold suspect, simply as Muslim, the refinements of Muslim civilization. Arabic influences percolated notwithstanding, and can be detected alongside those of France and Italy in the Romanesque architecture of the eleventh and twelfth centuries, best exemplified in the cathedrals of Santiago, Lérida, and Tarragona, the wealth of external sculptural decoration being especially noteworthy. By the thirteenth, features of a new, Gothic, style introduced by the Cistercians were firmly established: the pointed instead of rounded arch, groined vaults allowing greater height, the flying buttress, thinner walls, more windows, and the crowning with a spire of more elaborate towers. The cathedrals of Burgos, Toledo, and León and a number of palaces and public buildings in the greater cities show the notable wealth of Peninsular Gothic. Mudéjar art, a combination of Gothic and Arabic, is peculiar to the Peninsula. Decorative exterior brickwork, glazed tiles, panelled and painted ceilings, plaster relief, and the horse-shoe arch are its most distinctive features, to be admired in Toledo, Saragossa, Seville, and wherever substantial Muslim communities lived under Christian rule.

In the north-east formative influences were differently balanced. Mudéjar scarcely penetrated, French never received the same unquestioning acceptance as in Castile, Italian was always strong. The fourteenth century, Catalonia's great age in the Mediterranean, saw it lead the Peninsula too in architecture, both ecclesiastical and civil. Barcelona, Gerona, and Pamplona cathedrals are the three great fabrics of this period, the second boasting the widest vaulted nave in Christendom. The traces they bear of more northern inspiration became pronounced throughout the Peninsula generally in those of the closing phase of Gothic, covering the fifteenth and early sixteenth centuries, when Flemish and German architects and sculptors abounded. Seville cathedral, begun in 1402 on the site of a mosque and incorporating some of its features, is the largest medieval church in the world, its side aisles the equal in width and height of the main nave of Westminster Abbey. Polychrome sculpture was common throughout the Gothic period.

Painting was likewise an essentially ecclesiastical art. Flourishing first on parchment for book illumination, Alfonso's *Songs of the Virgin Mary* being one of the great masterpieces in this respect, and then on glass, to the glory of many a cathedral window, it progressed to murals and to painting on wood, the fourteenth century being rich in both. Italian, French, and Flemish artists once more supplied much of the inspiration, their conflicting traces often visible in the same work. Barcelona and

Valencia, ahead of Castile in the pictorial art, founded distinctive schools that flourished down the fourteenth and fifteenth centuries, the Valencian giving proof of greater originality in realistic observation. The first known Castilian painter – on wood – did not emerge until the end of the fifteenth century. During this closing period of the Middle Ages the *retablo* or altar setting provided the characteristic outlet for the painter, its series of panels allowing a narrative succession of incidents, each depicted in miniature, in which Flemish technique combined admirably with that feeling for exact local representation, even in religious art, which was soon to become the hallmark of Spanish painting.

Portugal can show comparatively little of the Romanesque. Lisbon cathedral, dating from 1150, suffered severely in the earthquake of 1755, while Coimbra's Sé Velha or old cathedral, clearly modelled on Santiago, is much overlaid with Renaissance reconstruction. As much holds for Thomar, where the Knights Templar had their seat. The Cistercians were already in Portugal by the mid twelfth century, and the monastery of Alcobaça, with the largest church and some of the finest sculpture – this much later – in Portugal, is counted outstanding among Cistercian buildings anywhere. Batalha, Portugal's Battle Abbey, was begun by John I to celebrate his vanquishing of the Spaniards at Aljubarrota in 1385, and represents the most ambitious and most elaborate medieval monument in the country. In its 'noblest Founder's Chapel in the world' lie the bodies of John and his English queen.

From this reign dates also the palace of Sintra, likewise basically Gothic yet so strikingly Moorish in many aspects of its architecture and decoration – it is the Portuguese counterpart of the Alcázar of Seville – that tradition long dated it from the Muslim rule of centuries earlier. In fact these Moorish features are late additions. The palace with its curious medley of styles and embellishments exemplifies the one original chapter in the history of Portuguese architecture, which, corresponding to the reign of Manuel I, is known as Manueline. This interlude between late Gothic and Renaissance was more properly a style of architectural adornment than of architecture, its keynote the free rein given to the imagination in the desire to express all the exuberance, vitality, and dazzling splendour with which access to the wealth of the Orient had suddenly endowed the Portuguese people.

Erecting caprice into a principle, Manueline juxtaposed elements old and new, however disparate, and in fact exercised itself more in reshaping existing monuments – Thomar, Alcobaça, Batalha, Sintra – than in original creation. In this last category is, however, to be found the culmination of the movement, in the Jeronymite monastery of Belem built by Manuel in commemoration of the Indian achievement. Here Gothic at its most flamboyant mingles with a luxuriance of vegetation in stone to produce an effect of the bizarre unique in European architecture. Such extravagance overreached itself. Belem showed too the penetration of Renaissance influences, French and Italian, and soon these had swept Manueline away.

In Portugal, as in Spain, illuminated manuscripts cradle the art of painting. The earliest known murals, in Braga cathedral, date from 1330. A hundred years later, visits of Italian and Flemish painters to Portugal and of Portuguese painters to Italy reveal an activity still imperfectly documented, out of which came the one notable medieval masterpiece. Nuno Gonçalves, only rediscovered in this century, is today held the greatest, perhaps the only great, painter of his race. His two 'Triptychs of St Vincent' (c. 1460), dedicated to the patron saint of navigators, present a series of life-size portraits, masterly in their realism, of the generation of Prince Henry the Navigator, and convey to us something of the vision and spiritual intensity of those who laid the foundations of their country's maritime splendour.

9

Involvement in Europe

THE century and a half beginning with Ferdinand's death in 1516 is commonly spoken of as Spain's 'Golden Age'. The term, accurate enough in literature and the arts, is for the latter half of the period politically a misnomer, for there set in then a precipitate decline from the greatness that over most of the sixteenth century proclaimed Spain the first power in Europe. Ascent and decline alike were part of the legacy of Isabella and Ferdinand, working itself out, it is true, in ways they could never have suspected, yet with its own inner logic. The apex is clearly discernible in 1588, the year of the 'invincible' Armada. Up till then Spain was supreme, and supremely self-confident. Thereafter, with the novel experience of defeat, came creeping doubt, doubt of her mission, of her ability to discharge that mission, and with it a weakening grip on the essentials of a policy in which from the beginning ideological strength had found itself at the mercy of economic weakness.

When Isabella died the unity for which she had striven was straightway endangered by Ferdinand's re-marriage to Germaine de Foix, his people desiring an heir specifically to the throne of Aragon. The hope, though thwarted, was an indication that Spain was still only nominally one. Isabella herself had pointedly underlined the fact in a codicil to her will excluding the Aragonese from trade with the New World, a hurt that was to last till 1778 and to rankle long after; and the persistence of regional Cortes and fueros continued to complicate administration for each successive ruler of the new Habsburg dynasty whose advent in 1516 brought Spain with a vengeance into the full current of European affairs. Ferdinand had wanted as much, but with Spain in control. Fate, in robbing him of a male heir, decreed instead that Spanish commitments should be determined by the alien interests of an alien line, interests dazzling enough, of a truth, to command the nation's whole energies and resources, but still unchosen and unrelated to what Spain might otherwise have achieved at home and across the Atlantic – and in the end disastrous.

Joanna, eldest of the three surviving daughters of the Catholic Monarchs and married to Philip of Burgundy, far from being another Isabella was mentally incapacitated and, while duly proclaimed queen of Castile in 1504, unfit to rule. Ferdinand with his new wife had withdrawn to Italy, leaving the regency of Castile to Philip: for a moment it seemed as though the union were undone, until Philip's sudden death two years later again altered the course of history. Ferdinand returned to Castile to act for his daughter and, shortly before his death, reverted to his first wife's corner-stone of policy by recognizing Charles, Joanna's elder son, as heir to his own throne of Aragon.

Charles's insistence that he be proclaimed king too of Castile, and not merely regent for Joanna, whose unhappy life dragged on to 1555, thus made this youth of sixteen, born and brought up in Flanders, the first wearer of the joint crown and ruler over an effectively united, if not yet unified, country in which he had never yet set foot and whose language he could not speak. As for Catalan, that tongue, vehicle of a great medieval literature, had fallen first victim to Isabella's marriage with Aragon and was now entered on a sleep from which it would not reawaken for another three centuries.

The foreignness of the newcomer provided an initial irritant in the body social and politic. Many vicissitudes had weighed on the Spanish crown in the eight hundred years since Covadonga, but never before had it passed to an outsider. To Charles (1516–56), reared in a pleasure-loving northern atmosphere and come to Spain in 1517 with a retinue of Flemish nobles and officials, the austerity and the seriousness of the Spanish court and of Spanish life in general proved stifling. From a bustling, thriving business community he found himself translated to a lean, sparsely-inhabited land – the figure of ten million has been advanced for the whole of Spain at this time – with a predominantly rural economy in which agriculture was still overshadowed by the pastoral activities of the *Mesta*, a vast sheep-breeders' corporation which annually moved several million sheep south to the plains for the winter and back to the Castilian uplands in summer. The excellence of the Spanish soldier, like the indefatigable hardihood and endurance of the conquistador, rested in large part precisely on the sobriety and dogged tenacity bred of a life lived close to the subsistence level and in a climate of harsh extremes.

The king's new subjects returned the antipathy with interest, and passed soon to an attitude verging on revolt when Charles began distributing high offices and wealthy sinecures among his fellow Flemings. The archbishopric of Toledo, after the Pope's the richest see in Christendom, he tossed to a youth who had not even come to Spain. Something of the Spanish temper was made known to him as he visited successively the Cortes of Castile at Valladolid, of Aragon at Saragossa, and of Catalonia at Barcelona to receive the formal oath of fealty, which none would swear till he had sworn to respect their rights and to right a mounting list of grievances. Grudgingly they voted him meagre supplies, taking his measure as he took theirs.

Far more important to Spain, however, than Charles's Flemish birth was an ambition for power that not even Spain and the New World could satisfy. This grandson of Ferdinand was grandson too of the emperor Maximilian, and when at Barcelona early in 1519, with the Cortes of Valencia still unvisited, word arrived of Maximilian's death, he leapt into the fray for the succession with a spirit befitting his youth. Bribing the electors as they had never been bribed before, he duly won for himself the imperial crown to the intense discomfiture of his rivals Francis I of France and Henry VIII of England – and of Spain. To his kingdom the shock of having a foreigner as king was nothing to that of seeing him accept, without even consulting his new subjects, distant dominion and responsibilities that threatened Spain straightway with second place. Charles I was one thing, Charles V another; and, anticipating history, it was as Charles V of the Holy Roman Empire that he already thought of himself.

Announcing his intention of leaving at once for Germany, 'for not more than three years', he foreshadowed for Spain long periods of absentee rule; and in demanding from the Cortes additional subsidies for the purpose and exacting a substantial loan from the Mesta he gave a foretaste of the extent to which Spanish resources, including the wealth of the Indies, were to be bled over the next two centuries on causes that were initially not

Spain's and, by the time Spain came to adopt them as such, were already lost. The electoral debts he had incurred with various German banking-houses proved an initial millstone round Spain's neck as well as his. With one, the Welsers, he tried to settle by a grant of territory in what is now Venezuela, but the foundations were laid of a financial chaos, the concomitant of power politics on a scale beyond any El Dorado, that would dog Spain's every policy while the dynasty lasted.

Another consequence of his election stood out clearly from the beginning. France and England could not view with equanimity such a concentration of power and territory – two empires, half Europe, a New World – in the hands of a rival. Germany, the Low Countries, the Franche Comté, Roussillon, Spain, half of Italy, the Indies: even without the dream of world dominion that many attributed to him, Charles became the inevitable focus of war after war, and Spain bore the brunt of them all.

Yet the main area of conflict for Spain, and the greatest of all her new complications, lay in the realm of ideas. We have seen how the triumphant conclusion of the reconquest had ended too a long and fruitful period of cultural coexistence and religious tolerance with Isabella's elaboration of a new ideal for her country based on religious unity and the defence of the faith. The change is reflected eloquently in the legislation evoked by the new art of printing, which reached the Peninsula in 1474. Welcomed in a first law of 1480 exempting foreign books from duty, 'in consideration of the profit and honour accruing from the bringing to these kingdoms of books from abroad, that men may thereby become learned,' by 1502 the book trade was already burdened with censorship, import permits, and a rigorous system of royal licences to print or sell.

Thereafter each successive law proved more severe, until in 1558 the death penalty would be prescribed for importing any work in the vernacular into Castile even from Aragon, Valencia, Catalonia, or Navarre, or for printing any in any language, without specific permit. Spain had become afraid of the free play of ideas, and Charles's straddling of two empires greatly sharpened both the fear and the threat. For Germany was the seed-bed of protest against the continuing blind acceptance of dogmatic authoritarianism in religion, the protest which, flowering into

Protestantism, was shortly to rend in two the essential unity of the western world; and henceforth the problem would be to keep the affairs of Spain immune from German contagion.

As king of Spain Charles's reign could scarcely have had a less auspicious start. Riots and a general atmosphere of revolt marked his departure for Germany in 1520; and his last act, the appointing as regent of a Fleming, the future Pope Adrian VI, touched off a general rising throughout Castile, the 'revolt of the Comuneros'. Beginning with Toledo, city after city repudiated, not their loyalty to the crown, but a royal authority delegated to foreigners and identified with abuse of traditional rights and privileges. The regent, mobilizing his forces, attacked and set fire to Medina del Campo, the great mart and depository of Spanish trade, thereby fanning still fiercer resentment throughout the country as a whole. Fifteen cities, meeting in the same Avila where, some fifty years before, popular opposition to Henry IV had likewise come to a head, formed a league binding for once nobility, clergy, and people to a common cause. Disowning the authority of a regent already discredited in the field, they sought to draw the unhappy queen-mother from her seclusion; and had Joanna's lucidity been less in question the country might then and there have turned its back on the great European adventure.

Advised in Germany of the hazards his crown was running, Charles astutely associated with Adrian two of the great Castilian nobles in a co-regency, a step which at once mitigated the basic resentment against foreign rule and led the nobility to desist from its unnatural alliance with the commoners, who in their ardour were now demanding redress against all their oppressors. Militarily, this sounded the knell of the communes. Their forces, confronted at Villalar in April 1521 by a strong royalist army, dissolved into a rabble and the rising was at an end. A year later Charles rubbed salt into the wounds by marching 4,000 German troops through the disaffected towns.

A second rising, in Valencia, though coincident in time sprang from curiously unrelated causes. The large Muslim population of the east coast had remained unaffected by the edict of 1502 imposing on those subject to the crown of Castile the choice between exile and conversion; and in Valencia they formed a bone of contention between the nobles on the one hand, who largely relied on them for the cultivation of their estates, and the common people on the other, in whom jealousy and suspicion were sharpened to fear by the frequent coastal raids of Barbary pirates. Charles had committed one error of tactics by not presenting himself to the Valencian Cortes for recognition. He soon afterwards committed another by authorizing the populace to band itself into an armed *germanía* or brotherhood. This seized control of the capital and developed a truculence which spread throughout the kingdom of Valencia, until Charles found himself compelled to oppose it with force. Here the nobles were on the side of authority from the beginning, and the movement was foredoomed to failure, though it dragged on to the end of 1522.

The chief victims were the Muslims of all three territories of the ancient crown of Aragon, on whom there fell in November 1525 a decree exacting the old cruel choice. Thereafter in Aragon too, in theory, the religious problem was solved, and none but Christians were now to be found throughout the length and breadth of Spain. In practice such conversion was again suspect, and rightly, for the outraging of their religious loyalties made the converts worse, not better, subjects of the crown. The pirate raids did not diminish, nor the collusion that had been alleged between the raiders and their erstwhile co-religionists, and a creeping economic decline descended on this most fertile region of the Peninsula.

With the breaking of the towns, Habsburg autocracy was firmly established. Isabella in her studied neglect of the Cortes had shown that popular representation, whatever the seeds of democracy contained therein, was to her but a means to her own ends. Those ends had still concerned the common people, whom they bound to the crown as never before, and it was the persisting strength of the bond that enabled Charles at once to flout them as king and still rely on their loyalty to the institution of kingship. As a political factor the towns would not count again for close on three hundred years.

Yet it would be wrong to argue a dictated subservience. The *quid pro quo* was Charles's gradual adoption of Spanish ideals. It may well have been for wrong reasons that he came to believe in what, to Spain, were the right things, but believe in them he eventually did. Marrying a Portuguese princess, supporting the Inquisition, stimulating conquest and proselytization across the Atlantic, he set himself to further the objectives of peninsular unity, of a Catholic faith inviolate, of a Hispanic New World; and his Spanish subjects, coming to identify themselves with the empire as the emperor progressively identified himself with Spain, were in the end well content with the association.

The Cortes were convened more frequently, not less, by Charles than by his predecessors, their interests being entrusted between meetings to the permanent commission which, long existent in Aragon, Castile too had instituted in 1525. Yet the request of the towns in 1544 to be dispensed from assembling oftener than once in three years, if argued on grounds of cost, implied recognition that they had ceased to be an effective power in the realm. The constraint imposed on them after Villalar to invest their deputies with full powers and to vote grants before raising grievances was only part reason of the decline. Another consequence of Villalar had been the monopolizing of municipal office by the *hidalgo* class (literally 'son of something') of the lesser nobility who, having sided with the crown, had their reward in this new field of exploitation. It was they who thereafter represented the towns in Cortes, where Charles found them for the most part agreeably pliant to his will.

The considerable prosperity that accompanied these decades of internal peace was the fruit of an expanding economy closely related to events in the New World. That adventure had for long hung fire. The conscripting of gaolbirds to man Columbus's third expedition, the total disillusion that enveloped the discoverer's closing years, and his death in penury had been the measure of his failure to give Spain the promised access to the riches of the Orient. 'If I had stolen the Indies and given them to the Moors, Spain could not have shown me greater enmity.' Balboa's sighting of the Pacific, 'silent upon a peak in Darien,' in 1513 was a second landmark in that it set the New World in geographical perspective and made clear that this new land mass awaiting exploitation was neither the Far East nor a feasible way to it. The realization provided an added stimulus to the search for what wealth it did possess, and the conquest of Mexico from Cuba by Cortés over the years 1519–22, with that of Peru by

Pizarro from Panama between 1531 and 1534, left Spain cause no longer to envy Portugal her rounding of the Cape.

Cortés's first consignment of Aztec treasure fell into the hands not of Charles but of the king of France, as many subsequent consignments from the greater wealth of Peru, especially after the discovery of Potosí, the silver mountain, in 1545, would into those of a queen of England. Enough would still reach Spain to obscure the fact that two great indigenous civilizations were destroyed in the getting of it and that the honest concern of crown and Church to seek the spiritual and safeguard the material welfare of the Indian population was consistently impeded, where not stultified, by the lust for gold and power that characterized the Spaniard at 3,000 miles' remove from the restraints of his home society.

The *leyenda negra*, fathered by a Spaniard, the humanitarian Las Casas, and exploited thereafter by Spain's enemies for political purposes, calls for assessment in terms of this profound cleavage between the will at home and the reality overseas. The crown's dilemma was not merely the lively fear on occasion that the Indies, won once from the Indians, might have to be won a second time from the Spaniards – in the 1540's it all but lost Peru – but that the growing and soon desperate need for ever more American bullion to meet ever vaster European commitments forbade even the royal conscience to scruple overmuch at the sufferings of the native tribes.

In the process the feudalism from which Europe was at last emerging became to the Indian the symbol of what Christianity and 'civilization' had conferred on him; African slaves, imported and treated as merchandise, degraded further the conception of personal dignity that to the Spaniard in Spain had always figured among the most sacred of human values; and the mingling of bloods consequent upon the arrival of Spaniard and Portuguese without their womenfolk – herein lying the most profound original divergence between Latin and Anglo-Saxon America – endowed the new society with a complex of racial and other tensions that the lapse of centuries finds still unresolved.

The conquest was still, in the material sense, a stirring achievement, that before the century was out had carried the Spanish flag from California to southern Chile and left the conquistadores still looking for fresh worlds to conquer. Coincident in time with the overthrow of the Aztec empire was the first circumnavigation of the globe that followed on the ill-fated voyage of the Portuguese Magalhães, sailing under Spanish auspices. This fructified in 1565 in Spain's occupation of the Philippine Islands, called after Charles's heir the future Philip II. Thus at long last Spain secured her footing in the Far East, administering it, in tardy justification of Columbus, from Mexico in the far west.

To these spacious if scattered domains, isolated so far as Spanish sea-power could ensure from trading and other contacts with an increasingly envious, as it was an increasingly heretical, outside world, flowed the products of Spanish industry. From them poured back the cargoes of gold and silver that to an age still innocent of economic science spelt the epitome of wealth. In the first quarter of a century after the discovery of Peru bullion receipts came to some two-thirds of the previous total gold and silver currency of Europe.

Seville, with its 'Casa de Contratación' or Trades House for all commerce with the New World, was the port of entry, whence there irradiated throughout Spain and to Europe at large a steady inflationary movement that by 1550 had on an average doubled commodity prices over the preceding three decades and by the end of the century would double them again. Paradoxically, Spain thus found herself the first victim of her dazzling new-found wealth that, come so easily, was to go even more easily, much of it in the service of the mounting foreign debts that were Charles's nightmare throughout the whole of his reign, until there came a time when consignments of gold and silver arriving at Seville were trans-shipped straightway to come to rest in the coffers of German or Italian banking houses.

The industrial boom scarcely lasted beyond the middle of the century. With soaring prices went a dwindling trade with the rest of Europe, with a gradually increasing self-sufficiency in the colonies a lessened reliance on the products of the home country, with easy wealth a contempt for honest labour, and with penal taxation and wrong-headed policies, such as the sacrifice of agriculture to the vested interests of the Mesta, a progressive thwarting of the country's economic development.

In its intellectual development over this same first half of the century there may be seen at play conflicting forces of which the more liberal originate from without, while the more conservative draw much of their strength from identification with specifically Spanish ideals. Aragonese, and later Spanish, possession of Naples had made it possible for generations of Spanish intellectuals and men of letters to travel and study in Renaissance Italy, a liberating experience that presided over the birth of Spanish drama, the rebirth of lyric poetry, and the reinvigoration, thanks to returning scholars and to the occasional Italian scholar who accompanied them, of Spain's universities, notably the already venerable Salamanca and its new rival Alcalá, founded as recently as 1508 by cardinal Ximénez de Cisneros and with a monumental polyglot Bible already to its credit. Charles himself, friend of Erasmus, tolerant of criticism and, so long as good government was not impeded, of the right to think for oneself, was prepared to move with the times and represented a liberal element in a northern tradition, and men like-minded found welcome at his court.

The Inquisition incarnated the denial of that right, and Charles was initially disposed to accede to petitions awaiting his first arrival in Spain for reform of its procedure and the clipping of its wings. In 1527 a conclave of theologians at Valladolid could still give official approval to the writings of Erasmus, and Charles subscribe a ban on further hostile criticism. It was his long absences from Spain that gave their chance to the religious orders, incensed as these were by Erasmus's criticisms of their short-comings.

Setting themselves through the monopoly of preaching that was theirs to confuse Erasmus in the popular mind with the archheretic Luther, they succeeded in equating humanism with heresy to the point where – as Luis Vives, one of the greatest of sixteenth-century humanists, commented – one could neither speak nor remain silent without getting into trouble. The Inquisition had by now come under the virtual control of the orders, in particular of the Dominicans, and successive *Indices expurgatorios*, the first of 1546, bore witness of the price to literature as well as to thought of the Inquisition's concern that all men should walk circumspectly. Vives and Juan de Valdés were of the number who preferred to live out their lives in exile.

Among those harassed both by the Inquisition and by the orders, the former imprisoning him when a student for the priesthood at Alcalá, the latter in Salamanca, was one Ignacio de Loyola, the same who in 1539 founded in Rome the Society of Jesus. This proved to be not just one order more. Its members added to the vows of poverty and chastity that of unquestioning obedience to the Pope, a provocative complication in a Spain where the defence of religion was held a sphere of state action by a crown traditionally jealous of papal interference, and much more so in Spain's New World with its *Patronato Regio* vesting in the Spanish monarch full ecclesiastical responsibility and control.

The Jesuits resuscitated the concept of the church militant, Loyola, formerly a soldier, continuing so to think of himself and of his fellow-members. And, a consequence of this, they transferred the emphasis from reclusion in monasteries to teaching in colleges, and were soon successful in penetrating the whole field of education. From the beginning the movement was international in scope. Prepared to go anywhere and do anything *ad majorem Dei gloriam*, Jesuits took the whole expanding world for their parish. Francisco Xavier, a founder-member, achieved canonization with his fellow-Basque Loyola in 1622 as one of the greatest missionaries of all time, his labours embracing India, Ceylon, Japan, and the Moluccas.

Withal, Spanish in origin, it long continued Spanish too in spirit and in its higher direction, and nowhere was its influence felt more deeply than in the Peninsula. In comparison the Inquisition was but defending a *status quo*, with weapons that spoke rather of fear than of conviction. The Jesuits placed themselves in the forefront of the ideological battle then rending Europe, and it was thanks chiefly to their zeal that Spanish religious fervour, as distinct from religious orthodoxy, knew the rebirth which underlay both the rare flowering of Spanish mysticism exemplified in a Santa Teresa or a St John of the Cross and such natural leadership of the Counter-Reformation as was to make of the Council of Trent predominantly a Spanish affair.

Many and diverse charges would later be laid at the door of the Jesuits; eventually, in the eighteenth century, a Spanish king would decree their expulsion from all his dominions. In the present context they symbolize that fierce Spanish passion of the spirit which could count a Renaissance well lost that dared impinge, in the name of reason, on the preserve of the irrational. Deep down in the consciousness of the Spaniard that preserve was identified with the essence of his national being: in its name he had fought the reconquest, and he was conscious of being called on to fight again now in defence of what he had then won, a close-knit society resting on a spiritual basis which none might call in question. The Jesuit as a soldier believed that the best defence was attack; as a Catholic that his noblest mission was to spread the faith; as both that the end justified at once the cost and the means. In all of which he spoke for Spain.

It was at the siege of Pamplona by the French in 1521 – an attempt to win back Navarre while Charles was in Germany and his regent had his hands full with the Comuneros – that Loyola, one of the defenders, had suffered a broken leg and seen the light. It would be stretching truth to hold the French monarch responsible thereby for the Society of Jesus, but the incident serves to point how soon and how inevitably the awareness had descended upon Spain of what association with the empire, in the person of her new king, portended. The four wars with France that span the years 1521 to 1544 sprang on the French side in part from the disgruntlement of a defeated rival in the contest for the imperial succession, that filled Francis I with life-long enmity, in part from the threat of encirclement by an emperor in whom, on grounds alike territorial and spiritual, there was suspected to lurk the ambition of universal monarchy.

For Charles these wars were largely unsought, save for one specific problem of communication. Since 1515 the duchy of Milan had been in French possession, and was vital to continuing French ambitions in Italy. But even more vital to Charles was the securing of safe passage between his Spanish and his Habsburg dominions, and through Milan all traffic had to pass. Once only, in 1538, was Charles able to cross peacefully through France on his way from Hendaye to Antwerp; once, in 1520, when first summoned to assume the imperial mantle, he had essayed the hazards of the long western sea voyage from Galicia to the Netherlands and thrice he would return that way, a route dependent on good relations with both France and England. But there could be no real alternative to a secure overland route. A campaign for Milan had to be waged, and, waged and won in 1521, the lasting hostility of France on this additional ground had to be accepted.

The brilliant victory at Pavia in 1525 of German, Spanish, and Italian troops over a French army led against Milan by Francis himself delivered the French king into Charles's hands and a year's captivity in Madrid. Papal sympathies veering to the weaker side, in a 'Holy League' contrived by a new and un-friendly Pope, there resulted the famous sack of Rome that scandalized Christendom in May 1527. The work not of Charles or his commanders but of a mutinous German and Spanish soldiery left too long unpaid – the Achilles' heel always of Spain in the field – it underlined the distinction then to be made be-tween the Pope as a temporal power and the Church he often so equivocally represented. There were indeed those among Charles's advisers who would have had him turn this unhappy chapter to account by putting an end once for all to the territorial sovereignty of the papacy.

The winning of Genoa to Charles's side now reinforced him where he was weakest, in naval power, and enabled him first to foil France in her attempt to turn the tables on him by investing Naples, and thereafter to take the offensive against the alarming expansion of Turkish power which, in its double advance up the Danube to the gates of Vienna and westward along the Mediter-ranean, threatened at once the empire, Spain, and the faith. Infidel raiders from bases in north Africa kept the coasts of south-eastern Spain in a constant state of alarm. In 1532 a Spanish army was fighting on the Danube in conjunction with a Genoese naval offensive in the Peloponnese.

The Turkish occupation of Tunis two years later spurred Charles to a supreme effort to regain control of the western Mediterranean. Leading the attack in person in 1535, he captured the city, liberating thousands of Christian captives and noting that many of its guns had come from the arsenals of the king of France, to whom the worsting of the emperor was a higher cause than the defence of Christendom. The escape of the Turkish garrison to Algiers robbed the victory of finality, and the battle remained to be fought again a generation later.

France meanwhile was preparing against him a third war, with Milan still the pretext; and in April 1536, before the Pope, his cardinals, and the assembled ambassadors of foreign powers, Charles protested at the injustice of France's enmity. An offer of accommodation over Milan having been rejected, he proposed to Francis that they should meet in personal combat, with Milan and Burgundy as the stakes. He spoke in Spanish, and it was as a Spaniard now, the emperor merged in the crusader, that he pleaded the cause of a united Christendom against the common enemy. But the most Christian king would not listen, and the war went on, indecisively, until in 1538 the Pope brought about a ten-year truce.

Freed for a time from the one danger, Charles turned again to the other. The piratical activities of the Turks, based now on Algiers, had intensified until trade and communication between Spain and Italy were almost at a standstill, and again, in 1541, Charles prepared and led a mighty expedition – his retinue in- cluding Cortés – against this threat to his whole polity. A winter storm turned incipient success into disastrous failure, and though Cortés pleaded for the chance to show once again, as he had in Mexico, how victory might be snatched out of the very jaws of defeat, defeat it remained, and marked the almost total abandon- ment of the Mediterranean to the Turk for the remainder of his reign.

Again the decisive factor was France, about to launch yet another campaign for control of Milan, which Charles had just settled on his son and heir Philip. Against the open support for France of the Turkish fleet, commanded by a French admiral, Charles could count this time on England, the heretic Henry VIII having agreed to a proposal to dismember France in the event of her total defeat; but Charles's attempt to march on Paris proved as abortive as that of Francis to invade Spain and, after three years, the two signed a peace of exhaustion in 1544.

The death of Francis in 1547 at length removed this bitterest of personal foes; but the reasons for French hostility to a Spain linked to the empire remained strong as before, as did the readiness to consort with allies of whatever religious hue. It was less the military might of his enemies that was wearing Charles down than the attrition of a Europe whose leaders, from the

Pope himself to the king of England, no longer found in religion the supreme principle of conduct and bond of loyalty. He, and the Spain he championed, found themselves in fact only not an anachronism in that certain others, not kings but common men, did still agree in so regarding their faith, for which they too were prepared to fight and die. And they were on the other side of the fence.

This was his other and heavier cross, that accompanied him throughout the length of his long reign. The year of his arrival in Spain, 1517, had been the year also when Luther nailed his ninety-five theses on the cathedral door at Wittenberg. Charles could not then know how great a disruptive movement had been born in the act, nor that his accession to the empire would cast him for the chief role in this struggle for the soul of western Europe that was to be fought out on his territories and to end with his defeat. That Lutheranism would be anathema to Spain was self-evident, and the hands of the Inquisition were greatly strengthened by fear of the consequences to be expected from the unsought association with this new breeding-ground of heresy.

To Charles the problem bore another and more complex cast, for within Germany religious dissidence fed on the same political apprehensions in reverse that had weighed on Spain at the news of his election. Neither country had wanted union with the other nor any subordinating of its interests to an alien policy. German unity, moreover, was superficial at best, and the invitation to independent thinking implicit in Lutheranism was not likely to stop at religion. If authority could be questioned in matters of faith, its vulnerability in matters secular followed; and soon Charles found himself using Spanish armies to quell rebellion in Germany, the Spaniards fighting, as they understood it, in defence of the faith, Charles in defence of his sovereignty.

Again and again France and the Turk would compel him to temporize and, if not to concede, to acquiesce in the principle that each prince might decide the official religion of his principality. For long he pinned his hopes to a general council of the Church which by prudent reforms might yet keep Christendom intact. But for this at least a semblance of amity among the Christian nations was essential, and not until December 1545, after peace with France, could it meet. It was to prove a long council, much interrupted, and dominated, as has been noted already, by the Spanish bishops, in whom there burned a religious zeal that left the Pope far behind.

The choice of Trent, in the Tyrol, had met the German demand that the council should convene on German soil; but from its proximity to the Italian frontier there arose such suspicions of imperial and of papal intentions alike that in the end the Lutherans refused to attend. Arming now in a Protestant league, Luther's moderating influence having been removed by death, they forced Charles's hand, and his last war, like his first, was fought against his own subjects. The Pope, proclaiming it a holy war, contributed his own contingent of 15,000 men.

Charles was equally convinced that the issue at bottom was the challenge to his imperial authority. It was not merely Christendom but the empire that was disintegrating. Summoning troops from Spain and the Netherlands, he won at Mühlberg in 1547 an apparently decisive victory that was dramatically reversed in 1552 when, his search for a definitive basis for compromise having finally failed, he was ignominiously routed at Innsbruck and only escaped captivity by flight. The Council of Trent dispersed for a decade, and Charles interested himself no more in its fortunes. In 1555 the Diet of Augsburg conceded religious freedom and equality to both persuasions.

The battle was over for Germany, and – if not for Spain – for Charles. Milan, where the Franco–Turkish power axis had crossed his own, was the symbol of the material conflict that had spanned his reign. This he understood, for it was cast in the traditional mould of territorial ambition, a trial of strategy and resources. Luther had symbolized the other struggle, for the control of men's minds: this was new, and lay beyond the reach of conventional weapons. Brought into the attempt to stem the tide, Spain was confirmed in the conviction of where her role lay, and grew still more resolute that the waters of heresy should not lap her shores. As Germany personified now the Reformation, so she the Counter-Reformation, taking her stand on the findings of the Council of Trent and identifying religion ever more closely with that unquestioning submission to dogma which, the Pope had insisted to Charles, meant so much more than morals.

But Charles could fight no more, and prepared to lay down his sceptre, concerned only with the knotty problem of how best to dispose of an inheritance that he was at last persuaded could no longer be held together. In a series of acts of abdication, he divested himself of the Low Countries in 1555 and of Spain with the Italian dependencies, including Milan, in 1556 in favour of his son Philip; the German empire he resigned in 1558 to his brother Ferdinand. 'Nine times,' he said at Brussels on the first of these occasions, 'I have been to upper Germany, six to Spain, seven to Italy, ten I have come here to Flanders, four – in peace and in war – I have been in France, twice in England, and twice in Africa: forty in all, not counting other lesser journeyings over my dominions. In all this I have eight times sailed the Mediterranean, three times the Atlantic between here and Spain, and now will be the fourth when I return there to die.'

The last words were significant. To Spain it had been a costly and unsatisfactory reign. For more than twenty of its just on forty years the country had been governed, in its monarch's absence, by a succession of regents. Charles had not set foot now in the Peninsula for thirteen years on end. Yet Spain had set its mark on him. To Spain he willed the Low Countries and Milan despite their historic affinity with the empire, and to Spain he now returned, to the monastery of Yuste in Estremadura, where death released him a few months after his final surrender of the trappings of power.

It was a revealing commentary on the reign of this colossus who bestrode half the western world that he had been unable to abdicate until funds could be had from Spain to pay off his household in the Netherlands. For near-bankruptcy had pursued him as a shadow throughout; and here Spain, that had never admitted the imperial mantle as extending to the Peninsula, was bled white notwithstanding. The true measure of what the crushing of the Comuneros at Villalar portended lay in the compliance thereafter of the Castilian Cortes, that over forty years approved twenty-one out of twenty-two demands for ever more crushing sums in taxation, their one refusal, in 1527, resting on the fact that the previous vote was still uncollected. Charles got revenues even out of the Church. The nobles proving more difficult, he had resort to the stultification of selling titles of nobility and thus exempting from the ranks of the taxpayers precisely those best able to pay.

But everything, even the confiscation as forced loans of private remittances from the Indies, was negligible compared with his needs, and his only remedy was to mortgage and keep on mortgaging the future on terms that grew more onerous as his credit declined. Tax-farmers extorted a fee for collection of up to twenty-four per cent; the cost of raising advances from his Flemish and Italian bankers reached on occasion forty-three per cent; and in 1555 Spanish revenue was already pledged and exhausted to the end of 1560. It was not for love nor primarily in pursuit of his grandparents' policy of peninsular unity that in 1526 he had married a Portuguese princess, but because the largest dowry was to be looked for from that quarter.

The first fruit of that marriage, dowry apart, was the birth of the future Philip II in May 1527, a fortnight after the sack of Rome, word of which put an abrupt end to the nation's celebrations and was by some accounted an ill omen. The second was not to mature for another half-century, when the falling of Portugal into Philip's lap would appear to proclaim in retrospect the far-sighted wisdom of his father's choice. In fact Spain and Portugal, matrimonial alliances apart, ran their separate ways during Charles's reign with a degree of mutual unconcern that was strikingly at variance with their earlier history.

Manuel I 'the Fortunate' (1495–1521), cousin of John II, had agreed, as a condition of his Spanish marriage in 1496, to follow Spain in expelling such Jews as would not abjure their faith, many of those driven out of Spain four years earlier having made their way into Portugal. Their importance to the nation's economy, allied to the fact that national unification was not to Portugal the problem it was to Spain, at once increased the pressure to secure conversion and mitigated the rigours of enquiry into its sincerity. The crown gave in fact a twenty-year undertaking, later prolonged for another sixteen years, not to enquire further into the beliefs of the *conversos*. This did not prevent mob massacres at Lisbon in 1506; but the religious intolerance that marked state policy in the neighbouring country was still strange to Portugal, as was its chief instrument, the Inquisition. Of much more immediate interest to Manuel was the consolidation of the royal power.

One factor in this, after his predecessor's grim humbling of the overweening rivalries that had threatened his throne, was the conciliation of a now chastened nobility and the attaching of it to his court. The process was furthered by the absorption in the crown of the grandmasterships of the military orders, a policy learnt from Spain of both political and economic prudence. Manuel initiated it by securing from the Pope in 1516 the right of nomination; John III would complete it in 1551. Another concerned the Cortes and the towns which, without any commoners' revolt as in Castile, suffered a no less drastic clipping of their powers, and at bottom for the same reason. John I had summoned Cortes twenty-five times in a reign of forty-eight years. Manuel convoked them four times in the opening years of his, not at all in the last nineteen. His successor found them amenable in 1525 to a proposal that they should meet only every ten years. The towns were the victims of a thorough-going revision of the country's municipal *forais* – corresponding to the Spanish fueros – which, part of a general overhaul of legislation, reduced what had been precious charters of rights as well as of obligations to little more than a code of taxation.

The reason why Manuel could so flout the third estate was that he no longer depended on it. Fortune, reflected in his sobriquet, had bestowed on him the inheritance of the labours begun by Henry the Navigator and brought now to fruition by Vasco da Gama. As the wealth of the east poured in on him, making him the richest monarch and Lisbon the greatest entrepôt of western Europe, the need to continue humouring the Cortes that they might be pleased to vote him subsidies dwindled to insignificance. From the beginning, to Portugal as to Spain, the imperial adventure had been a royal and personal, only indirectly a national, undertaking. John I had forgone a levy rather than admit participation by the Cortes in his expedition to Ceuta in 1415; and although Manuel did consult his council before launching that of 1497 which was to carry da Gama to India, the final decision, taken against their advice, was his own.

The empires that resulted made Spain and Portugal again partners, in the mighty enterprise this time of bringing new continents and oceans within the ken of Europe and the ambit of the Christian faith, as once before in the task of expelling the infidel from the Peninsula. There was rivalry too, reflected in the line of demarcation of 1494 and in the corresponding line drawn at the other side of the globe, 17° east of the Moluccas, in 1529, to the east of which, this time, stood Spain and to the west Portugal. The two powers had withal a common interest in trying to make of their new worlds a peninsular preserve, Portugal ceasing notably after 1500 to reaffirm her alliance with a still Catholic England.

It is important nonetheless to realize how different in character the two empires were. Both countries had gone overseas in search of India and trade. Castile, a nation of landsmen, found instead the Indies and, in lieu of trade, an invitation to conquer and to settle vast territories which soon yielded an unlooked-for reward in precious metals. The Atlantic once crossed, it was still a landsman's empire, from which the Catalans with their long maritime tradition were deliberately excluded. The Portuguese were a race of seafarers who, succeeding where Spain had failed in finding direct access to the spices of the east, concerned themselves with conquest only to the extent that their new interests demanded the securing of sea lanes and trading posts. The settling of Madeira, the Canaries, and the Azores was incidental, and the Canaries were eventually, in 1479, ceded to Spain.

Brazil, whether it was foreknowledge or contrary winds that in 1500 carried Alvares Cabral, India-bound to follow up da Gama's achievement, across the Atlantic narrows to make a landfall for Portugal too in the New World, likewise signified for half a century little more than another and lesser trading venture in brazil-wood, parrots, and monkeys. 'To Portingals,' runs an entry for 1505 in the accounts of Henry VII of England, 'that brought popinjays and cats of the mountain with other stuff to the King's Grace, £5.' The true importance of Brazil came later, when Portugal's hold on the east was already slackening: its significance at the time lay in the fact that, without Columbus, the discovery of the New World would have been delayed a mere eight years, with what consequences for its subsequent history none can say.

In the east Portugal found in possession races whose civilization, if not whose faith, there was no calling in question, and whose strength to defend their own far outweighed any land forces the Portuguese could muster at such a remove from home.

Man-power constituted in fact the major handicap throughout. The hazards of the sea journey alone exacted a toll that soon proved crippling. One-third of da Gama's men never saw Portugal again. Four of Alvares Cabral's thirteen vessels foundered at the Cape, the victims including Bartolomeu Dias, and only six reached their destination. Of the four ships that sailed for India in 1553 only one arrived, among its passengers a common soldier named Luis de Camoens who was to become his country's greatest poet; and that vessel too was lost on the return journey. Alongside *Os Lusíadas* of 1572, Camoens' memorable epic of Portuguese overseas achievement, there are to be set therefore the many heart-rending narratives that were later collected to form, in the *História trágico-marítima* of 1735–6, perhaps the most moving entry in the whole balance-sheet of empire.

Arab traders concerned to deny to the intruders any share in their monopoly of the Indian Ocean, rather than Indian merchants or potentates, proved the enemy. Their wiles, however, often manoeuvred the latter into hostility against the newcomers, and Alvares Cabral's unwilling bombardment of Calicut, where da Gama's reception had been friendly enough, altered the tone of subsequent relations. Land bases now had to be fought for, and the fleet of 1504 carried out a force of 1,500 men and a viceroy, who established his seat at Cochin. Afonso de Albuquerque, second and greatest of the viceroys (1509–15), seized Goa in 1510 and, encouraging his men to take native wives and settle, made of it the seat and symbol for centuries to come of Portuguese dominion in the east.

But trade, and further exploration as a means to more trade, remained the objective. The token shipment of spices brought back by da Gama in 1499 had paid the costs of the expedition sixty times over, pepper selling in Lisbon at forty times its price in India. With increasing supplies that rate of profit was before long halved and then quartered: it was still sufficiently lucrative to engage Portuguese energies beyond what the nation could spare and once again, as has been seen happen in Spain, to involve a profound disturbance of the home economy. In 1526 the dowry of Charles V's Portuguese bride could still be expressed as 50,000 quintals of pepper.

Albuquerque had found the Indian Ocean already in fee to his country's flag, for the Arabs proved no match for the Portuguese in naval encounters. His own seizure of Ormuz in 1515 carried that flag into the Persian Gulf; on the Red Sea it sailed at will after the defeat of an Egyptian fleet at Diu in 1509. A heavy blow was thus dealt to the rival spice route to Europe, with economic consequences both to the Mameluke empire in Egypt, that contributed powerfully to its overthrow by the Ottoman Turks in 1517, and to Venice, from which that proud republic never wholly recovered.

Soon, as erstwhile Africa, India too was rounded and Portuguese vessels were sailing the Bay of Bengal and into the China Sea. The capture of Malacca in 1511 was to the Portuguese what Darien and the first glimpse of the Pacific would be to the Spaniards two years later. From there the way opened up to Siam, Java, Cochin China, and the Moluccas or Spice Islands. Here was wealth indeed, and a commerce more profitable than even India had to offer. Magellan's voyage of circumnavigation, an exploit that, giving mankind a first true measure of its universe, captured the imagination as the greatest adventure yet, was a direct consequence of this mounting challenge to a still disappointed and thwarted rival and the indirect cause of the eventual transfer to Spain of sovereignty over her one foothold in the Far East, the Philippines. Sailing ever further, in whatever direction trade – even a share in local coastal shipping – was to be had, the Portuguese ranged northward to China and eventually to Japan, discovered in 1542 by a vessel disabled and carried for fifteen days at the mercy of the winds, and southward to Timor and New Guinea.

The 'State of India', as it was known to and administered from Lisbon, was thus never a territorial empire but a vast and loosely knit field of operations extending from Sofala and Mozambique in East Africa to Macau in China. After the trader, at some remove in time, came the missionary. On the establishment of the Inquisition in Portugal in 1536, again on pressure from Spain, there had followed in 1540 that of the Society of Jesus, which soon gained control both of education, with the ancient university of Coimbra as its particular stronghold, and of the king's conscience. Two years later the arrival of the first Jesuits in India marked the serious beginning of an enterprise notably different in its demands and in its results from the mass conversions of subject populations in America.

Enjoying by papal grant the same titular overlordship (*Padro-ado Real*) in matters spiritual in the east as did Spain with her *Patronato* in the west, the Portuguese crown created a bishopric – from 1557 an archbishopric – of Goa invested with a jurisdiction stretching from Africa to China. But apart from the common difficulty in commending a faith of which the generality of Portuguese in the east were themselves indifferent exemplars, and the fact that Catholic activities and institutions could only rest, in the absence of territorial sovereignty, on local tolerance, the Hindu, Buddhist, or Muslim was not easily detachable from beliefs powerfully identified, as in the caste system, with the intimate structure of his society. Surviving Portuguese settlements in the Far East remain Christian till today; for the rest, time has left only the faintest of traces to tell of centuries of devoted Christian effort.

On the material plane too the rewards began before long to dwindle. As supplies of commodities from the Orient increased the European price fell, while failure to block completely the Red Sea route resulted in a substantial recovery by Venice, from the mid sixteenth century, of her earlier trade. Had every vessel made the return journey safely and with a full cargo the venture might still have shown a handsome return for long enough; but the carracks and galleons, increasing in size till they became the largest vessels afloat, did not gain correspondingly in sea-worthiness.

Not uncommonly half of the six or eight hundred men they carried died of scurvy or other diseases on the six months' journey out, and the casualty rate to the vessels themselves reached on occasion to ninety per cent for the round trip. French and Dutch piracy had a hand in this: the Dutch in particular were soon to be found in the wake of the Portuguese throughout the east, waiting to step into their shoes. In conjunction these factors altered the balance of profit until the value of the traffic back to Europe via the Cape was outweighed by that of the carrying trade in far eastern waters, a monopoly of traffic between China and Japan proving especially lucrative; and this wealth stayed in the east.

For Portugal it was apparent by the middle of the century that the cumulative results must prove disastrous. The crisis was firstly one of population, the Indian adventure draining the country's life-blood until a languishing agriculture compelled the large-scale import of African slaves. An estimate of 1551 gave Lisbon a population of 100,000 of whom one-tenth were slaves, with sixty or seventy slave-markets. Moral decline reflected the collapse of economic values. Easy riches had replaced glory in the lure of the Orient and deprived honest labour at home alike of reward and of attraction. The corruption and incompetence that had become a byword across the seas cast their shadow no less over the home country, where a spate of sumptuary and other laws proved impotent to check the rot. And all the time, as crowning paradox, the state grew poorer and poorer until Portugal too was living a hand-to-mouth existence dependent on loans from foreign banking-houses at ever steeper rates and driven to declare moratoria on interest payments and to condition foreign alliances by the possibility or impossibility of paying a princess's dowry. When to all this was added the exhaustion and at length the total eclipse of the dynasty it seemed indeed that Portugal had overreached herself and fallen on the other.

That other could only be Spain. Philip II (1556–98), in inheriting the Low Countries and Milan, found himself burdened with commitments that, severed from the Germany to whose orbit they belonged, were to prove a major embarrassment. The Low Countries, to be governed and defended thenceforth from Spain by sea, were scarce defensible should France or England turn hostile, and scarce governable were Philip to insist, as he did, on exacting from all his subjects unquestioning submission to the Catholic Church. Milan, with Naples, made him the arbiter of Italy, and bound him to that arbitrament and to the continued blocking of French ambitions in that direction when his whole desire was to retreat within his peninsular shell, with the New World as empire enough. One first smell of battle he had, against the French while still in the Low Countries, and it sufficed him for life. Returning to Spain in 1559, he would never again set foot outside the Peninsula in the four decades that he too was to rule.

Son of a Portuguese mother, his first bride another Portuguese princess, he was a strange reversal to type, a medieval type with a mind closed and dominated by a single idea. Wishful, if not to have Africa begin, to have Spain end at the Pyrenees, he accepted as a sacred trust, since this could no longer be, the forlorn attempt to force Spanish dogma on the minds of other Europeans with whom time had not stood still. His personal misfortune was to be called to responsibility in an age of dissolving belief, and fate's blackest blow the realization, after the Armada, that to believe oneself to be on God's side did not necessarily commit God.

Certain aspects of Philip's policy have allowed the argument that expedience, and not religiosity, guided his actions, to the greater exalting of Spanish dominion, and that as Protestant or agnostic he would in fact have acted not otherwise: such his support of Elizabeth on the English throne against her Catholic rival Mary of Scots, his war in 1557 against Pope Paul IV, who had already excommunicated him and his father, or his constant rebuttal of papal infringements of the royal jurisdiction in Spain, where, since the days of the Catholic Monarchs, the Church stood as a branch in effect of the civil service.

But there is here a misunderstanding. The Pope was a temporal sovereign, elected as such and not for the sanctity of his character or the spiritual defence of Christendom: the rise of Lutheranism, the history of the Council of Trent, are conclusive on this score. With Rome constantly playing power politics for material ends, Philip had no choice but to do the same for spiritual ends, persuaded that he alone had the true interests of the faith at heart. The fate of Catholicism was in the balance, and it was a delicate balance. To have allowed France through Mary queen of Scots to dominate England would equally have inferred such a threat to Spanish supremacy in Europe as to jeopardize all he stood for. Here was no expediency but the cool pursuit of a single-minded objective only possible so long as Spain remained strong. And no opportunist would have risked, or need have lost, the Low Countries. Philip, who 'would rather not rule than rule over heretics', was to make their loss inevitable.

Meanwhile Spain herself must be kept inviolate, and Philip's first official appearance on his return to Spain was at an *auto de fe* in Valladolid. For the remainder of the century Spain and the Counter-Reformation were as one. The arrest by the Inquisition, in that same year 1559, of the very head of the Spanish Church, archbishop Carranza of Toledo, prelude to a trial that, dragging on for seventeen years, found him at length 'vehemently suspect' of heresies he was compelled formally to abjure, gave the measure both of the power the king allowed to the Holy Office and of its solicitude that doctrinal error should nowhere raise its head.

Charles for forty years had fought wars all over Europe, wars of armies, of squadrons, with territories as the stake. Philip for another forty would fight a war of ideas with men's minds – or, as he believed, their souls – as the battle-ground, and the first differential mark of his reign is that he sought to control his empire by paper-work and directed his campaigns from his desk. This, and a resolve inculcated by his father never to trust anyone wholly nor to leave to others any final decision, necessitated a new concentration of bureaucratic control.

Castile till then had never had a fixed capital, the capital being wherever a peripatetic court happened to find itself, with Valla-dolid and Toledo as preferred centres in the two previous reigns. Philip's choice for this purpose of Madrid, from 1561, betrays a strong symbolic significance, for Madrid stands at the geo-graphical centre of the Peninsula. Adopted for administrative convenience, it has stood out ever since as what it is, an arbitrary federal capital without a past, and unable as such to command the loyalties of the other kingdoms that likewise make up Spain. To a Catalan, a Basque, an Andalusian, even a native of Old Castile, Madrid is still today merely the city from which he is governed, and the object thereby rather of distrust than of affection.

Here on this bleak upland attuned to the austerity of his own spirit, and apparently without confiding to any at the time that it was his intention the court should move no more, Philip settled in to the castle-fortress that had earlier held Francis I a prisoner and gathered about him his series of councils, some charged with territorial responsibilities (the Councils of Castile, Aragon, Italy, the Indies), some with departmental (Finance, Justice, the Inquisition), with the Council of State over all. All were nominated by and answerable to the king, and all were purely consultative. Philip would seek advice, he could never bring himself to delegate responsibility, or even to inform his advisers fully on the issues he referred to them; and so he became with time the victim of his own cumbrous machine, a slave to papers whose mounting bulk outran the hours of the longest working day. Spanish dilatoriness became a byword throughout Europe. 'If death came from Spain,' remarked a viceroy of Naples, 'we should live a long time.'

Fortunately for Philip, the tempo of external events had notably slackened. Neither in Italy nor with France was he called on to fight any wars, and though England gave abundant motive, for thirty years he evaded the challenge. The peace of Cateau-Cambrésis, signed with France in 1559 after that initial conflict inherited from his father in which France, though it won back Calais from England, had appeared for a moment after St Quentin to lie at Philip's mercy, was wholly conciliatory. Spain gave back close on two hundred towns and villages on France's northern and eastern frontiers, France accepted the position in Milan and gave up her designs on Italy. It was the burying of the hatchet.

Two years after the move to Madrid Philip began the building of the Escorial, thirty-two miles away to the north-west, at once monastery, church, and royal palace, in fulfilment of a vow made at St Quentin, his one battle, in 1557. Its completion took over twenty years and it remains the most eloquent monument of the man and the reign. The contrast between this sombre pile rising out of a rocky desert and what was to have been Charles's monument, the unfinished Renaissance palace set in the precinct of the Alhambra at Granada, well reflects the change in atmosphere.

The desire for peace rested too on a more immediate compulsion, the economic. The spectacle of a Spain in process of financial strangulation in spite of all the wealth of the Indies was nothing new. 'The common people who have to pay the taxes,' he himself had written from Spain to his father in 1545, 'are reduced to such extremes of calamity and misery that many go naked, and this poverty is even greater on the estates of the nobles, many of whose vassals have not the wherewithal to pay their dues, and the prisons are full, and everyone is heading for ruin.' This, during the brief hey-day of industrial prosperity, was a telling sidelight on the decay of agriculture, which had never

recovered from the havoc of the Comunero rising and the in-
roads of the Mesta.

Philip had returned from the Low Countries not merely to an
empty treasury but to the first signs of industrial and commercial
decline, and the phenomena were not unrelated. Two ominous
measures marked the beginning of his rule, one a repudiation of
interest payments to foreign bankers, who soon forced him to
think again by threatening to have no further dealings with the
Spanish crown, the other the confiscation from 1556 to 1560, and
again in 1566, of all bullion coming from across the Atlantic. In
1560 he himself estimated the royal indebtedness at some seven
times the national revenue; by 1574 he was paying interest to his
German and Genoese bankers in excess of his total incomings.

Taxation he increased until it weighed like a millstone on the
country's whole economic life. A plague of beggars and vaga-
bonds became a major feature of the landscape, contributed to by
increasing aversion from honest labour, the fusing and confusing
of which with a mistaken sense of 'honour' were soon to foreign
observers the mark of the Spaniard. For this accumulation of
problems the king and his advisers had neither settled policy nor
firm solutions: the legislation of the period is a series of arbitrary
enactments, addressed to evils that were not answerable to treatment in isolation. Not infrequently decrees created such new
difficulties as compelled their speedy rescinding.

Political problems, on the other hand, Philip honestly believed
he did understand. Such was the question of the Moriscos of
Granada, whose forced conversion in 1502 had not led to their
expected full assimilation into the Catholic fold. Half a century
later they remained still suspect not merely of attachment to their
earlier faith and practices but of a close understanding with the
Turks, whose almost undisputed control of the Mediterranean
ever since Charles's discomfiture at Algiers in 1541 gave substance to very real fears that the *revanche* was at last at hand for
the Catalan adventure into the Near East of over two centuries
earlier.

More than once Charles had proposed a radical uprooting of
the Moriscos from the setting of their Muslim past; but this
prosperous community, knowing his financial straits, had each
time bought him off, and Philip's accession found them still

wearing Moorish dress, still talking Arabic, and still Muslims at heart. In 1567 Philip renewed the ban on Muslim practices and the Moriscos, convinced at length that the son was of different stuff from his father, finally confirmed much of what had been alleged against them by launching open rebellion.

This 'rising of the Alpujarras' of 1568–70, had it enjoyed full instead of merely token support from Islam, could have preluded another collapse of Christian Spain; for the might of this empire on which the sun never set, of this monarch whose will, it has been said, counted for more than the will of any other man in the world, was so widely dispersed as to be nowhere strong and was perhaps weakest of all at home. Troops were hastily summoned back from Italy, and eventually, after a campaign sullied with the utmost cruelty, the king's half-brother Don John of Austria smothered the outbreak. The Moriscos were deported *en masse* from the province of Granada and scattered throughout Spain, and 12,000 peasant families from the north moved in to take their place. One of the fairest regions of Spain had been laid waste.

The problem withal was still far from having been solved, for what from one point of view promised at last effective absorption threatened instead, from another, infiltration of the whole of Spanish society by elements none could trust and whose forced allegiance none could suppose their recent experiences to have strengthened. In effect the Moriscos were to remain unassimilable and a thorn in Philip's flesh to the end. Forty years later the dilemma would once again come to a head and invite a still more drastic solution.

Granada, moreover, was but one facet of a much larger whole. The defence of Christendom meant so much to Philip because on him, as the colossus of the west, its defence chiefly devolved. His relations with England and France, his sway over the Low Countries, Italy, and the New World, only mattered in the last analysis on the assumption that he could keep the Turk in check. Charles had failed, and the full consequences of his failure were now being brought home to Spain in her inability to secure, not alone her legitimate goings and comings over what had once been *mare nostrum*, but her own coasts against ever bolder pirate raids.

The Turkish seizure of Tripoli from the Knights of St John in the very year of his accession he had accepted as a challenge, making its recovery the key of his strategy for closing the Mediterranean to the enemy at its narrowest point. To this end he despatched from Sicily in 1559 a mighty naval force with over 12,000 men, Spaniards, Germans, and Italians, which, repeating the indecision of Charles's attempt on Algiers, paused to winter on the island of Las Gelves and was there surprised and destroyed utterly by the Turks in the following March.

The blow was still rankling, and still unavenged – though a Spanish fleet had in 1565 compelled the lifting of a long Turkish investment of Malta – when in 1570, on the morrow of the quelling of the Morisco revolt at home, there reached Philip an appeal from the Pope to join with Rome and Venice in a Holy League against the common enemy, who was then assailing Cyprus, the most easterly outpost of the Catholic west. Philip acquiesced, and Don John was named commander-in-chief of a combined fleet mustering over 200 galleys and some 28,000 men. Cyprus had by then fallen, and the foe, flushed with success, lay in the bay of Lepanto, near Corinth. There, in October 1571, he was brought to battle and, despite almost equal strength, experienced complete reversal of his fortunes in most devastating defeat.

This was in truth the victory Philip had been waiting for. At long last the Turk had been humbled to the dust, his naval power destroyed, and the Mediterranean was once again a Christian sea. Lepanto was to Catholic Europe what the taking of Granada in 1492 had been to Catholic Spain, the lifting of a long nightmare, the divine sanction of a righteous cause. Had Don John had his will, Spain would have pursued her advantage straightway, assailed the enemy in his citadel to make of Constantinople the capital of a new Christian empire of the east, delivered the Holy Land, Egypt, the Red Sea, the short route to India: there was no limit to what might be achieved.

The prudent Philip knew better. He knew that only a chance mitigation of pressures elsewhere had permitted the concentration of such a powerful striking force in the Mediterranean. He knew that the exorcizing of the threat on this front was Heaven-sent to allow him to brace himself for the dangers already threatening on other fronts. Lepanto would still lead to the recapture of Tunis in 1573, but for Don John a new and safer sphere of action awaited in the Low Countries. The visions of the two visionaries were incompatible.

In that of Philip no worldly ideal took priority over the goal of peninsular unity. The defence of the faith did not here enter, save insofar as Spain could never be too strong at home for the magnitude of the tasks abroad. But the Peninsula had been one, under Roman and Goth, before the Muslim avalanche of 711. Its fragmentation into the various medieval kingdoms had been a consequence of that irruption, and something to be laid accordingly at the door of the infidel. Hence the twin facets of the reconquest as seen by Castile, the expulsion of the infidel and the rebuilding of a unitary Christian state. The marriage of Ferdinand and Isabella had been a long step towards the achievement of the latter, and had preluded the fall of Granada which seemed to achieve the former, leaving Isabella free for the great American enterprise and Ferdinand for his scheming after a Spanish hegemony in Europe.

Philip, sitting at home, realized in a way in which Charles, roving constantly over half Europe in the exercise of that hegemony, never could, that in fact the slate was not yet clean on either count. The Alpujarras rising had underlined the continuing presence of Islam in Spain, and shown it to be still a threat: that issue he now believed to be disposed of. But after a century of nominal union Castile and Aragon were still something other than one, each having still its separate Cortes, its distinctive fueros and legislation, its own tax structure. Charles had tacitly recognized as much in his act of abdication, passing the two territories to his son in separate instruments. And Portugal continued outside the fold.

To west and to east chance was now to play into Philip's hand, and first to west. The tangle of marriage alliances arranged for their children by Ferdinand and Isabella had, it will be remembered, included Portugal; and the mantle of imperial greatness that shortly afterwards fell on Spain seemed to exercise a hypnotic effect on the Portuguese court, already drawn closer by the two nations' joint monopoly of expansion overseas. Manuel turned to Spain for each of his three wives, two of them aunts, the third the sister, of Charles V. They bore him in all thirteen children, and the number proved ominous, for his successor

John III (1521–57), himself marrying another of Charles's sisters, produced as his heir a weakling who, likewise taking to himself, at fifteen, a Spanish wife, died a year later, in 1554, without ascending the throne. The posthumous son to whom he bequeathed his rights was the ill-fated Sebastian (1557–78), last and most calamitous in a line of kings that, begun so brilliantly with John I, had now played itself out. The final act, like the first, would again be written in Africa.

Declared of age at fourteen, after an eleven-years' regency, Sebastian gave rein to a character compounded of headstrong self-will and morbid religiosity. The latter, fomented by his Jesuit tutor and confessor, had gradually bred in him the resolve to cross into Africa and there wage in person a holy war against the infidel. In 1574 he sailed to Ceuta and Tangier with a following wholly inadequate to serious campaigning, and was after some months constrained to return. But his appetite was only whetted the more. An interview with Philip, whose favourite daughter Isabella he would fain have in marriage, brought token offers of help, with no intention they should be implemented; for Philip saw clearly where such an adventure, led by such an adventurer, was bound to end, and was already making his own calculations.

Sebastian resisted all advice – in him absolute monarchy met its *reductio ad absurdum* – and drained his country's wealth and man-power to the dregs to fit out his expedition. This sailed at last from Lisbon in June 1578, some 17,000 strong in 500 ships; 9,000 camp-followers, many women among them, went too to witness the victory parade that was to overthrow the might of the emperor of Morocco. The emperor, with many descendants of exiled Moriscos under his banner, had little to fear. He drew the enemy five days' march into the interior, and at Alcazar-Kebir, in a four-hour encounter under a broiling sun, the might and flower of Portugal was utterly destroyed. The dead numbered 8,000, Sebastian among them; the captives, held for ransom or sold into slavery, another 15,000. Fewer than a hundred succeeded in regaining the coast and safety.

Portugal was stunned. Camoens, ill in hospital, was glad to die 'in and with' his country. The common people could not accept that their king had met so ignominious an end, and a succession of pretenders made 'Sebastianism' for long after a curious strand in the fibre of a nation whose supreme direction had so taken leave of reality. Had Sebastian triumphed, the rewards of victory would have been wholly insubstantial. Not so the price to his country of defeat, for he had left the succession to the crown unsecured, and several generations of intermarrying with Spain had given to Philip all the cards.

Sebastian's great-uncle, the aged cardinal Henry, was crowned a stop-gap king. His few remaining months of life saw the nation torn by fear and intrigue. Two Portuguese claimants there were, one a niece of John III, the other, Anthony prior of Crato, his illegitimate nephew, who enjoyed much popular support as the only hope of saving the country's independence. Philip, as both nephew and son-in-law to John, had no doubt of the superiority of his claim, and through bribery and the other arts of persuasion he won the clergy and a majority of the surviving nobility to his side. They were making a virtue of necessity: as Anthony's show of fight soon made clear, the country after Alcazar-Kebir was wholly defenceless. The Spanish king sent an army into Portugal, before which Anthony fled north to Oporto and thence to the Azores. In December 1580 Philip himself arrived in Lisbon. It was the first time he had left Spain in twenty-one years, and would be the last. As he saw it, it was in a good cause. Once again, after close on a thousand years, Spain meant the Peninsula.

Among the consequences was the falling to Spain of all Portugal's vast interests and commitments across the oceans, so that she now found herself in the impressive position of controlling Europe's every overseas colony and foothold from China to Peru. Access to the east, the goal that had first lured her into sailing west, was hers at last in full measure, and those among Philip's advisers who would have had him move his capital to Lisbon had the true vision of the greater Spain that might have been. But Philip was still tied to his past. Portugal was his, one more task accomplished, and – having confirmed to the Portuguese in a charter of 1582, under a governor or viceroy and a council of regency, all their rights, privileges, and offices, their language, Cortes, justice, and overseas trade, and undertaken to reserve all Portuguese affairs at Madrid to a Council of Portugal composed entirely of nationals – he withdrew early in 1583 and turned to the next.

In the result his successor at one remove would lose Portugal again, a consequence not merely of failure to honour these stipulations but of the absence of any real policy for the consolidation of the two kingdoms into one. And Portugal meanwhile would suffer a grievous further diminution of her sway over the Far East, which she no longer had the power, nor Spain the freedom from other engagements, to maintain as a peninsular reserve against enemies of Spain who were now her enemies too and could give full play to their depredations on the coasts of Africa, in the Indian Ocean, and beyond.

It was Philip's closing of the port of Lisbon to Dutch merchants in 1594 that first sent these, in retaliation, to India on their own, piloted round the Cape by a compatriot erstwhile in the service of Portugal. Elizabeth's East India Company of 1600 and the Dutch East India Company of 1602 laid the foundations of English and Dutch empire in the Orient; and soon there were Danish, French, and Swedish East India Companies as well. In 1624 a Dutch West Indies Company would carry the offensive across the Atlantic to Brazil. The Portuguese monopoly was gone, and when the events of 1640 brought a rebirth at home the wonder would be not that Portugal recovered so little of her overseas territories but that she recovered so much.

Aragon was a different problem. Nominal sovereignty there was Philip's already; but if Spanish was to mean Castilian the Aragonese, and in particular the Catalan, still felt himself something other than a Spaniard. Charles the Fleming, it was noted, had found himself much more at home in this part of his dominions than his son ever did. The activities of the Holy Office, the treatment of the Moriscos, the continued exclusion from the New World, all wounded alike the feelings and the interests of the Aragonese, and made them the more resolute in defence of their fueros, symbol and touchstone of their differential existence. Philip reciprocated the latent animosity, secretly determined, as the French ambassador reported at the beginning of his reign, 'to cut their claws and dock the privileges that make them insolent and almost free'; and between 1563 when they swore allegiance to one heir, the tragic and short-lived Don Carlos, and

1585 when they swore it again to the future Philip III, he never once summoned the Aragonese Cortes.

The opportunity to intervene came later and even more fortuitously here than in Portugal. In 1590 one Antonio Pérez, a high royal official, escaped from imprisonment on a charge of political murder involving the king's own name and took refuge in his native Aragon. The authorities there refusing royal demands for his surrender, the king, baffled and humiliated, invoked at last the overriding powers of the Inquisition. Pérez's seizure on a fabricated indictment of heresy caused riots in Saragossa, where nobles and commoners joined in setting fire to the Inquisition building. Once again Pérez escaped, this time to France, to pursue thereafter a violent vendetta against Philip, and the king left his sick-bed to raise and despatch an army against the insurgents. Saragossa was occupied, the *Justicia* or supreme officer of justice executed, in flagrant violation of Aragonese law which made him answerable only to the Cortes, and his and a number of other offices and rights were modified in the royal favour at Cortes specially convoked at Tarazona in 1592.

If this was as much as the king then dared, it still went a long way. That his objective was integration rather than subjection he had shown at the previous Cortes of 1585, when he conceded to the Aragonese equal rights with Castilians in the matter of holding office in the Indies. But the Aragonese did not want integration, and his new paring of their liberties they chalked up as one more on a mounting list of grievances which fifty years later would culminate in a determined attempt to detach themselves once again and for good from Castile, even at the cost of transferring their allegiance to France.

Within the Peninsula, in the Mediterranean, in the New World things were going well enough for Philip. The one running sore lay in the Netherlands, that most unhappy relic of Spain's attachment to the Holy Roman Empire. It had been a token of Charles's conversion from a Fleming into a Spaniard that, after suffering religious defeat in Germany, he should have thought to intimidate the Low Countries, his own birthplace and the home of Erasmus, into orthodoxy. Yet by a decree of 1550 he had imposed the death penalty there on all who bought or read heretical books, held or preached heretical doctrines. Even without the extortionate taxation and the quartering of Spanish troops as on an occupied country, Charles would have faced, and eventually lost, one struggle more.

Philip, incarnation of a national temperament poles apart, never had a chance. But by the same token he could not admit defeat; for in this conflict, which was to overshadow his whole reign, what was at stake was not territory or a pawn on the strategic chessboard but the whole conviction by which he lived. The sworn enemy of heresy could not just renounce his rule: he could only labour to the end to uproot the heresy. And as he laboured he drove the Low Countries into ever closer identification with a cause that had initially stood much less for repudiation of orthodox Catholicism than of Spanish rule.

In 1566 riots fomented by Calvinist elements from without loosed an orgy of destruction of churches and monasteries, including Antwerp cathedral, which provoked Philip to new extremes of rigour in his war on all dissidents, religious and political, and in particular on the great nobles, led by William of Orange, who were denounced as the instigators. In the following year the duke of Alba, his outstanding general, arrived with a fresh army and launched a campaign of terror which counted its victims by thousands – five hundred were sentenced to death on a single day – and made pacification for ever impossible.

By 1572, with the imposition of a new and still more crippling system of taxation, including a capital levy, the whole country was on the verge of revolt. The 'Spanish fury' of a day in 1576, when Antwerp was sacked by mutinous unpaid troops – the repercussions of Philip's spectacular bankruptcy of the year before were felt from the Low Countries to Italy, and across the Atlantic – proved the last straw and brought the royal authority to a new low ebb. Don John of Austria, sent to restore the situation, was compelled to promise observance of all traditional liberties and the removal of all Spanish troops before the States-General would agree to receive him as governor. The hero of Lepanto had thought, for he was still irrepressible, to use the Low Countries as springboard for an invasion of England: he soon found his power to be completely illusory. By the time of his death in 1578 only Namur and Luxemburg, of all the seventeen provinces, were still under effective Spanish control.

Thanks to an unwonted combination of military skill and diplomatic astuteness in his successor, Alexander Farnese, Spain won back her position in the still predominantly Catholic south; the seven 'United Provinces' of the north, the modern Holland, formally proclaimed in 1579 an independence they were henceforth enabled to maintain, in spite of the assassination five years later, engineered by Philip, of their leader William of Orange. For here England played openly a hand she had been at scant pains to conceal in the years preceding and in 1585 sent an army which, if it did not cover itself with glory, sufficed to save the day.

Its sending had other, more far-reaching, consequences, that merged the Netherlands issue in the great and now inevitable clash between Spain and England. Philip's relations with Elizabeth, it will be remembered, had for long been friendly. He had aided her accession to the throne, had succeeded by intervention at Rome in staving off for the first and vital twelve years of her reign the threat of papal excommunication, had offered to marry her as, in 1554, he had married Mary Tudor. Nothing of this had been done for love or through misapprehension of whither, under her, a Protestant England was tending, but simply because the alternative, an alliance between France under the Guises and an England under Mary, Queen of Scots, would have been fatal to Spanish hegemony. The short-term interests of Catholicism could not override the long-term interests of Spain in the eyes of one who held the two causes at bottom identical.

The sardonic delight with which Elizabeth exploited Philip's dilemma belongs rather to English than to Spanish history. She could seize his treasure-fleets on the Spanish Main or in the Channel, help the rebellious Netherlanders, probe his defences in the New World, and Philip had to smother his hatred while he still hated the Guises more. An understanding with them was thus the key to the situation, and gradually, in the years following the St Bartholomew's Day massacre of 1572, as France too became committed to the fanatical defence of Catholicism, that understanding came about. It was, incidentally, to cost Mary queen of Scots, fulcrum of their now joint English policy, her life.

With Elizabeth's open intervention in the Low Countries in 1585 all pretences were down. England, looking to the direction whence danger could come, was discovering in the need for a friendly Netherlands the first principle of all her subsequent foreign policy. Spanish plans hinged on the transport of Farnese's army thence to the conquest of England. The problem lay in the transporting, for though the Channel was narrow its control lay with the enemy, and Philip was only too conscious that the sea had never been Spain's element.

The launching of the Armada was the biggest naval enterprise the country had yet put its hand to, and disaster dogged it from the beginning. Drake's devastating raids on Cadiz and Lisbon in 1587 delayed it for a year; the death of the one naval commander who might have led it to success delivered it instead into the hands of a prince of incompetents; severely battered by a storm as it left Lisbon, it began by putting in at Corunna for repairs. The 130 ships and 30,000 men who eventually sailed suggested a strength that was totally belied by bad design and equipment, rotting stores, untrained crews, and inferior leadership, and in the Channel it met its doom. There was never a hope of embarking Farnese's army, and the only vessels to make Britain were those wrecked on her shores. Sixty-five ships and 10,000 men survived the hazards of the North Sea flight and the return by the west coast of Ireland.

To Philip the reverse was the first sign that Spain's star was setting, the expansive period of her greatness over. To mount another comparable effort would never again be in her power, and henceforth his communications alike with the Low Countries and with the New World lay open to attack from an enemy no longer to be impressed by his vaunted might. The spiritual reverse was even more devastating, for Philip had believed with utter conviction that he was doing God's work, waging a holy war – and God had forsaken him. There was no easy answer to this one. He and his country could turn back upon themselves, search their consciences, and, while heresy triumphed abroad, pledge themselves the more fervently to the defence at home, within the citadel, of the true faith. But the old certainty was gone, and with it the belief in a European mission. In their place came the creeping disillusion, the hypocrisy, the divorce between faith and action that were to characterize over the next century and more a Spain sadly fallen from her high estate.

Elizabeth sought, a year later, to press home the advantage

by despatching Anthony, pretender to the Portuguese throne, to Portugal with an army of 20,000 men. England, however, was still as weak at land strategy as Spain was at sea, and wholly mismanaged a campaign that could have restored Portuguese independence until it too turned into a rout, with the loss of more than half its numbers. Philip and Elizabeth kept at arm's length thereafter. English freebooters found a happy hunting-ground in the Caribbean; Philip subsidized a series of half-hearted expeditions to Ireland, thinking to find there the weak joint in Elizabeth's armour; but the dream of conquest was over.

The one remaining aspect of Philip's foreign policy concerns France and his struggle in alliance with the house of Guise to keep that country too from embracing Protestantism. Henry III's assassination of the duke of Guise in 1588, a few months after the defeat of the Armada, followed shortly after by the assassination of the childless Henry himself, gave a dramatic turn to events by raising the possibility that either Philip in person, by invitation, or his daughter Isabella as niece to the late king, might succeed to the empty throne.

The rival claimant Henry of Navarre, turning Catholic in 1593 when Philip had already resolved to occupy a sorely divided France by force and secure the crown for himself, won the day instead; and the Spaniard was left with the consolation that he had at least been largely instrumental in keeping France within the Catholic fold. In truth Spain's offensive energy had already drained away. Farnese with his veterans in Flanders was still a formidable fighting force, and showed it when he marched to the relief of Paris against Henry of Navarre in 1590. But the sinews of war had long since grown flabby.

Just before the Armada the old staple of taxation known as the *alcabala*, a ten per cent sales tax compounded a century earlier for lump sums which were then farmed out on a regional basis, had been increased to a figure two and a half times that of twenty years previous. Part of the legacy of the Armada was a new tax levied on basic foodstuffs; reckoned in millions of ducats, it became known and hated as the *millones*. Every device known to Philip for extorting more money at home or raising it abroad he invoked, until the people was pauperized, and still the gap widened between his commitments and his resources. The year

1596 brought a decree proclaiming for yet a third time the bankruptcy of the realm.

That the bankruptcy was not financial alone Drake proved in that same year with his further raid on Cadiz, when the richest city in Spain, containing in its harbour the greater part of the country's remaining naval strength, was sacked, its defences razed to the ground, and every vessel of the sixty-five there at anchor either sunk or burnt. Impotent abroad, defenceless at home, deep in penury despite the Indies: to this pass had involvement in Europe and the mirage of empire brought a Spain presumptuous beyond anything so pedestrian as the equating of ends to means in her self-appointed role of interpreter of the divine will.

Philip, now a sick and broken man, reflected on the price his country had paid for his father's legacy to him of the Low Countries, and decided to cut the knot. Flanders – all that was left of them – he now willed to his daughter Isabella and her husband-elect the archduke Albert as a sovereign state, charging them only to keep it true to the faith. The wisdom of this move he largely nullified straightway by providing for a continuance of Spanish garrisons and the reversion of the territory to the Spanish crown should its new rulers die without issue: it was ever his besetting sin to take thought for every contingency, and in this matter he was to re-tie the millstone about Spain's neck for decades still to come. He tied two more in leaving a national debt of 100 million ducats, some ten times the cost of fitting out the Armada, and as heir to his Spanish, Italian, and New World dominions a son, twenty years old and a weakling in both senses, whom he knew to be totally unfitted for the charge.

10

The Age of Retribution

THE seventeenth century began with Spain still nominally a great power. Sole mistress in the Peninsula, supreme in Italy, still extending her sway over north and south America, she was at the pinnacle too of a literary and artistic achievement which, in compensation for her forced withdrawal from the role of spiritual leader of Europe, made clear how much the Spanish genius still had to contribute to the cultural patrimony of the west. Cervantes in the novel, Lope de Vega in drama, Quevedo in satire, Góngora in poetry, El Greco and Velázquez in painting: these were household names with an influence far beyond their native land and that is not dead yet.

Yet real power had gone, and only the shell remained. That famous key passage in *Don Quixote*, 'This, Sancho, that I clearly perceive to be Mambrino's helmet seems to you to be a barber's basin, and to another it will appear as something else,' touches nearly on the nation's dilemma. The belief that truth was one and absolute, and that she held the clue to it, had for a century underlain Spain's policy and directed all her energies at home and abroad. Defeat and disillusion had at length opened some eyes: truth instead was multiple and relative, and the future lay with those nations which could seize the lesson and turn it to account.

Spain was not of them, if only because to propound such a doctrine were still heresy, and the compensatory reflexion that within her own domains she could at least to her own self stay true had as one consequence the strengthening of the Inquisition and its watchdogs. The eventual price to be paid for the quixotic flight from realism was heightened thereby, and religion added as one more sphere where outer forms concealed an inner vacuum. 'The Spaniards,' observed a Venetian ambassador, 'though they are immoral, are good Christians.' Immorality, beginning at the top and seeping downwards through the whole fabric of society, becomes the dominant mark of this age of retribution.

The legacy that passed to Philip III (1598–1621) was studded with ill-omen. To his father, shortly before his death, the Cortes of Castile had reported that 'No one has either money or credit, and the country is completely desolated. Any money that is made is hidden away and the owner lives poorly upon it until it is gone. Trade is killed by taxation. In the principal cities most of the houses are closed and deserted.' Upon this crisis of confidence the new king imposed straightway a crisis of kingship. Isabella had pulled Spain out of the slough of despond by her vigorous assertion, backed by the requisite personal qualities, of the doctrine of '*L'état, c'ést moi*', which set the throne on a new eminence of authority and responsibility. Charles V and Philip II remained true to the same guiding principle, with a differing but still adequate personal stature, and the history of these three reigns is essentially in consequence that of the three monarchs.

Philip II's death marked the great divide. In each of the next three reigns the monarch is a cypher, of importance to history only because of the responsibility incurred by his abdication of power. A new era of rule by favourites was to recall the Spain of two centuries earlier. There would, it is true, be no return to the factions of warring nobles as in the days of Alvaro de Luna, but the same disregard of the interests of the people and of the true ends of government would preside. In justification the last three Habsburgs, all manifesting a progressive deterioration in moral and physical endowment that bore relation to generations of close inbreeding, could allege that they were but recognizing their total unfitness to direct the nation's affairs. This was the contingency for which the doctrine and tradition of absolute monarchy had failed to provide.

The new king inaugurated his reign by dismissing his father's chief officer of state and entrusting the conduct of affairs to the duke of Lerma, who forthwith appointed his own relatives and creatures to high office, an uncle becoming archbishop of Toledo and inquisitor-general, a brother-in-law viceroy of Naples; and for the next twenty years Lerma monopolized effective power. This done, Philip alternated thereafter between the pursuit of pleasure and pious devotion, while Lerma, as unprincipled as he was ignorant of statecraft, ministered to his extravagances, without regard to the impoverishment of the nation, until the court became notorious far beyond Spain for its profligacy and display.

A new Cortes had been told that the king was totally without resources. Early in his reign the dignity of the crown sank to new depths when, after a suggested confiscation of all church plate and an appeal for contributions to prelates and the nobility, officials accompanied by a priest made door-to-door collections throughout the country to help meet his running expenses. Yet those expenses, which under Philip II had amounted to 400,000 ducats a year, now reached an annual 1,300,000. The sale of titles and offices lined Lerma's as well as the royal pocket and bred administrative corruption on a scale the country had never known before. Depreciation of the coinage added its quota to soaring costs and a dwindling economy, copper coins being declared by decree to be worth double their face value, one effect of which was the hoarding of silver until it disappeared from circulation. The chief sufferers were inevitably the common people, who grew steadily poorer as prodigal ostentation increased in high places.

Lerma's answer to mounting criticism and resentment in Madrid was, not to attack abuses, but to have Philip move his capital early in 1601 to Valladolid, the king issuing the decree one day and setting out the next, as though he would flee from his own shadow. The ruining of Madrid solved nothing, and five years later Philip was glad to accept a bribe from the city of 250,000 ducats together with one-sixth of all house rents over ten years to bring the court back again. Lerma received a palace. The incident was eloquent of the new dispensation, and official morality in Spain has never been the same since.

But the most disastrous blow to the national well-being was still to come. Lerma, as a Valencian and erstwhile viceroy of Valencia, had seen much of the Moriscos and shared all the popular prejudices against them. They were still Muslims at heart, or at least bad Christians; they were in league with Spain's enemies, from England to Turkey. So much was indisputable. That they were also industrious, frugal, and prolific irked no less in a society where these qualities, never more needed, were now at a discount. The Moriscos, consuming less, paid less than their fair share in consumption taxes. They married early, sending none of their numbers into the Church, whereas 'old Christians' had swollen the Dominican and Franciscan orders alone to a total of 32,000 monks. Landowners knew well, on the other hand, that Morisco labour was vital to the running of their estates and to the nation's agriculture as a whole, and nowhere more so than in Valencia, where the combination of the country's most fertile lands and most dangerously exposed coast made the dilemma particularly acute.

The problem had had a long history before Lerma took it up. Philip II, no longer able to believe that the events of 1568–70 had settled the matter even for Castile, had addressed decree after decree to its solution, Church councils had sat on it, the Pope had been brought into discussion. Gradually hope of genuine conversion and full assimilation had been abandoned. Some counselled total extermination, some mass deportation to the Indies to work in the mines: all seemed agreed that the time for half-measures was past. The Moriscos had got on Spain's nerves, to a degree conclusive not merely of her weakness but of her consciousness of her weakness.

Lerma decided on expulsion as early as 1602, but the many practical difficulties deferred the decree for Valencia to 1609. Others followed over the next two years for Castile, Andalusia, Aragon, and Murcia. Vessels and troops were brought from Italy to transport them to north Africa, a very few being exempted that they might instruct the settlers who were to replace them in matters agricultural. The total number exiled has been estimated at 500,000, the population of Spain being then some nine million; of the losses, hardships, and outrages they suffered there can be no estimate. This remains one of the blackest pages in the Spanish record, and the chief sufferer was Spain herself.

The change of régime in the Low Countries brought little relief to Spain, whose troops could alone maintain the new sovereigns in power and whose coasts and shipping felt increasingly the relentless weight of Dutch hostility. The two Spinolas from Genoa, Federico by sea and Ambrosio on land, at length succeeded in restoring a stalemate which disposed both sides to a brief truce in 1607, followed by another for twelve years, signed in 1609, in the text of which Spain explicitly recognized the sovereign independence of the United Provinces.

In theory the remaining territory, Flanders, was no less

independent under the archduke and his wife, but Philip had never approved his father's cession while military responsibility still fell to Spain, and his concern to keep the archduke's wings clipped, even to planning his arrest should his wife die first, fructified in 1616 when the loyal states formally accepted ulti- mate reversion of the sovereignty to the Spanish crown. Philip II had stipulated as much in the event of childlessness – and there would in fact be no heir – but his hope had been to see Spain finally rid of the inheritance. That hope Lerma and circumstance between them now defeated for another hundred years.

The other inheritance from the previous reign was hostility with England. Spanish weakness since the Armada counselled peace at any price. Spanish pride, unwilling to admit that one star was setting and another in the ascendant, counselled war. English Catholics here played the role of Spain's Moriscos in reverse and urged a renewed attempt at invasion. In 1599 another fifty ships were scraped together at Lisbon, only to be scattered by a tempest long before reaching the Channel. Two years later a further thirty-three were despatched with the lesser objective of helping Tyrone and O'Donnell drive the English out of Ire- land : some 4,000 men got there, to be either killed or driven out themselves by the English.

In 1602 the Spinolas received Philip's approval for a new attempt at invasion from Flanders. It too came to naught, and not only because of Federico's death in a naval encounter with the Dutch in May 1603. For two months earlier Elizabeth herself had died, before Spain's reserve plan of supporting any strong Catholic claimant to the succession could take effect, and James I, acceding, changed the international situation overnight by proclaiming his desire for peace. This he bought in his treaty with Spain of 1604 by undertaking not to support the Dutch or to allow English ships to trade with the Indies, terms that Elizabeth would have contemned.

With France the understanding reached at the peace of Vervins just before Philip II's death fortunately held good for a decade. It was an uneasy peace. Henry IV and his minister Sully were the exact antitheses of Philip and Lerma, men of character and resolve as effective in building a strong France out of chaos as the others were inept and self-seeking, competent only in working the ruin of Spain; and Henry's ultimate plans included the humbling of the house of Austria. He supported the Protestants in the Netherlands and in Germany, the anti-Spanish states in Italy, and the Moriscos in Spain. Lerma countered by bribes and intrigues with the disaffected French nobles, even with the Huguenots.

War seemed very near when once again a royal death completely altered the outlook, and again to Spain's advantage. In 1610 Henry was assassinated in Paris. His widow, Marie de Médicis, unlike her husband a Catholic first and always, succeeded as regent and set herself to re-direct policy, as James had in England, towards closer bonds with Spain. A double marriage followed, sending a Spanish princess as queen to the young Louis XIII and giving his sister as bride to the future Philip IV, and a treaty of 1612 bound the two nations into a close Catholic alliance. Both princesses formally renounced, for themselves and their descendants, all claim to the thrones of their respective countries; but the linking of the two crowns, here begun, was to prove of high dynastic consequence.

Meanwhile the settlement did much to restore Spain's waning prestige on the international scene. It allowed her, at peace now with England, with Holland, and with France, to devote some much-needed attention to the defence of her Italian interests. It nurtured also the fatal illusion of being still a great power which caused Philip, on appeal a few years later from the emperor Ferdinand II, to involve the country in the Thirty Years' War, in which it had nothing to gain and more than most to lose. Charles V's wisdom in severing Spain from the empire was cruelly undone just when, for the first time in a century, the country was enjoying a long perspective of peace.

The duke of Savoy, having looked to gain from Franco–Spanish hostilities, threw down an individual gauntlet to Spain when these were averted and in 1615 invaded Milan: two years of fighting ended in a treaty that left the frontiers as before. A more curious episode was another two years of undeclared war and naval attrition dating from 1618, between the duke of Osuna, viceroy of Naples, and the republic of Venice, then negotiating an alliance with Holland that threatened to bring the Dutch into the Mediterranean. The famous 'conspiracy of Venice' whereby

Osuna with his colleague of Milan plotted to overthrow that city and republic from within lies still under suspicion of being a Venetian invention. Venice turned it to fullest account in fomenting hatred of Spain, and killed a second bird by spreading the charge that Osuna was pursuing his own ends and aiming to make himself king of Naples, which secured his speedy recall to Spain. The occupation at this time of the Valtellina, connecting Lombardy with the Tyrol, by the viceroy of Milan proved of importance straightway in a larger context, by facilitating direct access to the German territories of the emperor.

Italy, with its northern half still a parcel of small conflicting states, was proving a temptation now to east as well as west, and Turkish ambitions to secure a foothold intensified the menace they continued to represent to Spain throughout the Mediterranean and, with their north African allies, all round the coasts of the Peninsula. Barbary pirates were now raiding as far north as Galicia and beginning to join forces with English, French, and Dutch privateers in interfering with the treasure fleets from the New World. Early in the reign an embassy from the shah of Persia had come to Madrid to propose an alliance for joint action, and the two powers declared war on Turkey in 1602.

Of this, however, nothing came, for Spanish naval strength had touched its nadir. Catalonia and Valencia were charged, like Naples and Sicily, with maintaining their own men-of-war. Here too the general corruption and incompetence of the reign had permeated, and fleets existed on paper at which the enemy could afford to snap his fingers. Of thirty galleons paid for by Naples only sixteen existed, of Sicily's twenty, ten. Isolated raids were made into Greek waters and along the coasts of Morocco and Tunisia: the threat remained, and the expulsion of the Moriscos, reinforcing the enemy with large numbers of recruits in whom bitter hatred of Spain was allied to detailed knowledge of her more vulnerable points, did little to lay it.

Exactly a century had passed now since Luther and his theses first raised the momentous issue of freedom of conscience, and Europe, long riven by the religious wars that were its consequence, had for the most part settled and declared its loyalties on the compromise basis advanced by Charles V. Rather than Catholics and Protestants there were Catholic and Protestant states, relearning at last the difficult lesson of co-existence. The exception was Germany, where the trouble had begun. There, as in the Low Countries, Protestantism was dominant in the north, Catholicism in the south: had the parallel continued with the emergence of two independent countries with the religious dividing-line as frontier there would have been no Thirty Years' War. Had Henry IV, alternatively, lived to carry to success his projected assault on the Habsburg empire, one probable result would have been a united Protestant Germany and an end to all hopes of a Catholic *revanche*.

His elimination from the scene had greatly strengthened the Habsburg cause when ten years later, in 1620, the newly elected emperor Ferdinand II struck at the newly dissident Bohemia. Spain was ready to come into the fray forthwith, for Philip and his advisers were incapable of learning from history, and once again the country was plunged into alien wars she could not afford for alien purposes that touched only her sentiment, and not her interests. An army of 8,000 men sent from Flanders largely decided the fate of Bohemia, thereafter once again a Catholic country, at the battle of Prague in that same year; Spinola with another 30,000 overran the Palatinate. Protestant Germany was quick to realize the challenge to her very existence, and took up the arms she had laid down so long before. The twelve-year truce between Spain and the United Provinces was now due to expire, and a renewal of hostilities there too became inevitable. Soon England would be at war with Spain, and the France of Richelieu, recovering her political awareness, would set religious considerations aside and range herself with the Protestant north.

Philip did not live to see these omens of disaster mount up. His court had continued to be the centre of spendthrift indulgence and riotous entertainment, inviting the deluge. The protests of now impotent Cortes at the woes of the people had long since failed of effect, but an undercurrent of resentment warned Lerma that blind respect for the monarchy did not necessarily extend beyond the monarch. In 1609 he allowed the impeachment of a secretary of finance whose peculations were estimated at a million and a half ducats. A subordinate in the same department had amassed a private fortune only slightly less. Two years later he threw to the wolves Rodrigo Calderón, second only to himself in the hierarchy of parasites, against whom the queen and the Church mobilized opposition as a first step to ridding the country of the favourite. Calderón was imprisoned and tortured. Lerma's own day came in 1618 when, bowing to a palace conspiracy headed by his son, he took refuge in a cardinalate. However immoral, he could still count himself a good Catholic, and the Church could still cater for such. His personal booty was reckoned at forty-four million ducats.

The king's eyes were at last being opened, and in that same year 1618 he asked his Council of Castile to report in detail on the state of the country and to propose remedies for its ills. The council confirmed what successive Cortes had represented in vain. 'The depopulation and lack of people are greater than have ever before been seen or heard of, and the realm is being totally ruined and exhausted. The cause of this is the heavy burdens which weigh upon your vassals, and drive them abroad to escape taxation.' Taxation should be reduced, and collected honestly. Crown grants and pensions should cease. Nobles should be sent away from court to live on their lands, ecclesiastics in their parishes. Extravagance in dress and living should be abolished, the king setting the example. All impediments to the free circulation of foodstuffs should be removed. And the flocking of men and women into the religious orders needed to be severely checked.

The report was received, and nothing done. It was late in the day to look for reform from a monarch not merely incapable of governing but a stranger to all ethical standards, and who was now and for the remainder of his reign as much in the hands of Lerma's son as he had been of Lerma. When, two months after Lerma's fall, his archbishop of Toledo died, the king claimed and duly obtained the primacy for his own son Ferdinand, then nine years old, on whom too the Pope conferred a cardinalate.

In 1619 the king set out on a five-months' state visit to Portugal, a visit due on his accession twenty years earlier that he might swear the customary undertaking to respect all Portuguese rights and privileges and receive in return the customary oath of fealty. He had promised to go in 1600, and again in 1612, and only went now from the necessity of having his son formally recognized as heir. The cost of the visit fell on Portugal, Lisbon's share of 200,000 cruzados being double the proposed assessment of seven years earlier. There had been good reasons for the so long deferment, for the broken promises on this head were only two of many and his reign coincided, as has already been noted, with the total collapse – at the hands of Spain's, not Portugal's enemies – of Portugal's great trading empire of the east. Philip and Lerma would not survive to see Portugal lost to the Spanish crown, but it was they who, betraying her and perjuring the crown, made the loss inevitable.

In direct violation of the statute Spaniards had been appointed to the Council of Portugal in Madrid, sent to Lisbon as permanent inspectors of the treasury, inducted to Portuguese bishoprics, granted Portuguese estates. Lerma had taken for himself two royal domains at Beja and Serpa. Save for the occasion of Philip's present visit the Cortes was never once summoned. Taxation was levied to be spent in Spain, and shady deals for the same end were made, and broken, with the Portuguese new Christians. From the Spanish point of view the country was being treated more and more as if it were one with Spain; from the Portuguese, it was being treated, and despoiled, almost as a conquered foe. Never had the two peoples been separated by a wider gulf. The assassination of Henry IV was mourned in Lisbon almost as a national disaster, for with him and his ambition to bring down the Habsburgs died their hopes of early deliverance.

Philip returned home from Lisbon having failed to give any satisfaction to his subjects there, and made acutely aware of the latent tension. But over his reign of twenty-two years he had given no satisfaction to his Spanish subjects either. 'A fine account we shall give to God of our government,' he said on his deathbed in 1621. In two things only could he compare himself with his father: his outward piety, and his anguish at the thought of the heir to whom he was bequeathing a country still prepared to accept its hereditary monarch, however unworthy by character or competence, as king by divine right.

Philip IV (1621–65) succeeded to the throne, as had his great-grandfather Charles V, at the age of sixteen. In him the century of decline that lay between the two was exemplified to the full.

Where his father had been weak and pious he was weak and vicious, his life already an open scandal before his accession. Under no illusions about the state of the country, and inclined at first to take some hand in the business of governing it, the realization of his unfitness was soon borne in on him, his father's example making it the easier to relinquish power and responsibility to one who had already established over him a total ascendancy.

The new favourite, known to history by his later title of count-duke of Olivares, had much in common with Lerma. He was ridden by the same boundless ambition, that would not be thwarted, and began, as Lerma had, by ruthlessly eliminating the pillars of the previous reign. Rodrigo Calderón, still in custody, he beheaded. Lerma's son and successor he cast into prison and left there to die. The great Osuna, viceroy of Naples, suffered a similar fate. His zeal in plunder was no less: attaching to himself a dozen offices and privileges, including that of sending an annual cargo to the Indies, he enjoyed an income, while Spain starved, of close on half a million ducats a year. He was intolerant alike of the established organs of government, largely nullifying the authority of the various councils, corresponding to modern ministries, by the creation of a series of committees answerable to himself, and of the counsel of experts, which he would override arbitrarily even in matters of war and peace.

Energy and ability he had, however, far beyond Lerma, and with these the resolve not to let the country drift at the mercy of circumstance in an international atmosphere heavy with challenge and the presage of change. For the next twenty years the subordination of internal to foreign affairs was complete. This was tragedy enough, given the condition to which Lerma had reduced the country, even had Spain found herself on the winning side. When the gamble failed and the smoke had cleared away, all would see that Spain had ceased to count in the concert of Europe.

Two convictions underlay all Olivares' acts and his policy for Spain. One was that the cause of the Counter-Reformation was again in the ascendant and that by throwing in all her weight behind the emperor in Germany Spain might yet restore her tarnished imperial greatness, on which the upstart shadows of

England, France, and Holland lay so heavily. For such a stake no sacrifice was too great. On this latter proposition hinged his second principle, that touched the very kernel of peninsular reality and showed the extent to which Olivares himself was but obeying Castile's great historical imperative. Strength abroad demanded unity at home.

A century and a half had elapsed since Ferdinand and Isabella had thought through their marriage to provide the political formula, and through the Inquisition the social formula, for such unity. The expulsion of Jews, Muslims, and now Moriscos had got rid in theory of all dissident elements. And yet, for all the professions of loyalty to a common monarch and a common faith, the country was still and manifestly not one, in virtue of the paradox whereby, from Valencia to Portugal, the Cortes of the ancient kingdoms swore a limited fealty on the very clearly understood basis of royal respect for their continuing right to govern themselves. They tolerated a viceroy on conditions, voted supplies on conditions, and the first condition was that the Castilian writ ran only to the borders of Castile.

As the national economy deteriorated, and with it the sense of dedication to a national ideal, so the temptation and the need increased to override those rights and conditions that cramped the effective mobilization of the country's total resources for a supreme trial of strength. There was logic therefore in Olivares' attempt to break down the barriers and achieve at last a truly unitary and integrated Spain, just as there was logic in the resolve of the regions, as they took stock of the fate of Castile in this new era of cypher kings and corrupt favourites, to resist to the death any further trampling of their fueros.

Olivares persisting, the inevitable explosion in due course took place, a double explosion, to east and west, that rocked the Peninsula to the point of fragmentation, destroyed Olivares himself, and superimposed on Spain's involvement in the European conflict twenty-five years of internal strife. Meanwhile the larger struggle was to develop for Spain into a mortal duel with France, Olivares and Richelieu taking up anew the same challenge for mastery in which Charles V and Francis I, a hundred years earlier, had over four wars fought themselves to a standstill.

The reign was but ten weeks old when, with the death of the

archduke Albert, Flanders reverted to the Spanish crown, his widow, Philip's aunt, continuing in office as governor. Albert had been all for the continuance of the truce with the Dutch. Had he lived, or had a son, the history of Spain and of Europe from this point might have been very different, but the Habsburgs were at times as unfortunate in their lack of heirs as in their heirs. Spinola too was for peace but, flushed with his recent success in the Palatinate and overborne by Olivares, he resumed hostilities. Apart from his capture of Breda in 1625 after a ten-months' siege, it proved a war of attrition on land and sea that when another ten years had passed still left the position largely as before. The issue had long since merged into the general conflict.

In this the England of James I was playing a minor and undignified role, that would not come into the present picture but for the egregious visit of Prince Charles and Buckingham to Madrid in 1622. James's pride had been hurt by the rude ejection of his son-in-law the Count Palatine, recently elected king of Bohemia – this being the immediate cause, already mentioned, of the outbreak of the Thirty Years' War – from both his territories, and he thought to recover for him at least the Palatinate without recourse to arms by marrying his son to Philip's sister. Charles's appearance in the Spanish capital, unbidden and unheralded, did nothing to enhance his or his country's prestige. The princess declined marriage to a Protestant, Olivares countered English importunity with Spanish pride, and after eighteen months of extravagant entertainment Charles returned home empty-handed, to wed a sister of Louis XIII and bind England instead to France in an alliance that failed equally of James's immediate objective.

France, threatened again with encirclement, had a more positive conception of where her interests lay, and the fact that her king was brother-in-law to the monarchs alike of England and of Spain was not one to deflect Richelieu, come to power in 1624, from making war on either or both in their pursuit. He began cautiously, in that same year, without formal commitment as yet in the Austrian struggle, by seeking to recover control of the Valtellina and so impede Habsburg communications. In this after two years he was successful, as he was too, after a longer and more arduous contest that lasted from 1627 to 1630, in thwarting Spanish ambitions to the succession to the duchy of Mantua, easing greatly thereby his own communications with Italy.

While the brunt of the war against the empire was being borne by the redoubtable Gustavus Adolphus of Sweden, Richelieu was content to see Spain become ever more deeply committed in Germany. After the Pyrrhic victory of Lützen in 1632, in which Gustavus slew 12,000 imperialists and lost his own life, and the emperor's revenge at Nördlingen two years later, largely due to the 18,000 Spanish troops led by Philip's brother Ferdinand, the erstwhile boy-archbishop, on his way from the viceroyalty of Catalonia to the governorship of Flanders, a compromise peace seemed possible.

This was the moment for decisive French intervention. To compromise could provide a religious settlement on the basis of mutual toleration, if one chose to forget that such an earlier settlement was precisely what the Habsburg emperor had wilfully destroyed by war. It settled nothing in the great issue of predominance in Europe, which was what interested Richelieu. Seen against the background of Spanish exhaustion, the revival of Spain's imperial ambitions in Europe was an anachronism. In the Low Countries and in Italy her rule, and the power this gave her of interfering in the affairs of other states, had lasted far too long: witness the emperor's cause in Germany, which lacking Spanish help would have long since collapsed.

France, possessed now, after the final defeat of the Huguenots, of the unity Spain still lacked, believed herself strong enough to deal with Spain once and for all; and the war went on, to last as a general struggle no longer for religion but for power another fourteen years, till the treaty of Westphalia of 1648, and as a particular struggle between France and Spain for another eleven years after that, until a thoroughly beaten Spain, capitulating everywhere, signed the peace of the Pyrenees in 1659. There would be many vicissitudes and complications by the way.

Richelieu's reaction to Nördlingen was an open declaration of war against both Spain and the emperor in 1635, with offensive action against Flanders, in Italy, and on the Franco–Spanish frontier, where attempts at penetration in 1638–9 gave to the French Roussillon and fleeting footholds in Irún and Catalonia.

The latter year saw too, in the Channel, the destruction by the Dutch of a Spanish fleet of seventy ships carrying 10,000 men. This was a blow not merely to the defence of Flanders: it sounded the death-knell of the hopes, on which Olivares had expended infinite time and energy, of a recovery of Spanish naval power. The navy had consisted on Philip's accession of seven vessels. Spain's fortunes seemed at their lowest ebb, and her hold on Flanders, Luxemburg, and the Franche Comté tenuous in the extreme, when there befell her within the Peninsula the double blow that made of 1640 one of the most critical years in her long history.

Philip's troubles here go back to 1625. In that year, Castile having been drained with repeated and ever heavier exactions, he gave ear to Olivares' apparently so reasonable contention that 'when any of the states was at war, the rest should be obliged to come to its aid and defence', and planned on his impending visits to the Cortes of Aragon, Valencia, and Catalonia to invite and if need be compel subscription to this doctrine. These regions accepted responsibility for their own defence and for an agreed tribute to the crown: their connexion with Castile bound them to no more, nor even to the tribute save on guarantees. If Castile chose to go adventuring in foreign wars the consequences were her own.

Aragon bluntly refused Philip's demand, when he met the Cortes early in 1626, for 3,300 armed soldiers and the right to enlist 10,000 more. It did, however, offer an increased sum of a million ducats to be paid over ten years, and with this Philip had to be content. The Valencian Cortes similarly rejected a request for troops, while the nobles, pleading ruin as a result of the expulsion of the Moriscos, held out against the other two estates when these had been browbeaten into conceding an increased money vote. Philip's blustering and threats at length intimidated them too. The Cortes was permanently weakened by the encounter, one of the stormiest sessions in its history; so too was Valencian goodwill to the crown and to Castile.

There remained the Catalans, wealthiest but most independent of all, who stood so firm on their insistence that Philip repay earlier loans before they would vote him anything at all that Olivares, fearing violence, unceremoniously bundled his monarch back to Madrid. Barcelona sought to repair the situation by intimating a readiness now to vote the sum asked. Madrid by way of acknowledgement threatened vengeance. Here too constitutional damage had been done. In 1632 Philip again approached the Catalan Cortes, and found it again obstinately intent on the reform of abuses and not to be moved to any increase of supply.

As to the war, Catalonia was not anti-Castilian in the sense of being pro-French: it was pro-Catalan. When Richelieu invaded the Roussillon in 1639 the Catalans were at once in arms and made common cause with the Castilian forces for that limited Catalan objective. But the constant passage of Castilian troops through Catalan territory, with all the abuses to be looked for from an under- or unpaid and indisciplined soldiery, allied to the multiplying of unconstitutional pressures from Madrid and their backing on the spot by a viceroy who was a creature of Olivares, eventually built up a situation there was no containing. 'Do not spare force, no matter how they cry out against you. I will bear all the blame,' wrote the viceroy. Olivares ended by ordering a forced levy of Catalans, to be carried out with complete disregard of 'provincial pettinesses'. This to Catalonia was an ultimatum.

The explosion came in mid 1640, over an order for compulsory billeting of the very troops who had fought alongside the Catalans in the Roussillon. Beginning in the country districts, it soon reached Barcelona, and with the murder of the viceroy and a general massacre of Castilians not merely civil war but a war of secession had begun. Leading Catalans had already been in communication with Richelieu, their late enemy, and now a formal agreement proclaimed Catalonia a republic under French protection. The pact was modified that same year, France demanding a *quid pro quo* for her protection in Catalan recognition of the sovereignty of Louis XIII, hailed as count of Barcelona, a castback to the ninth century when Catalonia had constituted the Marca Hispanica of the Frankish empire.

When Philip had scraped together yet another army for this new threat, it found Barcelona and Tarragona already garrisoned by French forces. This was Richelieu's opportunity, and soon French armies were pouring south of the Pyrenees. Philip, as a last resort, set out from Madrid to lead his troops himself. Arrived in Saragossa, capital of Aragon, late in 1642, he learnt that half of Aragon too was in French hands. No mere magic of monarchy could restore this situation. Philip had never led an army before, and made over the command to another, who suffered prompt defeat before Lérida. The king returned to Madrid shattered, unconsoled even by the death of Richelieu, and of Louis XIII shortly after, who for their part could die well content. The dismissal of Olivares was the least, and the most, he could do. The count-duke retired to his estates, lost his reason shortly after, and died in 1645.

Catalonia was not the only gall in the royal cup. Towards Portugal Olivares had pursued from the beginning a similar policy of absorption, to reap in the end a similar harvest. All respect for the undertakings of 1582 had long since been lost. Castilian officials were everywhere, Portuguese offices of emolument mere additional spoils for the favourite's minions. The imposition of a Castilian tax in 1636 led to a rising the suppression of which brought a new tax and a proposal to abolish the Portuguese Cortes altogether and substitute instead representation in that of Castile. The destruction of the country's national identity was clearly intended, and the intention was clearly perceived. Given a leader and the opportunity, revolt loomed as inevitable as in Catalonia.

In circumstance if not in character the duke of Braganza seemed indubitably cast for the former. Grandson of that female claimant to the throne in 1580 whose sex had proved her chief disqualification, he was the greatest noble in Portugal and, as the possessor of estates covering something like one-third of the country, by far the richest. What he lacked in energy and ambition his Spanish wife made up for him, no less resolved to see her husband rule over an independent Portugal than had been her distant forerunner, the Spanish princess who drove her Burgundian husband to the original proclamation of that independence. Alive to the danger the duke represented, Olivares made repeated attempts, ranging from kidnapping to the offer of the viceroyalty of Milan, to remove him from the scene. Braganza remained at his country home, awaiting the day. Seeking once more to engage his fealty, Olivares then appointed him to the military command of Portugal and sent funds for the repair of the country's defences, which were duly expended in a contrary sense.

The demands of the war abroad had already compelled the substantial withdrawal of Spanish forces. The crisis in Catalonia now denuded the country of those remaining, and when at length Olivares peremptorily demanded of the Portuguese nobles that they enlist under the royal banner incitement was added to opportunity. The uprising of 1 December 1640 proved a triumph of spontaneity. Three hours sufficed to overthrow Spanish authority in Lisbon, twenty-four to acclaim Braganza, still living in peaceful retirement, as king John IV, first of the house of Braganza, Portugal's third and last dynasty.

For twenty-five years Philip would cling to the hope of re-conquest, a hope vain from the beginning. Embassies were sent to France, England, all the enemies of Spain, and brought back varying degrees of support. With Holland, in view of the complicated situation arising out of Dutch depredations and conquests in the Far East and in Brazil, a ten years' truce was signed giving assurance of military and naval aid against Spain. The sovereign independence of Portugal stood out as something more than a profound peninsular reality: it had become overnight a major European interest. The Portuguese thereafter would look back on the black interlude as 'the sixty years' captivity'.

To Philip the crumbling of his inheritance to east and to west raised the larger fear of where the process would stop. Already, to the north, he had been faced in 1631–2 with the same spirit of revolt and the same threats of secession in the Basque provinces when Olivares thought to impose a salt tax in violation of their fueros. Now, hard on the heels of the Portuguese revolt, came an attempt at defection in the south. The duke of Medina Sidonia, captain-general of Andalusia and the greatest noble in Spain, was ordered to divert to punitive measures against Portugal an expedition then fitting out at Cadiz against the Dutch in Brazil. But Medina Sidonia, if he was Olivares' nephew, was also brother to the new queen of Portugal and harboured a corresponding ambition after personal royalty. Lacking something in spirit, he lacked too in Andalusia the strong separatist tradition on which revolt battened elsewhere. The conspiracy was discovered, and no new kingdom of Andalusia came to birth. An attempt to resurrect the separate kingdom of Aragon, that failed likewise, provided one more pointer to the glaring failure of the Habsburgs, over generations of misrule and misunderstanding, to weld Spain into a true national unity.

Outside Spain the same spirit of independence raised its head in territories that had been Spanish for centuries. A rebellion in Sicily in 1646–7 was put down without difficulty. Not so one in the latter year in Naples, the general cause being hatred of the viceroy and the Spanish rule he stood for, the specific again taxation. The populace, in control of the capital, proclaimed as in Catalonia a republic under the protection of France, who sent a fleet, and the movement spread all over the country. At long last France had it in her power to end Spanish dominion over Italy, when, rather than see Philip replaced by the duke of Guise, who had been acclaimed by the Neapolitans as their leader, she threw the opportunity away. It suffered, too, from being essentially a popular rising: the feudal nobility, with an outlook more medieval than existed anywhere else under the Spanish crown, soon reverted to the cause of authority, and by the following year the revolt had collapsed. It was the year too of the peace of Westphalia.

This series of disasters and near-disasters in the Peninsula and in Italy had greatly complicated the Spanish horizon during the closing years of the Thirty Years' War. Olivares had gone, and 'Our king is king at last. God save the king' had been the people's cry. But the nightmare remained, and Philip, soon realizing his personal impotence to cope with it, did as his father had done before him, on Lerma's fall, and promoted to fill the vacuum another favourite, nephew of the old.

From Flanders there came at this time perhaps the worst news yet, the catastrophic defeat at the hands of the French of a force of 20,000 Spanish veterans. Rocroi – May 1643 – was not just one defeat more: it was the final, irrevocable eclipse of that prestige of the Spanish *tercios*, which, first built up by Fernández de Córdoba in the Italian wars of Ferdinand of Aragon, had made them redoubtable ever since on the battlefields of half a continent. The repute had rested on the early adoption of new arms and tactics: it collapsed now on failure to meet the new tactics of the enemy, and the detail is symptomatic of that general hardening of the arteries which had overtaken a country wedded to a policy of standing still in a changing world.

The Armada at sea had signalized the first waning of Spain's imperial greatness; Rocroi on land closed the long chapter of decline, and its moral consequences far outstripped the military. From then onwards Spain was in retreat in Flanders and in Italy, as the emperor was in Germany, until the peace of 1648 set the seal of failure on the Habsburg dream that had brought thirty years of war on central Europe. Germany remained divided into Protestant and Catholic. The German states won their political as well as religious independence. France won Alsace. Holland, like Switzerland, won final recognition of her sovereignty.

Spain won nothing, not even peace. Holland, moved partly by apprehensions of her French ally, had now signed with Spain a separate treaty that gave her, along with final victory, rights of commerce with the Indies. France on the contrary, at peace with the empire, continued at war with Spain, in whose plight a disillusioned and ungrateful emperor no longer professed any interest. Prepared to write off Flanders and the Franche Comté, the French maintained their grip on Catalonia, where Philip was as far as ever from restoring his sovereignty in spite of his adoption, after the fall of Olivares, of a much more conciliatory tone.

A French viceroy, Condé, victor of Rocroi, was able to contain the now considerable resentment of the Catalans against forces who proved no less an army of occupation because they were French, and apart from the recapture of Lérida in 1644 the Castilians made no headway for close on a decade. At length the tide turned, with the waning of French interest in view of new troubles nearer home, and in 1651 they were able at last to lay siege to Barcelona. After fifteen desperate months the city surrendered, the French gradually withdrew, though retaining Roussillon, and the rebellion was over in fact, if not formally for another six years. The king had learnt his lesson, and did not quibble over confirming the cherished Catalan fueros, reserving only control of fortresses to the crown.

Philip sorely needed the respite, which left him still at war with

France. Driven to seek reinforcement from whatever source, he turned in that same year 1652 to the England of Cromwell, at some cost to his feelings against the government that had lately beheaded the king he once spurned for a brother-in-law. But Cromwell's conditions, including freedom of trade with the Spanish colonies, were too high even for his need. English ships went to the Indies on their own, capturing there another treasure fleet and, infinitely more important, Jamaica. The loss of this key to the Caribbean in 1655 was the gravest blow Spain had yet suffered in the New World and the beginning of the end of her monopoly of its resources.

When the desired ally went on in 1657 to make an alliance instead with France and to join in an all-out attack on Flanders, Philip, seeing stronghold after stronghold collapse, bowed at last to the inevitable and put out feelers for peace, which France had now her own reasons for welcoming. Mazarin had been nourishing for some years a peace plan that would bring nearer French ambitions concerning Spain than any victories in war – the marriage of the young Louis XIV to Philip's daughter María Teresa – and on this basis the peace of the Pyrenees was signed in 1659. For added to all Philip's public tragedies had been the private one of the death in 1646, not seventeen years old, of his heir Baltasar Carlos, a youth of much promise and greatly beloved by all. A second marriage, to his niece Mariana of Austria, the betrothed of Baltasar, had given him to take his place only a scrofulous epileptic infant then not two years old and doomed to die before it was four.

By the treaty France, while renouncing all claim to Catalonia, kept Cerdagne and Roussillon, thus making the Pyrenees at long last her southern frontier; she kept too Luxemburg and several strongholds in Flanders. María Teresa, as in the double marriages of 1615, renounced all rights to the Spanish throne, in consideration of her carrying to France a dowry of 500,000 gold crowns. The condition was important, for France counted, rightly as it proved, on the impossibility of Spain's ever being able to pay such a sum. There had been a day, not long before, when the Spanish monarch had dined in his royal palace off a dish of eggs, his steward having neither money nor credit with the palace tradesmen to provide richer fare. The crown too now knew the depths of impoverishment in which the country as a whole had been so long sunk. Spain's greatness lay in ruins. Not merely would she never rank as a power, or menace other powers, again: her own independence hung on the slenderest of threads. And even now she was not at peace, for there was still Portugal.

Philip had done what he could in this direction ever since 1640, but militarily his campaigns over many years had had little more than nuisance value. The men and the resources did not exist, and after Rocroi his offensive strength was less still. He made difficulties of another sort by persuading the Pope not to recognize John or to fill vacant sees, until by 1649 only one bishop remained in Portugal. He plotted John's assassination, and, having got hold of his brother, a distinguished soldier then serving the emperor in Germany, had him put to death. In the general settlement of Westphalia he secured the exclusion of Portugal. The treaty he then signed with Holland told doubly to Portugal's disadvantage, largely nullifying her own agreement with the Dutch and recognizing Holland's title to the conquered Portuguese possessions overseas. A further danger, that the Spanish troops now released might be turned against Portugal, was averted by Philip's continuing involvement with the Catalans and the French. Not until Barcelona fell in 1652 could any forces be transferred to Spain's western front, and the capture of Olivença, taking advantage of John's death in 1656, represented after sixteen years the paltry sum-total of reconquest.

Now France too was eliminated, though Mazarin continued to give surreptitious help to the enemy, and by 1661 Spain was able to muster armies for a two-pronged invasion, from Galicia and Estremadura. The outlook might well have been black for Portugal, defrauded of the hopes from France on which she had expended long years of negotiation, had she not been able to turn to England, making there the same proposal of matrimonial alliance that Louis XIV had turned down in favour of a bride from Spain and offering as dowry two million cruzados, the strongholds of Tangier and Bombay, and free trade with the Portuguese colonies. England accepted, Charles II at thirty being fortunately still unmarried, and undertook in return to defend Portugal by land and sea and to send troops and ships to that end. The marriage treaty and alliance were signed in 1661.

Catherine sailed for England; Tangier and Bombay were handed over, the former to be relinquished as unprofitable in 1693, the latter to become the centre of British power in India; and a British army arrived in Portugal in time to counter the immediate Spanish threat.

In 1663 political confusion in Lisbon enabled the Spaniards to overrun the Alemtejo and imperil the very capital; but demoralization in a soldiery so long unused now to victory allowed a dramatic turning of the tables. Driven back to the frontier, the Spaniards were caught at Ameixial and there suffered overwhelming defeat with the loss of some 8,000 men. This was the penultimate scene in the long-drawn-out drama. The final encounter took place at Montesclaros in 1665. Philip had withdrawn from Italy and Flanders every available soldier, had got together by every device he knew, legal and illegal, every last ducat, for a supreme effort, and managed to put 23,000 men into the field. The Portuguese and English were fewer in number but superior in spirit and tactics. For eight hours the battle raged; at its end 4,000 of the Spanish forces were dead and 6,000 captive. Portuguese independence was not finally recognized by Spain until 1668, but it would never again be in question. Ceuta in Africa, cradle of Portuguese empire, remained to Spain as solitary reminder of what had been thrown away. Now indeed the sun had set for good on her military might.

The news of Montesclaros broke Philip's heart. There was nothing more now that he could do for the redemption, or the ruining, of his country, and within three months he was dead. Philip 'the Great' Olivares had called him, in those far-off days of illusion when it had seemed possible to believe that a renewal of Spain's imperial splendour lay within his grasp; and the name had stuck. Great, commented Quevedo, after the manner of holes, which get greater the more you take from them. 'Of all his majesty's household,' an eye-witness noted as he lay in state, 'the marquis of Aytona and two other servants alone wept for the death of their king and master; and in all the rest of the capital there was not one person who shed a tear.'

It had been better for Spain had Philip left no heir. The Habsburg line was played out, physically, intellectually, and morally, and though it might have seemed that there were no lower depths to plumb, Charles II (1665–1700) plumbed them. Four years old on his father's death, he was the final, catastrophic fruit of generations of intermarriage with cousins and nieces, a cretin so malformed and under-developed that he never learnt to speak or to eat normally, so weak of intellect that he could not be taught the rudiments till he was ten, and whose mental age and tastes in manhood remained those of the nursery.

The fates had shown themselves pitiless to Spain ever since the beginning of the century: they reserved their cruellest blow till now, that this abortion, instead of dying at birth, should have caused the history of his country to revolve for thirty-five years around the question of what happened next, a tale of court intrigue, international conspiracy, and meaningless war that came back full circle to end where it had begun. The only factor that never came into the picture was the well-being of the Spanish people: they had made their bed long before, when they allowed the first Charles to accept election to the empire, and were left to lie on it.

The Portuguese people had once found themselves in not dissimilar case, faced in 1383 with the accession of a wholly unworthy monarch to the jeopardizing of their liberties and independence. Being moved to think and act for themselves, they ousted the heir, defying her foreign backing, in favour of a candidate of their own choosing, illegitimate but still a man, who started a new dynasty and led his country to new pinnacles of greatness. Spain had never stood in such need of such a leader as now, and as it happened he was available, again illegitimate but again a man. Don John of Austria, compact of all the virile qualities his half-brother Philip II lacked, had left his mark on the history of the previous century. Now another Don John of Austria stood out to proclaim what the Habsburgs might have been had they married on grounds of eugenics and not of dynastic alliance.

Philip IV's son by a Madrid actress – the only one of his thirty-odd bastard children to be recognized – Don John was now a man of thirty-six with a long and distinguished record in Catalonia, Naples, Flanders, and Portugal, a record dimmed only by the disaster of Ameixial, where his failure to recover Portugal for the crown he confidently attributed to lack of support born of malice in court circles. His popularity was great, and many would have liked to see him on the throne; but that degree of initiative was beyond a cowed people.

The new reign opened, therefore, with the stage set for a trial of strength between the queen-mother Mariana, now regent for her infant son, and Don John, in her eyes the would-be usurper, if not of her son's crown, of her authority. Already in Philip's last years she had foiled his ambition to be named first minister; for she had a part to play, the furthering at whatever cost to Spain of the Austrian connexion and the imperial interest, and to this he, a supporter of the new understanding with France that the peace of the Pyrenees had seemed to promise, was resolutely opposed. The conflict between them thus symbolized the two forces that throughout the reign struggled for possession of the king's person, his conscience and his inheritance.

Among Mariana's first acts was the appointment of her confessor, the German Jesuit Nithard, as inquisitor-general. Thus foisted ex-officio, though a foreigner, on the council of regency, Nithard soon became the power behind the throne. Don John took up the challenge. Withdrawing to Catalonia, he attracted to his banner the many discontented elements there and elsewhere to whom the Jesuit's elevation was a scandal not to be borne, and early in 1669 marched on Madrid with a small force and compelled Nithard's dismissal, content then for the moment to retire to Saragossa as viceroy of Aragon. The regent surrounded herself with an armed guard, a further offence to the populace she now feared, and found herself another favourite, one Valenzuela, whom she raised from obscurity to become her right hand in government and, rumour said, her lover.

Don John held his hand until 1675, when Charles at fifteen was deemed of age: it was planned that the king's first decree, lying ready to his hand, should name Don John chief minister. But the astute queen-mother foiled the plot, and Valenzuela ruled for another two years, when both fell before a mounting wave of public indignation. He was deported to the Philippines, she relegated to Toledo, and her guard to Sicily; Don John was at last supreme.

It proved a nominal supremacy, and the expectations of the nation, pitched high at his advent, soon wilted. For twelve years now Spain had been tossed impotently in the trough of external events and there remained little one man could do beyond seeking to thwart the efforts of such as, led by Mariana, would still bind the country ever more closely to Austria. French goodwill had scarcely survived Philip's death, and for the ensuing thirty years, apart from brief 'peaces' that were little more than spells of armed truce, the two countries were again at war, Spain's role that of the exhausted combatant who, repeatedly floored by his opponent, is as often set on his feet again only to be floored anew. The humbling of her hereditary enemy having been already achieved, it was impatience to begin the despoiling that now moved France, with Flanders over these decades as a first consistent objective. As against Spain, this was fruit ripe for the picking: the obstacle lay in the vital interest other powers had in preventing the assumption by France of a European hegemony so lately and at such cost wrenched from Spain, and Spain was now to have the strange experience of seeing other nations, late her enemies too, rush unasked to the defence.

Louis had begun by claiming the succession to Flanders in his wife's name, on the ground that the non-payment of her dowry annulled the earlier renunciation of her rights and invoking the precedent of 1598, when Philip II had left the Low Countries to his eldest daughter. Spain refusing, Louis prepared to use force. Counting on Charles's early death, and with no expectation that Europe would allow him simply to absorb Spain and her dominions whole, he already contemplated their partition with the emperor and sought, against that day, to strengthen his hand.

This explains a series of apparent failures to push his military advantage and a surprising readiness on occasion to surrender what he had seized. Thus, having overrun both Flanders and the Franche Comté in 1667–8, and thereby provoked a league against him of England, Holland, and Sweden, he gave back both, save for a number of fortresses in Flanders, at the peace of Aix-la-Chapelle in the latter year. The world could not know that he had already signed a first partition treaty with the emperor. Four years later he was invading Holland and, Spain being again drawn in, France once more occupied the Franche Comté, sent an army into Catalonia, and fomented a new rising in Sicily, where from 1674 to 1678 Spanish dominion came near to collapse. In the latter year a new peace was signed at Nimeguen, again forced on France by a coalition largely independent of Spain, who saw herself reduced to accepting such terms as others chose to offer. This time she lost the Franche Comté for good.

Don John, come to power in the previous year, turned the respite to account by arranging a marriage for Charles with a niece of the French king, Marie Louise of Orleans. The match as seen from Madrid was a check to the queen-mother, who would have had Charles marry the emperor's daughter; as seen from Paris, an opportunity to establish French ascendancy over the wretched monarch. None entertained hopes that he could have offspring; but the theory of monarchy still vested in him, how-ever pitiable his mental capacity, the right to dispose of his in-heritance by testament, and a wife could be the decisive influence. The triumph of the French party was short-lived. Before the princess had crossed into Spain, in 1679, Don John was dead: for the first, if not the last, time over these years one whispered poison. Charles promptly restored his mother to his side, and the new queen, who lacked all the qualities her role required of her, gave herself over to a life of frivolity until, ten years after, she too – and again mysteriously – died.

Louis had long before resorted once more to arms, and from 1681 was campaigning as of old in Flanders and Luxemburg, against Spain, Holland, and the empire to begin with but soon against Spain alone, and again a French army entered Catalonia. Once more a truce was signed, in 1684, at the price to Spain of Luxemburg, and once more Louis treated the agreement as waste paper. In the result he provoked Sweden, Spain, the empire, Holland, England, and even the Pope into a new league against him. The accession of another William of Orange to the English throne in 1688 had committed England more deeply than ever to the defence of the Low Countries.

With Marie Louise's death in 1689 the queen-mother had reverted to her earlier project and promptly found her son a second, Austrian, wife in Mariana of Neuberg, sister of the empress, an unscrupulous shrew who was to harry her husband unceasingly. This was an additional provocation to Louis and threat to his hopes, and that same year a new and general war began, to drag on for years and to strike Spain alike in Flanders,

Catalonia, and the Mediterranean, in Africa and in the Indies. French troops were on Catalan soil from 1689 to 1697, when Barcelona fell a second time into their possession, and with it control over the whole principality.

Peace came at length with the settlement of Ryswick in 1697, and Spain could take stock of how she stood after yet another thirty years of fighting. That she was no longer mistress of her destinies was accepted; the people had in any case no voice. National decline had gone hand in hand with the decline of representative institutions, and Villalar, in which the seeds of that decline were sown at the very beginning of the reign of the first Charles, bore as its ultimate fruit the decree of the regent Mariana in 1665, when the reign of Charles II was exactly ten days old, transferring from Cortes to the municipalities the function of voting grants to the crown.

Its last *raison d'être* disappearing therewith, the Cortes of Castile met not once during the next thirty-five years. It was not for the people to reason, or even to be informed; their role was but to pay, and die. The decree did not run, and, given the strength of local feeling, could not have been enforced, elsewhere. To Aragon, Catalonia, Valencia, and Navarre the monarch still had to go cap in hand asking for grants that were still only to be had on condition, and that were conceded at times so sparingly, with such waning confidence in the crown, as barely to cover the expenses of the royal journey.

From the beginning therefore the Habsburg autocracy had weighed more heavily on Castile than on the peripheral regions, and by the end it had completely crushed the spirit of a people that had first emerged on the canvas of history as fighting stalwarts of democratic independence. Herein lies part of the intimate tragedy of Spain, for Castile never fully recovered her earlier spirit, and the readiness with which she would lend herself to subsequent policies of centralization and on occasion of dictatorship is relevant both to the Castilian claim to leadership of the nation and to the vigorous repudiation of this by regions that point with pride to their long record of successful self-government and to the sacrifices they have ever been ready to make in its defence.

The Cortes had often in their earlier submissions laid bare

the nature of the country's woes, and seen their advice rejected, until now the economic collapse was complete. The reason was not wholly wilful blindness, nor a tale merely of incompetence, prodigality, and corruption. In a country at war expediency must always threaten the principles of sound economy, and where the stake is not conquest but survival expediency must win. The flow of gold and silver from the Indies had exposed Spain, as has been stressed already, to the particular confusing of wealth with money, a confusion that threw its shadow over the whole of the Habsburg era and obscured the appreciation of production as the true source and measure of a nation's prosperity.

But equally blighting to productivity was the fact that ever since the advent of the first Habsburg Spain had scarcely known peace. War was become her normal state, and now for some eighty years that war had been increasingly a struggle for bare existence. No principles of government remained: expedience was all. The nation groaned under the load of taxation, but ever more money had to be found, and more and more taxes were imposed in the full knowledge that agriculture, commerce, and industry were alike being strangled. Already, a century before, Philip II had dabbled despairingly in alchemy. The alchemist was only one of the tribe of ingenious propounders of *arbitrios* or projects for raising revenue by unorthodox means, and in the reigns of Philip IV and Charles II there was no *arbitrista* too absurd for a drowning exchequer to clutch at.

Manipulation of the currency had for long played havoc with the economic structure, and the tampering continued. Successive decrees raised the copper coinage to six times its face value; in 1680 another edict proclaimed the restoration of that face value, to the intensifying of confusion and hardship. In such circumstances foreign trade became impossible, even without the ban on trade with enemy countries. Without goods, or the ships to carry them, to maintain the commerce of the Indies, the colonies turned to contraband with those enemies. As for the remittances of treasure from the New World, with which Spain had once thought to be able to hold the old in subjection, it was estimated at this time that two-thirds of the total of all such went directly abroad in settlement of debt, while the other third gradually followed in payment for goods.

A denuded countryside no longer growing the food to feed the nation, the government's answer to food riots in the capital was, not to encourage agriculture, but to ruin what little remained by fixing prices far below the cost of production. When taxation failed, the crown resorted to forced loans, extortion, and confiscation: this, and the constant impressing for an army of unwilling conscripts, drove large numbers into hiding or exile. Marauding bands roamed the country, and gradually the last semblance of an ordered society collapsed.

The crown being all-powerful, responsibility clearly attached to the crown, and the people's loyalty was put to a hard test. One last stratagem was resorted to, that something might be saved of the façade, and it spoke eloquently of the depths of intellectual degradation to which two centuries of orthodoxy at all costs had reduced an intelligent people. Charles was declared to be in the grip of evil spirits. Allowing himself to be persuaded of as much, he never thought himself safe without his confessor and two friars by his side, whom he made to lie in his chamber every night, and as 'the Bewitched' he has gone down to history.

The terms of Ryswick proved once again unexpectedly generous for Spain. Instead of forcing on her, as she well might have, the further grievous loss of Catalonia, France restored this and Luxemburg as well, for reasons already apparent. As Charles's health grew steadily more precarious and all Europe hung on the outcome, France pitched her ambitions steadily higher and transferred the struggle from the battlefield to political intrigue. She was playing now not for a share in the spoils but for the whole, and since much depended on the strength of the French party at the Spanish court and on the general disposition to France there obtaining, it suited her to leave the whole intact.

As contingent insurance Louis continued to treat with the other powers in terms of partition. He and the emperor Leopold were both grandsons of Philip III, each had married a daughter of Philip IV. There could be no expectation of Europe's consenting to the wearing by either of the Spanish crown in addition to his own: the French candidate was therefore Philip of Anjou, second son of the dauphin, the Austrian the archduke Charles, second son of Leopold. A third candidate, the child-prince

Joseph Leopold of Bavaria, advanced his claim as great-grandson of Philip IV.

Louis put forward a proposal, and won for it the support of England and Holland, that Spain, Flanders, and the Indies should go to the Bavarian, Naples and Sicily to Anjou, and Milan to the archduke. Inasmuch as the plan made nonsense of the previous thirty years of warfare, its presumed real object was to divide and confuse France's rivals, in which it was eminently successful. The emperor's indignation knew no bounds, nor did Spain's, and Charles named the Bavarian his universal heir. This caused Leopold to protest more violently still, injuring his own cause thereby at Madrid, and signed the young prince's death warrant: he died shortly afterwards, under inevitable suspicion of foul play.

While the tug of war went on in Madrid, with the helpless monarch torn and bandied about between the Austrian faction, led by the queen, and the French, headed by cardinal Portocarrero, archbishop of Toledo, whose master-stroke was the replacing of the royal confessor, a queen's creature, by one of his own persuasion, a new plan of dismemberment was hatched in London early in 1700 between the same three powers as before. This would give Spain, Flanders, and the Indies to the archduke and the rest to Anjou. Again France's motives were suspect, again the emperor would have none of it, and again the Spanish reaction, especially violent now against England, was such as to make certain that whichever side succeeded in wresting from the dying king his last signature would be named heir to the whole.

Since it followed that the inheritance left entire should preferably go to that candidate who could give the better guarantee of so maintaining it, Louis' tortuous diplomacy was producing its effect. At length, in October 1700, Charles the Bewitched made his last will and testament, naming Philip of Anjou heir to all his dominions, and died. An age, and a dynasty, and the greatness that had been Spain died with him. The long battle for the unity of the Peninsula, for hegemony in Europe, for the supremacy of the Catholic faith, all was over, and lost. Material prosperity and spiritual ideals, self-respect and the esteem of others, all had crumbled; and the erstwhile arbiter of continents and oceans, now a country without visible or invisible means of support, accepted as the happiest fate open to it subjection to its bitterest enemy, the crowning indignity the manner in which it had been wrangled over and finally disposed of as a chattel across the death-bed of a degenerate. The bell tolled not indeed for Charles; it tolled for Spain.

These thirty-five years had begun with the final acceptance by Spain of an equally sovereign Portugal. The circumstances attending their close were once more to involve the smaller nation in the fortunes of the larger, and in war. Meantime, as Spain sank deeper and deeper into decline, the first Braganzas enjoyed several decades of peace and set about rebuilding their country. Its overseas fortunes had been the most deeply implicated, and the reluctance of Holland in particular to surrender gains made at Portuguese expense had much impeded both the re-establishment of friendly relations after 1640 and the process of recovery. The Dutch, who in the course of fifteen years from 1623 had seized over five hundred Portuguese and Spanish vessels in the New World, had set themselves seriously to the conquest of Brazil in 1630, and before the decade ended were in occupation of most of the vast coastal territory north of the São Francisco river.

When, after 1640, the colonies duly signified their adhesion to John IV, it suited the Dutch to regard them as still under Spanish dominion and so fair conquest, and in 1641 they sent an expedition from Brazil to the capture of Angola in West Africa. The motive was twofold: to command the source of slave labour for the sugar plantations and, by denying this to Spain, to strike a blow at that country's hold on the New World. The key to the recovery of Brazil thus lay in Angola, without whose black ivory the Dutch no less must suffer economic strangulation; and it was a notable triumph of Portuguese diplomacy that Angola should have been regained in 1648 with a modicum of force and without upsetting a truce so delicately poised. Dutch Brazil it had been hoped to recover by purchase, but economic difficulties following on exclusion from the slave trade, added to Portuguese risings against the intruder in Brazil, made this unnecessary, and in 1654 the Dutch were finally driven out. Portuguese sovereignty in the New World and in Africa was again intact.

In the Far East, where the interests at stake had been much more commercial than territorial, no comparable recovery could be looked for. As Portugal weakened under the 'captivity' the east too had been asserting itself, and Japan's expulsion of the westerner in 1639, costing Portugal control of the most lucrative branch of the carrying-trade in Asia, was only one of many blows. The Dutch, as the rival westerners, for their part were determined and able to strengthen, rather than see weakened, their hold; and, truce or no truce in Europe, they continued to invade Portuguese preserves.

Their seizure between 1655 and 1663 of Ceylon and Malabar dealt the *coup de grâce* to Portugal's tottering eastern empire, of which the surviving fragments, Goa and one or two minor footholds on the coast of India, Macau in China, and Timor off the Australian coast, are today but pale reminders. By a secret clause of the Anglo–Portuguese marriage treaty of 1661 England stood committed to the defence too of Portugal's overseas possessions; but the most that England could do was to offer mediation, thanks to which, and to the realism shown by Portugal in accepting that, given her present weakness, her oriental past was past, a comprehensive peace with Holland was signed at last in 1663. One empire had gone: she would build up another. In Brazil she had as yet barely touched the fringe of possibilities.

John IV had not lived to see that peace. He died in 1656, happy at least in the knowledge that his sway extended again over the whole of his Brazilian 'milch-cow', as he termed it, whose resources had fed and sustained Portugal during the long years of conflict with Spain, as they provided the dowry for the marriage with England; sad in the thought that on his death the new dynasty would be confronted, thus early, with crisis. His son Alfonso VI (1656–68) was thirteen and, a victim of paralysis at the age of three, less than normal both physically and mentally. 'Pitifully stupid, though on occasion apparently sound in the head,' was the English ambassador's description of this counterpart to Spain's Charles II. His assumption of authority in 1662, after a six-year regency by the Spanish queen-mother, meant as in the neighbouring country the rule of a favourite, the count of Castelo Melhor, who for five years wielded a personal dictatorship. Son of a distinguished soldier, Castelo Melhor had the qualities both civil and military the situation demanded, and saw his country through to final victory over Spain at Montesclaros.

His reward was dismissal, as the result of a palace intrigue arising out of Alfonso's marriage in 1666 to a French princess, Marie Françoise of Savoy, who came to Portugal – as Marie Louise would later to Spain – charged by Louis XIV to win her husband for French interests, and who had the liking and the capacity for political intrigue that Marie Louise lacked. Both royal husbands were impotent, and the stake in both cases was accordingly nothing less than the succession. This Marie Françoise settled in her own way by falling in love on first meeting with Alfonso's brother Peter, five years his junior, and applying herself to the triple objective of securing Alfonso's deposition in favour of Peter, the annulment of her marriage, and remarriage with the new king.

The programme, ably backed by her French Jesuit confessor, the French ambassador, and Peter, took eighteen months. Once Castelo Melhor, whose loyalty to his monarch made him the chief obstacle, had been sacrificed, the Cortes intervened to further the plot, demanding first, in the interests of good government, that Alfonso give way to his brother, and second, in the interests of the nation's finances, that the brother should take, with the throne, the queen – though the suit for annulment had not yet been heard – to obviate the return of her dowry to France. Alfonso, in himself a cypher, had no option but to acquiesce, the marriage was declared null and void, and four days later the second marriage took place and Peter ruled in his brother's stead as regent. The ex-king was sequestered first in the Azores, then in Sintra, till his death in 1683.

The new reign – technically still a regency – was ushered in with the formal conclusion in February 1668 of peace with Spain, that at long last concluded the unhappy chapter begun at Alcazar-Kebir in 1578. Relations, the treaty ran, would be restored as in the time of Sebastian, and Peter II (1668–1706) could contemplate for his country a long and welcome period of tranquillity and recuperation. The one threat was that of involvement in the continuing conflict between France and Spain. Spain tried repeatedly but in vain to engage Portugal on her side. French blandishments were even more persistent. The league with France, that Portugal had been seeking to reach ever since 1640, had been concluded at last in 1667, conceded by France in the hope of prolonging Spanish-Portuguese hostilities; and though it had contributed instead to the contrary effect by encouraging Spain to end them, French machinations continued. But Peter refused to be drawn, even when the bribe was help towards winning back some of the ground lost in the Far East, and the hard-won peace was preserved.

A threat of a different nature now arose over the succession. Peter's only child by Marie Françoise was a daughter born in 1669, and much hinged on her marriage. The Cortes would not hear of another entanglement with Spain and finally, in 1680, approved of a French prince as consort. The uncertain future this opened up for Portugal was averted by the prince's withdrawal from the match. Three years later the queen died, and in 1687 Peter married Maria Sophia, daughter of the elector Palatine, by whom he had four sons.

Internally, Peter's concern was the economic rehabilitation of a country that had been reduced, first by alien exploitation, then by a quarter of a century of war, to a shadow of its former self. In 1641, to help restore Lisbon's former proud position as a great mart of international trade, his father had thrown open the port to the flags of all nations. This step, and the English treaty of 1654, had told to the advantage of others rather than of Portugal; and Peter, having first reduced the army and dismissed all foreign soldiery on reaching peace with Spain, initiated with his minister Ericeira a protectionist policy that, allied to severe measures of economy at court and throughout the nation, at length produced its modest effect.

In all this Peter too governed as absolute monarch. The Cortes, that had continued under John IV to discharge their traditional function of voting supplies, was indeed convoked by Peter – three times in thirty-eight years – but merely to signify approval to questions affecting the succession. Its function as bulwark of popular liberties had been allowed silently to lapse, by a process less of attrition than of exhaustion over so many troublous years, and an event of 1699 sounded its death-knell for over a century.

In that year there reached the crown from Brazil the first substantial consignment – a ton and a half – of gold, earnest of the vast new sources of wealth just being tapped in that mighty dependency. It promised handsome compensation for the loss of the spice trade of the east; and though it again brought the threat, that had contributed so much to the undoing of Spain, of undermining notions of sound economy and honest labour at home, at least it would not be squandered on a mirage of European conquest and dominion. More immediately, it freed the crown once again from reliance on the Cortes for revenue; and though the events of 1700 in Spain were already casting their shadow before, and Peter knew that the neutrality he had already proclaimed it to be his intention to preserve would very doubtfully be of his deciding, he never summoned the Cortes again.

11

Literature and the Arts – II

THE 'Golden Age' of Spanish letters comprises the period from Garcilaso to Calderón, or approximately 1530 to 1680. Spanish now meant at last the language of Spain, for among the consequences of the union of Castile and Aragon was the eclipse of the Catalan tongue, which survived indeed as the speech of the countryside but would not again serve as vehicle for a people's literature until the second renaissance of the 1830's. The final expulsion of the Muslim, discovery and conquest in America, and the identification of Spain with the Holy Roman Empire were factors in the striking literary expansiveness of the age: all served to bolster national pride and to make the Spaniard free, as was no one else, of both the Old World and the New.

In one thing pride and freedom were at issue, for new intellectual horizons brought home just how circumscribed and peninsular the traditional outlook had been, and the early sixteenth century saw the country's leading thinkers and writers at school in Italy. Soon they were at school in Flanders too, and Erasmus would count among them some of his most cherished disciples. The northern wine was the headier, tempting into forbidden regions, until Luther, Protestantism, and Erasmus became to authority all one and the Inquisition pounced on their faintest echo. The Renaissance stimulus from Italy had too its implications in the realm of dogma, but the initial and strongest impact here was aesthetic. Spaniards discovered for the first time something of the range of experience, in particular of emotional experience, susceptible of literary expression, and turned to the Italians quite simply, and through them to the ancients, for instruction in the art of writing.

Garcilaso de la Vega (1503–36) succeeded, where earlier attempts had failed, in naturalizing in Spanish the whole gamut of Italian metres, sonnet, tercet, *canzone*, and blank verse, all on the basis of the hendecasyllable, his most effective form being the *silva*, a long verse paragraph with free rhyming scheme and occasional heptasyllables, and his most influential the *lira*, a fixed five-line stanza of eleven- and seven-syllable lines. The significance of these innovations was twofold. They demanded of the poet a mastery of technique and subtle effects that till then had lain beyond his ken and his capacity alike. And the longer line and more complex stanza forms constituted a challenge to the poet to think and analyse where previously he had been content to describe or narrate.

Garcilaso himself rose triumphantly to the double challenge. With his own emotions as central theme and an unfailing ear – he is one of the most musical of all Spanish poets – he effected a total revolution in poetry, and through a slender corpus of eclogues, elegies, and sonnets worked profoundly on all who came after. Herrera and fray Luis de León, his immediate heirs, show in their divergence the rich potentialities of the inheritance. Typifying anew the old dichotomy between Andalusia and Castile, Herrera the Sevillian wrote grandiloquent odes in *silva* form on national occasions, fray Luis the Salamancan made of the unpretentious *lira* the perfect instrument for introspective meditation and deep personal issues.

This too was realism, of a specifically Castilian stamp, that had its finest flowering in the great mystics of the later sixteenth century. Santa Teresa and St John of the Cross both wrote of the most sublime of spiritual experiences with the authority of those whose natural habitat lay on the heights, and none who aspires to scale these may dispense with their writings. St John distilled the travail and the ecstasy into some of the most ethereal poetry ever written. Santa Teresa, indefatigable foundress and reformer, contrived to keep one foot firmly on earth, and alike her *Autobiography* and the *Book of the Foundations* are masterpieces of warm humanity by any secular reckoning. In their wrestlings with the problem of expressing the ineffable the mystics, these two and a host of lesser but still significant figures, contributed much without knowing it to loosening the joints of the language and enlarging its penetrative scope. Shrewdest of psychologists and masterly in pinpointing those of whom she writes, Santa Teresa had in her the makings of a novelist.

The picaresque novel came to birth with the brief, anonymous

Lazarillo de Tormes (1554). The *pícaro*, a social outcast who saw life from below and delighted, as he passed from master to master, to prick the many bubbles of Spanish pride and idealism, provided the counterblast to the romances of chivalry. Lazarillo's satire spared the Church least of all, thus conflicting with the new official urge, taken over from the Council of Trent, to make literature subserve dogma; and when at length he had a successor, in Mateo Alemán's *Guzmán de Alfarache* (1599), the satirical was all but forgotten in the overlying doctrinal purpose. Artistically the formula proved sterile, plot being but the beading of episodes on a string and character static. In Quevedo's *The Rogue* (1626), irreverence became cynical contempt for all civilized values, including religious fervour. Here the author but mirrored the spirit of the age: in so doing, he finally dehumanized the picaresque, and it never recovered.

It was reserved to Miguel de Cervantes (1547–1616), a meditative artist who had pondered much on the relation of life to literature, to discover the true scope and technique of the modern novel and to write, in *Don Quixote* (1605–15), what the world still regards as the greatest in the kind. This began ostensibly as a parody of the chivalresque romance, indicted not for its high idealism but for utter remoteness from reality. Brought back into contact, it could be made the modern counterpart, in prose, of that sublimest of all literary forms to the ancients, the heroic epic, which the Renaissance kept trying, unsuccessfully, to re-acclimatize. Ercilla's *Araucana* (1569–89), written around the war of conquest in distant Chile, was the most gallant of the many Spanish failures. Cervantes's epic ranges over the whole of society and its problems, being concerned with incident and adventure only for the light these throw on character, and with character as something in a state of continual becoming. The constant probing into the nature of reality and of truth makes this too one of the great philosophical novels, that abounds further in an infinite humanity, unfailing humour, and a charm of style without parallel in Spanish letters.

The other great creative sphere of the age was the drama. Lope de Vega (1562–1635), to the envious Cervantes 'nature's prodigy', was prodigious not merely in his fecundity: an alleged 1,800 plays, of which some 700 are authenticated. He forged and established a new dramatic form, haughtily independent of the ancients, which was compact of action and intrigue and achieved a rare solidarity with its public through his success in mirroring that triple respect for Church, crown, and the human personality, symbolized in the 'point of honour', on which society rested. *Comedia* is a generic term for Spain's national drama: this does, in fact, reflect the spacious optimism of an age still sure of itself and legitimately proud of its achievements.

The theme was often medieval – Lope ransacked chronicles and balladry with an infallible ear for such chords as still vibrated in the national consciousness – and often again foreign: the play's appeal still resided in its essential contemporaneity of spirit, and on Lope's instinctive sense of theatre. A poet too to the finger-tips, with a mind of infinite imaginative resource, he breathed into his plays a gaiety and insouciance that compensate for the absence of any serious concern with character, verisimilitude, or questions of social urgency. *The Sheep Well*, *A Certainty for a Doubt*, and *No Judge like the King* may serve out of hundreds to characterize his historical plays, and *The Gardener's Dog*, the so-called cloak-and-sword comedies of contemporary manners. *The Star of Seville*, long held perhaps his best play, is now reckoned very doubtfully his.

A galaxy of lesser Lopes followed: Guillén de Castro, Alarcón, Tirso de Molina, and many more. To the first of these Corneille was to turn for *Le Cid*, to the second for *Le Menteur*. Alarcón, a Mexican by birth, supplied the missing concern with character and ethics. Tirso is memorable for having risen on occasion above theatre into drama (*Damned for Lack of Faith*, *A Woman's Prudence*) and for giving to the world, in *The Seville Deceiver*, the prototype of the immortal Don Juan.

The decadence that settled on Spain down the seventeenth century found its due reflection in literature. As values believed sacrosanct proved their hollowness, that fervour of conviction that had given to Spanish society its earlier cohesion and buoyancy yielded to an all-pervading disillusion, to be seen alike in the brutal cynicism of Quevedo, in the 'culteranism' of Góngora and the 'conceptism' of Gracián, in the formalism of Calderón. Quevedo, who wrote serious treatises, and poems, on the disordered state of the times, is remembered, after *The Rogue*, for

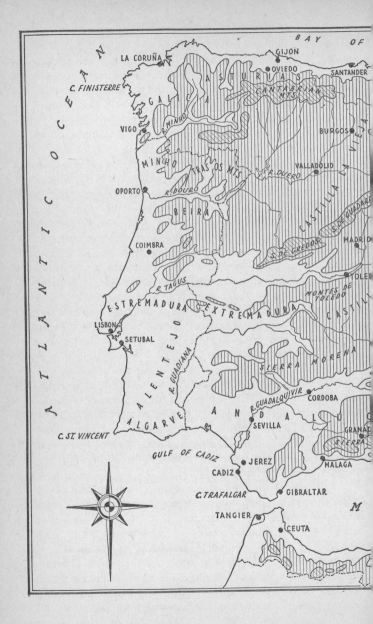

SPAIN
AND PORTUGAL

▯▯▯▯ THE HIGH TABLELANDS

▧▧▧▧ HIGH MOUNTAIN AREAS

∿∿∿ INTERNATIONAL FRONTIERS

SCALE

| 0 MILES 50 | 100 | 150 | 200 |
| 0 KMS 80 | 160 | 240 | 320 |

his *Dreams* of an underworld in which the follies and hypocrisies of mankind are unmasked more pitilessly still.

Culteranism and conceptism were twin aberrations nominally at issue each with the other yet eloquent of the same general malaise. The former, affecting poetry, can be traced back through Herrera to Juan de Mena, exemplifying the Andalusian's persistent exalting of form over thought. Latinization of vocabulary and syntax, recondite classical allusion, involved metaphor were here carried to the extreme, three elements among many in the deliberate search for an art that should be at once timeless and a closed book to the non-initiate. Around Góngora there raged a mighty polemic in his day: he was still a great artist in words, and his unfinished *Solitudes* (1613), a nominally descriptive poem in which the effects are all of a heightened lyricism, have set him on a pinnacle of esteem three centuries after, as a poet's poet, from which he is unlikely now to be dislodged.

Conceptism, in prose, fled not from everyday reality, and still less from thought, but from their everyday expression. It sought to be an art of the quintessential, and to shock the reader into attention through subtle play with and juxtaposition of ideas. Gracián formulated a whole elaborate doctrine for the 'conceit', and applied it in various brief treatises on the hero, the statesman, and the courtier. His underlying philosophy, a bitterly pessimistic view of life as a constant dying and of society as inevitably corrupting, found expression in *The Criticaster* (1651–5), a long allegorical novel of the three ages of man that would be more esteemed, and more easily, but for its over-density of style.

Calderón (1600–81), the last of the great dramatists, has been for centuries the best-known outside Spain. He too was dexterous in light comedy of the cloak-and-sword tradition, and greatest of them all in the *auto sacramental*, a peculiarly Spanish development of the old morality which, hingeing on and exalting the doctrine of transubstantiation, was become the central feature of the Corpus Christi festival. His fame abroad rests rather on a small group of religious-philosophical plays – *Life's a Dream*, *The Prodigious Magician*, *Devotion to the Cross* – which display great subtlety in dramatizing not character or life so much as certain key positions of the Counter-Reformation. There is in his style much both of the Gongorist and of the conceptist, and in his cast of mind clear evidence that the creative exuberance of the Golden Age has finally declined into a cautious concern with orthodoxy. Lyrical rather than dramatic, its philosophy close kin to casuistry, his is still a brilliant art, but it is art at the service of an ideology on the defensive.

Two names dominate Portuguese literature over this period. Given worthy successors to Gil Vicente (*c.* 1465–*c.* 1536), Portugal too might have had a national drama. Gifted beyond any Spanish playwright before Lope, he still lacked the sense of plot and technique that would have shaped and given purpose to his rare endowment for humorous probing and character creation. A retainer at court – many of his forty-four 'comedies, tragi-comedies, and farces' were formal allegorical pieces written to grace royal occasions – he could not engage the interest of the commoners he depicted so admirably. Having thus at command neither theatre nor public on which to build, his achievement perished with him. Read today, the plays delight not least for their profusion of sparkling lyrics.

In Luis de Camoens (*c.* 1524–80), the age's epic urge found at last its perfect expression. Discovery and conquest in the east had already inspired a distinguished line of chroniclers, Barros, Couto, Corrêa. Camoens raised the theme to the level of high poetry, and with it interwove, following Virgil, the nation's whole story, which Portugal ever since has studied in his pages. A classical education had its part in the formal excellences of *The Lusiads* (1572); its vibrant actuality came from the poet's own seventeen years of travail and travel throughout the Portuguese east. Without this, his country's greatest masterpiece, Camoens would still be its greatest poet, for his wealth of emotional and other experience he distilled too with rare felicity into more subjective vein.

The Lusiads had ended – it was one of its purposes – with a stirring call to the author's fellow-countrymen to show themselves worthy of their forbears and capable of inspiring poets yet unborn with deeds no less glorious. It was too late. Having lived to see his country's eclipse at Alcazar-Kebir, he knew the heroic age was over. Decadence in Portuguese letters thus anticipated that of Spain by the sixty years of the Spanish domination. An occasional writer of note would still emerge, like the poet and historian Manuel de Mello: in choosing to write his chief work, a history of the Catalan rising of 1640, not merely on a Spanish theme but in Spanish, as in his general indebtedness to both Góngora and Quevedo, Mello shows how serious the threat of Castile had now become to the cultural tradition of the peripheral nations. Both Vicente and Camoens had already written much, and with almost equal distinction, in Castilian too.

This was the Golden Age no less in the arts, which throve on the same pride in national greatness, on the influx of wealth from the Indies, and on noble patronage on a vast scale. Ease of access to Italy and the Low Countries, now but extensions to the Spaniard of his homeland, was another important factor which stimulated and enriched without impeding the development of distinctively peninsular styles. In architecture the first of these, the so-called plateresque (from *plata*, silver), resembled Manueline in Portugal in its concentration on exuberance of detail rather than on design. On a mixture of Gothic and classical elements it superimposed a flamboyancy of ornamentation inspired by the silversmith's art, to be studied in the Renaissance cathedrals of Salamanca, Segovia, Granada. Counter-Reformation austerity dictated the severe pseudo-Roman period of Philip II, whose direct personal interest in the planning and building of the Escorial helped make of that formidable pile the revealing document it is. Its architect, Juan de Herrera, gave a second expression to the same qualities in the cathedral of Valladolid.

In the later seventeenth century Churriguera gave his name to a school of architecture that once again abandoned restraint to plunge into an orgy of contorted extravagances. This was no longer the expansive spirit of the Renaissance but a subordinating of function and taste alike to mere passion for display. As with Gongorism in poetry, it produced estimable creations from the more talented: the palace of San Telmo in Seville, the Jesuit college at Salamanca, or the portal in Madrid of the much later Royal Hospice. In lesser hands it ran as inevitably to excess and abuse, proclaiming once more the progressive impoverishment, aesthetic and intellectual, of the nation.

The starkly realistic Christs and Madonnas of Luis de Morales (1517–86), Spain's first wholly native painter of note, show what the course of Spanish painting might have been but for its exposure, now greatly intensified, to foreign influences. Charles V's portraitist was Titian, Philip II's a Fleming, Antony Mor. In portraiture Flemish masters proved the more influential, in religious painting the Italian, though always Spain wrought subtly on what she accepted. This power of assimilation has never been better illustrated than in one of the greatest of all her painters, El Greco (*c.* 1548–1614) – his real name Domenico Theotocopouli – a Greek from Crete who studied in Venice under Titian, settled in Toledo about 1577, and there found himself strangely attuned to Counter-Reformation Spain, whose spirit he was to express better than anyone else. In the sense of religious ecstasy that informs his masterpieces, 'The Burial of the Count Orgaz', 'The Assumption', and 'The Day of Pentecost', and the constant reaching after something that defies expression, he is at one with the great mystics of the age.

Ribera, Ribalta, Herrera, and Zurbarán are other artists of note, concerned with the discovery and rendering, each in his own way, of a distinctively Spanish reality, who pave the transition from El Greco to Velázquez (1599–1660). Endowed with the visual imagination of the Andalusian and schooled by two years in Italy, where Titian and Tintoretto greatly enlarged his command of light and depth, Velázquez shook off the earlier subservience to religious themes and, as court painter from 1623, achieved through long experiment a technical mastery of impressionistic effect far outstripping all his contemporaries. His progress from 'The Topers', through portraits of court dwarfs and of Aesop, to the supreme art of 'The Spinners' or 'The Maids of Honour', in which he set himself and solved brilliantly the problem of 'painting empty space', is the most striking in the annals of Spanish painting. Murillo, the last great name in this beadroll, delighted more than any in the humours of the intimate and the lowly – melon-eaters, a flower-girl, peasant youths. His was an art wholly humanized, that fittingly closed the cycle. Spain would not produce another great artist on canvas for a century.

The brief span between the death of Manuel in 1521 and the catastrophe of 1578 belongs in Portuguese architecture to Italian Renaissance influences that have their chief monument in Torralva's Tuscan cloister at Thomar; only completed after Philip II's seizure of the throne, it is known as the cloister of the

Philips. Philip's interest in ecclesiastical building extended to his new realm but, thanks chiefly to the elegant taste of his architect, the Italian Terzi, did not succeed in imposing there the full rigours of his sombre genius. Terzi's masterpiece, the Doric church of São Vicente de Fora at Lisbon, is held among the finest of its time in Europe.

In painting Portugal knew no comparable distinction to that of Spain. Much in the early sixteenth century, still almost exclusively religious and predominantly Flemish in origin, is in fact of unknown authorship. One known name of merit, Vasco Fernandes, carries in consequence a host of dubious attributions. Gregório Lopes, in mid-century, bore the other, Italian, imprint, and was of greater though still only relative stature. Portraiture flourished during the decades of affluent patronage, but with the coming of the Philips good practitioners were drawn to the Spanish court, and Portuguese painting lost again an individuality it had barely achieved.

12

'No More Pyrenees'

THE accession of Philip V (1700–46), ushering in the new century with a new dynasty, kindled hopes of a total break with a disastrous past and, had it been a purely internal issue, would have commanded thereby widespread assent. Louis XIV might boast of the abolition of the Pyrenees, enjoin on his grandson the memory always that he was a Frenchman, and secure for his ambassador to Madrid membership of the Royal Council. The qualities of the French mind and genius were precisely those of which Spain then stood most in need; the rise of France had demonstrated her possession of that secret of national greatness which it was essential Spain should relearn; and the prospect of a durable peace now that the age-long rivalry across the Pyrenees had been laid was worth any sacrifice of traditional attachments.

The new monarch, aged seventeen, was not another Louis XIV 'Well fitted to creep through life in a humble station,' he was still a reasonable specimen of manhood, in itself a welcome change on the Spanish throne, and, if free from particular virtues, free too from vices. Born less to rule than to be ruled, he was governed by his child-wife Marie Louise of Savoy, who was governed in her turn by the redoubtable princess des Ursins, French by birth, widow of a Spanish grandee, and chosen by Louis as guarantee of the supremacy of French interests at his grandson's court. A Frenchman, Orry, was charged with the overhaul and reorganization of the national finances, first and most arduous of all the herculean labours awaiting. The constitutional intentions of the new dispensation appeared from Philip's failure to summon Cortes in due form for the customary oath of fealty: at no time throughout his long reign would they be allowed any initiative or responsibility in affairs. The nation could look to be better administered than before, and in the interests of the nation, not of the crown; but it would still be from above, and without consultation, for the whole of the ensuing century.

All this still hinged, however, on the prospect of peace; and peace depended on how Charles's will was taken, not by the Spanish people, but by the powers. Portugal accepted it. England and Holland held Louis bound by the partition pact he had signed with them; but on the argument that this would never have been accepted by the emperor France persuaded both into unwilling acquiescence. The emperor for his part had made no compacts, and if he would have spurned half the inheritance, even a half so substantial as Spain, Flanders, and the Indies, much less was he disposed to tolerate his total exclusion. Militarily he was no match for France, but it was a reasonable expectation that England and Holland would yet come to see their vital interests as no less affected than his by the elevation of France into another colossus bestriding Europe and the New World, in a position to dominate the Mediterranean and the Atlantic and to impose its will in all directions. Without waiting for assurances he sent an army into Italy to dispute France's new title at its nearest point.

The year was still 1700. The War of the Spanish Succession had begun almost before Charles was cold in his coffin and while Philip had not yet set foot in Spain. This was no longer Spain fighting for Europe but Europe fighting for Spain, and the old mainspring of all Spain's wars had by now been long forgotten: balance of power, not religion, was the stake. Herein lay the novelty for Spain, destined to find herself hereafter, in war after war, become the storm centre of Europe, with foreign armies tramping the country from end to end as foreign powers fought out their dissensions. The one familiar element in the new situation was the total disregard, once more, of the interests of the Spanish people.

England and Holland were swift to follow the emperor into the fray, signing an alliance with him in September 1701 that committed them to winning the Spanish crown for the archduke Charles, a youth two years younger than his rival. The centre of action was now transferred to Spain, where it was hoped to find that the Habsburg cause had not, after so long and so close a connexion, gone entirely by default. Separatist sentiment, and the repeated invasions of French armies in the previous reign, no longer by invitation, indicated that any fissure in loyalties was to be looked for first in Catalonia, where the pretender already held one trump card.

Prince George of Darmstadt had come to Spain at the head of an imperialist army in 1695 and proved himself thereafter the backbone of resistance to the French in the Catalan campaigns, endearing himself both to the Catalans and to Charles in Madrid who made him a grandee with all the honours of a prince of the blood and in 1698 appointed him viceroy of Catalonia. One of the new king's first acts three years later was to dismiss him; but he had done his work well, and left with the ominous remark that he would soon return, and under a different monarch. As liaison officer of the emperor with his new allies, prince George helped to shape British war counsels, and his was the suggestion of the naval expedition which sailed against Cadiz, Spain's chief arsenal and hub of the American traffic, in 1702.

The prince set out in advance for Lisbon, and there succeeded in winning over king Peter to the side of the allies. The attack on Cadiz failed, though the seizure of a silver fleet at Vigo on the way home afforded some compensation. Much more important was the collaboration now of Portugal, who early in 1703 renounced her understanding with France and, formally adhering to the new grand alliance, offered a basis for land operations in the west. With the known disposition of Catalonia in the east, the stage was set for a trial of strength in the Peninsula, and the archduke, proclaimed in Vienna Charles III of Spain, set out for Lisbon by way of England to assert his title, Darmstadt accompanying him as commander-in-chief and minister of war. With him from England sailed 10,000 allied troops, 188 sail in all.

The dilapidated state of the Portuguese defences indicated as a beginning the probing of Spain's eastern coast-line, where a first assault on Barcelona was thwarted by the apparent apathy of the Catalans, awaiting some political guarantee that would justify further sacrifice. This expedition too brought its contingent reward in the capture in 1704 of Gibraltar – on behalf, it is to be noted, of the Austrian pretender, though the British flag has flown over it ever since.

A second landing at Barcelona in the following year, headed by Charles himself, had been preceded by a formal English undertaking to the Catalans, given in the name of queen Anne, that she would 'secure them a confirmation of their rights and liberties from the king of Spain that they may be settled on a lasting foundation to them and their posterities'; and on this undertaking Catalonia ranged itself behind the Austrian cause, Aragon and Valencia soon following its lead. In the storming of the citadel of Barcelona Darmstadt perished. To counter this threat Philip was compelled to withdraw troops from the Portuguese frontier, where he had at first concentrated his forces, and he led in person an army of 21,000 men – all, but for two troop of horse, French – through largely hostile territory to the siege of the Catalan capital. An English fleet carrying reinforcements saved the day for Charles, and to complete Philip's discomfiture came word that the denuded Portuguese front had broken and the allies were marching on Madrid.

The Bourbon cause was now in retreat everywhere. Marlborough's and prince Eugene's brilliant joint victory at Blenheim in 1704 had retrieved a potentially disastrous situation for the emperor and driven the French out of Austria. Two years later the victors were to win new separate trimphs, Marlborough at Ramillies, prince Eugene at Turin, which proved equally decisive for Flanders and northern Italy. Henceforth the struggle would centre more and more in Spain, and in Spain it seemed lost. Philip, beaten before Barcelona, escaped ignominiously into France in May 1706 with the loss of 6,000 men and all his guns and supplies, and had to make his way back to Madrid through Navarre.

He arrived at the capital just in time to make a second retreat, this time to Burgos, for the allied forces advancing from Portugal were already at Salamanca and entered Madrid exactly a week after his departure. This was Madrid's blackest day in the six hundred years of its Christian history, to see in occupation an army of English heretics and upstart Portuguese and hear proclaimed as their sovereign the prince it had rejected, risen to power on the support of the dissident Catalans. But Charles, journeying slowly from Barcelona through Saragossa, where he received the fealty of Aragon, arrived too late; for Philip with reinforcements from Navarre had reoccupied the capital and compelled his enemy to fall back on Valencia.

The Balearic Islands and Naples now declared for Charles,

while the two Castiles and Andalusia remained faithful to the Bourbon. Again the cleavage was clear, running along the same historic fault-line that had always bedevilled Spanish unity: the kingdom of Castile on one side, the kingdom of Aragon on the other, each with its own monarch. The traditional connexions had suffered reversal, but the fundamental incompatibility went deeper than the passing allegiances that served to give it expression. So poised, the two commanders now summoned all their resources for a decisive encounter. This befell at Almansa in April 1707. The opposing forces – French and Castilians under their English leader the duke of Berwick on one side, Portuguese, English, Dutch, Huguenots, Germans, and Catalans led by a Frenchman, Henri de Ruvigny, on the other – would have been closely matched at some 25,000 men each had not Charles withheld 10,000 Catalans for the security of the principality. The precaution cost him the day, for the allies were routed with heavy losses, not least in leadership, and first Valencia and then Aragon were overrun in consequence and won back for the Bourbon cause.

Charles was master now of little more than the Catalonia with which he had started. Had Louis been able to succour his grandson at this point the war might have been won. But Louis' own resources had been strained to the pitch where he would have welcomed a composition. Already in 1706 he had offered the allies yet another partition: Spain and the Indies to Charles, Flanders to the Dutch, Milan, Naples, and Sicily to Philip; and again the emperor – now Charles's brother Joseph, who had succeeded on his father's death in the preceding year – and with him England, would have none of it. In 1709, after Oudenarde, Louis would try again, offering now to relinquish the entire Spanish inheritance. This time it was France's turn to be kept in the fight against her will and to be dealt one stunning blow on top of another: on Oudenarde followed Malplaquet, that saw the most fearsome carnage of the century with 40,000 dead and wounded.

Philip, far from being able to count on unlimited French aid, had instead to send many of his French contingents back home. The allied reaction to Almansa was to strengthen Charles thereafter with imperial troops no longer needed in Italy rather than with British conveyed the much longer distance from England, and the supreme command in Spain passed accordingly from British to German hands. Fighting continued inconclusively, neither side having the resources to pursue an over-all strategy; but the balance of advantage in men, if still not in territory, came gradually to lie with the Austrian.

The years 1710–11 were to settle the issue in a manner and a direction both wholly unexpected. While Louis again sued for peace, and again in vain, Philip affirmed his resolve to surrender nothing, and succeeded in engaging the French monarch in one last supreme effort against the allies. His own offensive against Catalonia could scarcely have been more disastrous. Defeat after defeat drove him back through Aragon to Castile, with Charles close in pursuit, until in September 1710 the allies for the second time entered Madrid in triumph, while Philip took refuge in Valladolid. It was a triumph muted by the sullen hostility of the Castilians: 'We are not masters, in Castile, of more ground than we encamp on,' wrote the English general Stanhope. Reinforced at length from France, Philip was able to retrieve his fortunes and compel Charles to retreat on Barcelona. This game of give and take still promised final victory over a united Spain to neither, and the issue might well have been stalemate and partition after all, when an extraneous event, allied to the advent in August 1710 of a Tory government in England pledged to make peace with France, totally altered the situation.

In April 1711 the emperor Joseph died childless, and Charles, succeeding to all his hereditary dominions, found himself chief candidate to the imperial throne, to which he was duly elected six months later. The War of the Spanish Succession, fought to prevent the union of Spain with France, would have been fought no less had Charles II left his empire instead to the Habsburg; and this new turn of events obviously vitiated, if not in Charles's eyes, the whole purpose of the grand alliance. The conference begun at Utrecht in 1712 agreed to a suspension of hostilities between England, Holland, France, Spain – for whom France spoke – and Portugal. The treaty of that name signed in the following year determined the shape of Europe for a century to come; yet the two parties most interested, Charles and Philip, were alike absent from the conference table.

Negotiations were much complicated by a mysterious and heavy mortality in the French royal family. The dauphin had died in 1711. Now, within a few months, there died also his eldest son and eldest grandson, leaving only a sickly two-year-old duke of Anjou, great-great-grandson of Louis XIV, between Philip and the throne of France. And Louis was 74. A solemn renunciation of all rights to the French succession having been at length secured from Philip, the treaty was signed. From Spain England gained, or kept, Gibraltar and Minorca, and won too the *asiento* or monopoly of the slave trade with the Indies, with ancillary advantages that counted for far more; from France Newfoundland, Acadia, Nova Scotia, and Hudson's Bay. Utrecht marks the beginning therefore of Britain's mastery over the Mediterranean, her dominion in Canada, and her recognized entry into Spain's New World, from which, too, vast consequences would in time flow. Spain accepted further as final the loss of the Franche Comté to France, and ceded to the empire, by the treaty of Rastadt of 1714, Flanders, Milan, Naples, and Sardinia, while Sicily was forfeited to Savoy.

This was a sore dismemberment, reducing Spain once again to her share of the Peninsula, along with Majorca, the Canaries, and the Indies. The last relics of the Habsburg imperial incubus had gone at last, to create new wars for Austria as down two hundred years they had for Spain. With them went Naples, and the still longer history of Spanish ascendancy in Italy ended too. But these were the pre-conditions of any attempt at internal recovery, and the country could now hope to resume its own development at the point where it had been diverted by the fateful death of prince John in 1497.

Isabella the Catholic's decision to marry east instead of west must always remain the watershed of peninsular history. But she had married east, and Catalonia remained the great problem, even for Utrecht. Charles's attempt to fight on alone was foredoomed to failure, and in 1713, having achieved nothing more in Spain, his troops were finally evacuated from Catalonia on British vessels. Only the British guarantee of their fueros and their own valour stood now between the Catalans and Philip's vengeance, this already portended in a decree of 1707, after Almansa, declaring extinct all the fueros of Valencia, Catalonia, and Aragon alike; and, although the Catalan question had echoed throughout the negotiations, in the end England defaulted on her guarantee.

A clause in the treaty offered an amnesty and 'all the liberties and privileges enjoyed by Castilians', which last, especially in the matter of freedom of trade with the Indies, England sought to represent, and thereby salve her conscience, as of more value than any differential political rights. It was a scurvy evasion, and the Catalans rejected it with contumely. Charles in his negotiations had sought to stipulate first that the territories of the crown of Aragon should fall to him; then, defeated on this, that Catalonia should be created a free republic collectively guaranteed by the allies. Lacking the strength to back these demands, he could achieve nothing.

To the Catalans this was the supreme crisis in their history. Whatever else they had lost in the past, even to Philip IV and Olivares, they had held on to their fueros, and they preferred death to dishonour now. Some indication of the depth of Catalan sentiment on this issue may be seen in the approach they now made, in vain, to the sultan of Turkey; a pointer to where England stood in a matter engaging her honour so nearly, in the despatch of British vessels, at Philip's request, to help reduce Barcelona. The thirteen-months' defence of the city against 40,000 French and Castilian troops constituted an epic of desperate heroism for parallels to which one must go back to Numantia in the second century B.C. or on to Saragossa in the nineteenth.

With its fall in September 1714 the struggle for the Spanish throne was over. Charles's testament had willed eleven years of war on the Spanish people and on Spanish soil. One of its provisions had been confirmed: a Bourbon reigned. Inasmuch as he reigned over a European patrimony diminished by nearly half, the main purpose of the will had been effectively defeated. Either of the partitions proposed in Charles's lifetime would have given Spain more. Against this, Philip could claim that, the Catalans being at long last politically no more than, nor different from, Castilians, he did at least reign, for the first time since the Visigoths, over a unitary Spain. Of a united Spain he could not yet speak, since to crush dissidents is not to suppress dissidence, and of Catalan dissidence much more would be heard.

Meanwhile a new citadel was built to command the ruins of Barcelona and symbolize Castilian military dominance; all Catalan universities were suppressed and their revenues attached to a new foundation at Cervera largely controlled by the Jesuits and intended as an instrument for the castilianizing of the population; the laws of Catalonia were formally revoked in favour of those of Castile, and when a simulacrum of Cortes did meet thereafter it met in Madrid for the whole country; the Catalan tongue was abolished from courts of law and gradually from the schools; and the office of viceroy gave way to one of captain-general.

Once more the prospect of peace proved illusory. Philip had two sons when in 1714, the year that saw all the fighting over, his wife died. By one more in the series of queer twists of fortune that had so often determined the country's destiny, the fact that the succession to the throne was happily assured, instead of removing anxiety, became this time the specific cause of international intrigues, alliances, wars, and rumours of wars that for some fifteen years would again deny to the Spanish people the right to a life of their own. Behind it all lay a woman's ambition. Philip had shown phases of energy and resolve during the late war, but with the years the weak strains in his character, in particular the melancholia that was later to disturb his reason, had been more and more in evidence, and eventually left him totally reliant on his wife. On her death that reliance was transferred to the princess des Ursins, who with Orry continued to be the real power in the country, and it became a matter of general and urgent concern that he should marry again.

The new queen, Isabel Farnese of Parma, was the choice of the princess, who showed herself thereby able to override the views and interests even of Louis XIV. A reputed docility had been the commending factor; but here the princess's sources of information had betrayed her, and on their first meeting she found herself unceremoniously bundled over the Pyrenees, all influence gone for good. In strength of character, tenacity of purpose, and subtlety of manoeuvre the newcomer proved herself another Isabella the Catholic, and Philip's submission to her was from this first act complete.

What Isabel lacked in comparison with her namesake was

the purity of purpose, the sense of high principle and devotion to her people which might again have raised a Spain so led to greatness. Isabel wanted instead sons and, bearing them, wanted greatness for them; and since they could not aspire to the throne of Spain she bent her whole energies, and succeeded in diverting those of her adopted country, to the carving for them of thrones in the direction whence she had come. And so, but one year quit of the long Italian entanglement, Spain submitted to the ironic fate of seeing her whole foreign policy turned away from France and back to Italy to the renewal of entanglements that could not but cause wars in the getting, more wars in the holding, and that had not the remotest connexion with her true interests. The death of Louis XIV in 1715 and the rivalry and ill-will between Philip and his cousin the duke of Orleans, now regent to the young Louis XV and still nurturing in his heart his own ambitions concerning the French throne, played in all this into Isabel's hands.

Her instruments were a succession of foreign adventurers promoted to highest office; they throw a vivid light on the extent to which Spain had lost control of her destinies. The first, Alberoni, an Italian priest representing the duke of Parma at Philip's court, had made the original suggestion concerning a successor to Marie Louise, and was in gratitude soon accepted by that successor as her chief adviser. This meant in effect that he was unofficial, and soon official, first minister. Orry was sent back to France, and in 1717 the queen secured a cardinalate for his supplanter, who had already launched out into the deep waters of European diplomacy.

The emperor, whose interests any Spanish return to Italy must threaten, found himself then at issue on his eastern flank with the Turks. Alberoni's first concern was therefore to create difficulties for him on the west by suborning his former allies, England and Holland, through trading concessions in America, while at the same time embarrassing France by fomenting plots against the regent. In so much scheming he overreached himself, for in the name of Utrecht and the peace that all Europe so sorely needed England, France, and Holland had already formed a triple compact. Ignoring this, Alberoni in 1717 judged the time ripe for action and despatched a fleet that without warning

attacked and overran Sardinia. Protests and the offer of dis-
cussions he rejected, and a year later sent a second expedition
against Sicily.

Reaction this time was swift. The adhesion of the emperor
made the compact quadruple. A British fleet destroyed the
Spanish forces off Sicily, and Spain found herself at war with
both Britain and France. Soon a French army was overrunning
first the Basque provinces, then once more Catalonia, stirring
up the ever latent disaffection there, while British vessels stormed
Vigo and Pontevedra and laid waste much of Galicia. Alberoni
sought in vain to create diversions within England and France
and to obtain help from Russia and Sweden. Everything failing,
he fell, and in 1719 left the country while Philip sought anew a
basis of coexistence with the other powers. By the peace of 1720
Spain gave up Sardinia and renounced again all title to Sicily and
to the emperor's Italian possessions in general. In exchange
Philip obtained, for his wife rather than for Spain, the reversion
for her issue of the duchies of Tuscany and Parma. A new rap-
prochement with France was cemented by a proposed triple
marriage, of Philip's eldest sons by both wives to the regent's
two daughters, and of his and the Farnese's infant daughter to
the child-king Louis XV.

Only the first of these unions was destined to take place, in
1722. But the prospect of peace seemed to have dawned once
more and encouraged Philip to put into effect a resolve that he
had already formed in 1720, on seeing an end to the Alberoni
misadventure. In January 1724, 'having considered maturely the
miseries of this life and the infirmities, wars, and turmoils which
God has sent me during the twenty-three years of my reign,' he
announced his abdication from the throne in favour of his son
Luis and retired from the world, the queen accompanying him,
to the palace of La Granja which he had built near Segovia to
remind him of the Versailles of his youth.

The retirement was short-lived. After a reign of seven months,
during which his stepmother had continued to pull the strings
from La Granja, Luis died of smallpox. His brother Ferdinand
being still a minor, the pressure on Philip to resume the throne
was compelling. The theologians absolved him from his solemn
oath of withdrawal; and what he had assumed, with a sense of

relief fully shared by the nation, to be his whole reign proved to be exactly half. Over the second half, moreover, there presided the same motive of the queen's Italian ambitions, leading Spain into the same unprofitable complications with other powers, which had so perturbed the preceding decade, with the added factor that Philip, for all his gloom and moroseness, showed signs now of an interest in the French throne totally at variance with his repeated professions of renunciation and which the other signatories of Utrecht could not but look at askance.

The suspicious had already queried the sincerity of the reasons alleged for his abdication. During the brief duration of this, proposals were in fact made to him from Paris, in view of the recent death of the duke of Orleans and of the delicate health of Louis XV, that he should revive his title there. His refusal, and his wife's continuing intrigues for her sons, undid the so recent understanding with France. Luis's French widow returned home, leaving an unflattering reputation behind her; the other two marriage contracts were broken off; and Spain's foreign policy turned instead to the search for a basis of agreement, after a quarter of a century of hostility, with the emperor Charles, whose opposition to the Farnese's personal scheming not all her diplomacy in the counsels of Europe had been able to win over.

In this Alberoni had a worthy successor in Ripperdá, a Dutchman who had likewise represented his country at the Spanish court and, turning Catholic, had likewise ingratiated himself with the queen. This unprincipled adventurer was now sent to Vienna to procure an alliance resting, if possible, on a double marriage of the queen's two eldest sons with the emperor's two daughters, and in 1725 a treaty was concluded. The emperor now finally abandoned his claim to the Spanish throne, promised help in the recovery of Gibraltar and Minorca, and recognized his namesake, the Farnese's eldest, as heir to Tuscany, Parma, and Plasencia. In return he too was offered valuable trading concessions in Spain and the Indies. The treaty, while it said nothing about the marriages, included a mutual defence pact. Ripperdá's reward was to be made a grandee in his turn, and shortly afterwards first minister.

But he too had wrought his own undoing with lies and much

indiscreet boasting at both courts which within a few months
provoked his fall and arrest. Escaping to England and thence to
Morocco, he changed his religion yet again, and again achieved
eminence as grand vizier of the sultan. His legacy to Spain was a
hostile combination of England, France, and Prussia, joined
later by Holland, Sweden, and Denmark, all concerned to stave
off this double threat to their trading interests and to the balance
of power. The violent *volte-face* in Spain had proved extremely
unpopular with the Spanish people, who perceived clearly the
underlying reason. To this the queen made reply by elevating as
her new favourite the Austrian ambassador and eliminating from
court and government such elements as favoured good relations
with France and England.

At once, however, the new alliance wore thin. The emperor
sent no help for the futile siege of Gibraltar in 1727. Louis XV
seemed to be dying, and from Paris came renewed approaches
regarding the succession there, which Isabel straight began to
dream of not for her husband but for her own first-born son.
Philip's melancholia was again weighing heavily on him, and he
wished more than ever to withdraw from the troublous scene.
One indication of this was his reversion to a Habsburg tradition
with a double marriage contract with Portugal, concluded in
1728, whereby Ferdinand wedded the eldest Braganza princess and
his half-sister Mariana, formerly betrothed to Louis XV, became
the bride of the future Joseph I.

This settled, Philip would again have resigned the throne; but
his wife insisted now that he remain while she still had family
interests to pursue. After long negotiations, greatly helped by the
queen's disillusion with the emperor, a first general treaty was
signed in 1729, excluding Austria, and a second in 1731, excluding
France, in which, among the series of reciprocal concessions, all
the powers confirmed her son Charles in the claim on the duchies.
On Gibraltar, that by contrast was a genuine Spanish interest,
the agreements said nothing. In the latter year the duke of Parma
died, and Charles sailed with a Spanish force, escorted by the
English fleet, to take up the inheritance.

Spain was back in Italy. Isabel Farnese alone had done it, had
in fact done more than she knew, as developments there were soon
to prove. It was some indirect satisfaction to Spain that the

queen's skill in keeping all the chancelleries of Europe on tenter-hooks had contributed more than all the wars of the previous hundred years to raising Spanish prestige among the nations. More directly, the emergence to power in this latest shift in policy of a new minister, Patiño, at once a Spaniard, a man of integrity, and an administrator of much acumen in the economic sphere and the first of a line of notable Spanish statesmen, contributed to a sorely needed rehabilitation both of the nation's economy and of its pride in itself. That pride still tended to think imperially, for it was in this sense that Utrecht had hurt most, and it was Patiño himself who suggested the next, more modest, adventure. As minister earlier of marine, then of finance, he had taken a particular interest in stimulating naval building; and the fleet that in 1732 sailed to the recapture of Oran, lost to the Moors twenty-four years before, was the largest and finest that Spain had assembled in over a century.

When the powers, and especially Austria, became entangled over another succession dispute, centring on the crown of Poland, Isabel readily dropped her first thought of angling for that crown too in favour of exploiting Austria's involvement nearer home. France gave a ready approval, and cemented it with the first 'Family Compact' of 1733, an offensive-defensive alliance aimed against both Austria and England which, if it served the queen's immediate purpose, was later to drag Spain in reciprocation into other and much less profitable enterprises. So fortified, Spain declared war on the emperor, and the Spanish fleet set sail to help Charles of Parma reconquer – for himself – the kingdom of Naples, still responsive to its long Spanish tradition. Naples was overrun, then Sicily, and by 1735 Charles had had himself crowned by the traditional title of king of the two Sicilies. After twenty-two years Spanish influence, if not Spain, was recovering something of the ground lost at Utrecht.

The Polish dispute had ended in that same year, and in the general settlement the powers incorporated recognition of Charles's conquests, on the double condition that they should never be reunited with the Spanish crown and that he should now renounce Parma and Tuscany, the former going with Milan to the emperor. This last greatly offended Isabel, who now wanted the two duchies for her second son Philip, and provided her with excuse for a renewal of plotting and intrigue at the expense of the peace of Europe.

Friction with England over trading rights and abuses in the Indies, with Gibraltar always in the background as an irritant, led in 1739–40 to the brief 'War of Jenkins' Ear', Jenkins being an English captain whose return from the Caribbean with the severed organ had greatly inflamed public opinion against Spanish 'atrocities'. Fought out mainly on the high seas, and remembered for the English sacking of Portobello, its chief interest lay in the demonstration that Spain had become once again a respectable naval power, able to hold her own even against England. The foiling of a determined English assault on Cartagena, nerve-centre of commerce in and with the Indies, was matched by the failure of a second Spanish siege of Gibraltar. But this conflict quickly merged in the general war that from 1740 to 1747 rent Europe over the imperial throne when Charles too, like his brother, died without male heir.

This resembled the Spanish situation of 1700 in reverse, and Philip, alleging descent from the great Charles V, duly laid claim to the whole inheritance. The gesture was made chiefly for bargaining purposes and at the instigation of his queen. What she wanted was the Italian dominions of Lombardy and the Milanese, to round out with Tuscany a kingdom for her second son; and to this end Spanish armies in northern Italy waged a series of campaigns fraught with many vicissitudes and set-backs. When, with general exhaustion, peace returned at last, the Farnese had gained neither Lombardy nor the Milanese and had seen Tuscany lost for good. Her son received instead his modest dukedom of Parma with Piacenza and Guastalla, undertaking in his turn to renounce these should he ever succeed to the Neapolitan or the Spanish throne. The powers continued firm in their resolve that Spain in Europe should mean Spain.

With this settlement of Aix-la-Chapelle in 1748, and the particular 'treaty of Aquisgran' signed with England in the following year, which was all to England's commercial advantage in the New World, Spain once more looked to enjoy a spell of tranquillity, the outlook brighter for the disappearance from the scene of the woman who for over thirty years had been the country's evil genius. For Philip, now a gloomy nonentity who in his last years had known long periods of derangement, had died at last, in 1746, when peace negotiations were already in train; and his second son Ferdinand, succeeding, had every interest in conserving resources so long and so rashly squandered on private ambition. With his accession Portugal again comes into the picture.

That country had emerged from the war over the succession in Spain, in which after Almansa it had played a very minor part, without substantial loss or gain. Utrecht merely provided for the return of Spanish frontier towns still held in exchange for some disputed territory in the New World. Portugal had, it was true, come out on the wrong side, for a Bourbon and not Charles III reigned in Spain; but a by-product of the negotiations that in 1703 had brought her into the grand alliance amply counterbalanced any apprehensions on that score. This was the famous Methuen treaty of the same year which, supplementing the more comprehensive agreement of 1654, taught the English to drink port and the Portuguese to wear English woollens and was destined to prove of immense importance to the economies of both countries, Portugal's new purchasing power born of the influx of Brazilian gold and diamonds being here a major factor. The defence clauses of successive Anglo–Portuguese commitments duly reflected the store set by what would be for long the most lucrative of all Britain's markets.

Peter II's long reign, an effective thirty-eight years, ended with his death in 1706, and his son entered at seventeen on an even longer one as John V (1706–50). Fortunate in being able to maintain his country at peace for decades when the rest of Europe was still a prey to war after war, enjoying sources of apparently inexhaustible wealth that brought back memories of the spacious days of Manuel the Fortunate, and endowed with strength of character, enthusiasm for the arts, and a lively intelligence that found relaxation in the study of languages and mathematics, John devoted himself after the pattern of Louis XIV to discharging with distinction the role of enlightened despot. Had the nation been drawn into a responsible share in the execution of his programme for it, this could have been one of its great epochs.

John had married the sister of Philip's rival for the Spanish throne, the archduke Charles, in 1708, and it was in fulfilment of a vow made while still anxiously hoping for a male heir – the future Joseph I was born in 1714 – that he constructed the vast monastery-palace of Mafra. This Portuguese Escorial-Versailles, begun in 1717, took eighteen years in the building and swallowed a large proportion of his Brazilian revenues: it remains the most expressive monument of a prodigal munificence that found out-let too in the creation of a Royal Academy of History and of the university library at Coimbra, in the protection of antiquities and a general patronage of the arts. The king showed a concern too to enhance the standing of the Church in Portugal, obtaining from Rome in 1716 the creation of a cardinal-patriarchate of Lisbon in addition to the existing archbishopric, the two even-tually merging in 1740. This came in appreciation of his response to papal appeals for help in a crusade against the Turk, though not until 1717 did a Portuguese force go into action, at the battle of Matapan.

It was John's only martial enterprise, for he consistently refused to be drawn into the political tensions and combinations of other countries. In matters affecting the prestige of his own he showed nonetheless a firmness, amounting to obstinacy, that threatened more than once to involve him in hostilities. Thus in 1724 he broke off relations with France over a question of protocol, the rupture lasting for fourteen years; waged diplo-matic strife with the Vatican for a decade in pursuance of his demand for equality of status for the papal nuncio in Lisbon with those appointed to Paris, Madrid, and Vienna, and in 1730 won his point, adding to it later the right of appointing to bishoprics; and in 1735 came to the brink of war with Spain over a violation of diplomatic immunity at his embassy in Madrid, a storm in a teacup that brought a British fleet to the Tagus and was only settled peacefully with the intervention of England, France, and Holland. In the penultimate year of his reign, in token of the extreme liberality of his many gifts to Rome, he received from the Pope the title of 'most faithful', corresponding to the 'most Catholic' and 'most Christian' traditionally borne by the kings of Spain and France.

These activities and achievements did not necessarily spell prosperity for his subjects. The Methuen treaty, while stimulating viticulture in the port wine country around Oporto, had placed the wine industry largely in the hands of Englishmen. A more serious consequence was its stifling of the textile industry that had been the object of so much concern in the previous reign. Royal affluence, squandered at the royal whim, left the exchequer in the end straitened rather than strengthened: from the beginning it accentuated the gulf between the luxury of court and capital and the misery of the provinces.

As before in Spain, the influx of gold, far from creating real wealth, discouraged throughout the land the spirit of industry and led to emigration on a scale that impelled the government as early as 1720 to forbid this altogether. In the closing years of the reign, when prolonged illness, following a paralytic stroke in 1742, loosened John's grip on affairs, the quality of his ministers too deteriorated and the influence of the Church increased, until one cardinal as prime minister and another as inquisitor-general between them ruled the country. A religiosity that had declined into gross superstition was one of the national characteristics thrown into vivid relief by the events of the years following John's death.

As with his father Philip V, the most important thing about Ferdinand VI (1746–59) was his wife, Barbara of Braganza. Portugal under her father John V, once free of the question of the Spanish succession, had kept resolutely out of European power politics. John had offered his mediation to help end the Austrian succession dispute in which Ferdinand's accession found Spain still committed; and once this was over Ferdinand and his Portuguese queen embraced a similar resolve. It was a novel experience for Spain, this phenomenon of a king who refused to go to war, and infinitely salutary. After Aquisgran, in consequence, the country's external history is limited for more than a decade to the signature of a few peaceful agreements and to the successful parrying of attempts by France and England to draw it into one or the other camp.

A treaty of 1752 with Austria, Tuscany, and Parma confirmed the *status quo* in Italy and gave promise that conflicting ambitions there would cease to kindle European wars. It signified to the world that Spain had finally dissociated herself from the policies of Isabel Farnese, still intriguing from her retreat at La Granja. A year later a concordat with Rome at last normalized relations which had been less than harmonious ever since the papacy had identified itself with the Habsburg claimant to the throne. Ferdinand for all his piety shared the Bourbon determination, at one in this with the earlier dynasty, to suffer no intromission of Rome in the secular affairs of his kingdom; and he secured now, along with confirmation of the crown's right of nomination to all save a few reserved benefices, the suppression of a number of Church prerogatives through which an appreciable part of the nation's wealth had been finding its way annually into the Vatican coffers.

France, having over two centuries waged – and in substantial measure won – an unrelenting struggle against first the Spanish and then the Austrian branch of the house of Habsburg for supremacy on the mainland of Europe, saw now approaching a no less momentous clash with England for supremacy in India, in north America, and on the high seas. The 'diplomatic revolution' of 1756, bringing France and Austria together and reversing thereby the system of European alliances, proved the signal for the outbreak of the Seven Years' War that was to decide these mighty issues.

Ferdinand's two chief ministers, Carvajal and Ensenada, inclined respectively to England and to France, and this equilibrium helped defeat the unceasing efforts of both countries to win from Spain a definite allegiance. Presuming on Carvajal's death in 1754, Ensenada had entered into secret negotiations with the French king and might have overridden Ferdinand's obstinate neutrality had he not been discovered in time and disgraced. For the remaining five years of his reign, Ferdinand persevered in his refusal to become involved, even when Minorca, now held by the French, was dangled by them as a bribe, or Gibraltar by the English.

This respite – it was no more, for when the fates at last gave Spain a good king they brought him to the throne in middle age and made him childless – Ferdinand used to good purpose. A national stocktaking revealed something of the dimensions of the problem. Eighteen thousand square leagues of good farming land were found to be entirely uncultivated, while 2,000,000 people, out of a total population estimated in 1748 at 7,500,000, existed on the verge of starvation. Ferdinand had thought to begin by paying off the vast legacy of debts that encumbered the treasury at his father's death, but found the resources did not exist. A conclave of ministers, lawyers, and theologians then assuring him that no man was bound to the impossible, a composition with the state's creditors was arrived at.

Already under Philip a beginning had been made with fiscal reform, the most notable stimulus to economic recovery being the abolition of all internal tolls and customs which the suppression of regional fueros had at last rendered possible. The experiment made at Valencia in 1717 of replacing a cumbrous structure of sales taxes and imposts by a single tax on salt had had a remarkable effect on the local textile industry, which in five years septupled the number of its looms until it once again supplied the entire home market. Ferdinand's outstanding contribution in this field was the ending of tax-farming, to the great relief of his subjects and benefit of his exchequer. In Castile alcabala and millions remained, oppressive and hated as ever; Ensenada was planning, after the Valencian model, to replace them too by a single salt-tax when he fell from power.

The entrenched power of the Mesta, with its separate jurisdiction and its claim on a sheep-run ninety yards wide reaching from Estremadura to Old Castile, also claimed his attention. Here too radical reform had to wait till the following reign, but some restrictions he did impose, compensating for the resultant fall in flocks by establishing factories for the processing of the wool, till then sent abroad – it was Spain's most valuable export – to be reimported after manufacture, so that its wealth now remained at home. Mining he encouraged by the opposite method of removing a ban on exports, and mines long abandoned were working once more.

The long uphill task of reinvigorating the cultural and intellectual life of the nation had now been in progress for half a century. Philip had found a Spain sunk in a stupor of ignorance, prejudice, and superstition scarcely to be conceived, after the greatness of a century earlier, until it is recognized as the inevitable fruit of blind adhesion to outworn doctrines and of the long denial of the right of free thought and free enquiry. There was little to be looked for from the universities, which down the century constituted the last and most formidable bulwark of obscurantism. Salamanca in 1761 rejected a proposal to establish a department of mathematics as 'fraught with dishonour'; Alcalá as late as 1781 had in the 17,000 volumes of its library a mere fifty representative of contemporary science and thought. In the end, forfeiting all claim to respect, they compelled the government interference that turned them into the state institutions they still are today.

The independent thinking of the century was done elsewhere, and notably in the many academies that derived a fruitful impulse from official initiative. First of these was the Academy of the Language founded in 1713, the year of Utrecht. Others followed, of Medicine in 1734, of History in 1738. Ferdinand launched that of Fine Arts in 1752, founding too the first botanical gardens and an astronomical observatory: like his father-in-law in Portugal he showed himself a constant patron of art and learning. It was a portent of the age that its greatest writer should have been the Benedictine monk Feijóo, who from his monastery cell at Oviedo published between 1728 and 1760 thirteen volumes of critical essays – he is Spain's first essayist – ranging over the whole intellectual horizon of his day and dedicated to one supreme purpose, that of uprooting superstition and ignorance and inculcating the spirit of independent enquiry. Ferdinand, showing enlightened despotism in action, intervened in the violent polemics Feijóo stirred up by forbidding in 1750 the publication of further attacks upon him.

The strain of piety and melancholy that Spain bred in successive Habsburgs and Bourbons alike was only less marked in Ferdinand than in his father, and towards the end of his short reign he too had periods when his reason was disturbed. The death of his wife in 1758 left him inconsolable, and just a year later he died, knowing his country appreciably more prosperous and more contented than it had been in two hundred years. By his will he recognized the right to the succession of his eldest half-brother Charles, in whom, as Charles III (1759–88), Isabel Farnese saw her highest ambitions crowned at last.

The new king duly renounced the throne of Naples in favour of his third son, his eldest being of unsound mind, and came to Spain accompanied by his second, who in due course would reveal himself to be far below the calibre of kingship. But Charles himself had proved a very acceptable and successful ruler in Italy, and at forty-three he was still in the prime of vigour and wedded to an active conception of royal statesmanship. He wished Spain great in order that she might play the part of greatness on the international stage. Already from Naples he had protested, and intrigued, against Ferdinand's policy of neutrality; now, the Seven Years' War having not yet run its course, that policy clearly would not last.

The third Family Compact of 1761 bound France and Spain, together with Naples and Parma, in a defensive alliance that involved Spain straightway in war against England. The first victim was Portugal, whose refusal to join the pact Charles chose to interpret as partiality for the enemy; and once again a Franco–Spanish force crossed the border, once again speedy succour came from England and the invaders retired with the winter, having achieved nothing. To the far west and the far east, with England now free to attack openly, Charles soon had cause to regret his presumption. In the Caribbean Havana fell, with enormous booty, and various other strongholds; in the Philippines Manila. France was faring no better, and both countries were glad to get out of a disastrous war with the peace of 1763, which cost Spain Florida, though Havana and Manila she recovered.

France, anxious to keep Spain faithful to a pact whose first fruits had been so inauspicious, now transferred to her the vast but still valueless territory of Louisiana, the inhabitants of which were not induced to accept their new allegiance without some display of force. Farther north, the loss of Quebec marked the end of French supremacy in Canada. In India too her pretensions had collapsed, while nearer home she was constrained to restore Minorca to Britain. These events carried their lesson for Charles, impressing on him the need to extend his reforming zeal to the Indies. The first intendant, an official sent out with a roving commission and wide powers of inspection, supervision, and report, was posted to Cuba in 1765. Before the reign ended they numbered thirty-six and covered all Spanish America save New Granada, the modern Colombia.

An ominous beginning abroad had its matching troubles at home. Charles had returned to Spain a foreigner after his twenty-five years in Naples, and found Madrid by comparison a squalid city, unpaved, undrained, and unlit, lacking in all the urban amenities and made over, the dress of its inhabitants suggested, to conspirators and cut-throats. Europe, it seemed to him, still stopped at the Pyrenees. A Walloon guard, an Italian minister of finance, Squillaci, and a leaning towards French tastes and ideas, the latter strongly tinged with the new secularism, were indications to his new subjects that it was they, and not himself, of whom he expected change. He expected it of a people whose whole history and cast of character made for conservatism, and he expected it by decree. The situation repeated that of 1517 with Charles I newly come from Flanders, Squillaci playing the role now of the earlier cardinal Adrian, and the famous 'Esquilache revolt' of 1766, bringing long simmering grievances to a violent head, the modern rising of the Comuneros.

Charles had presumed to compel the citizenry to abandon overnight their long capes and broad-brimmed slouch hats for short coats and tricorns, and stationed officers in the streets with shears to enforce compliance on the spot. The populace rose in fury against Squillaci, the Walloons, and everything else foreign, and Madrid fell prey to a sudden reign of terror that only subsided when Charles, who had fled for safety to Aranjuez, withdrew the obnoxious measures. It was nine months before he again dared, or condescended, to resume residence in his capital. The particular end had by then been achieved, more tactfully, by making the traditional garb the official uniform of the executioner; but there would be no more foreign ministers, and whatever Charles thought of the Spanish people, who 'cried when they had their faces washed', he realized that they had recovered something of their earlier spirit and could only be led, not driven, along the path of reform.

One major obstacle to reform he saw in the Society of Jesus, to whose activities he had already become disaffected in Naples. Since the first loyalty of Jesuits was not to their sovereign but to the Pope, they had always stood exposed to the charge of being bad citizens; and for long now the Society had been incurring a growing odium throughout Christendom, not merely in circles receptive to the liberal doctrines emanating from France but in the eyes of secular authority everywhere and of the religious orders themselves, on the general ground of an insidious and intolerant striving for power far removed from the ends of true religion. Portugal had expelled them *en masse*, as representing a threat to the interests of the state, in 1759, the year of Charles's arrival in Spain, France on similar grounds in 1764.

In every insurrection or intrigue from the revolt of the Indians of Paraguay in 1753 to the Esquilache riots their hand was seen; and in 1767, without warning even to the Pope, Charles too decreed their expulsion from Spain and all her dominions. To avoid controversy the decree stated no reasons, these being reserved to the royal conscience, and public comment was forbidden: 'I impose silence regarding this matter on all my vassals, it not being incumbent on them to judge or interpret the commands of their sovereign.' This time Charles and Aranda, his new and equally liberal first minister who had likewise lived long abroad, had taken the measure of what the crown might do, and some 10,000 members of the Society from Spain and the Indies were shipped to Italy. In 1773 France and Spain obtained from the Pope, after some pressure and a display of force, its total suppression.

This did not spell the end of priestcraft in Spain, or make of every Spaniard a secularist; but it was a long step towards ending the strangle-hold that the Church had exerted for centuries over the civil fabric of society. And it made possible two other steps. The Jesuits had come to exercise a monopoly not only over the king's conscience, through a long succession of royal confessors, but over the Inquisition, whose rights of jurisdiction in the sphere of the individual conscience, like its constant impingement on that of civil justice, the temper of the age was beginning to call in question.

No less than the Society itself, the Inquisition tended to consider itself a state within the state. And Charles was nothing if not a regalist. The years following on 1767 saw therefore a series of measures all aimed at clipping its prerogatives and restricting its scope. It was forbidden to execute orders from Rome without specific sanction of the Council of Castile, to detain on suspicion, to ban writings until the author had had opportunity to defend himself, to pass judgement on other than strictly religious offences, and was ordered finally to remit to the crown for trial any noble, minister, or other servant of the king. The time approached when Spaniards would once again be able to think and speak like free men. In 1780, in Seville, the Holy Office burnt its last victim, an old woman accused of sorcery; in the next reign it too would hover on the verge of extinction.

The going of the Jesuits meant further the breaking of their hold on education, where secularization was long overdue. The 120 colleges and seminaries which the Society possessed throughout Spain, and especially the College of Nobles in Madrid, founded in 1725 by Philip V and now under its control, had enjoyed a prestige closely related to the entry they commanded to high public office, and were identified with an educational system suggestive of a vested interest in the closed mind. To the universities the competition had been one powerful factor in their decadence. The crown, its interest deeply engaged in the new pattern of studies that should take the place of the old, earmarked for education the sequestered property of the Society, and set itself to a drastic overhaul likewise of the twenty-four so-called universities, few of which had any real claim to the title.

An edict of 1771 required the modernization of all textbooks and curricula in the light of contemporary science, and the filling of chairs, as of places in the aristocratic colleges, by competition. All theological chairs formerly associated with the Jesuits were suppressed. The experimental method in science and in medicine was introduced, and Bacon, Descartes, Locke, and Kant were read and discussed, to the scandalizing of the ultramontane. The crown appointed further a director of each university and instituted visits of inspection. As always, much was decreed that did not take effect; but a new wind was stirring, and the universities felt it.

In the economic field no less the reign witnessed a new upsurge. The abolition of sales- and food-taxes in favour of a single impost remained the dream of successive ministers, but the alcabala, which had soared to fourteen per cent, was reduced by half, and the millions correspondingly lightened, both being remitted where sales were local. In substitution a five per cent tax on land and property rents and a state lottery were introduced, this latter to prove with time the one genuinely popular formula for raising revenue. Thanks to the building of new roads and canals, government stage-coach services made it at last possible, in combination with a new rural police, to journey across country in safety, while agriculture benefited from the double stimulus of irrigation and readier access to markets. Foreigners were brought to Spain to teach new industrial processes in government-established factories or just to settle on the land, the 6,000 Bavarians who, wishing to go to the Indies, were induced instead to found thirteen new communities in the Sierra Morena being the most notable experiment in this sense.

Behind all this activity lay the desire to inculcate anew the spirit of industry and a belief in the nobility of honest labour that the riches of the New World, allied to a false sense of honour, had in an earlier age done so much to kill. A decree of 1773 enunciated the doctrine that there was nothing derogatory for the hidalgo in the exercise of a craft. The creed found an echo in many members of the privileged classes who through education or travel now subscribed to the teachings of the new philanthropy with its corollary of social responsibility. Their energies were canalized in the 'Economic Societies of Friends of the Country' which, originating in the Basque provinces in 1765, spread to Madrid ten years later and thence irradiated over the country, exerting everywhere a powerful influence on charitable enterprises, education, and agriculture. The nation's response to these many and fruitful stimuli was seen in a buoyant revenue and a population increase, over the twenty-nine years of the reign, of one-sixth, to a total of ten and a half million.

In two directions the crown showed itself still loath to take radical measures. Church and nobility, whose self-seeking in earlier times had done so much to depress the third estate, continued to be preserves of privilege and power. The king, as has been noted, had had much clerical support in his action against the Jesuits, but the Church itself lay open to social charges no less serious. Its wealth made the crown seem poor, and rested in large part on the maintenance of a still medieval feudalism. No fewer than 3,148 towns and villages, according to the census of 1787, belonged to ecclesiastical overlords.

The Habsburgs had often turned to the Church for loans or gifts when secular taxation failed: that immunity at least the Bourbons down the eighteenth century did whittle steadily away

until the clergy too paid alcabala, millions, and numerous ecclesiastical dues as well. Reforming ministers concerned themselves
further with the extravagant numbers who sought in the Church
a parasitic existence – the same census returned a total of 2,067
monasteries and 1,122 convents, sheltering 62,000 religious and
71,000 adherents – and with the widespread moral laxity that
inevitably followed. But in many respects the cloak of religion
continued to cover a social cancer, and a power thrown always
on the side of reaction, that down the following century would
have explosive consequences.

The nobility too retained, on the coming of the Bourbons,
much of the power and privilege of centuries before. Philip V
abolished the right of life and death over their vassals still held
by the lords of Aragon, but remained generally respectful, as did
his successors, of their many prerogatives and exemptions before
the law, and even added liberally to their numbers by conferring
titles in reward for services to the state. The Order of Charles III,
founded by this monarch for the purpose, soon greatly exceeded
the number of 60 grand crosses and 200 knighthoods originally
intended. Seventeen cities, 2,358 townships, and 8,818 villages
were in 1787 recognized as pertaining to the nobility and outwith the royal jurisdiction. Administrative and judicial offices,
and even on occasion Church benefices, lay in the gift of their
overlords, to whom the fief paid dues and services several times
higher than accrued to the crown.

The crown did what it could to extend its effective sovereignty,
inquiring into titles and impeding their sale or transfer, sub-
jecting appointments to crown confirmation, reincorporating
estates and townships in the royal patrimony wherever possible,
and levying succession or commutation payments. The exemption
from taxation it left untouched, to the grave detriment of the
exchequer and the perpetuating of social injustice: this was but
one of the anomalies in a social structure that had long outlived
all justification and would become harder of solution the longer
it persisted.

While engaged in so complex and arduous a campaign of
internal reform, Charles was again caught up in an Anglo-French
conflict that posed for Spain a particularly delicate problem.
The revolt of the English colonies in north America in 1776

offered at first glance the eagerly awaited opportunity for a joint settling of accounts with England; and France, approached by the colonies two years later, moved with alacrity in their support. In terms of the Family Compact Spain's place was at her side, and the chance of humbling the great rival of Spanish dominion in the New World no less tempting. To aid colonies in revolt suggested, however, a dangerous undertaking for a colonial power whose grip on its own it knew to be none too secure; and it was with a lively sense of Nemesis to come that Charles first temporized, combining surreptitious help with an offer of mediation, and then in 1779 took the plunge into war, Gibraltar again presenting itself as the immediate target.

Spain was stronger now on land and sea than she had been for a long time, and in conjunction with France the plan of campaign in Europe – invasion of England, siege of Gibraltar, assault on Minorca – seemed feasible enough. The invasion proved one more miserable failure; Gibraltar survived an exacting ordeal. Minorca was, however, recaptured in 1782. Across the Atlantic Florida once more fell into Spanish hands. France as before gained nothing, beyond the embarrassing of England; and once the independence of the British colonies had been accepted as inevitable the disposition of both France and England to make peace brought Spain unwillingly – for she still nourished hopes of Gibraltar – into the settlement of 1783. She had profited something from the war, a rare and gratifying experience. She had also made the eventual loss of her own colonies inevitable.

Charles was now an old man, and had lost much of his ardour for foreign adventuring. One external enterprise remained. Muslim attacks on Spanish shipping, laid it had been hoped for good by a treaty with the emperor of Morocco in 1767, had resumed some years later when the emperor and the dey of Algiers banded together to throw the Spaniards out of Africa, and began by laying siege to Ceuta and Melilla. In 1775 Charles sent an army to their relief, success in which led him into the launching of a major expedition against Algiers that met with overwhelming disaster. Now, in 1783–4, he returned to the attack, and though again repulsed at Algiers he reaped eventually a series of treaties with the various Muslim powers of north Africa, and with Turkey, which by 1786 had put an end to the long grim chapter of piracy in the western Mediterranean, with its concomitants of coastal raids and the enslavement of Christian captives.

A small matter compared with other international issues of the day, this had been a running sore in the country's body politic ever since Isabella captured Granada in 1492; and its healing was a fitting end to a reign which had done more for the advancement of the Spanish people than any other since the days of the same great queen. Charles died in 1788, aged seventy-two, a prey at last to the hereditary melancholy of his line, which a life of intense activity had for long staved off. It was intensified by the intimate personal tragedy that had assailed so many of the kings of Spain on their deathbed, the knowledge that he too was leaving his country to a son wholly inadequate to a responsibility destined, on the eve of the French Revolution, to be heavier than ever.

In Portugal, as in Spain, the second half of the century stands out through the emergence of a strong, enlightened ruler who laboured to the utmost to bring into line with the age a country likewise in danger of remaining stranded on the fringe of progress. Pombal was not a king but a minister, raised through his monarch's insignificance and the challenge of a national disaster to a personal dictatorship that lasted for twenty-six years. The concluding decade of John V's reign Pombal had spent abroad, first in London from 1740 to 1744 as minister plenipotentiary, then in Vienna as mediator for his government in the War of the Austrian Succession. The years in London had a particular influence on his thinking and subsequent policy, implanting in him the double concern to try to raise his country to a comparable pitch of commercial prosperity and to lift it socially and intellectually out of a still largely medieval stagnation.

In 1749 Pombal returned to Portugal, and to ministerial office under the new monarch Joseph I (1750–77), already aware that this programme must involve him in open conflict with the nobility and the Jesuits. Joseph had neither taste nor capacity for public affairs and, noting Pombal's energy and clear-cut ideas, was content he should exercise them. For the next five years he was much occupied, nominally as minister for foreign affairs, with the development and control of commerce with

Brazil, his English experience having convinced him of the greater security and profitability of colonial over foreign trade, and with combating England's grip on the Portuguese economy.

Then befell, on a Sunday morning when the churches were crowded for All Saints' Day masses, the Lisbon earthquake of 1 November 1755. The dimensions of the calamity shocked all Europe. In less than fifteen minutes two-thirds of the city collapsed in ruins, a tidal wave inundated the low-lying districts, and by evening a hundred conflagrations had taken possession of what remained. Churches had caved in on top of their congregations; the magnificent patriarch's palace and forty-two great houses of the nobility, thirty monasteries and a score of convents, many large public buildings, and countless private houses were reduced to rubble. Estimates of the dead ranged from 6,000 to 80,000. Panic, soon degenerating into anarchy, gripped the living.

It was the earthquake that made Pombal all-powerful and his position impregnable. When the king and everyone else lost their heads he kept his, and emerged from the crisis as prime minister. 'Bury the dead and feed the living' was his simple prescription for the moment, but out of the ashes he planned and built the new Lisbon that is still today one of the world's finest capitals. Out of the destruction of records and dislocation of business he succeeded too in dealing British interests in the capital, and in the port wine industry in the north, a number of shrewd blows.

The Wine Company of the Upper Douro, created in 1756 to develop this industry in the national interest, had other consequences as well, control over production and quality causing a rise in prices which touched off riots in Oporto in the following year. These were put down by Pombal with an individual and collective severity – twenty-six death sentences, the billeting of 3,000 troops on the city, and suppression of the municipal council – indicative to the nation at large of the iron rule in store for it. Soon it was found convenient to accuse the Jesuits of having instigated the uprising.

They, and the nobility, held the centre of the stage for the next two years. Pombal had already clashed with the Society over the earthquake, which it interpreted to the populace as divine retribution for the people's sins and for lack of piety in high places, while he would have it accepted as a natural phenomenon. As the first anniversary approached, some of its members prophesied a second convulsion; and one Malagrida, the most prominent of their number and a man of infinite prestige both in Brazil, where he had won the reputation of a Portuguese St Francis Xavier, and at home, published a pamphlet calling on the people to renew their faith and to contribute to Jesuit funds. This to Pombal was a direct challenge. Waiting till the day had passed without earthquake, he denounced the pamphlet in a royal edict as heretical and the author and his fellow-Jesuits as having used the disaster 'to terrify feeble and superstitious minds', and had Malagrida banished across the Tagus. A struggle for the soul of Portugal was engaged.

It had in fact begun in Brazil, as a trial of strength between the missions and secular authority, over a transfer from Spain of the Jesuit reductions in Paraguay agreed in a boundary treaty of 1750 in return for the River Plate colony of Sacramento. Pombal's brother, a governor in Brazil, had been a member of the frontier commission on that occasion, when an Indian uprising took place, instigated by Jesuits, which lasted for three years; 'the regulars', he later reported of Brazil in general, 'are the most powerful enemy of the state.' In 1755 Pombal declared all Indians in Brazil to be free and forbade to priests the exercise of civil authority. These decrees, not enforced till two years later, likewise provoked resistance and disturbances, and a number of Jesuit missionaries were deported. News of this was published, and the action officially defended, in Lisbon shortly after the Malagrida incident, and all Jesuits in the palace, where they were confessors to the whole royal family, were evicted. The Society was thus thrown forcibly into the opposition camp.

The issue with the aristocracy came to a head over an attempted assassination of the king. Pombal to the nobles was an upstart, and he had never forgiven them for their haughty refusal to admit him to their circle. The rift bound them the more closely to the old order which was their natural intellectual climate; and, the king being completely under the sway of their enemy, they centred instead round his brother Peter. Joseph and his Spanish queen had four daughters, no sons: Peter was the suitor most canvassed for the eldest daughter's hand, and a papal dispensation for the marriage had already been obtained in the previous reign.

When the years passed and no marriage took place, Maria being now twenty-three years old, suspicion fell inevitably on Pombal. There were grounds therefore for wishing either him or Joseph himself, without whose support Pombal was nothing, out of the way, and Joseph offered the easier target. On a September night in 1758 his carriage drove into an ambush. It failed, and Pombal, soon knowing where to look, arrested members of two of the most illustrious houses in the land, the Aveiro and Távora families. Their guilt being established to Pombal's satisfaction, five were broken on the wheel and strangled and one, a woman, beheaded.

Nothing comparable had been known in Portugal since the fifteenth century, when John II set himself to break the power of the nobles by violent despatch. That power was now infinitely less, but Pombal was more determined even than John to brook no opposition; and having dealt now with this potential enemy he went on, or back, to the next. From evidence at the trial, given under torture, the Jesuits emerged as only less deeply implicated in the crime, and Pombal seized his opportunity. Thirteen leading members of the Society, including Malagrida, were arrested, and throughout the country troops surrounded their seminaries while the fate of the Society was discussed.

The Pope, reading the portents, asked of Joseph that it should be reformed and not expelled; but Pombal kept the letter from reaching the king, and in the end diplomatic relations with Rome were severed. The decree of expulsion, indicting the Society as 'corrupt, deplorably alienated from its divine institution, rebellious, and perfidious', bore date a year to the day after the abortive attempt on the king's life, his minister being at pains to associate the Society and the nobility in the same crime and the same condemnation; and over a thousand of its members were shipped to the papal dominions and there thrown on the papal charity.

Not all suffered expulsion. For many, including the thirteen aforementioned and those identifiable as having led the uprising in Paraguay, exile was too gentle a fate and they were consigned to prison, to rot forgotten. Malagrida Pombal did not forget.

Preferring to trial for treason – he had wrung from Rome, but never used, consent to the trial of religious before a civil tribunal – the subtler vengeance of condemnation by the Church itself, he revived against him his first charge of heresy and delivered him to the Inquisition, the inquisitor-general being Pombal's own brother. In 1761 the accused was burnt at the stake. Shortly before, the long-deferred royal marriage had taken place, a preventive rather than positive act of state, to guard – with memories of 1383 in mind – against the complications and dangers of admitting a foreign prince as consort.

Pombal's attention up till now had been centred on civil affairs, the one thing he had taken over from the previous reign being the general desire for peace. When Spain and France, at war now with England, would make a place for Portugal in the Family Pact, he scorned the invitation and remained faithful to the English alliance. But he scorned no less the intimidation to which that fidelity forthwith exposed him and, all unprepared for hostilities, declared war in 1762 against those who would presume to free Portugal 'from the heavy shackles of British dominion'.

The situation of fifty years earlier was renewed, with Anglo-Portuguese troops fighting Franco-Spanish on both sides of the frontier; and equally inconclusively, for the main conflict lay elsewhere and neither France nor Spain was faring well. After six months of skirmishing and another six of negotiations the war ended. Portugal had survived unfreed, finding common ground now with her late aggressors in the attitude of all three to the Society of Jesus. When, under joint pressure suggested by Pombal, a new Pope finally acquiesced in its extinction, Portugal resumed relations with the Vatican, to the latter's considerable relief; for it had feared Pombal capable of going the whole way to the declaration of an independent national Church.

No more shocks of war disturbed Pombal's rule. The repercussions of the attempt on Joseph's life had gone far beyond the trial, more and more of the nobles falling suspect in ever widening circles of delation or implication until the prisons were full and an atmosphere of terror permeated society. The dictator knew himself now all-powerful, and hated as he was feared. He moved surrounded by a guard of royal dragoons who watched over him with swords drawn day and night, and what he willed was law. Yet he found, with all dictators, the destructive part of his task easier than the constructive, and, like his contemporary Charles in Spain, that to decree was one thing, to effect another.

One difficulty lay in the lack of an educated middle class to implement his reforms. The degree of literacy in the country was inadequate even to its business needs, and in the end Pombal found himself another Philip II buried in paper work, with state business at a standstill when he was not there to attend to it. A second was the pathetic fallacy that a people could be carried along, without consultation, in directions in which it did not wish to go. A thousand years of tradition did not yield to one man's desire to create overnight a secular state, and the ground had still to be prepared in which French philosophic or English economic doctrines might hope to take root. Hence the ease and rapidity with which so much of his accomplishment would, on his going, be swept away.

At bottom, as he perceived clearly, the question was one of education; and since the expulsion of the Jesuits meant for Portugal even more than for Spain the collapse of the existing system, there offered here a first and most urgent field for action. The university of Coimbra had fallen into Jesuit hands early in the sixteenth century, to the eclipse of a budding intellectual renaissance from which, with the recruitment of eminent foreign scholars, much had been hoped. Ever since, it had sunk steadily lower until now, as Pombal knew from his own student days, it retained of a university only the name. In 1559 another Jesuit university had been founded at Evora which had languished no less until, in 1759, he suppressed it as no longer serving any purpose.

Thereafter he set his own hand to the plough, creating grammar schools, a College of Nobles in 1761, and a royal board of censorship which, replacing that of the Inquisition, proceeded to license much that till then had been forbidden and which exercised also many of the functions of a modern ministry of education. Crowning the whole was the elaborate reform at Coimbra begun in 1772 in which, appointing himself 'lieutenant-general of the university', he personally supervised every detail as though it were a military operation. There could, however, be no improvising teachers by decree, and much of this too proved still-born. The Inquisition lost much of its remaining power when in 1769 he made its tribunals subject to civil procedure and declared their hearings open to the public. Four years later he formally abolished slavery in Portugal, and put an end too to the so galling distinctions still made between 'old' and 'new' Christians.

In the economic life of the country the dictator was likewise indefatigable, reorganizing the exchequer, bringing in foreign experts to stimulate old industries or found new ones, setting up control boards and trading companies, regulating everything by *ad hoc* decrees which not infrequently contradicted one another. His reforming zeal extended to Brazil, where his spacious gesture of emancipation of 1755 had, to the extent that it proved effective, the incidental result of greatly stimulating the demand for negro slaves. Removing the capital from Bahia to Rio de Janeiro, he did much to centralize administration; and by ending serious discrimination against creoles in the matter of public office he removed a chief incentive to the cry for independence which was shortly to rock the Spanish colonies.

Joseph died in 1777. The only purpose of his long years as king having been to keep Pombal in power, men hailed his death as ending a reign of terror. The prisons were thrown open to reveal the full horror of Pombal's arbitrary rule; and the great dictator knew the greatest stroke of fortune in his close on eighty years in being allowed to retire to his country house and there live unmolested – apart from the stigma of 'infamous criminal' pronounced on him by a royal decree of 1781 – till his death in 1782.

Maria I (1777–1816) and her consort Peter were crowned together. She was forty-three, he sixty: both had been excluded by Pombal from all contact with public affairs, and were too old now to learn the art of government, while their interests were completely domestic and pious. Apart from the reopening of the conspiracy case against the nobles, which resulted in the rehabilitation of all those who had suffered save only the duke of Aveiro and three of his servants, and from the dispensing of much sympathy and beneficence to ex-Jesuits, the new rulers professed no policy beyond the undoing of all that Pombal had done, especially in the matter of Church and state; and power fell straightway into the hands of the leading nobles, now recalled to court, as though the dictator had never been.

They found an empty treasury, with a record of salaries, dividends, and pensions unpaid since 1763; and for years the watchword was perforce retrenchment. All public works were suspended, subsidies to industry cut, and the royal establishment severely pruned. Peter's death in 1786 plunged Maria into a depression which, soon aggravated by the grim tidings from France, eventually unhinged her judgement. In 1792 her son John assumed responsibility, though not the title of regent until seven years later. Maria was to survive, long bereft of her faculties, till 1816.

The events of the closing decade of the century were such as to make both countries wish fervently that the Pyrenees could be reconstituted the effective barrier they had so long proved. France, with its fearful object lesson in 1789 of what could happen to a country which sacrificed everything, including the people, on the altar of royal aggrandizement, lay uncomfortably near; and Family Pacts and much intermarriage of princes made it nearer still. The peoples of Spain and Portugal continued firm in their religious and monarchical sentiment; but they had been ruled no less autocratically from above, by rulers who had looked precisely on France as the source of political and social enlightenment, and some contagion was inevitable. Strength and wisdom in their rulers now might still have averted the worst blasts of the storm, or allowed at least the two ships of state some semblance of control over their respective courses. It was the tragedy of both that at this juncture of destiny they should have fallen instead into the hands of weakness and folly, and drifted aimlessly in consequence until, colliding, together they were swept into the maelstrom.

In Spain Charles IV (1788–1808) was dull, amiable, and forty, wholly lacking experience in statecraft and thus one more monarch doomed to be ruled by an imperious wife, María Luisa of Parma, grand-daughter of the Farnese, and whatever favourite she might elect. The French Revolution broke before he was well seated on the throne, and his every act was done therefore under the shadow of the terror. Suppression of all newspapers, a watch

on the frontier, the requiring from every foreigner in Spain –
half of them Frenchmen – of an oath of allegiance to the Spanish
throne and the Catholic faith: these availed nothing.

In Paris the National Assembly had proclaimed its sovereignty,
which other powers had either to acknowledge or defy, and
Louis XVI was a prisoner, his life in danger. Acquiescence
carried the gravest implications for Charles's own throne;
defiance meant war, for which Spain was utterly unready. Late
in 1792 the Assembly forced the issue with a blunt demand that
Spain choose between a close alliance and open hostilities. It was
at this moment, when the future of Spain hung in the balance,
that the last of the old ministers surviving from the previous reign,
Aranda himself, was jettisoned and the favourite appeared.

Godoy was a young guards officer whom María Luisa had
advanced to the rank of grandee, councillor of state, and now, at
twenty-five, prime minister. Though she was twice his age and
the mother of a large family, he was also notoriously her lover:
responsibility and respect were thus dragged down together.
But for the international situation even the Spanish people could
doubtfully have swallowed the double insult; but the execution
of Louis XVI, whom Charles had done his utmost to save, forced
the larger issue, and in 1793 Spain found herself again, as in the
old Habsburg days, in a war with France that for once commanded intense popular enthusiasm. Under successive defeats
the ardour soon evaporated, and after two years Spain gladly
agreed to a settlement and the invading French armies once more
evacuated Spanish soil. Godoy, having shown no genius for war,
received the title of Prince of the Peace.

His next step showed his statesmanship. Offering the Convention, by the treaty of San Ildefonso of 1796, an offensive and
defensive alliance against England, he not only made inevitable
a war with the latter from which renewed humiliation and loss
could alone be expected, but tied his country to the chariot
wheels of a republic still bound on courses predictable in nothing
save in that they must prove anathema to everything Spain had
ever stood for. Convention, Directory, Consulate, Empire,
Napoleon, all alike treated Spain thereafter with contempt as a
tool ready to their hands.

The war against England was declared forthwith, and for

Spain proved disastrous from the start. Her fleet suffered an overwhelming reverse at Cape St Vincent, Trinidad was lost and again, for a spell, Minorca; while France showed complete unconcern at abandoning her ally and seeking, if in vain, a separate peace. She went further, overrunning the duchy of Parma and making of an accommodation with its ruler an excuse for extorting from Spain the return of Louisiana. Spain now had more to fear from her friend than from her enemies. Paris had begun giving orders to Madrid, and Godoy's reward for his extremes of compliance was his removal from office early in 1798, at the demand of Paris, as not compliant enough, specifically in the matter of forcing the hand of Portugal.

Portugal had shared all Spain's initial alarm at the events of 1789, had proposed that her neighbour adhere to the alliance with Britain and, when eventually Spain déclared war on the Convention, had sent an expeditionary force to her help. In return she had been treated by Godoy as France was now treating him. Left out of the settlement of 1795, she found herself still technically at war with France while she watched Spain change sides. Godoy now served Portugal with the same choice which had brought him to power, alliance with France or war; while France for her part made impossible demands – the cession of a large part of northern Brazil, trading advantages, a vast indemnity – as the price of peace. In fact the treaty of San Ildefonso made secret provision for compelling Portugal to abandon the English connexion. But Portugal, whatever her military weakness, had at least been spared a Godoy, and remained faithful. In the summer of 1797 English forces, military and naval, arrived in the Tagus, and a Portuguese squadron served in the following year at the battle of the Nile and in the blockade of Malta, to the intense annoyance of Napoleon.

Charles tried hard to arrive at some solution which would spare him the embarrassment of attacking his Portuguese son-in-law, and the even greater embarrassment of seeing the French troops offered in support enter Spain. To open the gates to the dread contagion of atheistic republicanism threatened a calamity only comparable in peninsular history to count Julian's act in bringing in the Muslim in 711. Rather than this he contemplated for a moment invading Portugal on his own account before

Napoleon could return from Egypt; but the moment passed, and the First Consul showed himself more intransigent by far than the Convention. Godoy, who had continued to be the force behind the scenes, was restored to power, as committed to France as ever, and in 1801 France and Spain agreed on a joint ultimatum.

Portugal would close her ports to English ships, open them to those of France and Spain, pay indemnities, and deliver to Spain as pledge one-fourth of her territory, or she would be jointly occupied, France contributing 15,000 men for the purpose. On her refusal Spain invaded, and Godoy himself led his army in what proved to be a military parade through the Alemtejo. An orange-branch plucked on Portuguese soil, which he sent to María Luisa as proud trophy, gave a name to this three-weeks' 'War of the Oranges', that ended of necessity in capitulation; for England had had to withdraw all her forces and Portugal stood defenceless, still paying in this direction too the price of Pombal. Much squabbling, and some double-dealing, followed between the victors over the terms to be dictated. France was to receive her territorial concessions in Brazil, a heavy indemnity, and, most important, the banning of English shipping from Portuguese harbours; Spain held on to the frontier town of Olivença, Portugal's one irredentist claim ever since.

Something not in the settlement mattered vastly more. While Spain had been invading Portugal, the 15,000 French troops, unneeded for that gallant enterprise, had invaded Spain. Godoy, returned home with the title of generalissimo of the army and the navy and flushed with martial prowess, demanded of Napoleon that he withdraw the unwanted guests. 'Is the king of Spain tired of reigning?' was Napoleon's reply, and without troubling to ask permission he sent further large forces across the Pyrenees. The gesture made, he subsequently withdrew them; but in negotiating with England the peace of Amiens, signed in the following year 1802, he sacrificed Spain's title to Trinidad, regaining all his own colonial losses, without deigning to inform Spain.

From that date, and especially from the marriage in October 1802 of prince Ferdinand, heir to the throne, with María Antonia of Naples, there began to form in Madrid an opposition party, centred in the palace itself. Ferdinand hated his mother and Godoy, María Antonia hated France, and the Spanish people hated the whole trend and conduct of the country's affairs. When in 1803 England and France renewed hostilities and Napoleon, to raise funds, sold Louisiana to the United States in violation of a treaty obligation to Spain never to alienate the territory, the feeling was exacerbated.

But the giving of orders continued, and that same year, summoned to make immediate declaration of war on England under threat that Spain herself would otherwise be occupied, Godoy held himself fortunate to be allowed to buy a nominal and temporary neutrality by agreeing to a monthly payment instead of 6,000,000 francs, Portugal being assessed at 1,000,000. Neutrality proved not to be in France's gift, for England was not deceived. Seizing a treasure fleet from the Indies, she forced the luckless Godoy into the open. War was redeclared in December 1804, and Napoleon's concentration now on the invasion of England started a chain of events which led ten months later to Trafalgar, where perished, with French hopes, the naval might of Spain.

Another Isabel Farnese, Godoy cared nothing for Spain. Driven by the lust for power, he sought now, in the redrawing of the map of Europe he saw in progress, to carve out for himself some principality. Since the adventure into Portugal his gaze had been fixed in that direction and he had tried repeatedly to compromise Napoleon in this sense, Napoleon using the knowledge thus gained to bind Godoy the more closely to his own purposes. Trafalgar foiled the possibility for a time; but in compensation for the failure to invade England the emperor could now boast himself, after Austerlitz, supreme on the continent and in a position, it seemed, to take Portugal by a nod. In May 1806 Godoy paid over to Napoleon 24,000,000 francs from an impoverished exchequer to forward a project, of which the emperor had feigned acceptance, whereby southern Portugal would go to Godoy, the northern part to be at the disposal of Napoleon, who was to take also for France the Portuguese overseas empire.

For the moment he was content to take the money, and Godoy saw in this, and in the new coalition then forming against France, the shape of things to come. A clumsy attempt to change sides, promptly rebuffed by the English, reached Napoleon's ears at Jena, and he vowed in revenge to destroy utterly the Bourbons of Spain. His plans, laid with guile, were unexpectedly furthered by Ferdinand, who chose this moment to imitate Godoy in self-abasement to the emperor, supplicating a matrimonial alliance – his Neapolitan wife having lately died – and asking French help in overthrowing the detested favourite. Godoy meantime was himself trying to recover lost ground, and, blind as ever to the national interest, sent 15,000 Spanish troops to join the emperor's forces in Germany.

Napoleon by this time had decreed his continental blockade of England, in which Portugal had a vital role to play, and he despatched an ultimatum to Lisbon demanding an immediate declaration of war. Being assured of British naval support, Portugal again refused, as had been foreseen; and France and Spain thereupon signed, in November 1807, the treaty of dismemberment under which Napoleon, while guaranteeing the independence and integrity of Spain, would march through Spain 26,000 men, and another 40,000 if need be, to the conquest of Portugal.

How much his guarantees amounted to appeared from the fact that nine days earlier Junot had already crossed the Pyrenees without asking Spain's leave. None knew then that the consequences of so doing would determine the fate of Napoleon himself. The ensuing drama was played out in three acts and an epilogue. The first concerned Portugal, the second Spain; the third would make of the Peninsula a common battle-ground for the struggle against Napoleon. The epilogue, set across the Atlantic, was to ring down the curtain on both countries' overseas empire.

Junot, marching straight across Spain, reached Lisbon late in November. There had been no opposition: all that the British fleet anchored in the Tagus could do was to blockade the city. But in one vital particular the enemy had been foiled. On British advice, and escorted by British warships, the regent John with the royal family and the court, some two thousand persons in all and much treasure, had sailed for Brazil two days before Junot arrived. Much in the history of both Portugal and Brazil was to hinge on the decision. Meanwhile Napoleon was denied any title to sovereignty or claim to loyalty that a cowed or complacent crown might have placed in his hands; and though Junot duly declared to a bewildered and leaderless people that the house of Braganza had ceased to reign, the reality proved to be far other.

There was no mention, needless to say, of Godoy. Junot, who was to intrigue himself, equally in vain, for the vacant throne, would govern in the name of the French emperor. Improving on a precaution already taken in Spain, he disbanded the Portuguese army, regrouped its core as a Portuguese legion, and sent the nine regiments of this to fight for Napoleon elsewhere, in Spain, Germany, Russia, and eventually at Waterloo. French generals administered the country as military governors, and delivered it up to brutal spoliation and outrage.

13

The Great Experiment

In Spain the year 1808 was a year of destiny. It opened ominously with the arrival, unbidden and unheralded, of two French army corps which proceeded to occupy the north of the country. Shortly before, Godoy had uncovered a plot of prince Ferdinand to dethrone his father and, it was alleged, murder his mother; and the Escorial had seen re-enacted the events of 1568 when Philip II in person arrested his own son and heir, the tragic Don Carlos, on a similar charge. Charles IV, the last shred of personal dignity gone, announced the treachery to his people and to Napoleon. The former refused belief, for Ferdinand was their only hope against the hated Godoy, whom they suspected of having engineered the whole; the latter saw the time ripe to sweep away the entire pathetic brood, and forbore even to consult further with Madrid. Godoy and Ferdinand tried each to convince himself that the French troops were coming to advance his own purposes.

By March, when the invaders, numbering now over 100,000, were in possession of Barcelona, Pamplona, and most of the other northern fortresses, and a demand came from Napoleon for a new treaty which would cede to him Spain north of the Ebro, the grim reality stood unmasked at last, and too late. Godoy's base plans for Portugal were Napoleon's for Spain, except that there would be no partition. As Murat marched south on Madrid the court in panic fled to Aranjuez; fortune holding, it would continue thence to Seville and, following the Portuguese example, to America. In Aranjuez a tumultuous mob stirred up by Ferdinand's agents stormed and sacked Godoy's mansion, thirsting for his blood while he lay concealed in a roll of matting. Close by, in the royal palace, the king and queen trembled for their lives and Ferdinand stalked triumphant. Charles bowed to the inevitable and announced his abdication, and Ferdinand returned to Madrid as king to find that Murat with his army had occupied it the day before.

The remainder of this sorriest chapter in the history of the Spanish crown is soon told. Immediately repenting his act, Charles asked Napoleon to restore him to the throne. Ferdinand, aware that he depended entirely on the emperor's recognition, and deluded by a report that the emperor himself was on his way to Madrid, was persuaded to set out to meet him and lured step by step to Burgos, to Vitoria, to the frontier, till he found himself, wholly disillusioned now and virtually a prisoner, in Bayonne. To Bayonne came too, with a French escort, Charles and María Luisa, and Godoy, to plead their suit. There Napoleon forced from the son a renunciation of the throne in favour of his father, from the father another in his own favour, and, appointing them residences in France, dismissed one royal line more from his mind. He had already offered the throne to his brother Joseph. Later, in St Helena, he would trace his downfall to that day's work.

The occasion of the rising of the Madrid populace on 2 May 1808 was the departure for France, again at Napoleon's orders, of the remaining members of the royal family. Its significance lay, not in the demonstration that Spaniards were still indissolubly wedded to the monarchy, however corrupt, or in the brutality and carnage of the ensuing retaliation by the French, but in the lighting of a spark which was to fire the country from end to end and would not be put out till the last Frenchman had been killed or driven back across the Pyrenees.

In the *dos de mayo*, that has been held ever since Spain's proudest hour, the Spaniard found himself again after two centuries of repression. In many ways he would be fighting, over the ensuing years, for the wrong ends; nor would he pause to consider that the only justification he could have alleged for his continuing devotion to the crown was this opportunity, arising out of its gross betrayal of him, to show himself still a man and not a chattel. But the immediate motive was sound, and clear, enough. After wars of imperialism and wars of religion and wars of succession into which he had been plunged unconsulted, this was a war of independence, and his own.

In Madrid French strength was overwhelming, and both the Council of Castile and the government Ferdinand had left behind him proved the equal of their master in sycophancy. But

Madrid was never Castile, still less Spain, and the country witnessed now a resurgence of that local, even separatist, spirit which had so often been its strength. Within weeks there sprang up in the various provincial centres from Galicia to Cadiz, from Valencia to Badajoz, *juntas* for the organization of defence and the raising of militia which often had to begin by overthrowing the symbols and henchmen of central authority and which showed an initial reluctance to merge their own effort, even for military advantage, with those of neighbouring provinces. The first region so to organize itself was Asturias, where that other reconquest of Spain from the Muslim had had its origin so many centuries before.

French troops continuing to pour into the country – the 120,000 of early June had become by mid-August 160,000 – the Asturians sent an urgent appeal to England, the late enemy, which met with an immediate response. But, unaided, Spain still inflicted some heavy defeats on the enemy. Bailén, where a French army capitulated in July, and Saragossa, which withstood a furious assault, a six-weeks' siege, and desperate street-to-street, house-to-house fighting when at length the French broke through, only to fly in the end, gave Napoleon the measure of his new enemy; and when Joseph 'the Intruder' was forced to abandon Madrid late in July, after a reign of ten days, to join the French armies then retreating beyond the Ebro, he knew that he must himself come to Spain.

By now the cause of Spain and of Portugal had become one, and the two countries were together again in spirit as they had not been since the expulsion of the Muslim. The rising in Spain had compelled Junot to release some of his forces for the new front, while his Spanish contingent, which had been garrisoning Oporto, changed sides and crossed back into Galicia. In Portugal too, therefore, the liberation movement began in the north, with the formation as in Spain of defence juntas first in Oporto and soon everywhere.

The appeal to England had reached London just as Wellesley was about to sail with 10,000 men for an attack on Spain in the Indies: he sailed instead to attack France in the Peninsula. Moore followed with as many more, and soon the British navy was able to transport back, from Denmark, 10,000 of those Spanish troops which Godoy had made over to Napoleon. One battle, at Torres Vedras in August 1808, settled the issue momentarily in Portugal, and by the convention of Sintra Junot and his forces, with much of their booty, were allowed to sail for France in British ships, to fight again another day. John's council of regency again governed the country, and an Englishman, Beresford, was appointed commander-in-chief of the Portuguese army.

Napoleon with the 300,000 French troops he assembled in Spain succeeded in reversing the tide of battle. Throughout the war the Spaniards were to prove as inept strategically as they were redoubtable in the harassing attrition of the guerrilla tactics which down the centuries they had made peculiarly their own. Madrid would change hands several times, a matter rather of political than of military import; but 1809 was the year of the French. Moore fell back in his disastrous retreat on Corunna, Saragossa succumbed at last after a second and no less desperate siege lasting two months, and Gerona after eight. Soult on the French side fared worst in his two attempts to reoccupy Portugal, finding his match in Wellesley, but the latter's great victory at Talavera, though it won him his dukedom of Wellington, was largely thrown away by Spanish failure to cooperate in following it up; and Ocaña, where a Spanish army equally suffered resounding defeat, laid Andalusia wide open to the French. By the spring of 1810 the enemy were in possession of Cordoba, Granada, and Seville, and had laid siege to Cadiz, now the last refuge and hope of the patriot cause.

Had it not been for the activities of the *guerrilleros* everywhere, and for Portugal, that cause might have been deemed lost. But Portugal, and the old alliance, held the key to independence even for Spain. Napoleon realized as much, and after occupying Andalusia he launched, early in 1810, what was intended to be a supreme effort in the west under Masséna, Soult holding a second army in reserve in the south. Wellington drew the former back to the lines of Torres Vedras, now so fortified that the Frenchman judged them inexpugnable and eventually returned to Spain having wasted nine months and achieved nothing. When Soult at length moved to his support it was several weeks too late. By May 1811 the French were out of Portugal for good.

Napoleon had had to leave the Peninsula, conscious of having overcommitted himself, for the still more calamitous campaign awaiting him in Russia; and Wellington, his caution and patience now handsomely rewarded, advanced into Spain to reap a series of victories – Albuera, Ciudad Rodrigo, Badajoz, Arapiles, Valladolid – that compelled the enemy to lift the siege of Cadiz in August 1812 and evacuate the whole of Andalusia in order to counter the threat to Madrid. Wellington made his triumphal entry into the capital that same month, withdrawing shortly after to winter again in Portugal.

The news from Russia, and the summoning of Soult's division to that front early in 1813, gave promise that that year's campaign would be the last. When Wellington advanced once more, his plan now to cut the road to the north, Joseph left Madrid for the last time and with as much plunder as he could carry hastened through Valladolid and Burgos towards the French frontier. At Vitoria he found Wellington awaiting him, and there in June the last major battle took place. Joseph lost most of his treasure, including his own coach and private papers, but was able to cross into France.

Some pockets of French resistance in Catalonia, Aragon, and Valencia were not finally cleared till the following spring; but the Peninsular War – to Spaniards and Portuguese the War of Independence – was for all practical purposes over, and won. Wellington, continuing his victory march into France, saw Napoleon, the master of Europe, reel under blow after blow until, within fifteen days of the last surrender in Spain, the un-maker of kings and forcer of abdications had himself abdicated and seen his empire shrunk to the island of Elba.

These six years had witnessed, in one sense, merely the latest, as it would not be the last, in the long series of invasions, of struggles for the soil and the soul of the two peninsular peoples. Their true importance lies rather in the complex political history which followed on the administrative vacuum left by the collapse of the throne and all its institutions, and in the paradox that the invaders did not in fact suffer total defeat, inasmuch as they left behind a ferment of ideas that set Spaniards – and Portuguese – at issue among themselves and sowed the seeds of what has been in effect a continuing civil war ever since.

By 1814 the Spanish people held its destiny in its own hands, and for the rest of the century would be freer from external molestation or involvement than it had ever been in the modern age. Yet over the century it was to know more years of war than any other country in Europe, and social peace only when and to the extent that it again resigned that destiny into the hands of autocracy. Much the same, in its degree, can be said of Portugal. The legacy of the French Revolution went deep.

Joseph had been at once aware of the political problem, and within a week of his proclamation by Napoleon as king of Spain had convoked a Cortes at Bayonne for June 1808. Attended by some sixty-five renegade nobles and others who had followed Charles and Ferdinand in their subservience to the emperor, it had before it, and approved, a draft constitution which, since it could never be put into effect, became an empty gesture. It was nonetheless an enlightened document, such as Ferdinand could never have subscribed to, and stressed thereby the acute dilemma of the intelligent patriot, who throughout the war was constantly exposed to finding his intelligence and his patriotism pulling in opposite directions. An independent judiciary, a common law for all, freedom of the individual and of the press, parliamentary control over finance, and a moderating second chamber were among the principles it enshrined.

On the other side meantime authority had disintegrated, and its reintegration was soon felt by the regional juntas as a pressing need. By September 1808 they had constituted in Aranjuez a Central Junta which organized itself as a government and assumed direction of the war. Napoleon's coming drove it, in December, to Seville, and a year later to Cadiz, where it too planned to hold Cortes. The initial problem of representation in a country largely in the hands of the enemy was met by choosing provisional delegates for the occupied provinces, and for the Indies, from such nationals as were in or could reach Cadiz.

The real issue was the nature and function of a new assembly. Some wanted simply to restore the old, going back to Villalar and assuming an eventual return of the monarchy as before; others looked forward to building a régime of constitutional guarantees secure against relapse into personal autocracy. Eventually the conservative view prevailed, with the important modification that there should be no calling by or distinction of the traditional three estates; and the Central Junta resigned its powers to a regency council of five, still more conservative in cast, which eventually summoned Cortes for September 1810.

From the very first session, however, the initiative passed to the reformers; and out of their deliberations there came an attempt to reshape the nation's whole political structure, of which it may be said that almost everything in Spain's subsequent history is the direct consequence. The circumstances have their importance, for this most solemn and fateful chapter in the country's political record was embarked upon while the enemy hammered at the gates, and was carried through by a body whose representative character and authority were, like its deliberations themselves, largely a matter of faith.

In retrospect two considerations proclaim that the moment could only be then or never. Only the *de facto* vacancy of the throne made possible free discussion on the fundamental question, the relationship between crown and people. And only the total collapse, brought about by the French and the war, of the traditional fabric of society made possible a new concept of national unity based not alone on the ending of regionalism and differential fueros – to the achieving of this earlier Bourbons had already gone a long way – but on the suppression of the feudal jurisdictions still wielded by Church and nobility, spheres of anachronistic abuse into which, as has been noted, the crown had scarcely dared to venture.

The 105 deputies, forty-eight of them substitutes, acting as a constituent Cortes, the first in their country's history, declared this to be the depository of national sovereignty and of the legislative power, the executive vesting in the regency council, and proceeded thereafter to legislate. Discussion quickly revealed the profound cleavage between reformers and conservers: 'liberals' and 'serviles' they came to call each other, and the former added a new term to European politics. The charter they eventually evolved, the constitution of Cadiz of 1812, was destined for long after to serve as a cause and a banner for which men would fight and die.

In many respects a compromise, in others it bears only too clearly the imprint of the background against which it took shape. In the main the liberals won the day and produced a liberal and even revolutionary document whose 384 articles aimed at creating, if not a new heaven and a new earth, an unrecognizably new Spain. Much of its reforming vigour was contributed by spokesmen for the New World, who had their particular interest in drafting the terms of what to them, even more than to peninsular Spaniards, constituted a declaration of rights.

The nation, 'free and independent and the patrimony of no family or individual,' was defined as comprising all Spaniards of both hemispheres, and its territory, 'the Spains', as Spain together with the 'overseas provinces', a Spaniard being any free man born and domiciled therein. Sovereignty, and hence the right to establish fundamental laws, resided in the nation, the form of this being declared to be a limited hereditary monarchy and its religion, to perpetuity, Catholicism. The making of laws was the prerogative of the Cortes with the king, the latter having right of deferment but not of veto; their application the prerogative of the courts.

An elective single-chamber Cortes – one deputy to 70,000 citizens throughout both hemispheres – would meet for three months each year, with a permanent deputation, half its number to be from overseas, bridging the sessions, and would be totally renewed every two years. Its functions were to include, with the making and interpreting of laws, control of taxation, of expenditure, and of the size of the armed forces, and a watching brief over freedom of the press and the responsibility of ministers and public servants.

The monarch was held answerable for public order and security, justice, appointing magistrates and bishops, choosing his ministers, declaring war, and making peace. A council of state appointed by the king on nomination by the Cortes would advise him, four only of its members being ecclesiastics and four only grandees, this being the extent of the recognition given to the two upper estates of tradition; a minimum of twelve others would come from overseas. The inviolability of the subject, an independent judiciary, a common law and common taxation for all without exception or privilege were, with one other, the chief remaining provisions.

That other, being the first of twelve restrictions on the royal power, laid down that on no pretext might the king prevent, suspend, or dissolve any meeting of Cortes, any so advising him to be proceeded against as traitors. In this the deputies had laid their finger on the one reason above all others why the medieval Cortes had failed to develop into the bulwark of popular liberties they had given promise of becoming.

The constitution was proclaimed with much ceremony and rejoicing on 19 March 1812, the fourth anniversary of Godoy's arrest and Charles IV's abdication. It embodied an eloquent commentary on the nature and causes of Spain's ills in the past; it postulated a country genuinely one, territorially and socially, and in its guarantees against tyranny, abuse, and domination from the centre would have removed the main plank of regional separatism; it was full of hope for a future of justice, prosperity, and enlightenment. In three respects, however, its generous idealism rested on over-large assumptions.

The integration of the Indies and the Philippines with Spain in one political society completely ignored overseas realities: impossible at any stage in their development, it was never more so than at this particular moment, and impracticability in one so important section of the constitution inevitably affected the viability of the whole. Concerning the monarchy, the efficacy of this circumscribing of its functions and prerogatives stood or fell by the monarch's agreeing to be so circumscribed. Ferdinand, unconsulted, remained uncommitted, and the document while proclaiming him king made no provision for a refusal to swear to it or, should he so swear, for failure to keep his oath: 'The king's person is sacred and inviolable, and is not subject to responsibility.' Nothing that was known of Ferdinand warranted optimism here.

Concerning the sovereign people, it was assumed firstly that it too accepted and held itself bound by the constitution; secondly that it understood the nature and implications of popular sovereignty; and thirdly that the system was workable in terms of a population wedded to tradition, a stranger to responsibility, and so unlettered that the constitution itself allowed a period of eighteen years before literacy should be made a condition of election to Cortes.

The subsequent proceedings of the Cortes were indicative of the shape of things to come. Reforming enthusiasm soon turned to intolerance towards such as could not go the whole way; and the bishop of Orense, an original member of the council of regency, was expelled from Spain and deprived of citizenship for swearing the constitution with reserves. Friction between Cortes and council was constant thereafter, and became an open break with the proclamation in 1813 of a decree suppressing the Inquisition, which stirred up among the clergy a widespread spirit of revolt. One element of far-reaching and tragic consequence in all this was that the liberals, seeing in the Church the buttress of reaction, were driven more and more into a camp not of their own choosing; and the Church would rely ever after on the alleged identification between liberalism and anti-clericalism for one of its most potent weapons of social and political propaganda.

The epilogue to the War of Independence, it has been said, was written across the Atlantic. It was already in the writing while the constitution of Cadiz was being framed, and the fact explains why that document never refers to 'empire' or 'colonies'; why the nation is now 'the Spains' and all, creoles, mestizos, Indians, and even negroes, if free, are Spaniards in the fullness of a common citizenship going far beyond anything that the New World had ever asked for itself; why Americans were given a hand in the shaping of the new Spain and promised such representation in future Cortes as would have swamped the native Spanish element. The colonies had been pondering on the events of 1776 to the north, and Spain had seen the writing on the wall. The constitution of Cadiz was a desperate attempt, the last peaceful attempt, to keep the Indies in the commonwealth, and the more desperate because the war in Spain, with the collapse of authority, was the Indies' opportunity.

Britain's surprise seizure of Buenos Aires in 1806 had been repulsed before the British could establish their new bridgehead in what is now Uruguay. It was, however, repulsed not by the viceroy, who fled ignominiously, but by the citizenry, and the militant anti-Spanish movement can be held to date from that discovery by the creoles that they could act and fend for themselves. The ground had been long prepared in the realm of ideas – precursors like Miranda had been actively canvassing British help from the year of the French Revolution itself – and concerted action would soon follow. The British army that first stemmed the tide in Portugal in 1808 we have seen diverted from its original destination in Spanish America.

But if the events of 1808 turned Spain overnight from foe to ally of England, and placed England thereby in an ambiguous position towards the Indies, the attitude of the Indies towards Spain remained unchanged. Independence was rendered no less desirable because it now seemed suddenly within reach, and in colonies where public opinion had not yet pitched hope so high it took on desirability with opportunity. Action committees first called into being out of loyalty to Ferdinand and in indignant protest at the Napoleonic presumption of pronouncing Joseph king of Spain and the Indies saw their responsibilities widen as the invaders overran the Peninsula.

The year 1810, that witnessed the convening of Cortes in Cadiz, witnessed too the deposition of the viceroy in Buenos Aires by a provisional junta of the River Plate Provinces, where the authority of Spain was never thereafter re-established, and in Caracas the overthrow of captain-general and *audiencia*, followed a year later by the declaration of the independent United Provinces of Venezuela. From these two centres the two great leaders of emancipation, San Martín and Bolívar, were to set out to work the final expulsion of Spain from the New World, until by 1826 her flag would fly nowhere on the American mainland, north, central, or south, her citizenship a privilege no one wanted or needed.

In Spain, with the final defeat of Napoleon, the constitution was put to the test. The reign of Ferdinand VII (1808–33), commonly dated from his father's abdication, only began in any real sense with his return from captivity in 1814. Received everywhere with a frenzied enthusiasm, he was met too with representations from army, Church, and many traditionalist deputies in favour of asserting his unconditional sovereignty, restoring the Inquisition, and generally undoing the work of the constituent assembly. Two days before he entered Madrid, the populace awoke to read on its walls a royal decree annulling the constitution and every act of the Cortes responsible for it, and to learn of the wholesale arrest of regents, ministers, deputies, and prominent defenders of constitutionalism.

The gage had been thrown down, and – most significant factor of all – the crowds, crying 'Death to liberty and the constitution!', were with the king. So long conditioned to their chains, they felt lost without them. The death penalty was decreed for any who dared to speak well of the charter that was to have given them their freedom, and the Inquisition came back. The reign of privilege and abuse had returned, even to the re-establishment of the seignorial jurisdiction over thousands of towns and villages that weighed so heavily on the crown's own interests.

The next six years were among the blackest in the history of Spain. Ferdinand, the most contemptible monarch ever to occupy the throne, turned back the clock not to the eighteenth but to the seventeenth century, to the worst days of Philip IV. Choosing as his ministers time-serving reactionaries in comparison with whom Godoy could appear an enlightened statesman, he disregarded them too for a camarilla of his own stamp, and the country was governed by backstairs politics to the total contemning of every national interest.

From persecution of the liberal patriots who had fought his cause for him while he cringed to Napoleon in captivity, even to congratulating him on his victories in Spain, Ferdinand turned to the pursuit of those who, with perhaps greater realism, had looked to a brighter future for their country from a French victory, and sentenced 12,000 by one decree to perpetual banishment. Of all foreigners in Spain the English, to whom he owed most, were treated worst. Rigorous censorship forbade publication of journals other than official gazettes and seized foreign books, while society was honeycombed with spies. A promise given on his return to summon Cortes he conveniently forgot; and, having taken no oath to anyone or anything, he had not even the stirrings of a perjured conscience to restrain him.

Against such a background administration, and notably the national finances, relapsed with incompetence and neglect into chaos, and abroad the prestige of Spain knew again its lowest ebb. At the congress of Vienna, called in 1814 to settle the affairs of Europe after Napoleon, she was ignored, and when Napoleon escaped from Elba to disturb the peace anew a Spanish contingent was sent back with disdain. One member of the camarilla was the Russian minister; through him, and without the knowledge of his own minister of marine, Ferdinand purchased in 1817 eight warships as transport for an expedition against the rebellious American colonists at a price and in a condition so outrageous that the czar, to help quieten the scandal, threw in another three frigates. Two years later a settlement of differences with the United States cost Spain Florida, lost this time for good.

It was in vain that Ferdinand forbade the use of the terms liberal and servile. Against so much tyranny and servility, liberalism was driven to the only protest now open to it, invoking that same right to rebellion and in the last resort to regicide which, under the Habsburgs, even ecclesiastical writers had held justified. Secret societies, among them freemasonry, now got their footing on Spanish soil, and conspiracy became incumbent on true patriotism. Within four months of Ferdinand's return to the throne the first flag of rebellion was raised in Pamplona, in the name of the constitution of 1812; in 1815 another attempt was made in Corunna. A plot aimed at Ferdinand himself was uncovered in Madrid in 1816; a rising in Catalonia followed in 1817, and in 1819 another in Valencia. These all failed, and many paid with their lives; but that of 1820 succeeded.

Cadiz, the cradle of liberalism, had remained its home. It was also Spain's chief port, and the point of assembly in 1819 for a disgruntled expeditionary force of 22,000 men under orders to sail for America. There, on 1 January 1820, one commandant Riego raised the cry of the constitution anew and found an echo this time not only among the troops but all over the country. The army did not sail, and the last hope of winning back the colonies by force was lost. With Riego a new feature had appeared in political life, the *pronunciamiento*. The liberal temper could make bold to challenge a despotic monarchy, but no alternative principle of authority yet existed apart from the army. And it may be noted here that the army, having pronounced once in favour of liberalism, would rarely do so again.

Meantime from Corunna, Oviedo, Saragossa, Barcelona, Valencia, and Pamplona word reached Ferdinand of risings all with the same demand, and he capitulated in terror, agreeing at last to swear to the constitution. 'Let us walk frankly, and I the first, along the constitutional path,' ran his manifesto in the official *Gazette*. The uneasy nuptials lasted for three years. The king was forced to dismiss all his ministers and accept a pro-visional junta till Cortes could be elected. Liberalism was in power for the first time, only to find its problem to lie within rather than without. On the inevitability of gradualness, first and most difficult of lessons for the reformer in a country with such a political past, there developed a split forthwith into moderates, being the old constitutionalists of 1812, and a younger generation of extremists, including army elements, already inclining to demagoguery.

Riego was of the latter, and had to be removed by guile from his command in Cadiz, from where he was seeking to dictate to Madrid. Many 'patriotic societies' were suppressed, and a party committed to the freedom of the press was itself driven to censor-ship through the decline of freedom into licence. The unreality of the constitution as a charter for Spaniards grew daily more apparent; in many ways it worked against itself, as in its ban on the re-election of deputies, which threw away experience and exposed successive Cortes to increasingly extremist opinion. The chamber of 1822, presided over by Riego, proved little more than a forum for wrangling. Before the year was out risings of the right and of the left amounted across northern Spain to a state of civil war and gave warning that the régime, left to itself, must soon go down in disillusion and disorder.

It was not to be left to itself. Ferdinand, who had been skil-fully exploiting disaffection in both camps, had been exploiting no less the concern felt by monarchies north of the Pyrenees at the contagion to which they in their turn were now exposed. Where Charles IV in 1789 had tried to seal off his Pyrenean frontier from French revolutionary ideas, Louis XVIII did the same in reverse with his *cordon sanitaire* of 1822, aimed at more than the yellow fever epidemic then raging in Spain. The congress of Verona of that year had the position of the Spanish monarchy on its agenda, and only England of the five powers concerned opted out of the secret treaty entrusting France, at the common charge of the remaining four, with the restoration of 'order' in Spain. The ultimatum of the Holy Alliance of January 1823 was followed by the entry into Spain of Angoulême's 'hundred thousand sons of St Louis' early in April.

Devoid of military strength, as Godoy in 1808, government

and Cortes withdrew to Seville, carrying the king with them a prisoner, then to Cadiz as Angoulême entered the capital un-opposed and pressed on in pursuit. The liberal triennium was over, and against this second French invasion there was no second *dos de mayo*; for if the Spanish people had no cause to like the French more than before, in the mass they liked liberalism still less. Surrendered to Angoulême in October and restored to his once more absolute throne, Ferdinand tore up promises right and left with the vengeance he now exacted for the three years, six months, and twenty days of his 'most ignominious slavery'. Riego, hanged and quartered, was an early victim. Hundreds of others went to the gallows, until even the Holy Alliance powers protested in horror, and thousands fled into exile.

His appeal to the Alliance had achieved its object. In one direction it achieved considerably more. Britain had followed with some concern the French march through Spain. More con-cerned still at a proposal for another congress on the affairs of Spanish America, she informed France in October 1823 that any attack on Spanish America would mean war with her. In Decem-ber the United States enunciated the Monroe doctrine. Spain had lost her New World, and lost it for good. Ferdinand VII pro-claimed for all to see her unfitness to hold it. If Spain was still his it was thanks to the 35,000 French troops who, at his request and the country's expense, continued until 1828 to hold its chief fortresses.

The ten years following on 1823 are associated with the name of Calomarde, minister of justice and personification of his sovereign's hatred for every principle of representative govern-ment, the rule of law, or the rights of a free society. The university of Cervera, beginning a loyal address with the words 'Far from us the dangerous novelty of thinking', epitomizes the intellectual climate of the period. Yet even the universities were closed for the last two years of the reign as threatening Calomarde's declared policy of stamping out for ever any trace of the idea that sovereignty could reside elsewhere than in the person of the monarch. A 'Society of the Exterminating Angel' gave scope to clerical bigotry, and the earlier liberal division into moderates and extremists now found its counterpart on the right in this ultra-reactionary régime.

The overthrowing of the constitution did not result, however, in equal advantage to all the interests this had assailed. Ferdinand, concerned to recover and strengthen every crown prerogative, remained self-centred as ever. It was a small but revealing matter that, the Inquisition having been resuppressed, he did not trouble now to re-resurrect it. In its place there sprang up extra-legal *juntas de fe* which, like a threatening intimation from the Catalan clergy that the Church expected from the throne a more whole-hearted devotion to its interests, were evidence that for a section of his subjects, early known as 'apostolics', Ferdinand had not put the clock back far enough.

The constitution likewise, it will be remembered, had had no place for regional fueros. Neither had the crown, and in fact they had lost their reality long before. But the only thing that could make the loss tolerable to Basques, Aragonese, Catalans, and Valencians – namely, government as good and guarantees no less effective, which had been the professed objective of the constitution – was the last thing they could look for from Ferdinand; and one of the most significant developments of this decade was the re-emergence of regionalism, timid at first, soon explosive. These two political forces met in Catalonia in 1827 in connexion with the clerical protest just mentioned; and a 'Federation of Pure Royalists', issuing a manifesto of adhesion to a rival candidate for the throne, touched off a six-months' rising throughout the north and north-east that if put down easily – with a ferocity even Ferdinand had not matched before – remained significant nonetheless.

That candidate, who could still disown complicity, was the king's own brother Don Carlos, destined to be long remembered through the popular rebaptizing of the 'apostolics' as Carlists. At once devout and sympathetic to the regionalist cause, as Ferdinand was not, Don Carlos wrote his name so large over the history of nineteenth-century Spain in virtue of a new dynastic crisis that arose in the late thirties. Ferdinand's third wife died in 1829, leaving him in failing health and still childless. The succession of Don Carlos seemed assured, and Carlists and regionalists were alike jubilant. But that same year Ferdinand married again, the choice falling on his niece María Cristina of Naples, of allegedly liberal leanings, who bore him in 1830 not the looked-for son but a daughter.

Two civil wars were to hinge thereon, their origin lying over a century earlier in Philip V's promulgation in 1713, the year of Utrecht, of the Salic law which, by excluding female succession, would prevent the union ever of the two crowns of France and Spain in one person. The act had laid down further that the heir to the Spanish throne must have been born in Spain. This affected Charles IV, who was born in Naples, and in 1789 he secured the approval of a Cortes bound to secrecy for its rescinding, a measure which he then chose not to publish, doubtless preferring to let the issue lie unless others should raise it. Ferdinand's new marriage had created a tense family situation with his brother and had bitterly divided the country; and, while María Cristina was still with child, anxious to secure the succession to his line in either event, the king bethought himself of his father's pragmatic sanction of forty years earlier and caused it to be proclaimed.

The rage of the Carlists was unbounded, and when the child proved to be a daughter Don Carlos asserted openly that he would fight for his claim. In 1832 Ferdinand fell seriously ill, and the intrigues in court and in his bedchamber reproduced those spun over Charles II's deathbed in 1700, while the country's future hung on threads no less slender. The queen, persuaded at length by Calomarde, a Carlist at heart, that her daughter's accession would loose civil strife, induced her husband when apparently at the point of death to sign a revocation of the instrument, thus making Don Carlos again the legal heir. But here another woman, the queen's sister, intervened, and with her famous slap on Calomarde's face changed the course of Spanish history.

Wresting the decree of revocation from the keeping of the president of the Council of Castile, she destroyed it, and persuaded a Ferdinand believed dead but come back most opportunely to life to change his mind yet again and to make a clean sweep of his ministers. Calomarde, sentenced to imprisonment, succeeded in escaping to France, where he died. Ferdinand now publicly withdrew his annulment of the pragmatic sanction, caused a Cortes of traditional stamp to swear allegiance to his infant daughter, declared María Cristina, who had just borne him a second daughter, sole regent, and in September 1833 died, his last bequest to his country a now inevitable civil war. There was irony in the thought that, had he remained true to his constitutional oath of 1820, there would have been no dispute and no civil war, for the constitution of Cadiz had specifically reaffirmed the traditional Spanish right of female succession.

That war, equally inevitably, would involve Portugal. Don Carlos was married to a Portuguese princess, whose influence as so often before had told strongly in his extreme religiosity; and to Portugal he betook himself early in 1833 to lay his plans. The issues which Napoleon's invasion had bequeathed to the two countries bore of necessity a common stamp, though with a sufficient divergence in the reaction to them to make Spain's confused political history over these twenty years appear simple by comparison with that of Portugal.

The complicating factor here had been the transference of the court to Rio de Janeiro in 1807. Among the unpredictable consequences of that step was the reluctance of prince John to return home once the French had been expelled. The spectacle of thrones tumbling all over Europe made his seem safer in Brazil, and even with the eclipse of the arch-tumbler in 1815 there remained uncertainties over the state of Portuguese opinion. As in Spain towards Joseph, there had been a certain element of support for Junot and the constitution he would have given the country, and the Spanish charter of 1812 aroused lively interest across the border.

Brazil, declared a kingdom in 1815 on the advice of a Talleyrand anxious to safeguard the principle of monarchy in the New World, made Portugal now seem the colony; and John's investment of Beresford in that year with full powers over the army and a charge to look to his interests in Portugal, while he still refused to return, stirred up resentment at once against the crown, against Brazil, and against England that found a triple expression in liberalism, freemasonry, and republicanism.

Beresford's harsh repression of a revolutionary plot in Lisbon in 1817, which was aimed partly at him as the target now for all internal difficulties, especially the economic, merely shifted the plotting to Oporto. There, following Riego's pronunciamiento in Spain, it came to a head in 1820. In August of that year, Beresford being again in Brazil, the Oporto garrison revolted and, that of

Lisbon joining, the regency council was displaced bloodlessly by a provisional junta professedly loyal to John VI – the death of the mad queen Maria in 1816 had made him king at last – but resolved he should find himself committed, when he did return, to a constitutional monarchy. Beresford, back from Rio in October, was refused permission to land.

After the same discussion, leading to the same conclusion, as in Cadiz over old-style Cortes or new, and against a background of army pressures, an elected Cortes assembled in 1821, appointed a new regency-council, and at length evolved its new constitution based closely on the Spanish model, with the basic postulate again that sovereignty resided essentially in the nation. Again Church and nobility were to suffer loss of all seignorial privilege, again the Inquisition was declared suppressed, and again intolerance leapt to the saddle and sentenced to forfeiture of citizenship and to exile all who refused to take the oath.

Alarmed at stirrings so unorthodox, John had at length set out for Portugal, where he arrived in 1821 to find the constitutional debate still in progress. No such upsurge of royalist enthusiasm greeted him as had emboldened Ferdinand, on his return in 1814, to refuse to be bound to anything, and when the constitution was finally promulgated in 1822 he duly swore to observe it. His queen and their second son Dom Miguel refusing, they were forced to leave Lisbon and became increasingly identified with the many elements of conservative dissidence.

John's departure from Brazil, where he left his elder son Peter as regent, precipitated developments there too. The Cortes in Lisbon, having got its king back, summoned Peter as heir to return likewise, intending that his regency, and therewith the status of Brazil as a kingdom, should lapse. But the Brazilians thought otherwise, and persuaded Peter to refuse compliance: now twenty-three, he had been in Rio from the age of nine and felt himself a Brazilian. His cry of September 1822 on the banks of the Ypiranga, 'Independence or death!', signalized the birth of a free Brazil, and a month later he was acclaimed constitutional emperor.

The striking difference may here be noted in the manners in which Spanish and Portuguese America threw off their colonial bonds. Spanish America disintegrated over many years of bitter and sanguinary conflict into a cluster of new republics, so shattered in the process that Bolívar on his deathbed could speak of 'having ploughed the sea', and condemned to carry into independence a legacy of disruptive misgovernment and civic irresponsibility that left them a prey for the rest of the century to civil war, tyranny, and dictatorship. With infinite possibilities still ahead – her area in 1822 was as yet only a quarter of that of today – Brazil gently detached herself from tutelage under the guidance of a prince of the Portuguese reigning house and as a unitary nation still wedded to monarchy. Her vast extent found its answer not in disruption but in the principle of empire; and when, nearly seventy years later, the throne gave way to republicanism there too the transition would again be peaceful and the new republic would again preserve its territorial unity. The day chosen for the proclamation of the empire in 1822 was 12 October, the anniversary of Columbus's first landfall in the New World in 1492. Brazil was fortunate in having fallen to Portugal.

With the French invasion of Spain in 1823, those opposed to the new constitution in Portugal hesitated no longer. Three days after the Holy Alliance had replaced Ferdinand on his throne a pronunciamiento in Vila Franca brought together army, Church, and nobility. Government and Cortes capitulated without a fight, and John regained his 'inviolable rights as absolute monarch'. But John had temporized with the enemy. Dom Miguel was the extremists' man, and the Lisbon garrison, reversing its earlier stand for liberalism, revolted again and hailed him as king instead. Dom Miguel was got out of the country, but thereafter he was to his father what Don Carlos was to his brother in Spain; and civil war in Portugal, without need of dynastic pretext, could be seen to be merely a matter of time.

There existed notwithstanding a succession problem here too. Peter, John's heir, was emperor of an independent Brazil. That independence John and Portugal at length recognized, in 1825, partly on British insistence, partly also because as wearer of one crown and heir to the other Peter might conceivably yet bring the two countries together again in some way. Peter's own solution, on his father's death in the following year, was to renounce the throne of Portugal in favour of his seven-year-old daughter Maria II (1826–53), with two conditions: the Cortes would accept a constitution of his devising – it cost him one morning's work – in replacement of that of 1822, already held defunct, and Dom Miguel should in due course marry Maria.

So ingenious an attempt to square the circle proved in the long run disastrous. It condemned the country to another protracted regency over a most critical period; and though Dom Miguel professed acquiescence, he and the constitution, any constitution, were incompatibles. Spanish support for absolutism led to incursions from across the border, denounced from Lisbon as unprovoked aggression, that brought once again an English army to Portugal, and soon there developed an intolerable situation. Peter's nomination of his brother as regent in 1827 did nothing to ease it; for Dom Miguel's return from abroad early in the following year again made the country over to reaction and tyranny, and Peter's charter too became a scrap of paper. Thousands of liberals, frustrated in a rising in the north, found asylum in England and from there succeeded, between 1829 and 1831, in making themselves masters of the Azores. Peter from Rio confirmed his abdication, but when a packed Cortes proclaimed Dom Miguel the rightful king he denounced the projected marriage for Maria.

In the latter year Peter was constrained to a second abdication, this time of the throne of Brazil in favour of his son; and by way of England, where he was able to raise men, money, and ships, he too came to the Azores to fight his daughter's cause. There was no disguising now the state of open war. A liberal force landing in the north in 1832 won Oporto, traditionally the home of liberal sentiment, where it withstood a long and rigorous investment. A second expedition sailed to the Tagus, destroyed there the Miguelist fleet, and in July 1833 was in possession of Lisbon. After a last vain attempt to storm Oporto Dom Miguel hurried south, too late, to the relief of the capital, and Oporto too was free. Though he still held much of the north, and though Miguelism like Carlism was to be a political force for decades yet, his cause militarily was on the wane; and in September, with English recognition already accorded, Maria arrived from England to claim her throne.

In that same month Ferdinand died, and in Spain as in Portugal the crown passed to a child-queen relying for support on liberal elements in a country where liberalism was still on trial and where, in Canning's words, 'a vast majority still entertained a decided attachment to arbitrary power and a predilection for arbitrary government.' In this community of situation alike those prizing their recent freedom and those hugging their traditional servitude would join with their fellows across the frontier; for the real clash was still to come, and it would be that new kind of war whose advent Canning had so much feared, not between contending nations but between conflicting principles, a war less of armies than of opinions.

The long, unhappy reign of Isabella II (1833–68), that began with the civil war and ended in flight, provided from first to last eloquent commentary on the impossibility of governing through representative institutions a country where the area of political agreement was so much smaller than that of disagreement. María Cristina as regent had found herself identified with the liberal camp, whose support alone could ensure her daughter's throne; and her first acts were to reopen the universities and declare a political amnesty which brought back from abroad the many thousands Ferdinand had driven into exile. But liberalism meant above all things a constitution with popular rights and elected Cortes, and this down the century was to prove the country's repeated undoing. The attempt to apply the charter of 1812 had not only ended in chaos: it had left behind a dilemma as insoluble as it was inescapable.

No constitution could command the respect of both sides in a nation profoundly divided against itself. A constitution that enshrined the principles of one was of necessity directed against the other and became in effect an incitement to civil war; a constitution that kept to the middle position was respected by neither and inevitably succumbed to attacks from both. And the enemies of constitutionalism, holding to the simpler creed of no change, were far more united than the friends. There is thus only a morbid interest in cataloguing the successive charters of 1834, 1837, 1845, 1852, 1855, 1876 that punctuate the political history of the next fifty years. As each broke down, respect for the rule of law was correspondingly weakened and authority gravitated away from parliament to the only residuary source of power, the army. As each new one was drafted, the pathetic fallacy was again shored up that profound social realities were amenable to pious enactments. In the end Spain was a country rotting from constitutional disease and crying out for the strong hand that would save it from itself.

Outside the debating chamber the issues were stark. Even before Don Carlos issued from Portugal his call to arms in November 1833 there had been risings of his partisans in the Basque provinces, Catalonia, and Valencia, making apparent that the first Carlist War would be a war not merely for religion and autocracy but, in the minds of many, for the fueros; though conviction on this last did not suffice to win over to the pretender the chief cities like Barcelona and Bilbao. It would again be a war of *guerrilleros* fought out in mountainous regions where knowledge of the terrain could be decisive.

This threat to both peninsular thrones and to the cause of constitutional government in both countries inevitably interested other powers; and on the joint request of Lisbon and Madrid England and France signed with them the Quadruple Alliance of April 1834 whereby, *inter alia*, they promised cooperation in expelling the two pretenders from Portugal. Herein lay no problem, however, for Dom Miguel had gone from defeat to defeat and in May he was obliged, accepting the convention of Evora-Monte, to renounce his claim to the throne and again leave the country, this time for good. Don Carlos escaped on board a British warship to England.

The Alliance had made no provision for the eviction of the Spanish pretender from Spain. In England no guarantee was asked of him or given regarding his future actions; and within a few weeks Don Carlos was at the head of his forces in Navarre and five years of devastating and merciless strife had begun. Britain recognized, with a twinge of conscience, her share of responsibility therefor, and in August agreed to supply the Spanish government with arms, munitions, and at need a naval squadron. Within the year the Foreign Enlistment Act was suspended to allow the enrolment of a foreign legion, soon 10,000 strong. Non-intervention as a British policy had gone by the board, a tribute incidentally to the strength of the Carlist movement.

The year 1835 saw risings of the left too, to whom the concept of popular sovereignty remained a heady wine; from Aragon, Catalonia, Valencia, and Murcia they spread before long to Old Castile and Andalusia. Beset by enemies on every hand, the government seemed at times within measurable distance of losing the day to the absolutist cause. This enjoyed the diplomatic support of Austria, Prussia, and Russia, the old Holy Alliance powers, and only needed for the free flow of war material command of a major port. Bilbao was thus from the beginning its chief strategic objective, and three times the city was subjected to, and three times withstood, close siege. The daring exploit of the Carlist general Gómez in 1836 when he led an expedition west and southward through Asturias, Galicia, León, past Madrid, and into Cordoba and Estremadura, returning after six months with a vast train of booty and a force larger than when he set out, brought back to memory the great raiding days of al-Mansur and revealed how tenuous was the government's hold on so-called 'loyal' territory. Normal administration was at a standstill.

The régime found, for a moment, its strong man in Mendizábal, the wandering Jew come back to politics, like Pombal by way of an embassy in London. With more financial acumen than any Spanish minister had possessed since the expulsion of his race in 1492, he is remembered chiefly for his radical solution of 1836 for a now crushing national debt, the confiscation and sale of all Church and monastic property. But he too fell victim to the total confusion now reigning in the constitutional realm, and lost office within the year. Three months later a palace revolt at La Granja forced the regent to proclaim anew the constitution of 1812, pending the elaboration of a new compromise charter which the Cortes approved a year later; and the régime looked again like succumbing rather to its well-wishers than to its foes. In 1836 too another leader emerged, in Espartero, adequate to the military crisis, who in December of that year fought and won the most desperate battle of the war, for the third relief of Bilbao.

Thereafter the eventual defeat of Carlism was inevitable, though it still had successes. Don Carlos himself in the early summer of 1837 led an army through Aragon, Catalonia, Valencia, and New Castile that for a moment threatened Madrid. The long stalemate was broken in the end by discords in the pretender's camp, where a renewal of the old quarrel between apostolics and moderates reflected the long years of frustration in the field. In 1839 Maroto, leader of the moderates and now openly at odds with Don Carlos, made contact with Espartero; and at Vergara in August both generals met on the field in the presence of the two armies and embraced. It had been a cruel and unnecessary war, stained on both sides – particularly on the Carlist – by such savagery, notably in the slaughter of prisoners, as shocked the conscience of Europe. In Catalonia hostilities were to continue for another year, but with Vergara the cause was lost. Don Carlos and 8,000 of his faithful withdrew to France; and in Spain too constitutionalism and parliamentary government, however tarnished in their application, appeared firmly established in principle.

Maroto had sought to stipulate, as terms of peace, acceptance into the queen's forces of such of his men as so wished, a marriage between Isabella and the pretender's son, the departure from Spain of the regent queen-mother, and respect for the Basque fueros. The first condition Espartero accepted, refusing the second and third. The fourth he undertook to have the government commend to Cortes, where it was finally conceded 'without prejudice to the constitutional unity of the monarchy', and the Basques were left with their administrative autonomy and their exemption from national conscription and from Spanish customs dues.

Espartero's emergence from the war as a national hero coincided with a period of great political instability in Madrid, where the rise and fall of governments, the convoking and dissolving of Cortes, were bringing the régime again into disrepute. A new law of municipalities then in angry debate proposed to alter the elective basis of these to the crown's advantage. Espartero, proclaiming himself the champion of the constitution, cried infringement, and delivered to María Cristina a veiled ultimatum which Madrid and the other leading cities backed with acts of open rebellion. The regent capitulated to the extent of charging Espartero to form a ministry, but would not repeal the law; and the impasse was only resolved by her resigning the regency in October 1840 and taking ship – she was then at Valencia – for France. She had long since disappointed the nation's early hopes, and by her secret marriage shortly after Ferdinand's death to an obscure but handsome guardsman, one Muñoz, to whom she bore many children, she had once again dragged the good name of the crown in the gutter. Her daughter would besmirch it even more.

Espartero, prime minister, succeeded as regent and, like the soldier he was, thought in terms of military rather than political solutions for the legacy of violent disorder throughout the country, largely of his own creation, which he now inherited. His treatment of María Cristina provoked a strong reaction in her favour, with numerous risings; and the ruthlessness of his suppression of these cost him too all his earlier popularity. The Church's long tale of grievances since 1833 was not properly to be laid to his account; but it was brought home to him nonetheless when, in 1841, the Vatican attacked the régime in what amounted to a declaration of hostilities.

The Basques needing only this encouragement to rise again, Espartero suppressed by decree in that same year the most important of the fuero provisions he himself had secured to them only two years before, thereby laying the foundations for another civil war. When Barcelona rebelled in 1842, demanding new constituent Cortes, he bombarded the city into submission, and that too the Catalans chalked up against Madrid and long remembered. He was in short Spain's first military dictator, and as such rode rough-shod over the constitution he had sworn to defend. At length even the army turned against him, and in July 1843 it was his turn to take ship, from Cadiz bound for London, into exile.

The decade of nominally liberal constitutional rule that Spain had now enjoyed invited contrast with the preceding decade of absolutism under Ferdinand. The one had bequeathed to the other the five years of the Carlist War, but this provided only part explanation for the sorry record that the exercise of popular sovereignty had to show. The years had seen no advance in efficient administration, in political stability, or in civic virtue. The nation stood as far removed as ever from real unity, the ancient kingdoms still leaping to every opportunity of disowning Madrid. As for the corollary of representative government, acceptance of the majority will, that no one in power or out found easy to learn. In this yawning gulf between political theory and practice, the rights of the individual and the interests of the nation were alike going to the wall. But the nation remained committed to the experiment, and the experiment went on.

The answer this time to the vacant regency was to declare Isabella, now thirteen, of age: a polite fiction, for she never grew to discretion, that inaugurated a long and calamitous rule by reactionary generals and palace intrigue, the latter much stimulated by the return of María Cristina. Narváez and Serrano, who would share with the queen most of the responsibility, had both achieved prominence through armed rebellion – Narváez had been exiled in 1838 for treason – and their way with opposition was, in Narváez's phrase, to 'use the stick and hit hard', a policy exemplified in his shooting in 1844 alone of 214 persons accused of political offences. Come to power in that year, he began by promoting yet another constitution, the preceding years of anarchy having derived in his opinion from the defects of that of 1837. The sovereign people was now quietly jettisoned, the senate – an 1837 innovation – made a crown preserve, freedom of the press much restricted, and the queen freed from any say of the Cortes in a matter soon to be of national and international importance, her choice of husband.

Scheming over the 'Spanish Marriages' had begun while Isabella and her sister were still in their cradles; and when in 1846 they were adjudged of marriageable age the old diplomatic rivalry between England and France in matters south of the Pyrenees broke out with a violence that for a moment threatened war. England had been consistently sympathetic with the liberal cause in Spain, helping it discreetly as opportunity offered. The France of Louis Philippe was no less identified with reaction. It has been seen that, when forced to resign the regency, María Cristina had fled to France, Espartero to England; and each government was now pushing candidates of its own persuasion. At length England gave way to the French king's proposal that Isabella should marry her cousin Francis – son of a reputed son of Godoy and of that sister of María Cristina who slapped Calomarde's face and secured Isabella the succession – while her sister should marry Louis Philippe's own youngest son the duke of Montpensier.

Since this raised the possibility that the throne might one day again fall to a Frenchman – liberal Spanish opinion protested that the choice of the effeminate Francis was designed to the specific end that Isabella should not have children – England's agreement was conditional on the postponement of the second marriage until the first had produced an heir. The celebration, in flagrant violation of this, of the double wedding in October 1846 was not a Spanish responsibility, save in its consequences; but Louis Philippe paid heavily for his fleeting triumph, the resulting rupture with Britain costing him, in the revolution of 1848, his throne. As for the queen and her consort, temperamental incompatibility was such that within weeks they were living apart; while her conduct, in particular her fondness for the company of Serrano, whose handsome bearing redeemed in her eyes his liberal leanings, augured ill for her good name.

The general revolutionary contagion of the year 1848, with its chain sequence of popular uprisings across half Europe, did not spare the now frankly reactionary régime in Spain. The influence of the new republic in France coming to reinforce, and no longer to combat, that of England, there were risings in Madrid, Barcelona, Valencia, and Seville; while in northern Catalonia and the Basque country the Carlists were again in the field, the more incensed that the queen's marriage had finally ruled out the hopes they had continued to pin on that solution of the quarrel. Narváez, invested by Cortes with dictatorial powers, dissolved this and rode out the storm alone, much helped by the injudicious interference of the British ambassador urging that Cortes be resummoned and martial law repealed.

The ambassador was given his passports, relations with Britain were broken off, and Narváez was hailed as the bulwark of Spanish dignity and independence. Austria and Prussia at long last recognized Isabella's title, and the Holy See restored the amicable relations severed in 1841. In return Narváez in 1849 sent an expeditionary force to help replace the Pope on the throne from which he too had been toppled in the general turbulence. This fleeting and inglorious reminder of the days when Spanish power in Italy had been supreme spoke eloquently of how far to the right the Spain of Narváez had veered.

What all the revolutionary forces in the country had been

unable to achieve came about shortly after through palace plotting. The queen's consort had arrived at length at a basis of co-existence with his wife and, now comptroller of the royal household, nurtured ambitions for a larger sphere of action. In 1849 he succeeded in ousting Narváez from the premiership for the space of one day. At the end of it Narváez was back in office and Francis had forfeited his comptrollership; but the palace as a whole had tired of a dictator so dictatorial, and drove him to resignation early in 1851.

There succeeded a government under Bravo Murillo which did little more than delay – in a sense it hastened – the impending storm. Ministers and programmes now might be good or bad: if good they rarely lasted long enough or commanded the support in the country to carry through reform. But the pretence had long since vanished that they rested on and derived their authority from a system of responsible representative government. Under Narváez only lip-service to political principle had remained: the principles themselves had wilted away. To criticism from the Cortes dissolution was become the routine answer, followed by manipulation of the ensuing elections.

In 1851, a year in which one parliament was dissolved and a new one twice suspended, a concordat with the Vatican, concluded without submission to Cortes, signified a resounding triumph for clerical interests. By it Catholicism was confirmed as the exclusive religion, to which all education public and private must conform, and the Church received a state endowment, the right again to hold property, and power of censorship. Louis Napoleon's *coup d'état* in Paris that same year, making of the republic once more an empire, came to strengthen Bravo Murillo's policy of reaction. Proposing one more revision of the constitution which would finally destroy the representative principle, muzzle Cortes, and empower ministers to legislate by decree – in all which he would have been merely legalizing recent practice – he forbade discussion, threatened to hang dissident generals 'in their own sashes' and, overreaching himself, for he was no Narváez, lost even the queen's support and fell in December 1852.

Early in 1854 a liberal petition was submitted to the queen reciting constitutional abuses and demanding redress. When she

replied by proclaiming a state of siege in Madrid and banishing
the opposition leaders from the country, there could be no more
burking the issue. The enemy of the constitution stood revealed
as the queen herself, and it was she, and not merely tyrannical
ministers, who must go. The revolution broke out in the streets of
Madrid, led by another general and veteran of the Carlist War,
O'Donnell, whose manifesto called for a return to morality in
politics, for a throne not dishonoured by a camarilla, a national
militia to guarantee popular liberties, and – a shrewd note – for
regional autonomy 'to save the provinces from the centralization
that is consuming them'.

Valladolid, Saragossa, Barcelona, and Seville joined the
rebellion. The Valladolid junta had as president the retired
Espartero. Summoned to Madrid, where the queen had capitulated and undertaken to dismiss the entire palace household, he
joined O'Donnell, the two representing left and centre liberalism,
and together they set about implementing the manifesto and convening new constituent Cortes. The second decade of the reign,
governed from the right, had ended like the first, governed from
the left, and after a record not dissimilar, with the same appeal
to violence as the only means of securing a return to first principles. The significant difference lay in the decaying prestige of
the crown. That process was progressive, not cyclical.

The return to constitutionalism under the guidance of two
generals did not prove easy; and when in 1855 the Cortes had
elaborated its new charter, much more radical – even to venturing
a first timid approach to religious freedom – than that of 1845,
it took fright to see the monster of popular sovereignty again raise
its head and left it unpromulgated, so that the document has
remained a museum piece. Twenty-three deputies, one in ten, had
voted for ending the monarchy.

A law regulating the sale of the remaining Church property
declared confiscated in 1836 – less than half had been disposed
of – led to a violent clash with queen, Church, and Rome that
nearly carried Isabella off to lead a new Carlist war in the north
and again provoked a diplomatic break with the Vatican. In the
provinces, where economic distress was greatly intensified by
famine, the new national militia was making the country over to
mob rule and causing O'Donnell and his fellow-moderates to

regret their own manifesto. Gradually he edged away from the Cortes and back to the palace for support, and in 1856 adroitly manoeuvred Espartero into tendering his resignation and the queen into accepting it.

Such betrayal, showing political morality back where he had found it, did not go unchallenged. The national militia took up arms, but Espartero failed to respond. O'Donnell had the army behind him, and revolts in Madrid, Barcelona, and elsewhere were easily put down. For the next five years reaction, still calling itself liberal, caused the manifesto of 1854 to be forgotten, and nothing more, it need scarcely be said, was heard of regional autonomy. The militia was dissolved, the 1845 constitution re-established, the law concerning the disposal of Church property repealed. Then, having served the queen's purpose, O'Donnell too was manoeuvred out in 1856 and Narváez recalled, his year in office before he too fell a victim to palace intrigue being remembered for his creation of an Academy of Moral and Political Sciences. The nation had need of it.

The ensuing lustrum belonged again to O'Donnell. His 'Liberal Union', the answer to the queen's tactics, was a coalition so broad as to leave her, save for Carlists and republicans, little choice outside it. That it held together much longer than any other administration in the whole hundred years of the constitutional experiment derived largely from the fact that it had no policy. Its watchword 'Dynasty and constitution' meant everything or nothing: content to accept the situation as it existed, it would let sleeping dogs lie, and administer. In this it found an ally in a nation grown allergic to politics. For a quarter of a century now the great constitutional debate had been going around in circles, getting nowhere. Politics had become a game for politicians, till the ordinary man refused to be stirred or to believe any longer that the way to the millennium lay through the ballot-box.

It was helped further by the considerable economic activity that marked the beginning of the railway era in Spain. Between 1848 and 1858 some 500 miles of railway had been opened, to the accompaniment, it is true, of financial scandals and palace stock-jobbing, involving particularly María Cristina, that led to the sacking of the queen-mother's palace and to her eviction from the country, this time for life, in 1854, when mobs and even the press demanded her head. In the following ten years another 3,000 miles were laid; and the easing of communications, a problem that in so mountainous a country weighed even more heavily on the national economy than internal customs barriers, was reflected in the doubling of imports and exports over a decade. The government proved no more successful than its predecessors in handling the nation's finances, its one windfall being the Pope's final acquiescence in 1859 in the disposal of Church property in gratitude for Spanish interest in his continuing difficulties in Italy. But the life of the country, left to itself, was slowly picking up.

O'Donnell was the first ruler since Godoy to lead Spain into adventure abroad, and his modest degree of success here contributed likewise to his hold on power at home. The ending of Moorish piracy at sea had not ended aggression against Spain's footholds on the north African mainland, and in 1859 O'Donnell declared war on the sultan and himself led a force from Ceuta to the taking of Tetuan. Britain had tied his hands in advance by refusing to countenance any conquests on the coast facing Gibraltar; and he was hampered from behind by an attempted Carlist invasion from the Balearics, planned to take advantage of the withdrawal of the army to Africa, which however collapsed of itself. The campaign brought therefore only a token advantage in return for 7,000 Spaniards killed; it was still accounted, from its very novelty, a glorious victory, and gave O'Donnell on his return a momentary apotheosis which disposed him to look for fresh laurels.

Across the Atlantic, where Cuba and Puerto Rico alone recalled the great days of Spanish sovereignty in the New World, it seemed that something might yet be recovered. In 1861 Santo Domingo, tiring of independence under the threatening shadow of Haiti, submitted once again to the Spanish crown. Four years later, the rediscovery of what Spanish colonial administration meant impelled it to throw off the yoke a second time. That interlude cost 10,000 Spanish lives.

Intervention in Mexico in the same year 1861 was of a different nature. There England, France, and Spain had agreed on a joint demonstration to bring to heel the Juárez government, in default on its international obligations. Spain had harboured some hopes that Mexico too might come back into the family, or at least abandon republicanism for a monarchy under a Spanish prince; but when Louis Napoleon, emboldened to flout the Monroe doctrine by the civil war then raging in the United States, made clear his determination to establish there by force a monarchy for his own candidate Maximilian, the Spanish general Prim and the English withdrew, having received the financial guarantees they sought. His anger at this major disappointment O'Donnell vented on Prim. When, after three years, Maximilian's puppet empire collapsed, Louis Napoleon vented his anger on Spain, and broke off diplomatic relations.

After Mexico O'Donnell's star began to sink. His packed Cortes tired of the monotony of one-party politics; the glory of his military excursions had faded, leaving public opinion to weigh the gain against the cost; and by the ferocity with which he suppressed an agrarian riot in Andalusia, sentencing six to death and 400 to penal servitude in Africa, he finally forfeited the country's esteem. Few now credited him with liberal views, and when, as an attempt at a liberal gesture, he recognized the recently proclaimed kingdom of United Italy, the queen too withdrew her support and in February 1863 he fell.

The five years of stability had been bought at a price. Opposition had thriven on exclusion from the Cortes and now rejected the invitation to return to party strife within that suspect forum. 'Democratic' and 'progressive' manifestoes exposed anew the hollow sham of so-called constitutional government with its rigged elections and backstair pressures: 'if by revolutionaries are meant the enemies of a tyrannous faction', true liberals were revolutionaries, and the atmosphere was heavy from now on with omens of impending disruption. Narváez reappeared, and O'Donnell, as the only leaders commanding any following among those still prepared to play the parliamentary game: their cabinets legislated, squabbled, and repressed in a world of increasing unreality.

Attempts at further intervention in America brought further humiliation and discredit. In 1864 a Spanish squadron seized the guano islands of Peru as an act of 'revindication' and, tactlessly suggesting to Madrid a resumption of the hostilities that had ended with Peruvian independence in 1824, which Spain had never recognized, brought an indignant Chile, Bolivia, and Ecuador into the fray. The Spanish offensive, limited to the shelling of Valparaiso and Callao, the former an open town, was wholly inglorious. Peace with the four republics came only in 1879, and involved at last the recognition of Peru. The illwill and suspicion so fruitlessly engendered lasted for long after.

At home an incident of 1865 was likewise long remembered. The treasury being in desperate strait, Isabella offered to make over to the nation two-thirds of the royal estates, receiving back one-fourth of the amount realized; and much was made of a patriotism so self-sacrificing. Castelar, a Madrid professor of history, in a newspaper article entitled 'The Gesture' stripped off the pretence by showing that the royal patrimony was the inalienable property of the nation and that the real effect of Isabella's proposal would be to put a vast sum of public money into her own pocket. Castelar and the rector of the university were dismissed, student riots followed, involving loss of life; the Madrid city and provincial councils, sympathizing, were superseded, and the government of the day fell. It marked the beginning of active student intervention in politics.

The queen was vulnerable too, as her mother and grandmother had been, from yet another side. While her husband had continued to be a cipher in her domestic life as in that of the country, she had had children: a first son born in 1850, who died after two days, a second, the future Alfonso XII, born in 1857, and several daughters. She had also had a succession of favourites, stretching from the now distant Serrano to the present Marfori, son of an Italian pastry-cook and raised by her, like another Godoy, to be marquis, cabinet minister, and governor of Madrid. When liberals spoke now of 'traditional obstacles' that must be swept away, all knew what and who were meant; and not all the repression of a Narváez, despotic as never before, could impose silence, much less respect. From 1864, when Prim, the moving spirit now of the republican cause, made the first of several abortive risings, the end was no longer in doubt. O'Donnell died in 1867, Narváez in 1868. Isabella stood defenceless.

The pronunciamiento came on 18 September 1868, again from Cadiz, this time from the navy. The army joined in, and the generals' manifesto, entitled 'Spain with Honour', made the sufficient indictment that 'the person charged with the defence of the constitution should not be its irreconcilable enemy'. Isabella, in San Sebastian, looked in vain for her supporters, then bowed to the inevitable, and with the words 'I thought I had struck deeper roots in this land' crossed into France.

The course of events in Portugal over these thirty years, if it did not reach to such a climax of disillusion, ran in channels closely parallel. At bottom the issues were the same, first the political stature and morality of those called on to govern on an untried basis of constitutional rights and limitations, and second the realistic or unrealistic nature of the constitution itself, in terms primarily of the loyalties it could command. Two such instruments had now been adopted by the Cortes in quick succession, the fundamental differences between them lying in the single-chamber assembly, not dissoluble by the king, of the 1822 document and the two chambers, the lower indirectly elected, the upper the preserve of the hereditary nobility, deriving from that of 1826, which gave back to the crown, in the powers of veto, of creation of peers, and of dissolution, the effective authority that the other had been at pains to deny it.

A third, Miguelist, position of utter repudiation of constitutionalism would re-emerge whenever there was hope of profiting from the incompatibilities between the other two; but the main battle would be fought on this central issue of the political function of the monarchy. Inevitably, in consequence, the monarch was deeply involved, and required gifts of acumen, objectivity, and tight-rope walking scarcely to be looked for in a girl of fifteen who had been born and brought up 3,000 miles away.

The defeat and banishment of Dom Miguel in 1834, celebrated by the suppression of all religious orders and confiscation of their property, were a bare four months old when Peter died and Maria, though three years younger than the charter laid down, was declared of age. That same year she married a prince of Leuchtenberg, only to be widowed almost immediately. Early in 1836 she married again, choosing prince Ferdinand of Saxe-Coburg. The charter had laid down that she might not marry a foreigner. Meticulous respect for its spirit and provisions was clearly going to be difficult to inculcate; and when the queen insisted on appointing her new husband, not yet twenty, as commander-in-chief, thereby provoking a cabinet crisis on the very day of the wedding, respect for the throne was called in question straightway.

To remedy a critical financial situation, the legacy of Napoleon and Dom Miguel, that was infinitely more critical now that the wealth of Brazil no longer lay at call, successive governments in 1835 and 1836 had been driven to sell many national and crown properties, to the consequent enrichment of favoured individuals rather than of the exchequer. When the treasury building was burnt down in the latter year, respect for the queen's ministers too fell under well-earned suspicion. This, together with the palace revolt at La Granja which had led to the re-proclamation in Spain of the Cadiz constitution of 1812, provided the background for the stormy events of the autumn of 1836: a dishonest election, a barracks rising which overthrew the government and forced the queen to revoke the charter in favour of its predecessor of 1822, an ill-judged palace attempt at counter-revolution backed by English bluejackets and Belgian gold, Ferdinand being a nephew of the king of the Belgians and cousin to princess, later queen, Victoria. The gold was to be secured on one of the African colonies.

Maria thought better of this just in time, and saved her throne, but under new masters. Septembrists and chartists, the names given to supporters of the 1822 constitution now restored in that month and of the charter of 1826, were not merely liberals and conservatives within the common fold of monarchism. In practice they stood at opposite poles, separated by the concept of popular sovereignty, alike only in that human nature and political competence remained the same whatever the creed.

That under the Septembrists the upper house disappeared was clearly an aggravation of the gulf between them, throwing the aristocracy into extra-parliamentary plotting to bring back the charter. The inevitable outbreak of Miguelist activity was thus secondary to the risings stirred up by chartists which over the next two years plunged the country into turmoil. A single day in March 1838 saw three proclamations, one of them an appeal by the queen asking all patriots to help rescue the country from anarchy; they preluded sanguinary street battles in Lisbon between conflicting army units, with heavy slaughter of innocent citizens.

A fortnight later a new compromise constitution was promulgated conceding an elective second chamber. It provided an ironic commentary on the growing unreality of parliamentary government, which gave men banners to fight under or against, but did not govern. It spoke also of a mounting revulsion from a cult of liberty that either declined into or provoked violence; and Septembrism lost ground steadily thereafter to the feeling that the principle of authority represented by the crown called for strengthening rather than weakening. Some notable conversions to the chartist camp took place, the most significant that of Costa Cabral, governor of Lisbon and for two years, from 1839, minister of justice.

A royal amnesty for political offences – save always those of the Miguelists – committed since the Septembrist coup of 1836 accompanied the launching of the new constitution, and men hoped for a fresh start. The queen had now two sons to secure the succession; friendly relations had been restored with the Vatican; Austria, Prussia, and Russia at last recognized the régime. Elections in 1840 returned, however, a strong chartist majority; and when in 1842 even Oporto pronounced strongly in the same sense Costa Cabral went north, in intelligence it was alleged with the queen, and from there headed a march on Lisbon. A show of resistance in the capital collapsed, neither government nor garrison having any longer the courage of its Septembrist convictions. The queen accepted that the sovereign people had changed its mind, and proclaimed yet again the charter.

Costa Cabral, the first strong man the régime had thrown up, dominated the years 1842–6. His first concern being that of all strong men, to keep himself in power, he manipulated elections for the lower house more shamefully than ever before, created thirty peers to make the upper house, now again composed of nobles and crown nominees, still more subservient, and muzzled opinion throughout the country. The opposition was driven to unnatural extremes, Septembrists allying themselves with Miguelists and even subscribing tentatively, in their search for allies across the border, to the arch-heresy of pan-Iberianism or union with Spain, a creed with a specious liberal appeal in that country but which in Portugal could never prove other than political suicide.

While its immediate interests were not touched, the mass of the people welcomed the strong arm; and this brief dictatorship, marked by a programme of road-building and the like public works and by first measures for the mechanization of the wool industry, did witness a measure of economic resurgence. For the country's financial problems Costa Cabral had no solution. Over these four years the national debt increased by another forty per cent, and a serious attempt at tax reform resulted only in an outbreak of violent opposition from those affected.

It was over an apparently innocent matter, the banning on health grounds of burials in churches, that the storm broke at last. Called after a villager in the extreme north, one Maria da Fonte, who early in 1846 led an impulsive local protest, the rising took on national proportions as political dissidents of every shade fanned popular indignation into rebellion for their own ends. Martial law proved impotent against a movement so amorphous, to which in many parts the soldiery too adhered; revolutionary juntas usurped local authority up and down the country, and the dictator accepted at last his dismissal and escaped in disguise into Spain.

His dilemma had been a repetition of Pombal's a century before: the despair of effecting reform by consent, since some interest must always be hurt, an authoritarianism born in all sincerity of the simple observation that the nation was incapable of equating rights with responsibilities, and despair again, the vicious circle complete, at the knowledge that cumulative resentments would eventually mean overthrow and the sweeping away of all reforms effected. For the Portuguese people too cried when its face was washed; and now Maria, trembling for her throne, duly revoked the offending taxation and burial laws, conceded, though the concession proved still-born, what amounted to universal suffrage, and – the exchequer still further undermined by a rebellion that was reckoned to have cost as much as the entire internal debt – sought a return to 'normality'.

This was not easy to achieve, a restored freedom of expression having opened the floodgates of recrimination, and Maria looked for another strong man. She found him in Saldanha, a prominent chartist who for five years had been filling diplomatic posts abroad. The palace coup which brought him to power in October 1846 offended the country so profoundly as to threaten both his head and the throne; but Maria took the risk knowingly, preferring to lose her crown rather than live 'thus openly insulted and calumniated day after day'. When again the nation was torn by civil war, an announcement of her assumption of absolute powers, coupled with the appointment of her consort Ferdinand to lead the army in the field, intimated that everything was at stake, and she appealed to the other members of the old Quadruple Alliance for help.

There was difficulty, in the year of the Spanish marriages, in any proposal for concerted action from England, France, and Spain; but Spanish forces were sent to the frontier region and one more British squadron appeared in the Tagus. This sufficed to save the day, the help arriving when opposition forces, centred as so often on Oporto, were already at the gates of Lisbon and Maria was about to board a foreign warship. The queen still had her throne, Saldanha smoothed the transition back to Costa Cabral amidst infinite precautions against the general revolutionary fever of 1848; and from 1849 to 1851 the history of the latter's earlier administration was repeated, even to the pronunciamiento made by Saldanha himself on a Septembrist basis, that again drove him to exile in Spain. Political principles were now merely battle-cries, to be forgotten with victory. Saldanha held office for the record period of five years, but he held it, as he had won it, by methods scarce distinguishable from those of the man he overthrew.

Midway in this new spell of authoritarianism, in 1853, Maria died, leaving eleven children and the record across a long and troublous reign of a sincere attempt, within her lights and limitations, to preserve the throne in good repute as the one steadying influence in a nation intent on pulling up its anchors. With the same disruptive forces at work as in Spain and a raw material of ignorance and superstition below, of self-seeking and improbity above, just as unpropitious, she had averted the ultimate disaster, the collapse of the crown and the abandonment of the country to chaos, that were Isabella's legacy to her people.

The great battle of the constitution she had lived to see ended, with the 1852 appendix to the charter. In this Saldanha had salved his Septembrist conscience by instituting the direct voting and universal suffrage promised six years earlier, annual budgets subject to Cortes approval, and a fuller measure of local government. So modified, it was to remain in force until the fall of the monarchy; and chartists and Septembrists, restyling themselves 'regenerators' and 'historicals', transferred their contentions to fields of debate other than the throne or the upper house and tacitly agreed to forgo the pronunciamiento as a political weapon. Historicals looked back in the old liberal sense of still working for the fuller popular liberties associated with 1822, regenerators forward on a conservative basis of authority and realism as the first condition of advance.

Ferdinand's two-year regency, until Peter V (1853–61) became of age to succeed, benefited directly from the accommodation, as from his own tactful and conciliatory spirit; and Saldanha was able to pursue his manifold policy of reform in an atmosphere of unwonted if still only comparative tranquillity. A ministry of works was created for the encouragement of agriculture, commerce, and industry; road development was intensified alongside the building, from 1852, of the first railways; and financial measures affecting customs, taxation, and loan conversion were carried, in face of second chamber opposition, by the old expedient of creating a score of new peers.

Saldanha's fall in 1856 was eloquent of the subtle change in the political climate. It came about not, like Costa Cabral's on both occasions, through violence, but from Peter's refusal to allow further recourse to the packing of the upper house. Peter had travelled and studied much abroad and showed himself an infinitely conscientious ruler with a high sense of royal responsibility. He had his reward now, for the new government of historicals under Loulé succeeded in passing the stringent financial reforms that had brought Saldanha down; and after this exemplary display of seriousness, where tradition had lain rather in rejecting and undoing the work of one's predecessors, it was itself rewarded by a three-year tenure of power. To cloud it there came devastating epidemics of cholera and yellow fever, killing between them over 8,000 people in Lisbon alone between 1855 and 1857, and the affair of the *Charles et Georges*.

The arrest of this French slaver off Mozambique in 1857, and its impounding against the captain's denial that the natives on board had been enslaved, gave rise to angry French protests and the despatch of French warships to the Tagus. When Portugal appealed to arbitration, there followed a peremptory demand for the vessel's release and for a heavy indemnity. To such a display of power politics Portugal had no option but to yield, and Loulé was forced to resign. As postscript there sprang up a heated controversy around French sisters of charity who had come to Portugal to help in the cholera epidemic: innocent victims of gallophobia and of a new wave of the anti-clericalism which had lain dormant since 1834, they were shipped back to France in 1862. Before then the historicals were back in power, again under Loulé, there to maintain themselves – thanks on one occasion to Peter's acquiescence in what he had earlier refused to Saldanha, the creation of new peers – for another lustrum, till 1865.

Late in 1861 the throne, that under Peter had much enhanced its prestige throughout the country, was struck a heavy blow from an unexpected quarter. Peter and his younger brothers Augustus and Ferdinand, returning to Lisbon from a hunting expedition, fell with typhus. Ferdinand died after a brief illness, Peter five days later: he was twenty-four. Luis and John, second and third of the five brothers, were then travelling abroad and were recalled at once, Luis being proclaimed king: within five days John too succumbed. Peter, who had been widowed two years earlier, after but a year of married life, and died childless, was mourned as few kings of Portugal had ever been mourned before, and neither crown nor country recovered from the loss.

Luis I (1861–89) was by profession and enthusiasm a sailor. Having had no expectation of the throne, he had not received the careful education into responsibility that had so distinguished Peter; and the translation to court and politics he accepted with ill-concealed distaste. His marriage in 1862 to Maria Pia, daughter of Victor Emmanuel first king of Italy, brought strained relations with the Vatican. At home the problem of the national finances continued to overshadow all others. The nation never had been solvent since the loss of the Brazilian revenues, to replace which recourse was now had more and more to foreign borrowing, at a price not to be measured in financial terms. Bold programmes of public works were launched on loans, against budgets which never balanced, while every new taxation proposal provoked a new outcry. In 1865 a coalition cabinet of historicals and regenerators betokened both the obscuring of party lines and the difficulty of providing stable government in a country increasingly conscious that it was not paying its way, yet unable to agree on how it should.

That ministry's civil marriage bill raised a storm of protest indicative of the continuing deep attachment of the people to its religious tradition. To it were added two other highly unpopular measures – the absorption of small districts and parishes into larger units for economy of administration, and a sales tax – which together threw the country into an uproar. While Lisbon rose in violent protest and troops were called out, the merchants of Oporto announced a suspension of business until the tax was withdrawn. The date, 1 January 1868, is remembered still today in the title of Oporto's leading newspaper, *O Primeiro de Janeiro*, founded in that year.

Failing to get the king's approval for vigorous action against such a challenge, the government resigned; and Luis, abandoned this time by all the leading statesmen of the day, entrusted to one far below the necessary stature the task of forming a ministry whose first duty would be capitulation on both fronts. This was the year of crisis too in Spain, where Isabella's deposition and the problem of the vacant throne were to have repercussions across both frontiers.

For the second time in sixty years Spain found herself without a monarch and with the national administration in collapse. The political vacuum was again filled, as in 1808, by revolutionary juntas throughout the country, whose impetuous pronouncements made much harder the task of the provisional government set up by the victorious generals and admirals under Serrano and Prim. All had been agreed on overthrowing Isabella, no two on what came next. Universal suffrage, freedom of conscience, of the press, of teaching, and of association: these were promised as a matter of course. On the form of government the nation would speak; though the makers of the pronunciamiento, if less through love of the institution than fear of the alternative, assumed it would still be monarchical. As always when a strong hand at the centre was removed, the country again threatened to fall apart; and regionalism and republicanism were seen to go hand in hand.

Conservative opinion thus found itself in a dilemma. Support of the fallen Isabella meant in effect voluntary disenfranchisement: that was the most lost of lost causes, as Isabella herself at length recognized by her abdication in 1870 in favour of the twelve-year-old Alfonso. Support of Alfonso meant acceptance of another regency, and none wanted a return to that. In the end many, especially those swayed by religious conviction – and a national petition in favour of maintaining Catholicism as the only faith claimed 3,000,000 signatures – transferred their allegiance to Carlism, now led by Don Carlos the third, grandson of the original pretender, and bold to think its opportunity come at last.

Even before the constituent Cortes convened in February 1869 took up the drafting of yet another constitution, it had and gave proof of how tortuous showed the path of principle ahead. No rallying-cry for the revolution had been more effective than the abolition of conscription: a country truly free at last would be defended by a free army. But the country was already a prey to such armed disorder that it became essential to raise an army at once. Conscription went on, and the process of disillusion had begun.

The charter of 1869, drafted by a committee which excluded the republicans, though these now numbered seventy out of a total of 350 deputies, prescribed a limited monarchy with sovereignty again resident in the nation, a second chamber elected by the provinces, and the basic freedoms. Civil marriage was legalized, but religious freedom, the most hotly debated proposal of all, was whittled down till it applied only to foreigners and to such Spaniards as made formal renunciation of Catholicism. This still constituted a major infringement of the 1851 concordat.

With Serrano as regent and Prim as premier, the search for a king began. It lasted for over a year, during which time Cortes and country, having lost all sense of urgency and purpose, drifted perilously near to anarchy. 'Finding a democratic king in Europe,' said Prim, 'is like looking for an atheist in Heaven.'

The lively interest taken by the other powers was another limiting factor. Prim, a Catalan, was that other variety of regionalist, the pan-Iberian, and offered the throne first to king Luis of Portugal, with a union like that of Austria and Hungary in mind; then, on Luis's refusal, Britain having intimated sharply that she would permit no fusion of the two crowns, to his father Ferdinand, who was interested, on conditions, and warmly supported by France, but eventually withdrew under pressure of Portuguese feeling against any threat, however remote, to the full and free independence of Portugal; then to Leopold of Hohenzollern, whose readiness to accept touched off the Franco–Prussian War and thereby altered the balance of power in Europe; and finally to Amadeo, second son of Victor Emmanuel and brother to the queen of Portugal.

Amadeo acceded, was approved by 191 to 120 votes in the Cortes, and accepted with indifference if not hostility by the population at large, who like the Portuguese could not forgive his father's usurpation of papal territories and dignities, culminating in the occupation of Rome in that very year 1870. His crowning handicap was Prim's death by assassination on the very day, 30 December, of his arrival on Spanish soil.

Himself an estimable person in every way and scrupulously observant of his constitutional position, Amadeo I (1871–3) thus never had a chance. To republicans 'the king of the 191', to the nation in general simply 'the foreigner', without Prim he was lost. Carlists and republicans joined hands in an unholy alliance to defeat him and – numbering between them 110 deputies in his first Cortes, the Carlists with 64 stronger than they had ever been – they dominated a now hopelessly divided liberal party and made parliamentary government impossible. Outside parliament the republicans, greatly strengthened by the proclamation of the third republic in France and the struggles of the Paris commune, gained a sweeping victory in the municipal elections of December 1871.

A month later the government outlawed the first International, whose seeds had fallen on particularly fertile ground in Spain, growing from a first Madrid chapter of 21 members in 1868 to 153 chapters with 15,000 in 1870, two-thirds of the total being in Barcelona, and threatening now under the new banner of socialism the complete disruption of Spanish society. In April 1872 Don Carlos from France called for a general rising against 'the foreigner': it was the signal for the outbreak of the second Carlist War, which was soon raging, if intermittently, throughout the Basque provinces and Catalonia, the chief cities refusing as before to throw in their lot with reaction. Across the Atlantic large numbers of Spanish troops were pinned down in a desperate struggle for Cuba, which ever since the revolution of 1868 in Spain had been fighting for its independence. This demand Prim would at one stage have conceded, at least to the point of full autonomy, had the rebels been willing to lay down their arms.

Sagasta in the midst of all this succeeded in returning a new Cortes with a majority for the monarchy, but by means that violated every norm of honesty and principle and that, when challenged, forced his resignation. Serrano, again in office, asked Amadeo for dictatorial powers as the only means of carrying on the government; these Amadeo's conscience would not allow him to grant, and he in turn was forced to an alliance of liberal extremists and republicans. In July 1872 an attempt to assassinate Amadeo and his queen failed, but the end was clearly in sight.

That autumn saw stalemate in the Cortes, while the republicans, anxious not to lose the day to the Carlists, provoked risings from Ferrol in Galicia to Malaga. Early in the new year the artillery corps which was holding the line of the Ebro against the Carlists mutinied. The government's act in dissolving the corps again offended Amadeo's constitutional conscience, and he resigned forthwith the thankless task of reigning over Spaniards, courteously thanking the nation, as he left Spain in February 1873, for 'the great honour it had conferred upon him'.

There could be no question now of seeking another king, and the republicans had their republic, born not only in anarchy but without legal sanction since it was ushered in, in double defiance of the constitution, by the two houses of a non-constituent Cortes sitting together. Throughout its brief and chequered course, however, legality mattered nothing, and though a constituent Cortes was elected it never had a constitution. Conscription was declared abolished, and the armed forces took the decree as licence to go home while the Carlists still held the northern provinces. The new Cortes declared the form of the republic to be federal. This the provinces interpreted as cantonalism, disregarding thereafter the authority of Madrid and proceeding each on its own to abolish absentee landlordism, taxation, individual property, and whatever other symbols of law and order offended the sentiments of good republicans.

The age of the *taifas* had returned. Catalonia had already pronounced itself an independent state. In Cartagena the populace took possession of the arsenal and the harbour, where lay the bulk of the Spanish fleet, and sent this cruising up and down the coast to help spread the revolutionary doctrine: only with the help of British warships was it eventually restored to government control. So disturbing a first taste of federalism converted many back to the unitary principle, and Madrid, a prey to chaos in the streets, was further torn by the resulting conflict in Cortes and government.

Before the year was out the republic had had four presidents. The first fled the country without the formality of resignation: his successors described themselves respectively as federalist, unitarian, and 'possibilist', and possibilism imposed itself as the only approach to a realistic policy. Castelar, its exponent, has been met already as the author of 'The Gesture'. He accepted that, whatever the ideal, order came first, and, Cortes being in recess, took to himself the supreme powers the situation demanded. With conscription reimposed and the army high command on his side, he achieved the seeming impossible by containing two civil wars at once. Andalusia, given over to cantonalism, saw its cantons fall one by one before the army of Pavía, who left behind him a grim trail of devastation as he advanced at last to the storming of the final redoubt, Cartagena.

Castelar had saved the republic: he had also destroyed it. When in January 1874 a hostile Cortes overthrew him, Pavía, now captain-general of New Castile, quietly overthrew the Cortes, ordering the deputies out of the chamber. The pronunciamiento had come back, invoked this time not in the name of this constitution or of that but of order and a truce to politics. A cabinet of generals was formed under Serrano and suspended constitutional guarantees while the army, freed from the menace in the south, got to grips with the even graver one in the north. Once or twice it had seemed that the Carlists, better led, might have made themselves masters of Spain. On their investment now of Bilbao, only to be relieved after a long and agonizing four months, the whole fate of Spain appeared to hang. From Catalonia in July they occupied Cuenca, a mere sixty-six miles from Madrid. But neither side had the generalship to enforce a decision, and by the end of the year deadlock had again been reached.

Politically, too, the country had been at a standstill ever since the January coup. No Cortes met, and no one missed it. Federalism was disowned, and the republic marked time against a dénouement that everyone now expected and that the vast majority were prepared to welcome. In November 1874 Alfonso, a cadet at Sandhurst, reached sixteen, the age for accession to the Spanish throne. A month later, in response to a prudent manifesto in which, 'as a good Spaniard, a good Catholic, and a liberal', he called on all Spaniards of good will to rally to the cause of constitutional monarchy as the only remedy for the country's 'cruel disorders', the last pronunciamiento of the century, made at Sagunto by Martínez Campos and seconded in Madrid by the new captain-general, one Primo de Rivera, tore away the façade from the republic, to reveal that there was no longer anything behind.

It had been a circuitous and costly way back that the country had taken, whence the striking measure of concurrence now that on this particular journey it was better to arrive than to travel. The sovereign people had learnt some hard lessons in the process, and had worked a certain amount of poison out of its system. 'We republicans,' Castelar confessed to the Cortes, 'have many prophets and few politicians; we know much of the ideal, little of experience; we embrace the entire heaven of thought and stumble over the first hole in the road.' It remained to be seen how much the Bourbons had learnt.

Alfonso XII (1875–85) thus came to the throne under happier auspices than the monarchy had known since the accession of Charles III over a century before. He landed in Barcelona early in January, and even the Catalans were tumultuous in their welcome. Like Peter V of Portugal he added to qualities of character education in a good school, away from his mother's baneful influence, and returned to Spain with a high opinion of

English parliamentary government and the hope that its virtues of moderation and stability might prove capable of translation.

Only to the Carlists did his accession, blessed by the Pope, bring dismay. They could now no longer claim to be fighting the cause of religion against secularism, while the legitimate issue of 1833 had receded into the very far distance and even the fueros, after the experience of cantonalism, had for the time being lost much of the earlier magic of their appeal. Rejecting a proffered amnesty, they fought on; but first in Catalonia, then in the north, they gave ground until in February 1876 Estella, their stronghold and capital for two and a half years, fell. Don Carlos crossed the frontier for the last time: the second Carlist War was at an end, and Spain again at peace.

Martínez Campos, to whose command most of the fighting had fallen, was now sent to Cuba with another 14,000 troops – 32,000 had already gone out in the first year of the restoration – and at last, in 1878, succeeded in halting the separatist revolt there with promises of substantial autonomy. The price was high, but the ten-year struggle had by then cost Spain at least 100,000 lives. Madrid's failure to keep faith with the Cubans over this settlement would raise the price higher still before the century was out.

Meanwhile at home Alfonso had found in Cánovas del Castillo a strong conservative minister, and in peace the opportunity to convene, again for the last time in the century, a constituent Cortes to prescribe under what fundamental laws the new régime would live. Though elected under the universal suffrage of the 1869 constitution, it proved by its homogeneity and cooperativeness the country's notable change of temper. The republicans of yesterday were now content for the most part to be liberals again, forming under Sagasta a constructive opposition. For twenty years these two leaders alternated peacefully in power, and the cataclysm through which Spain had passed was forgotten.

The constitution of 1876 proved conservative in a realistic sense, and deliberately conciliatory. Universal suffrage gave way to a property qualification, the second chamber became mixed in character, part hereditary or *ex officio*, part crown-nominated part elective, the jury system was abolished, civil marriage restricted to non-Catholics, and religious toleration interpreted as freedom of belief unaccompanied by external manifestations of any save the Catholic faith. Limitations were set to the right of public meeting and association and to the scope of municipal and provincial initiative. Cortes would be summoned, prorogued, and dissolved by the king, any dissolution to be followed by the summoning of a new Cortes within three months: a provision this last which was to prove of crucial consequence nearly fifty years later.

In the nature of things the new charter satisfied neither Church nor liberals; but it proved workable, and remained in vigour until the second collapse of the monarchy in 1931. By it the powers of the central government were firmly reasserted, and the Basques, defeated in war, could not this time claim preferential treatment. They protested strongly nonetheless at being declared subject with the rest of the country to conscription and taxation, and eventually salvaged the right to raise their own contingent for the army and to apportion and collect themselves their assessed contribution to the national exchequer.

The exchequer remained the one department of government intractable to change of régime or policy. Civil war and war in Cuba over so many years had swollen expenditure and depressed revenue beyond any hope either of meeting claims or of a balanced budget. The total income from taxation barely covered the cost of the army alone, while equity in assessment and efficiency and economy in administration still fell far short. In 1876 the Cortes was informed that the cost of collection exceeded one-third of the total collected, and in 1880 that 173,000 small holdings had been seized for tax arrears. As centuries before the Moriscos, so now the peasant class was being driven in increasing numbers into exile, emigrating both to Africa and to America.

It was here, in the broad field of social justice throughout the provinces, and no longer in political or dynastic wrangling in the capital, that the seeds of future trouble lay. Political rights did not of themselves feed the starving or pay the landlord, and selective suffrage remained a hollow satisfaction while ignorance and illiteracy denied effective representation to those, the bulk of the nation, most in need of it. The ease with which elections could he manipulated in such a society, the temptation to priest or landowner to dictate the votes of men unable or afraid to judge political questions for themselves, the very fact that the country had issued into an atmosphere of apparent tranquillity: all this had much to do with the gradual transformation of politics once more into a profession for professionals who, growing more and more detached from the tense social realities around them, would eventually discredit the whole constitutional fabric that now at long last seemed so firmly established.

Cánovas at length demitted office in 1881 before a coalition led by Sagasta which demanded a more liberal interpretation of the constitution and began by freeing university professors from the narrow subservience to the principles of Church and throne that Cánovas had required of them. The measure inevitably brought the universities into the political arena and led on occasion to head-on collision with authority, as in 1884 when Cánovas and the conservatives were again in power.

But there was in fact little of substance in the conflict between the two parties. Each in opposition flagellated the other for its alleged abuses and betrayals of principle, each in office pursued identical tactics and a scarcely distinguishable policy. In part this rested on a genuine concern never again to split the nation or to incite to arms. But it conveyed also with time the impression of a cynical abandonment of principle in favour of a tacit agreement to alternate in power at decent intervals and to share less the responsibilities than the spoils of office.

Alfonso took little part in the political game, but that little had its infelicities. His state visit of 1883 to Germany, to which country Spain had been inclining, against France, since the restoration, and his attendance there at military manoeuvres and acceptance of the colonelcy of a regiment of Uhlans provoked such hostile manifestations on his return through Paris as to cloud Franco–Spanish relations. Again, in 1885, he intervened against his government on the burning question of free trade and protection.

This, and not the fueros, was now the issue which divided Catalonia, insistent on a sheltered market for her industries, from the rest of Spain and especially from the depressed agricultural provinces of Andalusia, where social betterment was closely tied up with cheap imports. It was with a conservative and not a liberal government that England was seeking a trade agreement when Alfonso, taking sides impetuously with the Catalans, brought the negotiations to nought until after his death. But he tried honestly to interest himself in the national welfare; and his death at twenty-seven was tragic not only in that it confronted the country with one more problematical succession, his queen María Cristina of Austria having borne him only daughters and being now again with child.

Six months later this proved, to the great relief of all save the Carlists, to be a son, and Alfonso XIII (1886–1931) was thus born a king. They were a difficult six months, followed by a long and difficult regency under María Cristina. Though still almost unknown to her people, the queen-mother discharged her duties with tact and dignity that won universal respect, and that to those with long memories offered the strongest possible contrast to the behaviour of her namesake during that other so disastrous regency of fifty years earlier.

The reign began with a party truce and an agreed transfer of power to Sagasta, who held office for the next five years and whose first general election in 1886 may be mentioned for the fact that the results were published in a government newspaper in advance of the polling. The making of elections, down to the allocating of seats to each minority group, was now accepted practice on both sides, and made completely unreal the running debate on what the basis of suffrage should be or any claim that Spain was now firmly set in the ways of true representative government. The principle of universal suffrage at the age of twenty-four won final acceptance in 1890.

One reform Sagasta was not able to carry: his proposal to remove the army from politics by declaring the holding of a commission incompatible with civil employment. In this he trod on what, after the Church, constituted the greatest vested interest in the country. The army had brought in the republic, driven out the republic, and conceived of itself as the predestined saviour of the nation in every crisis. Patriotism grew confused in the military mind with the defence and where possible the extension of army prerogatives, until now the generals were demanding trial by court-martial for all cases involving the army with the press, seeking thereby to place themselves above criticism.

In 1890 Sagasta gracefully yielded another turn to Cánovas, who thus had to conduct the first elections under the new extended suffrage, which he had consistently opposed. The electoral machine proved equal to the challenge, the results turning out exactly as the new government had intended they should. It was notwithstanding an uneasy administration, for symptoms of decomposition began to multiply within and without the Cortes, bringing home at last the lesson that playing at politics and governing were two different things.

The year 1892 evidenced, in the fourth-centenary celebrations of Columbus's discovery of a New World, a considerable rebirth of goodwill towards Spain on the part of the erstwhile colonies, where experience of independence had by now induced in many the rueful reflection that in exchanging political colonialism under Spain for economic colonialism under the United States all was not gain. It was a year of portents at home, the socialism underlying a miners' strike in Bilbao yielding in significance to the first outbreak of bomb-throwing in Barcelona, a city to be tragically associated thereafter with anarcho-syndicalism and crimes of violence.

Anarchism, dating from Bakunin, had derived a great impetus from the eclipse of central authority and the emergence of cantonalism as a substitute for the state that marked the republican experiment of 1873, by which year it counted some 270 centres and 300,000 adherents. Its stronghold lay in the south among the *latifundios* whose origin has been seen to lie centuries earlier in the circumstances of the reconquest. There it fed on agricultural distress, exploitation of absentee landlords, and the cynical disregard of governments in Madrid towards the most urgent of social problems. Barcelona, as the country's chief industrial centre, exerted a natural attraction on a starving peasantry; and the flood of invasion, from Murcia in particular, of a generation later was already a significant trickle under the pressure of catastrophes such as the floods in 1879 which, sweeping away whole villages and bringing ruin to the towns, spread devastation throughout that province.

The anarchist movement soon came to centre its activities on Barcelona, its appeal to the Catalans lying not in the doctrine of violence – for this it would continue to recruit Murcians – but in the rejection of the centralization symbolized by Madrid and the exalting of personal freedom; and from 1888 it there joined forces with the syndicalist National Confederation of Labour, grown out of a 'Workers' Association' of six years earlier and likewise committed to decentralization.

On this issue hinges therefore the profound gulf that for the next half century would divide Spanish labour into two competing and fiercely antagonistic camps, Catalonia and the south anarcho–syndicalist and tending politically to devolution, industrially to workers' control, and socially to disintegration, Madrid and the Castiles identified through the General Union of Workers with belief in centralized authority and national solutions for national problems. The overlaying by this labour complex of the regionalist issue proper was to prove the tragedy of modern Catalonia. The Cortes reacted in alarm to the new phenomenon, passing laws against violence and the preaching of violence of a severity which incited in itself to further violence in Barcelona, and a plot was discovered to blow up parliament.

It proved a year too of mounting economic difficulties, with a dwindling of export markets in France, England, and Cuba; and Cánovas came at last to frank admission of the great game of bluff that both parties had been engaged in ever since the restoration. For fifteen years, he confessed, the country had never had an honest, still less a balanced, budget, and now it was bankrupt. Unable to find anyone to accept the ministry of finance, he pressed the whole cabinet into the confecting of estimates. When another major scandal broke over the municipality of Madrid, in which too Cánovas was deeply implicated, the nation realized at last how widespread was that 'administrative immorality' out of the allegation of which political capital had been made for years, and Cánovas resigned. In Madrid at least the electorate awakened; combating the machine at the ensuing elections, it captured six of the eight seats for avowed republicans.

Notice had been served. But even with the will to do better, governments now found themselves caught in toils of their own spinning: with dishonesty and irresponsibility as their own norms of conduct, they could in vain look for a high civic seriousness from the nation. Sagasta, doing violence with one hand to the municipal roll in the capital in order to prevent the republicans from carrying the municipal elections too, had no real cause for surprise when, on presenting with the other a first realistic budget including heavy tax increases, he provoked opposition so vigorous that the proposals had to be dropped. It was, however, the army, that grossly over-officered force that for a minor police operation in Melilla in 1893-4 had mustered 29 generals to 25,000 men, which this time brought him down by taking the law into its own hands a year later over criticism in a republican journal. From this direction another most ominous threat to the régime was clearly developing.

Cánovas entered on his last tenure of office in 1895 again under the shadow of Cuba, where the settlement of 1878 proved to have settled nothing and civil war once more raged furiously. He had a long record of opposition to fundamental reform in the island, holding that Spanish sovereignty demanded first complete sub-mission; and though Sagasta had at length abolished slavery, Spanish opinion as a whole was still for repression and against autonomy. To the Cubans autonomy, being dependent on Spanish good faith, was no longer enough. Martínez Campos returned to the island with a fresh army but could make no head-way, and in 1896 was succeeded by Weyler, a general whose record of cruelty in Catalonia paled before the inhumanity of his concentration camps and scorched-earth policy in Cuba. In-evitably the United States was moved to protest, in the name not only of her large Cuban interests; and behind the protest lay the scarcely veiled threat of intervention.

The assassination of Cánovas in 1897, in revenge for his repressive measures against anarchism in Barcelona, allowed Sagasta to reverse policy by recalling Weyler and finally con-ceding autonomy alike to Cuba and to Puerto Rico. It came too late; and indeed both Spain and the United States had been making preparations against a collision now held inevitable, for which the mysterious explosion that sank the United States cruiser *Maine* in Havana harbour in February 1898 provided merely the excuse. War, declared by the United States in April, began in the Pacific with an attack on the Philippine Islands, where too Spain had been engaged in trying to quell an inde-pendence movement. In the Caribbean, by July, Spain had suffered ignominious defeat all along the line; and in October the peace of Paris rang down the curtain on her overseas empire, with Cuba in the temporary custody and Puerto Rico and the Philippines under the sovereignty of the United States.

The year 1898 thus marks the end of the second great cycle in Spain's history, that had begun four centuries earlier in the same year which marked with the capture of Granada the conclusion of the earlier, longer cycle of the reconquest. The reconquest had formed the Spanish character; the overseas imperial adventure, bringing out both the best and the worst in that character, had perhaps in the end impoverished even more than it had enriched the homeland. In any material sense the loss of the remaining colonies was to be acclaimed as relief from a nightmare; for the drain on manpower, on resources and on reputation over the preceding thirty years had been a large part of Spain's weakness at home.

In her self-esteem, however, this was a most grievous hurt; and the humiliation prompted a mood of introspective analysis among her serious thinkers, later to be known collectively as 'the generation of '98', which, if it reached no finality on the crucial question of Spain's true role in time and space, threw a penetrating light on certain aspects of the national genius, formulated a challenge to the nation's will to survival and to greatness, and provoked incidentally a literary renaissance which for the first time since Cervantes' day enabled Spanish writers – Benavente, Unamuno, Ortega y Gasset – to make some impact on the intellectual life of the western world.

A small but not negligible sign of the new seriousness that marked the close of the century was the creation in 1900 of an independent ministry of education; for the one detail that had escaped the generous enthusiasts of popular sovereignty was the consideration, brought out so vividly throughout the whole long chapter, that no conferring of rights can be fruitful that does not go hand in hand with education into responsibility.

Portugal too had known her moments of uneasiness in the difficult situation created for Spain by the fall of Isabella in 1868. Prim's pan-Iberianism, that spread a natural alarm in the neighbouring country, found one ally in the veteran Saldanha, then ambassador to Paris and still a name to conjure with in military circles. Returning to Lisbon by way of Madrid, he issued in May

1870 a one-man pronunciamiento that resulted in his appointment by the king to a one-man ministry. This coincided with
renewed Spanish efforts, after the withdrawal of the Hohenzollern candidate, to win Ferdinand's acceptance of the vacant
throne; and in fact Ferdinand was so agreeable, though with the
stipulation – which Prim found himself unable to accept – that
the two crowns should never be united.

With the collapse thereby of Prim's 'great idea', which as
seen from Lisbon involved, in the unanimous opinion of the
chamber of deputies, 'infamous designs against the nation's
independence', the octogenarian dictator was defeated by the
weight of public opinion and withdrew from public life to the
embassy in London. His few months in office had seen the
creation by decree, for Portugal now too, of a ministry of education. Orderly stable government was restored with the advent to
power late in 1871 of Fontes, a regenerator with considerable
gifts of statesmanship who held office, with one short break, till
1879.

If the course and fate of the republican experiment across the
frontier helped to underline the virtues of conservatism, this
proved notwithstanding a period of much political activity, in
which the signs could be read of changes to come. The events of
1870 in France greatly stimulated the re-thinking of traditional
assumptions; and in the following year a series of lectures given
in Lisbon by a number of leading writers and thinkers – one,
Theófilo Braga, will be heard of again – dared to distinguish
between Catholicism and Christianity, holding the former 'inimi-
cal to tolerance and to all true education', and to inveigh against
the crown as an instrument for the exploitation of the many in
favour of the few. The government, intervening to put a stop to
such temerity, produced inevitably the effect opposite to that
intended. A few months later, in 1872, the country's first strike
gave warning that in socialism a new political force had come to
birth.

The creation in 1876 of a republican party provided a stimulus
to monarchism to close its ranks, and that same year historicals
and their offshoot the reformists merged again under the new
banner of 'progressives'. These and the regenerators corresponded to liberals and conservatives in Spain, not only in the

scant difference to be found between their policies, but in the working agreement soon arrived at in consequence to alternate peaceably in power and share its prerogatives. The system in Portugal was known as rotativism, and while again it seemed to preserve the peace, and to function, inevitably there were engendered the same cynical abuse of constitutional principle and purpose and the same disregard of fundamental social problems.

Parliamentary elections were falsified without scruple; while the packing of the upper house, where in order to provide complacent majorities sixty new peers had been created in the two years 1879–81 alone, had become a scandal to the nation. The progressives first secured office in 1879 – in the elections of this year the new republican party, intervening for the first time, won a solitary seat in Oporto – and for the next decade, until the death of Luis in 1889, they and the regenerators played the political game without serious impact on the nation's real interests.

These years proved notable nonetheless in a different direction, and here the paths of Spain and Portugal did diverge, to the manifest advantage of the latter. For while events across the Atlantic preluded the final eclipse of Spanish imperialism, Portugal in Africa was laying the foundations of yet a third vast empire that has survived intact till today. Angola and Mozambique had originated as supply and trading stations on the Cape route to the east, with little intrinsic importance. The loss of that first empire to England and Holland during the 'sixty years' captivity' had left to Mozambique merely the sentimental value which forbade any thought of voluntary relinquishment. With the development of Brazil, however, Angola took on its new role as source of slave labour for the New World, and the story has already been told of how it was overrun by the Dutch in 1641 and recovered from them seven years afterwards.

Not until the loss of Brazil, Portugal's second empire, and the establishment of a liberal régime under Maria II did the home government take serious concern for the betterment and expansion of these two territories. For the first time, in 1836, civil governors were appointed, and in that year Lisbon decreed the abolition of slavery throughout all the colonies, a measure that of necessity invaded many spheres of interest and took time to

effect. Gradually the frontiers of both were extended, alike along
the coast and in depth, until in the last quarter of the century the
other powers awoke to the potential importance of the continent
and the scramble for Africa began. From 1876 first Belgium and
then France began to stake claims to the Congo area, and Portugal was made conscious of the need to define and defend her
interests.

In 1877 Brito Capêlo, Ivens, and Serpa Pinto were sent out to
Angola – their mission a curious pendant to that so distant
expedition of Pero da Covilhã in 1487 to see whether Africa
could be circumnavigated – to see whether it could be crossed.
Serpa Pinto penetrated to the Victoria Falls and so to Pretoria
and Durban; the other two, striking north-east, reached to the
head-waters of the Lualaba or upper Congo. Already the
ambition was taking shape of a Portuguese belt across the continent that would join the two colonies.

Its achievement was greatly complicated by the Berlin conference of 1884–5, which had been convened at Portugal's
suggestion to discuss the protests directed by France, Belgium,
and Germany against an Anglo–Portuguese treaty of 1884
recognizing Portuguese rights north of the Congo. The conference
enunciated the new doctrine of effective occupation, not prior
discovery, as the touchstone of sovereignty, one consequence of
which was the invalidation of the treaty with England aforesaid
and a cooling of relations between the two allies; while the vast
Congo basin, that Portugal had discovered in 1482, was appor-
tioned to Belgium and France. With France and Germany, who
had no objection to seeing Anglo–Portuguese relations weakened,
Portugal now signed agreements in 1886 which secured the consent of both countries to her proposed expansion, Germany's
price being substantial concessions of territory between Angola
and German South-West Africa and between Mozambique and
German East Africa.

So fortified, the Portuguese government presented to the
Cortes its plan for a belt across Africa, the 'rose-coloured map'.
It was the misfortune of the two allies that there was now no
averting a head-on clash between the ambitions of a Portugal
intent on driving from west to east and those of an England
similarly bent on driving, from Cairo to the Cape, a belt which on

the map would be coloured not rose but red. The result could be foreseen. Had Portugal then possessed an empire-builder of the calibre of Rhodes, the name of the intervening territories would still today be the Rhodesias. But the strain on the old alliance was severe.

Britain at once protested against Portuguese pretensions on the ground that Nyasaland and Matabeleland were under British protection; and when, notwithstanding, Portugal in 1889 sent out a second expedition under Serpa Pinto that, moving inland from Mozambique, should meet another eastward-bound from Angola and establish a claim to effective occupation, the protest was followed by the famous 'ultimatum' of 1890 threatening a severance of relations should the territories in dispute not be evacuated at once. Portugal could but accede and accept, in the treaty of the following year, the loss of vast areas to which she believed her title to be indisputable.

The explosion of popular indignation was the more bitter because of Britain's refusal to refer the issue to arbitration in terms of the Berlin treaty: the other treaty powers, with whom lay much of the ultimate responsibility, looked on. That indignation found one outlet in a national subscription to help build a navy capable of guaranteeing the security of Portuguese possessions against the new enemy. The sum contributed did eventually purchase one cruiser, baptized – from the symbolized figure of the Cape in Camoens' great epic – the *Adamastor*.

With this collapse of an ambition there still remained enough for greatness and, in terms of Portuguese possibilities, a vast field of opportunity. Angola today, with an area of 480,000 square miles, Mozambique with 300,000, are together some twenty times the size of Portugal; added to the Cape Verde Islands and Guinea, Portuguese India, Macao, and Timor, they place that country still in the first rank of colonial powers. For the nation that, one of the smallest in Europe, has been a colonial and imperial power longer than any other, it is a proud record.

The immediate significance of the crisis of 1890 lay less in the toppling of governments than in its turning to account by the republicans. These, duly encouraged by the declaration of a republic in Brazil in 1889, sought now to fasten responsibility not on ministers but on the régime. Charles I (1889–1908) could

scarcely have acceded to the throne under less auspicious circumstances. The fall of the empire in Brazil and the ultimatum
from England coincided with the first weeks of his reign. There
followed a period of political strife and intrigue that went far to
discredit parliamentary institutions and party government, and
a catastrophic worsening of the chronically diseased national
finances.

Charles, with scarcely a statesman of stature and integrity left
to advise him, found himself in the hands of the politicians and
identified in the popular mind with their shady manoeuvres and
ineptitudes. A rising in Oporto in January 1891, rashly proclaiming the republic, was easily suppressed and led to the outlawing
of the republican party. This did nothing to restore confidence in
a régime which showed its awareness of being on the defensive
by an increasing disposition to invade constitutional liberties.

Four months later a government confession of what amounted
to national bankruptcy caused a panic collapse of banks and the
currency, and provoked a demand from foreign creditors for a
say in the country's financial administration. To balance the
budget, it was said, it would have been necessary to suppress
the army, the navy, the civil service, and all public undertakings.
One competent financial administrator did emerge in 1892-3,
Ferreira Dias, who succeeded by stringent economies, if not in rebuilding the national credit, in mitigating somewhat its discredit.

When he turned from reform to further taxation the public outcry forced him from office; and the crisis continued to dominate
alike the political scene and the life of the nation, under still
rotating governments whose frequent recourse to dictatorial
methods steadily strengthened the republican opposition. One
measure of 1896, authorizing the banishment to Timor without
trial of any individual held dangerous as an anarchist, enabled
the government to get rid straightway of sixty-six opponents; it
was to have a devastating repercussion a decade later.

A new threat to the colonies developed from 1897 with a tentative approach for financial help to England, with whom, thanks
in part to a state visit to London by Charles in 1895, friendly relations had now been restored. Germany, still eager to fish in
troubled waters and assuming that the colonies would of necessity
figure as security, demanded a share in any arrangement. To

press the demand, which England at first had rejected out of hand, she made play of her sympathy and influence with the Boers in the impending struggle for South Africa. By the Anglo-German convention of 1898 spheres of interest were recognized for both countries.

Germany's concern lay, naturally, with extending her own African territories into southern Angola and northern Mozambique; and while an England not over-easy in conscience pinned her hopes to the need's never arising, Germany bent her efforts to forcing Portugal into the desired borrowing. In mid-1899 a German and an English squadron arrived in the Tagus within a day of each other, one to apply pressure, the other to help Portugal withstand it. Portugal withstood, and that autumn a secret Anglo–Portuguese declaration reaffirmed the full validity of the earlier treaties of alliance, the most vital provision of which, it may be well to recall from the text of that of 1661, bound England 'to take the interest of Portugal and all its dominions to heart, defending the same with the utmost power by sea and land, even as England itself'. The rift had been healed, and in the troublous times ahead that guarantee would continue to be Portugal's sheet anchor.

The new century brought a split in the ranks of the regenerators, early in 1901, which foretold the approaching end of rotativism and of much besides. Franco, the dissident, based his defection on the need for a stronger colonial policy, and carried with him sufficient deputies to form a new party of 'liberal regenerators'. The title popularly given them of Franquistas was however truer, for he was a man of immoderate ambition playing for power; and though the elections of that year were so controlled, on the basis of a new electoral law promulgated for the purpose, as to deny election to every republican and every Franquista save one, he knew how to wait. The next few years were marked by outbursts of anti-clericalism in Oporto, of student turbulence in Coimbra, of violent indignation in Cortes and in the press over any allegation of scandal that could be turned against the crown. Even a momentary cessation of political strife, such as accompanied Edward VII's visit to Lisbon in 1903 and the return visit of Charles to London a year later, became memorable.

At length, in 1906, Charles himself put an end to the system that for so long had sought to delude the nation with the pretence of representative institutions. Turning his back on both parties, he called Franco to power with a charge to follow 'a different path' from the old. The new path soon revealed itself as arbitrary dictatorship, begun under the shadow of a major outcry concerning unauthorized advances made to the king, who thereby lost all claim to be considered above the mêlée. Having decreed cuts in official salaries, Franco proceeded to increase those of army officers. Early in 1907 he threw off all constitutional disguise, dismissed the Cortes by decree, and by his personal rule, backed by the king, found himself at war with monarchists no less than republicans.

In due course the Council of State reminded the king of his obligation to call new Cortes. His refusal tore up the constitution and created a situation out of which there was no escape for him or his minister. The Lisbon municipality, protesting similarly, was dissolved and replaced by an administrative commission; those of other cities soon suffered the same fate; and launched now, in desperate self-defence, on a career of despotism, Franco went on to suppress newspapers, suspend immunities, and create new political offences and new tribunals to try them. A revolution planned for 28 January 1908 was foiled; and Franco, proclaiming martial law in the capital, obtained from Charles the revalidation of the decree of 1896, since allowed to become a dead letter, empowering him to deport his political enemies to Timor without trial. In signing this Charles signed his own death warrant. On the following day, 1 February, returning to Lisbon with the royal family from a brief holiday, both Charles and his eldest son fell victims to assassins' bullets. Manuel, the second son, was slightly wounded.

Fearful that the monarchy itself must succumb, Franco turned at once to England and Spain for help. The former duly sent a squadron to Lagos, the latter a force to the frontier. But the army remained loyal, while Franco himself, dismissed by the new king, sought refuge in Spain. It was to prove but a brief respite for the crown. Manuel II (1908–10), another prince who, having no expectation of the succession, had followed the traditional calling of the sea, was eighteen years old and wholly inexperienced in politics. He wished a ministry and a policy of conciliation, but there were no new men capable of forming the one or implementing the other; and once the most offensive of Franco's decrees had been rescinded and the liberty of press and of association restored, the political game resumed as before, while republicanism, working through a secret society, the *Carbonária*, which rapidly infiltrated into the armed forces, laid its plans for final victory.

Six changes of government in two years were the indictment of a régime and a system no longer capable of governing. The elections of August 1910 gave the republicans a substantial moral victory in the winning of fourteen seats, eleven of them in Lisbon: they had already captured the Lisbon municipality, and knew the army now with them. The question was no longer whether the republic would come, but how soon, and how. It came on 5 October 1910, and triumphed with an ease none would have dared to foretell. A cruiser in the Tagus shelled the royal palace, and Manuel, discovering his advisers fled, fled himself in the royal yacht to Gibraltar and thence to England, there to live and, twenty-two years later, to die. Minus a king to fight for, the monarchists gave up the fight. The cruiser that fired the shells was the *Adamastor*.

14

Disillusion

THE chastened mood in which Spain entered the twentieth century did not prove in itself sufficient for regeneration. Inevitably, since no one could claim that the nation as a whole had yet been drawn into a responsible share in government, the disaster of 1898 was laid at the door of the politicians, to the further discrediting of politics. It was thus of particular ill-omen for the new reign that Alfonso XIII, declared of age at sixteen in May 1902 and formally sworn to observe the constitution, should have revealed himself from the beginning as much less a constitutional monarch or a statesman than as one politician more. Even had there been men immediately capable, like the Cánovas and Sagasta of the previous generation, of maintaining at least the semblance of continuity and tranquillity, the convention of conservative and liberal alternation in office had long since worn thin.

One reason was the emergence of new political forces, socialism and Catalanism in particular, that could not be accommodated within the two-party framework, with the consequent tendency to disintegration under new pressures of the two older groupings; another a growing resort to violence for political ends which often removed the struggle from Cortes to the streets. Of the notable political figures of this reign one of each major party, Dato and Canalejas, was eventually assassinated. Such political unease found early expression in the long series of cabinet crises and the eight prime ministers thrown up over the first four years, a period culminating in the attempted murder of Alfonso himself on the day of his wedding in 1906 to an English princess, Victoria Eugenia.

Collapse of empire had not freed Spain entirely from overseas commitments and anxieties. There remained Africa. Spain's share in the general scramble over that continent had been limited to the acquisition between 1884 and 1886 of the barren wastes of Río de Oro, to the south-west of Morocco. After 1898 the national mood was all for retreat, not expansion; but the threatening disruption of the Moroccan empire shortly afterwards compelled a renewal of interest in that direction. The Anglo–French convention of 1904, basis of the Entente Cordiale, and the Algeciras conference of 1906 brought Spain with France into a general responsibility for Morocco, which the Franco–Spanish agreement of 1912 made explicit by establishing a Spanish protectorate over the north-western zone. This gave Spain both an Atlantic and a Mediterranean coastline in Africa and provided a substantial hinterland to the individual strongholds, from Ceuta to Melilla, which for centuries now had been under Spanish sovereignty.

Pacification of the zone added one more to the accumulating problems at home, where the unpopularity of service in Africa and the liberal denunciation of this 'policy of conquest' provided constant scope for agitation. In 1909 tribal attacks on Melilla – the same spark that fired O'Donnell's war of 1859–60 – and the hurried despatch of reinforcements from Barcelona led to a major uprising, a general strike, and a death-roll of a hundred in the latter city. The execution in reprisal, among others, of the pedagogue and doctrinal anarchist Francisco Ferrer proved a tactical error, if not too a miscarriage of justice, which stirred liberal and socialist opinion throughout Europe. Maura, the conservative leader, was forced out of office after two and a half years, the first tenure of any length that the reign had seen, and there long persisted a violent antagonism to conservative rule.

This 'tragic week', though instigated by anarcho-syndicalists and unrelated to Catalanism, added a further count in the developing tension between Catalonia and Madrid. Since the elections of 1901 Catalan 'regionalists' had had representation as such in both houses of parliament, their aim 'to work by all legitimate means for the autonomy of the Catalan people within the Spanish state'. The cause received strong impetus from the passing in 1906 of a notorious 'law of jurisdictions', one provision of which enacted the long-standing army demand that activities directed against the armed forces should be tried by military tribunals. This frankly political weapon aimed directly at Catalonia became the most hated, as it was the most illiberal, measure of the whole twenty-five years during which it remained in force.

Among its results was the formation of a united front on the regionalist issue, the Solidaritat Catalana, which though soon sundered contributed to the winning of a first notable concession from Madrid, the creation in 1914 of a 'Mancomunitat' or federation of the four Catalan provinces invested with certain powers and functions – notably communications, education, and social services – hitherto reserved to the central government. A modest instalment of the full autonomy demanded, and far from settling the 'Catalan problem', it marked a reversal of that policy of centralization which the Habsburgs had begun and Philip V so ruthlessly completed, and it allowed the Catalans to demonstrate once again the capacity for running their own affairs which had always been the envy and despair of the Castilian.

In one direction Canalejas and the liberals sought to march with the times. The Church's monopoly control of education in a country where half the children received no schooling and its intolerance of religious dissent continued to irk the more enlightened sectors of public opinion; while the religious orders, greatly swollen after the expulsions from France of 1905, had come under heavy criticism as parasitical. In 1910 Canalejas proposed to the Vatican revision of the 1851 concordat, required the civil registration of orders, and forbade the establishment meantime of new religious houses. An outburst of anti-clerical agitation led to another period of strained relations with the Vatican, but again this proved too strong for the reformers.

The World War of 1914–18 found Spain deeply divided. Army, Church, and conservatives generally inclined to Germany, who dangled the old baits of Gibraltar and a free hand with Portugal. Liberalism had with it in supporting the allies the bulk of popular opinion, together with the Basque and Catalan regionalists, who knew well on which side their interests lay. Neutrality was thus the only possible policy, and the war years witnessed in consequence a rapid industrial expansion, with corresponding strains in the social fabric. Among these must be numbered the now large-scale influx into Barcelona of unskilled labour from Murcia and Almería. In 1917 labour unrest on the railways developed into a general strike with revolutionary ends in view.

It had the support, exceptionally, of both socialist and anarcho-syndicalist unions, normally engaged in bitter strife against each other, and for three months the country was under martial law.

Much more sinister was the emergence in the previous year of army 'defence juntas', the equivalent of a military trade union. Behind the direct challenge these implied to government authority some suspected the hand of the king himself, who in his personal relations with the armed forces had from the beginning laid himself open to the charge of unconstitutionalism. The defence juntas marked the beginning of the end. So supported, the army won every time it saw or imagined it saw its interests invaded, and normal government became impossible. The year 1917 witnessed four governments and a long succession of crises; a cabinet in 1918 of all the talents composed of ex-premiers fared no better.

The end of the war found the country a prey therefore to both social and political unrest. Early in 1919 a threat issued in Barcelona that any 'strike aggression' would be dealt with by military courts was accepted as a direct challenge and led to yet another general strike, which this time labour won, bringing down the government. Anarcho-syndicalism with its creed of violence that respected neither authority, property, nor life constituted an even graver threat to society, for which no government had the answer. In 1921 a prime minister was assassinated, in 1923 an archbishop. Catalan autonomists, confronted with this increasing lawlessness in their midst, had thus strong reason for renewing their claim to responsibilities which Madrid manifestly could not discharge. They had already, in November 1919, made petition to Madrid for full autonomy, with the support of ninety-eight per cent of all municipal and rural councils throughout the four provinces; and on rejection had gone to Versailles to invoke its concern for the rights of small nationalities and to ask for recognition in this category.

The dividing line between autonomy and separatism was crossed in 1922 by the launching of an out-and-out nationalist party, Estat Català, and for many the die had been cast: only within a federal Spain could they still want to be Spaniards. To this right wing of the movement there soon corresponded a vigorous left wing, Acció Catalana, which in 1923 concluded an alliance with similar forces in the Basque provinces and Galicia. Once more the fate of Spain as a unitary concept was called in question: if it should collapse, warrant abounded for the contention that it would prove to be not the regions but Castile, its original maker, who now unmade it.

From Morocco in 1921 derived one more crisis, the most damaging of all. Ever since the events of 1909 the task of pacifying the protectorate and civilizing the Rif tribes had been making slow if unspectacular progress, geographical conditions being infinitely more adverse, and economic rewards less, than in the French zone. A general uprising now under Abd el Krim took the Spanish forces by surprise, and the disaster of Anual in July, when the tribesmen destroyed a force 20,000 strong and all but pushed the Spaniards into the sea at Melilla, staggered the nation. This was the army that at home was presuming to set itself above the state; and this, to many, was the crowning result of Alfonso's constant meddling, over the heads of his ministers, in spheres that were not his to invade.

There was an immediate demand, in and outside the Cortes, for a probe into responsibilities that would spare neither feelings nor reputations. The result of the enquiry was awaited, with burning national interest, in the autumn of 1923. On 13 September of that year Primo de Rivera, captain-general of Barcelona and a nephew of the namesake who as captain-general of Madrid had in 1874 proclaimed the restoration, made his *coup d'état*, disbanded government and Cortes, and, with the king's support, replaced the parliamentary farce by a military dictatorship. No more was heard of the Anual report.

The new régime enjoyed a large measure of initial goodwill, inasmuch as civilian government had manifestly broken down and the country at large was less immediately interested in the causes therefor than in the reimposition of public order. This was true even of Catalonia, until the veil was torn from the dictator's first glib professions of benevolence towards Catalan aspirations. The things a dictatorship can do well Primo de Rivera did: public security, public works, and much that lack of authority and of continuity had repeatedly frustrated before. Through joint operations with France, made possible when Abd el Krim imprudently advanced into the French zone, he rescued the army in Morocco from contumely. The Rif leader surrendered in 1926, and the reoccupation and final pacification of the whole zone followed. This in its turn lifted a crushing burden from the treasury; and in the following year, for the first time in two decades, the budget was balanced without recourse to a loan.

Political problems were less amenable to solution. The dictator, having set out to free the country from party politics, merely drove the parties underground. Catalonia he antagonized completely by the obdurate centralism of a policy that culminated in 1925 in the abolition of the Mancomunitat. The change in that year from a military 'directorate' to a partly civilian cabinet, the formation of a 'Patriotic Union' in 1926 and of a National Assembly or pseudo-Cortes in 1927, failed completely to win the popular support he grew increasingly conscious of needing or to compensate for the suspension of constitutional guarantees, press censorship, and government by decree; while by his clericalist policy in education he ranged the intellectuals and the universities solidly against him. The university of Madrid he closed on one occasion for eighteen months. As always, it had proved easier to liquidate an old system than to create a new. When the repercussions of the world economic crisis of 1929 reached Spain he lost the support of the army too; and in January 1930 he confessed to defeat and left the country, to die in Paris six weeks later.

The king was left with his problem. By failing to summon new Cortes within three months he too, like Charles earlier in Portugal, had broken his coronation oath; and for that crime, to a nation concerned now only to find its way back to constitutional paths, there could be no condonation, not even the defence that in so doing he had thought to serve the higher interests of the country. A first stop-gap administration under a general, a second under an admiral, meant only that politicians concerned whether with principle or with reputation refused to serve under a perjured monarch; and persecution and imprisonment were impotent to stifle their views.

When elections could no longer be denied, it was the municipal elections of April 1931, the first opportunity for a free expression of opinion in eight years, which decided the issue. Over the country as a whole the returns alleged a monarchist majority; in the large cities the republican vote was overwhelming. Alfonso accepted their verdict and followed his late dictator into exile, though without abdicating the throne, to die in Rome ten years later.

The long chain of causation begun at Anual had brought Spain back to another 1868, with the difference that a search for another occupant of the throne did not now arise. Not only the king stood discredited, but kingship too; and there was no one in 1931 to argue that this had followed on and could be held the direct result of the total discrediting first of representative government. That conviction would gain ground with the experience of the years immediately ahead. Meantime the second republic came overnight.

Primo de Rivera, in a political testament written in Paris, had observed that, whatever his failures, one undeniable success he could claim: the Catalan question would raise its head no more. Within six months, in a pact signed at San Sebastian in August 1930 by the various anti-monarchist forces, the new republic had laid its plans on the basis of full recognition for the principle of self-determination. This, to some at least of the signatories, meant clearly a federal constitution on which not Catalans alone but Basques, Galicians, and any other region so minded would have claims, a forthright reversal of the unitary trend which had presided over close on 500 years of Spanish history.

When the monarchy fell, Catalonia in its enthusiasm leapt momentarily ahead of events with the proclamation, even before the republic had been hailed in Madrid, of a Catalan state 'which we shall endeavour to incorporate in a federation of Iberian republics'. For 'state' an anxious Madrid, emphasizing that regional autonomy and a federation of republics were two very different things, secured the substitution of the historic and less provocative term 'Generalitat'. A first and profound rift had appeared before the new régime was a day old: its development would further underline fundamental realities in Spanish history which no mere change of régime can obscure. Castile is, of its essence, centralist and in consequence authoritarian. The peripheral regions are, of their essence, centrifugal and egalitarian.

Another immediate problem was public order. Dictatorship and the mailed fist had put down terrorist outrage. Their removal brought it back; and a wave of anti-clerical violence, with much burning of churches, followed by another of syndicalist strikes, spread over the country, which authority was powerless to check. It was to prove the tragedy of the republic that from the beginning its gravest dangers came precisely from the republican ranks; and before the constituent Cortes could frame its new constitution it had to pass, and later to incorporate in the same, a 'law for the defence of the republic' vesting in the government and in provincial governors powers over the press, the right of association, and the individual as arbitrary and illiberal as any invoked by the dictatorship, only, as it proved, much less effective.

By the constitution of 1931 Spain was declared a 'democratic republic of workers of all classes', with authority derived from the people and without official religion. It instituted a single-chamber Cortes, and gave suffrage to both sexes at the age of twenty-three. The Church was disestablished, the religious orders forbidden to teach or engage in trade, and the Society of Jesus once more deprived of its property and expelled. Divorce by consent was recognized, and primary education made compulsory. As for regionalism, groups of provinces might seek from the Cortes a statute of autonomy, but no federation of autonomous regions would be tolerated.

Regionalism apart, it was the charter of 1812 over again, in a twentieth- instead of a nineteenth-century setting, and charged not merely with inherent contradictions, like the coupling of the ban on the teaching orders with the declaration of compulsory education while the state still provided at most for some twenty-five per cent of the school-age population, but with direct threats to the continued existence of the republic itself. One such was the giving of votes to women – more than half of the 1933 register – of whom the vast majority might be relied on to use them as their Catholic conscience, if not the priest, dictated.

The anti-clerical clauses in particular were thus political dynamite. Their formulation caused the first prime minister himself, Alcalá Zamora, and his minister of the interior to resign in protest. Azaña, succeeding as premier, might assert that Spain was no longer a Catholic nation: such wishful thinking in face of all the evidence was at one with the old presumption, never more dangerously exemplified than now, that a constitution need only reflect the society aimed at, and that the competence and the will of society as it existed to make it work could be taken for granted.

The charter safely on the statute-book, government and Cortes proceeded with the social revolution. The objectives were clear: to take the army and the Church out of politics, to break up the *latifundios* and give the land to a starving peasantry, to make all men economically free and politically equal, to educate the nation, beginning with the children, into civic responsibility on a wholly secular basis, in short to make a modern society overnight out of one which was still in many respects medieval. For two years the Cortes legislated, against a background of syndicalist and communist attempts on the left to disrupt the state and of conservative, Catholic, and monarchist attempts on the right to defend the interests at the cost of which the revolution was to be effected.

The right too had been quick to show its readiness to resort to force, as in the abortive monarchist rising in Madrid and that of the army in Seville in 1932. Azaña, who had retained the ministry of war after his elevation to the premiership, had already ranged the army effectively against the republic by abolishing alike the notorious law of jurisdictions, the supreme military court, and the captaincies-general of the eight military regions, by retiring – on full pay – many superfluous senior officers, and by a serious attempt to overhaul and make efficient what was much less a fighting force than a political organization.

An agrarian law, also of 1932, proposed the expropriation of large estates against indemnification and the leasing of them to the peasants in small holdings. It was centuries overdue and, had it been carried into effect, would have changed the social face of Spain: but for that twenty or thirty years, and not the five the republic lasted, were needed. The Catalan autonomy statute passed in the same year had been greatly changed and weakened in Cortes from the draft approved by the Catalans in an almost unanimous referendum. Catalonia accepted it loyally, but the disillusion went deep, and was readily fanned by later events into resentment. The corresponding Basque statute, likewise submitted in 1932, was not approved until October 1936, after the outbreak of the Civil War, and therefore never achieved reality.

Still less did that for Galicia, where autonomous sentiment and the prospect of its successful implementing had alike lagged far behind.

The elections of November 1933 produced the violent swing to the right which, even without the many other factors tending in that direction, female suffrage alone would have made inevitable. Where the Cortes of 1931 had been predominantly left-wing, the right now numbered 207, the centre 167, and the left only 99. There followed another two years, therefore, in which policy was centre–right, with the right chafing for full power and undoing as much as it could of the work of the preceding biennium. Discontent was soon rife in Catalonia and among the Basques over the treatment they were receiving from Madrid, as in Andalusia over the dimmed outlook for agrarian reform.

A cabinet reshuffle towards the right in October 1934 loosed the avalanche with a general strike throughout the country, the proclaiming anew in Barcelona of the Catalan state within a federal republic, and in Asturias a rebellion that became a minor civil war. The revolt in Catalonia was speedily quelled by the army, now with the government and always instinctively against regionalism. That in Asturias, broken within a week with the help of Moroccan troops, left a trail of 1,335 killed, 3,000 wounded, and the city of Oviedo largely in ruins. For two months the country was under martial law. The Catalan statute was declared in abeyance, and administration again centred in Madrid. Over the question of the death penalty for rebellion the government fell, and there ensued a long period of political instability and general stultification. By the end of 1935 there had been twenty-eight governments in less than five years; and although there was now much talk and evident need of revision of the constitution, against such impermanence in office this could never be undertaken.

New elections in February 1936 ended all hope of a republic for all Spaniards, or even for all republicans. They had become a battle for power between right and left coalitions more deeply hostile to each other than. ever extremes had been under the monarchy. Whichever side won, the victim would be not merely the other, but the liberal republic, and Spain. The one brought together, in a Popular Front, a strange assembly of bedfellows:

republicans, socialists, syndicalists, anarchists, communists. The other boasted at least much greater cohesion in composition and coherence in programme. Between the two the centre parties were all but eliminated. In this clear-cut issue where those who had everything to lose confronted those who had nothing, there was no longer room for a middle-of-the-road policy.

More formally stated, the conflict lay between order and 'progress', the two apparent incompatibles of modern Spain. The right polled slightly under or slightly over half the total votes, according to the interpretation given to marginal groupings in an election contested by close on a score of parties. The electoral system gave to the left an absolute majority of seats; and behind the façade of government its extremist elements, already wedded as all knew to direct action, set about the disintegration of the bourgeois society that was their real enemy. During the next five months there befell such a relapse into violence and chaos as had not been seen since the cantonalism of 1873. Church-burnings, strikes, and political assassination paralysed the life of the country. The record for the first four months of Popular Front rule, as presented to the Cortes, was 269 murders, 170 churches, 69 political clubs, and 10 newspaper offices set on fire, and 113 general and 228 partial strikes.

And again the violence was not all on one side. Extremism on the right had begun to retaliate in kind, its instrument the Falange Española, a Spanish brand of fascism founded in 1933 by a son of the late dictator Primo de Rivera. In the south peasants were taking the agrarian law into their own hands and parcelling out the estates. The government had lost control, and the republic was already dead before it received the *coup de grace* with the military rising launched from Morocco on 17 July 1936. Here was proof of its failure to destroy the political power of the army, as it had failed in education, in agriculture, and – with only one regular budget in its whole course – in finance. Least of all had it succeeded in inculcating the qualities of tolerance, compromise, and integrity without which there could be no self-government. And now the pronunciamiento had returned.

The Civil War of 1936–9 was fought with all the savagery and bitterness of which civil war is capable. It cost 1,000,000 lives and wrought incalculable destruction. Symbolizing in theory –

for the reality was infinitely more complex – the clash between the democratic and the totalitarian way of life which was then profoundly exercising the whole of Europe, it threatened to bring all Europe into the fray. Russia poured in help to the left, Italy and Germany to the right, while England and France fought a tense and losing battle to secure from the powers more than lip-service to the principle of non-intervention. The republicans were at heavy initial disadvantage in having to build up a people's army from nothing; but the issue was not the people against the army. The nation itself was almost equally divided.

Regionalism became one major factor in determining allegiance: it threw Catalonia, Valencia, and two of the Basque provinces, Guipúzcoa and Vizcaya, into the republican camp. Catholicism was another, and identified most of the agricultural provinces with the insurgents. Where the two were in conflict – and united, it will be remembered, they had provided the support for Carlism – there resulted for many a cruel dilemma of conscience, and the other two Basque provinces, Alava and Navarre, were with the army.

Organized labour knew clearly where it stood; but the socialist-syndicalist battle for control continued behind the other battle-front, and communism, thriving on the flow of arms from Russia, was soon disputing that control with both. In Barcelona in May 1937 an anarcho-syndicalist attempt to seize power led to what was in effect a second civil war within the first; and when in the following October the republican government, which already in November 1936 had abandoned Madrid for Valencia, removed to the Catalan capital, the presence of two governments and of so many conflicting forces in one city gave rise to a political tension that would only end with the war itself.

Apart from occasional local successes – the routing of the Italians at Guadalajara in March 1937, the crossing of the Ebro in July 1938 – the republic was on the defensive throughout. The fall of Badajoz in August 1936 had early given Estremadura to the insurgents and allowed their forces in northern and southern Spain, centred respectively on Burgos and Seville, to join hands to the west of Madrid. Vizcaya and Guipúzcoa, cut off from the other republican territories, were overrun by the end of 1937. Striking east in the following year, the insurgents reached the Mediterranean at Vinaroz near Castellón by the spring, thus cutting the remaining republican area in two. A final offensive against Catalonia was launched late in December; and when, in January 1939, Barcelona fell, the war in effect was over. Valencia had in itself no powers of resistance, andMadrid's withstanding of a long investment dating from November 1936 bore only a token significance. It surrendered at the end of March, and on 1 April 1939 the war was declared officially at an end.

There had been long periods of stalemate over the two years and eight months, and ground for suspicion on both sides that the conflict was being dragged out in the interest and at the behest of the intervening powers. To Germany and Italy it was at once a try-out and a diversion of their potential enemies as they prepared for the second World War which was to follow so soon upon its heels. To Russia it represented one long political manoeuvre aimed to ensure, should the republican cause triumph, a communist Spain; to which end the winning of the Civil War often took second place to the furthering of the prole-tarian revolution.

Behind the insurgent or 'nationalist' lines political develop-ment, much less confused, became with victory the more impor-tant. The second republic, like the first, had gone down in blood and chaos; but the victors this time could not simply revert to what had gone before. Out of the ruins they had to build a new social structure. The army, which had not lifted a finger when Alfonso was overthrown, had not fought this war to bring him back. It looked to Franco, its victorious generalissimo, for a new political structure as close as Spanish conditions would allow to the totalitarian dictatorships of Germany and Italy; and found it in the 'twenty-six points' of the Falange, this name being commonly if inaccurately accepted as abbreviation for the uneasy amalgam imposed by Franco in April 1937 on the three disparate political elements which had supplied most of his civilian support.

The Falange itself was frankly authoritarian, violent in its hostility to representative government and to any suggestion, however remote, of regionalism. The traditionalists were Carlists under a new name, intransigent in their attachment to the creed of a Catholic autocratic monarchy and to their fueros, and forced into a camp where they could have only the scantiest hopes of achieving their end. National-syndicalism dated from early 1931, while Spain was still a monarchy, and had thus originated not, like the Falange, as a challenge to the republic but as an alternative challenge with the republic to the monarchy. It too was anti-clerical, and demanded the separation of Church and state. It had joined forces with Falangism in 1934, and it was largely national-syndicalist doctrine which now, in 1937, supplied the basis of state policy.

The new state envisaged in the twenty-six points would be totalitarian, one-party, unitary ('All separatism is an unpardonable crime'), based on 'a military sense of life', anti-capitalist, anti-Marxist, and – the one concession to the traditionalists – profoundly Catholic. This last was in deference too to foreign opinion, Franco having made of the defence of religion an important plank in his propaganda platform. The specifically Falangist contribution was the theory of the 'vertical' syndicate or trade union with joint representation of workers and employers at each level.

One profound difference from the totalitarian régimes of Italy and Germany lay in the fact that in Spain it was not the party which had seized power and imposed collaboration on the army, but the army which, embarking on revolt without preconceived political objectives, then pressed into its service such political movements as lay to its hand. The party in consequence never captured the state nor won substantial authority. Franco, emerging from the Civil War as head of the state, of the government, of the armed forces, and of the party, showed repeatedly his determination to retain ultimate power in his own hands. During the war he had caused Hedilla, then leader of the Falange, to be arrested and sentenced to death for insubordination – the sentence was commuted through German intervention – and he did not hesitate to provoke a second crisis with the party by his rehabilitation, with even more rights than before, of the Jesuits.

The World War of 1939–45, breaking out within months of the nationalist victory, added greatly to the difficulties of economic and material reconstruction; while the ideological kinship and military indebtedness that bound Spain to the Axis powers, already reflected in her signing of the anti-Comintern pact in March 1939, was to turn to acute embarrassment once the tide of war began to flow in the allied direction. Neutrality was again, as in 1914, the only possible policy until, with the collapse of France and Italy's entry into the war in June 1940, the expectation of imminent Axis victory appeared to justify a change to 'non-belligerency', accompanied by much talk of Spain's new-found 'will to empire' – already in the twenty-six points – and the occupation by force of the internationalized city of Tangier. The presence now of German troops on the Pyrenees made very real the danger of military involvement, willing or unwilling, especially after the allied landings in north Africa in November 1942, when partial mobilization was decreed.

In the following month an 'Iberian Bloc' was formed with Portugal, consolidating a non-aggression treaty of March 1939 – signed within four days of adhering to the anti-Comintern pact – and its protocol of July 1940, the whole speaking eloquently of Franco's cautious concern for reinsurance. The collapse of Italy and of fascism in 1943, of Germany and nazism in 1945, proved how wise that caution had been, but left the régime still in danger from the severe landslide to the left that with the ending of the war swept the continent from Britain to Greece.

Branded by the Potsdam declaration of July 1945 as unfit to associate with the United Nations, one-third of whose members were the daughter republics of Latin America; excluded a month later from an international conference on Tangier which compelled the Spanish evacuation of that city; formally ostracized in December 1946 by the same United Nations, which demanded for Spain too a government deriving its authority from the governed and recommended all member states to recall their ambassadors or ministers from Madrid: nationalist Spain found herself all but friendless. Only Portugal and Argentina still lent their support.

Some concessions to foreign sentiment the régime had already begun to make, abandoning the totalitarian label for that of 'organic democracy', inaugurating in March 1943 another pseudo-Cortes with a membership part *ex officio*, part nominated and part elective on a functional basis and given a watching brief over legislation, allowing the Falangist party to sink into the background until in July 1945 it had no single member in the cabinet and Franco could announce to the world at large that it no longer wielded any political power, a statement clearly meant for consumption abroad and often later contradicted at home, and dropping hints of an eventual restoration of the monarchy, these never failing to provoke strong Falangist protest.

Repeal of the divorce law, with the restoration of religious education and of budget provision for the Church, led in 1941 to a *modus vivendi* with the Vatican, and eventually to a new concordat in 1953. Only in 1945, six and a half years after the close of the Civil War, did an amnesty for political 'offences' committed during the same put a term to the rancour with which the nationalists had pursued their political opponents: tolerance was still the hardest lesson for any Spaniard to learn.

Foreign indictments proved, however, to have the effect, opposite to that intended, of rallying Spanish opinion instead to the defence of the régime. In part a preference for internal over external dictation, if dictation there must be, in part also it reflected the profound disillusion born of the second republic and the desire to avoid at all costs any recrudescence of civil war. Other governments recognized at length the failure of the policy, and one by one resumed diplomatic relations. In 1955 Spain was admitted to the United Nations. Two years earlier she had signed an agreement with the United States whereby the latter granted economic aid in return for defence bases on Spanish soil.

In lieu of a constitution, the régime promulgated between 1938 and 1947 five 'fundamental laws of the nation': a labour charter, the law creating Cortes, a charter of rights, a national referendum law, and a law of succession. By the last-named Spain was declared once again, 'in accordance with tradition', a kingdom; in the absence of a king, Franco continued in power as regent. His successor, of the blood royal, would be required to swear these fundamental laws together with fidelity to the principles of the Falangist movement. In 1954 Franco agreed with prince John, third son of Alfonso and claimant to the throne, that the latter's eldest son, the sixteen-year-old Don Juan Carlos, should receive his education in Spain.

Meanwhile the régime continued to rest on authority, not on

consent. Compared with the brief and troubled span of the dictatorship of Primo de Rivera, many factors told in its favour. From fascism and nazism Franco learnt much of the technique of dictatorship, and learnt too how to avoid the mistakes, notably the foreign adventures – Morocco's achievement of independence in 1956 closing the one remaining chapter of Spanish imperialism – and the forfeiting of army support, that brought them down.

In maintaining public order and the public credit and pursuing at the same time a policy of economic development and social reform, especially in social services and guarantees assured to workers through the syndicates, he won to his side the many who felt that political freedoms can exact too high a price. Those holding to the contrary, their numbers reinforced by a generation which had grown up since the tragedies of the second republic and the Civil War, were of necessity unable to show in advance what they would or could make of yet another experiment in full self-government. Over the centuries Spain's choice had continued to lie between anarchy and hierarchy.

The coming of the republic to Portugal in 1910 had found that country no better prepared than Spain for political responsibility. Again everything externally was in its favour: the monarchy fell without a struggle, the army acquiesced, popular enthusiasm was nation-wide and foreign goodwill immediate. And again everything went wrong, from the belief that a society can be revolutionized overnight and that freedoms bring automatically in their train the corresponding sense of responsibility.

A provisional government under Theófilo Braga, the iconoclast of 1871, decreed the separation of Church and state, expulsion of the religious orders, and the secularization of education, with the suppression of the faculty of theology at Coimbra and the creation of new universities in Lisbon and Oporto. Conflict not merely with the Church but with the religious conscience of the nation was thereby ensured. Labour was granted the right to strike, and straightway invoked it on a scale and with a casualness and even irrelevance that promised not social advance but economic decline.

By August 1911 constituent Cortes had approved the new constitution. With the now inevitable preamble that sovereignty resided in the nation, this guaranteed freedom of conscience and worship, of expression and association. Parliament would consist of a chamber of deputies and a senate both elective, for three and six years respectively, by direct suffrage of all citizens over twenty-one years of age who were either literate or heads of family, and could only be prorogued by joint vote of both houses, while neither president of the republic nor prime minister would have power to dissolve. The judiciary was declared independent and the armed forces to be 'essentially obedient' and without right of petition or unauthorized assembly.

In fact the constitution proved to be of little consequence. With power, republicanism took on so many party shades that a first constitutional government was formed with great difficulty and lasted a mere two months. General strikes and bomb-throwing soon presented a much graver threat to the régime than the monarchists who, encouraged by a pact of 1912 between the exiled Manuel and his cousin Dom Miguel which at last buried the Miguelist hatchet, attempted in that year a fruitless incursion from Spain.

On the outbreak of war in Europe in 1914 Portugal sought initially, on British advice, to remain neutral, while despatching forces to the defence of Angola and Mozambique. German incursions there soon led parliament at home to authorize the government to enter the war whenever this should be judged necessary 'to the high interests and duties of Portugal as a free nation and ally of England', and meanwhile to take any necessary measures. These measures early in the following year led the army to intervene in politics despite the constitution; and the advent of a military cabinet, duly denounced as a dictatorship, provoked an abortive rising with naval backing in Lisbon which led to its fall and to the resignation of the first president of the republic.

In March 1916 Germany declared war on Portugal, the immediate motive the seizure at Britain's request of thirty-six German vessels immobilized since the beginning of the war in Portuguese waters. The declaration followed on earlier German protests, amounting almost to an ultimatum, against the services Portugal was rendering to the allied cause. Entry into the war led to some closing of the political ranks, and in January 1917 an army of 25,000 men embarked for France and Flanders, there to play a heroic role at the battle of the Lys in April 1918. But the worsening economic conditions at home provoked a further wave of strikes, oppressive counter-measures, and, in December 1917, another military revolt which drove the second president into exile and gave to the army leader, Sidónio Pais, autocratic powers.

His 'new republic', like the unitary republic in the Spain of 1874, had come with the help of the armed forces to save the republic from itself; and public opinion, recognizing the need, was substantially with him alike when he nominated himself president and when he abrogated measures against the Church and, after a rupture that had now lasted eight years, renewed relations with the Vatican, a first step on the long road to the eventual signing, in 1940, of a new concordat. The political parties, in contrast, boycotted the régime, then plotted its violent overthrow, and in December 1918, a month after the war had ended, Pais was assassinated.

Thereafter stability, order, and passable competence in government were no more seen. The politicians fiddled while the country burned. A succession of four governments in 1919, of seven in 1920, of five in 1921 accompanied a precipitous collapse in the country's financial and economic affairs. The escudo, worth 4s. in 1917, had fallen to 2s. 10d. in 1918: by 1922 it was worth 2½d. Strikes and outrages bore ever more frequent witness to the powerlessness of the rulers to rule. The revolution of October 1921 was stained with the murder of the prime minister and of a number of other leading figures of the republican right. Primo de Rivera's *coup* in Spain came soon after to point to the only possible outcome; and the three army risings in the course of 1925 were significant, in spite of their failure, as showing that that outcome would not now be long delayed.

It came with the successful movement of 28 May 1926, which put an end to one of the most calamitous periods in Portuguese history. The republic of 1910–26 was wholly negative in its achievements and, where positive in its views, rested these on assumptions early proved to be wholly unwarranted. The basic assumption of 1910 was that the monarchy had failed. What had failed was the liberal experiment, resting on representative parliamentary government, of the preceding ninety years. The change of figurehead from king to president gave in itself no guarantee of betterment; the granting of new liberties before the old had proved both merited and workable was at once naïve and disastrous; and neither a people's character was to be changed, nor a competent new governing class to be improvised, by paper constitutions. Over the sixteen years the republic had known an average of one revolution and close on three governments per year. By the end only one of six presidents had completed his four-year term, while 500 individuals had held cabinet office. Political integrity lay, with financial solvency, in the dust.

What followed was dictatorship; and here, where so much had run so closely parallel to the experience of Spain, a notable divergence arises. The sequence in Spain was to be monarchy, dictatorship, republic; in Portugal monarchy, republic, dictatorship. When in 1936 the second Spanish republic disintegrated, the earlier collapse of dictatorship left little to choose between the two for the next experiment: the nation's sympathies were in fact almost equally divided, and civil war was the result. The collapse of the Portuguese republic in 1926 left the solution of dictatorship still untried, and so widespread a revulsion from the republican nightmare that only the professional politicians, and such as they could play on for interested purposes, were left to mourn its passing. In Portugal, moreover, there was no regional consciousness to overlay the issue, nor, in a country still on the very threshold of industrialism, a complex and explosive labour situation.

The 'New State' that came to birth in 1926 was not firmly nor recognizably established as such until years afterwards. In its beginnings it seemed to betoken but one pronunciamiento more, clear on what it came to overthrow, completely vague on what was to take its place. The public order that was its first objective was itself severely shaken by risings in Oporto and Lisbon in February 1927 more desperate and costlier in lives than anything that had preceded, and army revolts continued until 1931. And the triumvirate that originally seized power and, having summarily dismissed parliament, formed a three-man government, lasted a mere six weeks, the two generals first deposing the one civilian, the second general then deposing the first and offering him the choice of elevation to the presidency or relegation to the Azores, for which latter he opted. Carmona, the survivor, then nominated himself prime minister and interim president.

Assurance of permanence or success did not come till 1928, with the appearance on the scene of a Coimbra professor of economics, Salazar by name, as finance minister. In that year the government had appealed to the League of Nations for a substantial loan, which was only forthcoming on such conditions of external control as Portuguese pride refused to accept. Salazar imposed similar conditions from within, starting with the resolve that, at whatever cost, Portugal should thereafter live within her means, retrenching on the heroic scale, and exacting for himself full authority over all spending by other ministers. In 1928-9, for the third time in seventy-five years, the budget balanced; and no subsequent budget failed to balance. Carmona, no longer premier, was confirmed in the presidency by plebiscite in 1928 and re-elected for successive seven-year terms until his death in 1951, when another general, Craveiro Lopes, took his place. On him followed, in 1958, vice-admiral Thomaz.

In 1932 Salazar became prime minister, and revealed his conception of government by forming a cabinet not of politicians but of technicians. The minister of justice was a lawyer, of foreign affairs a diplomatist, of public works an engineer, of war a soldier; the economist still held, and would until 1940, the ministry of finance. 'The people,' said Salazar, 'has less need of being sovereign than of being governed.' A 'National Union', the one party to replace parties, was formed in 1930 and gave to the régime a basis of political support; but the long-heralded new constitution was only submitted to plebiscite in 1933, from which year the New State can claim to have legalized itself, and its implementing with the first meetings of the new National Assembly and Corporative Chamber did not take place until January 1935.

The constitution, resting much less on liberal doctrines of political rights than on the ethical principles underlying successive papal encyclicals, made no crude concessions to the sovereignty either of the people or of parliament. Government responsibility lay directly to the president, and only through him to the nation. The function of the Assembly being fundamentally advisory, its composition was determined accordingly. The ninety members – the number was increased by one-third in 1945 – would be elected on a four-year mandate by block-list, a device to prevent the re-emergence of parties, an official list being drawn up by the National Union. Opposition lists were provided for, but in a manner to give them negligible possibilities of success. While the Assembly might initiate legislation, within the severely limiting condition that proposals must not involve any increase of expenditure or diminution of revenue, the government could legislate by decree-law at any time, and only laws promulgated during the annual three-months' session of the Assembly required its approval.

The Corporative Chamber was not an upper house in the accepted sense. Intended as the final representation of the nation's economic interests – these being organized, unlike the vertical formula of Falangist Spain, horizontally, with integration of labour syndicates and employers' guilds only at the highest level – it was composed of members nominated either directly or indirectly by the government, and met to consider proposed legislation not as a body but in technical sections. From the nature of both organs it followed that parliament was held useful rather than essential to the régime, which claimed to be judged by its success or failure in governing, not by the functioning of its mechanisms.

The fundamental rights all figured in the constitution, freedom of speech, of worship, of teaching, of association, and immunity from arbitrary arrest; but all were made subject to the higher interests of society and of morals, and it would fall to the government to define those higher interests. The régime sought thereby to identify itself with the state, and tended inevitably in consequence to regard all opposition to the one as being subversive of the other. Thus the outbreak of the Civil War in Spain led not merely to the formation of a Portuguese Legion 'for the moral defence of the nation' but to far-reaching commitments on the nationalist side in that conflict, it being openly confessed that the régime would be gravely endangered by a republican victory. In the second World War Portugal was fortunate this time in being able to remain neutral to the end, her loyalty to the alliance with Britain being never in doubt, but that ally's alliance with Soviet Russia giving rise to much embarrassed apprehension of the possible repercussions in the Peninsula of allied victory.

That the political turmoil which characterized so much of

Europe in the immediate post-war years passed Portugal by provided substantial evidence that Salazar was right in his main presuppositions. His régime might not indicate a path for others, and doubtless he would not have continued to affirm, as he did in 1935, his conviction that 'in twenty years from now, unless there is a setback in political evolution, there will be no more legislative assemblies in Europe'. Nor could he claim to have behind him all the more politically conscious elements in the nation, where again there had grown up a generation that did not remember the years before 1926.

But to have given to Portugal thirty years of tranquillity and orderly development within the possibilities allowed by the strictest financial integrity, and to have enabled the nation to raise its head again in the councils of the powers, was no mean achievement. The empire, administered on the same austere principles – since 1935 no colonial budget failed to balance – was still one of the largest in the world, and had held together when others were fast disintegrating. Granted collective continuity of resolve – and the régime continued very conscious of this, the basic problem, and of the extent to which it rested in the last analysis on the education of the nation 'in a thirst for social justice and a hungering after responsibility' – the potentialities of greatness still open to this 'garden of Europe planted by the edge of ocean' remained far from exhausted.

15

Literature and the Arts – III

THE eighteenth century was a period of intellectual regeneration, as Spain and Portugal were gradually brought back into European currents of thought and initiated in the critical disciplines they had earlier spurned. It was a slow process, that did not get under way until near the middle of the century, and it produced no great creative writers. Luzán's *Poetics* (1737) launched a far-reaching polemic on rules and the unities in drama. Feijóo (1676–1764) performed a herculean task in his attempt to re-awaken the nation through the hundreds of essays he poured forth on every conceivable subject from his Benedictine cell in Oviedo. *Fray Gerundio* (1758–68) by Francisco de Isla, the one novel of the century, is primarily a satire on pulpit bombast.

Jovellanos used his role as elder statesman to play mentor to a generation of poets, the most estimable among them Meléndez Valdés, who sought to rediscover from scratch the elements of their art and to raise this to philosophical heights worthy of the enlightenment. As the century ended, Moratín, its most effective because least pretentious writer, brought the unities to earth with his social comedies in prose, to which Ramón de la Cruz had pointed the way in his *sainetes*, brief playlets of manners abounding in wit and acute observation. Set to music, the *sainete* became the *zarzuela*, Spain's nearest approach to a native opera.

In Portugal the same influences were at work, with an added concern to uproot that of Spain. Inspiration there too continued at a low prosaic level: poetry was become a thing of Arcadias, and prose the preserve of erudition.

Romanticism, to the extent that it had its roots in the past, overleapt the age of reason and that of an earlier social cohesion alike and sought its affinities in the Middle Ages. French and English example was the stronger for the return after 1833 of thousands of liberal exiles, but the movement was still dispersive and shortlived, without recognized leader or received doctrine. In the drama half a dozen plays by as many authors – the more memorable Angel Saavedra's *Don Alvaro* (1835) and Zorrilla's *Don Juan Tenorio* (1844) – tore conventions and passions to shreds and presented the hero so at odds with society that all perforce ended in stark tragedy. The one lyric poet of the period, Espronceda (1808–42), made a serious attempt to live his romanticism, and reflected this, along with an element of Byronic pose, in his dramatic legend *The Student of Salamanca* and the unfinished *Devil-World*, a would-be philosophical vision on the grand scale of struggling humanity.

The historical novel in imitation of Scott proved for Spain a wrong turning, that was rectified thanks largely to a group of *costumbristas*, essayists and painters in little of the regions and characters they knew best. Among these Larra (1809–37) stood out as the most penetrating observer and critic of the social, political, and literary scene of his day, and its best writer. Soon the sketch of manners had grown into the novel, and this, its field of action and its technique now clearly defined, dominated literature down the second half of the century. The greatest of these regionalists was Pereda, his *patria chica* Santander. Others wrote of Asturias (Palacio Valdés), Andalusia (Alarcón, Valera), and Galicia (Pardo Bazán, Valle-Inclán). Pérez Galdós (1843–1920), come to Madrid from the Canaries, by contrast saw the country whole and in two series of *National Episodes* and *Contemporary Novels*, some eighty titles in all, recreated the life of nineteenth-century Spain and acutely analysed many of its social problems. He was the first Spanish author of international stature and appeal in 200 years.

In Bécquer poetry produced a late romantic whose handful of *Rhymes* (1871) is of a lyric depth and sincerity denied to his contemporaries Campoamor and Núñez de Arce, the one greatly esteemed in his day for his facile philosophizing, the other still for much earnest wrestling with doubt and disillusion. The drama, that had declined from the heady passions of romanticism into social comedy and one notable tragedy, Tamayo y Baus's *A New Drama* (1867), produced eventually in Echegaray (1832–1916) a connoisseur in violent melodramatic effects who in more serious vein introduced to the Spanish stage the themes and techniques of Ibsen and won for Spain her first Nobel prize for literature.

In Portugal wars Napoleonic and civil likewise made of the

first three decades of the nineteenth century a cultural desert, relieved at length by two returning exiles, Almeida Garrett (1799–1854) and Herculano (1810–77). These towered above all those of their time and, bestriding the whole field of letters with a seriousness of purpose equally in evidence in their public life, disregarded the current romantic debate in a concern to recover a genuinely national inspiration. Almeida Garrett distinguished himself as epic poet, lyricist, and historical novelist, but most of all by his valiant if finally unsuccessful attempt to resuscitate single-handed a national drama that had ended where it began, with Gil Vicente, 300 years earlier. Two of his half-dozen prose plays, *An Auto of Gil Vicente* and *Frei Luiz de Sousa*, are outstanding. Herculano, poet, historian, and again historical novelist, brought the same thoroughness that characterized his labours of research and interpretation to the imaginative evocation of the medieval past, in his *Legends and Tales* and the two parts, spanning seven centuries, of the *Monastic Chronicle*.

Castello Branco (1825–90) led the novel back to the present, his considerable output ranging from the sentimental to the cynical, from fantasy to naturalism. Uncertain often in purpose and direction, he was stylistically the outstanding artist of his age. Others who made a name for themselves in their delineation of the Portuguese scene were Júlio Diniz, his sphere the subdued idyllic tones of country life, and Eça de Queiroz, who took his stand, if with gradually dwindling conviction, at the opposite pole of French naturalism.

Romanticism, less a creed in Portugal than a vague something in the atmosphere, received a frontal attack in 1865, launched in the name of 'good sense and good taste' by a new generation of poets who scorned sentiment for sincerity. Quental, their mouthpiece, led by German philosophy into a respect for reason that early betrayed him, gave noble reflection to an anguished mind in his *Modern Odes* (1865) and *Sonnets* (1881). João de Deus, born a poet, drew poetry back to the countryside and interpreted the life of nature with unmatched spontaneity and charm. A generation later, Guerra Junqueiro, the most notable Portuguese disciple of Victor Hugo, returned to the same source and drew from it his finest poetry. Two names, António Nobre and Teixeira de Pascoaes, may stand for a revived cult of tradition, in particular the tradition of *saudade*, which took hold of northern poets towards the end of the century and led them in the direction of a vague pantheism. Others followed Eugénio de Castro into symbolism and the search for a cold, detached perfection that lies much more strangely on the native muse.

In Spain the turn of the century marked once again the end of an era and the shattering of its literary and intellectual assumptions. The 'generation of '98' bent its concern to the riddle of national decline, seeking to shock the nation out of the apathy that was held one major factor therein. Novel and essay were the chief instruments to this end, the novelists turning their backs on regionalism, naturalism, and the like criteria, and subordinating plot, description, and characterization to the discussion of ideas. Chief among them were two Basques, Miguel de Unamuno (1864–1936) and Pío Baroja (1872–1956). The former, poet, philosopher, and essayist as well, groped always after the ultimate reality, the inner kernel of personality, a faith rooted precisely in doubt and in ceaseless striving with the unknown. His novels, stripped of every external circumstance, are deliberately timeless. Baroja was equally unorthodox in more orthodox fashion: 'anti-monarchical, anti-historical, anti-Catholic', he too questioned every received value, but tried to make the reader look forward and outward instead of back and in.

Pérez de Ayala and Gabriel Miró, standing at some remove in time from the crisis, restored to artistry its place and in their novels savour with the reader, the one the rich spectacle of human character and foible, the other the delights of the miniaturist. Ortega y Gasset (1883–1955) brought the most acute Spanish mind of his day, nurtured on German philosophers, to bear on the contemporary social and political scene (*Invertebrate Spain, The Revolt of the Masses*). He was too, in the narrower sense, a great writer, an artist in words as well as in ideas. The essays of Azorín (*b.* 1863) constitute an impressionistic reassessment of Spain's literary past.

The movement in poetry associated with the term 'modernism' coincided closely in time with the generation of '98, but in ideals stood far removed. Introduced to Spain by the Nicaraguan Rubén Darío and compounded, with New World abandon, from elements of romanticism, parnassianism, and especially symbolism, it aimed to rescue poetry from the materialism of the age and to make of it, as earlier Góngora, a thing of beauty reserved to the initiate. The ivory tower gave way with time to a concern for things spiritual, and poets came back to grappling with life and experience with an instrument greatly enriched in suppleness and musicality.

Juan Ramón Jiménez (1881–1958), the outstanding follower of Darío and most influential of twentieth-century Spanish poets, evolved at length his own conception of quintessential poetry bared of every element of sensuous appeal. Other figures of note were the brothers Machado, Manuel an Andalusian to the end, Antonio a Castilian by adoption, who exemplify the continuing deep cleavage in spirit between the two regions. García Lorca (1898–1936) interpreted the traditional life and spirit of Andalusia in its more elemental aspects with a sense of the dramatic which informs, too, half a dozen powerful plays. Among leading poets of the present day are Dámaso Alonso, Vicente Aleixandre, and Rafael Alberti.

In the drama Jacinto Benavente (1866–1954), another Nobel prize-winner, as was Jiménez, showed himself a master of characterization and of gentle irony, gifts he used with devastating effect on the false standards and hypocrisy of a parasitical upper class. To this extent he was one with the writers of '98. His repute abroad rests rather on a number of psychological dramas and allegorical plays (*Bonds of Interest, The Mistress, Passion Flower*) written on a larger canvas. Martínez Sierra wrote with delicate intuition, especially into feminine psychology, on abiding facets of Spanish life, skirting most skilfully the dividing line between sentiment and sentimentality. The brothers Alvarez Quintero collaborated in some 200 sparkling comedies set in a care-free, irresponsible Andalusia; their aim, pure entertainment, they achieved with unfailing dexterity and humour.

Nothing is more striking in the peninsular cultural scene down the nineteenth century than the renaissance of Catalan letters dating from the 1830's, after an eclipse of over 300 years. Related in part to the romantic movement and its new sense of literary nationalism, in part to the industrial revolution that cast Catalonia for a new and leading role in the nation's economy, it gave fresh life and vigour to a tongue which had first to be recovered from the countryside, then enriched and disciplined for a resump-, tion of purposes long forgotten. The movement captured the popular imagination and soon fructified in a succession of writers, especially lyric poets, comparable with the best of their contemporaries in Castile and Portugal. Rubió i Ors sounded a clarion call, and made his name, with his volume of poems *The Llobregat Piper* in 1839. Jacint Verdaguer showed the language adequate too for epic and made this similarly serve to stir a national consciousness in his *Atlàntida* (1877) and *Canigó* (1886).

Joan Maragall (1860–1911), content just to be the great poet he was, showed by looking inward instead of back that the combative period was now over and that Catalan letters had again won their place in the sun. In that victory a prominent share falls to a group of Majorcans led by Costa i Llobera and Alcovar, the former's poetry classicist in inspiration and intention, the latter's of an elegiac intensity born of personal suffering. Josep Carner, Josep Maria López-Picó, and Carles Riba may stand as later leaders of a poetic activity which speaks eloquently of the ground recovered in the course of a century.

Imaginative prose came more hesitantly to maturity, and found expression first in the realistic sketch and short story, with Emili Vilanova, Narcís Oller, and Joaquim Ruyra among the masters in a kind that has proved peculiarly acceptable to the Catalan genius. Oller went on to cultivate with equal distinction the longer vein, and heads a long list of novelists who too underwent for a spell the influence of France, and Russia, but soon reverted to the more genial peninsular conception of realism as embracing equally, and preferably, the brighter side of life. Joan Puig i Ferreter, Alfons Maseres, Carles Soldevila, and Josep Pla are among the outstanding names.

Drama played its part no less in awakening and shaping the new Catalonia, and produced in Angel Guimerà (1847–1924) a figure of European magnitude, whose sombre masterpiece *Lowlands* (1896) has been translated into a dozen languages and inspired operas in France and Germany. Santiago Rusiñol won distinction as both painter and dramatist, his plays ranging from the satirical comedy of manners to the symbolical. The stature of Ignasi Iglesias has suffered from over-preoccupation with didactic purpose in his forceful social dramas.

The disruption that seized on the Spanish literary scene with the Civil War of 1936–9, which claimed among its victims some outstanding writers and drove others into exile, to the country's permanent impoverishment, was paralleled earlier in Portugal with the long chaos of the years 1910 to 1926. No stimulus comparable to the shock of 1898 or to the advent of modernism had invited there to a reappraisal of national character and destiny or of the literary art as such. Lyric poetry continued to be the most congenial mode of expression, and poets abound, with reputations still in the making. Fernando Pessoa, António Botto, Miguel Torga are three names among many. José Régio is novelist and dramatist as well. Their impact on the outer world has still to be made.

There was no second great age of Spanish painting. The obscurity that descended on this with the death of Velázquez was not lightened for a century and a half. Goya (1746–1828), another highly original genius and again a court painter, documented the decadent entourage of Charles IV with a cynicism, and the brutalities of the French invasion with a pathos, that place him on an eminence alone. His intensity of vision had as little use for tradition as for externals, and though he handled colour in masterly fashion he preferred to draw his effects from massed light and shade, and could discard it entirely, in his 'Caprices', and be more masterly still.

The century following Goya was again undistinguished, with no name of note until Joaquín Sorolla (1863–1923), a lesser master both of design and of the dramatic use of colour. His contemporary Ignacio Zuloaga, another vigorous exponent of the Spanish scene and character, relied rather on the play of masses and shadow. Pablo Picasso (*b.* 1881) belongs to cubism and the world at large, as Salvador Dali (*b.* 1905) does to surrealism. They have left Spain, and tradition, far behind them.

In one other art modern Spain has achieved fame transcending her borders. Music has always played a prominent part in the life of the Spanish people. In its beginnings the influences were largely oriental, as in that most substantial surviving corpus from the Middle Ages, the accompaniments to Alfonso the Learned's *Songs of the Virgin Mary*. The traditional ballad was sung, not recited, and song had its integral part in the drama of the

Golden Age. Till the end of the sixteenth century the *vihuela*, forerunner of the guitar, was the most popular instrument, and the early Renaissance period boasted a notable school of *vihue-listas*, the best known perhaps, for his treatise on the instrument, Luis Milán. Luis de Victoria (*c.* 1540–*c.* 1604) was an outstanding exponent of religious music for the organ, his influence extending beyond Rome, where he composed most of his works, to Germany.

Centuries of relative eclipse followed in this sphere too, though the eighteenth-century Vicente Martín and Vicente García made a reputation at home and beyond in the Italianate opera. When, eventually, there came a rebirth of interest and accomplishment, it centred to a striking degree on the folk-music of tradition, to the recovery of which Felipe Pedrell (1841–1922) gave a life-time of inspired effort. Three composers whose names have become familiar far beyond the Peninsula testify to the brilliance of the revival. They are Isaac Albéniz (1860–1909), remembered among much else for his *Spanish Suite* and *Iberia*, Enrique Granados (1868–1916), composer notably of the *Spanish Dances* and *Goyescas*, and, the greatest, Manuel de Falla (1876–1946), who wrote chiefly for opera and the ballet (*Fleeting Life*, *Nights in the Gardens of Spain*, *The Three-Cornered Hat*).

The vitality of the Catalan renaissance was seen vividly too in the arts, and not least in architecture, in which the rest of the Peninsula has nothing of modern significance to show. Antoni Gaudí (1852–1926) initiated a determinedly original style, characterized by conical towers and an ornate profusion of external adornment, that compels attention if not always admiration. He was followed and supported by Lluis Domènech i Muntaner. Their masterpieces are Gaudí's Church of the Holy Family and Domènech's Palace of Catalan Music, both in Barcelona. In sculpture Geroni Sunyol, Manuel Oms, and Marian Benlliure all made international reputations in the late nineteenth century, as have Arístides Maillol and Carles Mani in the twentieth. Marian Fortuny (1838–74), much travelled and much influenced by Rome and Paris, was in his day the greatest name in peninsular painting, being esteemed particularly for his colour. Martí i Alsina headed a long and distinguished line of landscape painters: Vayreda, Urgell, Mir. Rusiñol, the dramatist afore-mentioned, found his inspiration preferably in gardens.

Pedrell, in addition to his yeoman services to Spanish tradi-tional music in general, as a researcher and collector of genius, was the father of modern Catalan music and musical activity and the outstanding composer of his age in Catalonia. His best-known works are two operas, *The Pyrenees* and *Celestina*, and a choral poem, *Count Arnau*. While Albéniz, Granados, and de Falla took their inspiration where they found it and are held to belong to Spain rather than to a region, it should be remembered that the first two were Catalans and the third of Catalan–Valencian descent. The artistic resurgence of Catalonia has in fact scattered its fruits far and wide. Picasso received his early training, and first displayed his powers, in Barcelona, and Dali is a Catalan.

In Portugal painting and music can show over the past 250 years a continuing record of creditable achievement rather than names of international significance. The long reign of John V (1706–50) provided much royal patronage, especially in con-nexion with the building and adornment of the palace–monastery of Mafra, Portuguese counterpart to the Escorial and the largest building in the country. Among the more notable artists, most of whom studied in Italy, were the religious painter Francisco Vieira de Matos (1699–1783) and another Francisco Vieira (1765–1805), whose canvases include alike religious, his-torical, and mythological subjects. António de Sequeira carried the Italian influence well into the nineteenth century in historical paintings and portraits. Miguel Lupi typified the eventual reaction of a group of romantics against so much academicism, finding inspiration in native themes with an appeal to the imagination and revealing in his portraits a completely honest and pene-trating realism. Silva Porto (1850–93) showed himself a delicate interpreter of the Portuguese landscape. Malhoa and Columbano carry the tale down to the twentieth century.

Musical history in Portugal is strongly linked with opera. Accompaniments in the early *cancioneiros*, compared with those of Spain, show fewer Muslim influences, a reflection of the differ-ing and much shorter course there of the reconquest. In the songs which so enliven the plays of Gil Vicente a negro element is already in evidence. Another divergent factor is the relative insignificance of balladry in Portugal. The sixteenth century saw emerge, in the intimate association of music with the tragicomedies to which the Jesuits were much given in their colleges, a type of religious opera that was to engage the interest of composers for some 200 years.

John V's patronage extended in particular measure to church music. Musicians too he sent to Rome to study, the best known of these António de Almeida, composer of court operas and serenatas, and from Italy he brought composers and executants to Portugal, among them Domenico Scarlatti. José da Silva (1705–39) composed five operas, in part witty parodies of Jesuit tragicomedy, which enjoyed great popularity in their day; he perished at the stake, a victim of the Inquisition.

This emancipation from religious tradition was completed by Sousa Carvalho, whose part proved decisive in the creation of a genuinely national vein of opera, its hey-day the closing decades of the century, its home first the royal palaces, then, from 1793, Lisbon's magnificent São Carlos opera-house. António Fonseca (1762–1830), whose operas were long popular in Italy, and Domingo Bontempo (1775–1852) carried the tradition triumphantly into the nineteenth century, until the Napoleonic invasion and the migration of the court to Brazil violently interrupted all cultural activities. Folk-music continued, and continues, to live a life of its own, the *fado* and the *modinha* its most popular current expressions. Today a group of young composers – Rui Coelho, Lopes Graça, Ivo Cruz – is still engaged in winning its laurels. Opera retains its prestige, and a recently restored São Carlos presents at least one native work every season.

Chronological Table

1035	Castile and Aragon emerge as monarchies on death of Sancho the Great of Navarre
1085	Toledo recaptured by Alfonso VI of Castile and León
1086–90	Al-Andalus reunited under Almorávides
1094–9	Cid, exiled from Castile, seizes and holds Valencia
1095	County of Portugal given as marriage dowry to daughter of Alfonso VI
1118	Saragossa retaken by Alfonso I of Aragon
c. 1130	Alfonso VII founds school of translators in Toledo through which Arabic and Jewish learning reaches western Europe
1143	Portugal recognized as sovereign kingdom by Castile and León
1146	Almohade invasion from Africa
1158–66	Founding of military orders of Calatrava, Santiago, and Alcántara
1162	Union of Aragon and Catalonia in kingdom of greater Aragon
1179	Treaty of Cazorla delimiting Castilian and Aragonese interests in reconquest
1188	Towns first given representation in Cortes, in León
1212	Christian victory at Las Navas de Tolosa, leading (1236–48) to recapture of Cordoba, Valencia, and Seville
1213	End of Catalan dominion north of Pyrenees
1229–35	Conquest of Balearic Islands by Catalonia
1230	Definitive reunion of Castile and León
1238	Emergence of Muslim kingdom of Granada
1257	Alfonso X elected Holy Roman Emperor (title renounced 1275)
1267	Cession by Castile of claim to Algarve completes territorial integration of Portugal
1282	Peter III of Aragon conquers Sicily
1291	Castilian-Aragonese treaty partitioning north Africa into spheres of interest
1310	Gibraltar taken (lost again 1333–1462)
1322–86	Catalan duchy of Athens
1369	Assassination of Peter the Cruel of Castile by Henry of Trastamar
1385	Battle of Aljubarrota secures Portugal from Castilian designs for 200 years
1386	Anglo-Portuguese alliance entered into, 'for ever'
1412	Compromise of Caspe
1415	Capture of Ceuta launches Portugal on overseas conquest
1424	Canary Islands settled by Portugal (Azores in 1445)

1443	Kingdom of Naples conquered by Alfonso V of Aragon (left to illegitimate son in 1458)
1469	Marriage of Isabella of Castile to Ferdinand of Aragon
1474	Introduction of printing to Peninsula, at Valencia
1478	Institution of Holy Office or New Inquisition in Castile (extended to Aragon 1485)
1479	Canary Islands ceded by Portugal to Spain
1487–94	Grandmasterships of Spanish military orders incorporated in crown
1488	Bartholomeu Dias rounds Cape of Good Hope
1492	End of reconquest with capture of Granada
	Expulsion of Jews from Castile and Aragon
	Columbus discovers New World ('America' from 1507)
1494	Treaty of Tordesillas delimits Spanish and Portuguese spheres of discovery and conquest (corresponding agreement for Far East in 1529)
	Ferdinand and Isabella given title of 'Catholic Monarchs' by Spanish Pope Alexander VI
1498	Vasco da Gama reaches India by the Cape
1500	Alvares Cabral makes landfall in Brazil
1502	Muslims in Castile offered choice of expulsion or conversion
1504	Naples reabsorbed by Ferdinand in crown of Aragon
1509–15	Portugal establishes naval supremacy in Red Sea and Persian Gulf
1510	Capture of Goa, thereafter seat of Portuguese viceroyalty of India
1511	Seizure of Malacca opens to Portuguese way to Indo-China and Spice Islands
1512	Spanish Navarre (under French rule since 1234) reincorporated in Spain by Ferdinand
1513	Balboa discovers Pacific Ocean
1516	Accession of Charles I, Castile and Aragon being now first united under one crown, brings Habsburg dynasty to throne of Spain
1519	Charles elected Holy Roman Emperor as Charles V
1519–22	Cortés overthrows Aztec empire and adds Mexico ('New Spain') to Spanish crown
1520–3	Revolts of *Comuneros* and *Germania*
1527	Sack of Rome by imperial troops
1531–4	Pizarro overthrows Inca empire and conquers Peru
1535	Charles captures Tunis from Turks
1536	Holy Office extended to Portugal
1539	Ignacio de Loyola founds Society of Jesus

1542   Portuguese discover Japan to Europe
1545   Discovery of silver mountain of Potosí
1545–52   Council of Trent initiates Counter-Reformation (reconvened 1562–3)
1546   Publication of first Spanish *Index Expurgatorius*
1554   Philip marries Mary Tudor
1555–8   Successive abdications of Charles, leaving Low Countries and Italian dependencies to Spain, the German empire to his brother
1561   Philip II establishes his capital in Madrid
1565   Spain takes possession of Philippines
1568–70   Rising of Moriscos in Alpujarras
1571   Don John of Austria vanquishes Turkish fleet at Lepanto
1578   Eclipse of Portuguese power and sovereignty at Alcazar-Kebir
1579   'United Provinces' of Low Countries (modern Holland) proclaim their independence (recognized by Spain in 1609)
1580   Philip incorporates Portugal and her dominions in Spanish crown
1588   Defeat in Channel of 'Invincible Armada'
1601   Philip III moves Spanish capital to Valladolid (till 1606)
1609–11   Expulsion of Moriscos from Spain
1620   Spain enters Thirty Years' War
1630–54   Dutch established in north-eastern Brazil (and, from 1641 to 1648, in Angola)
1640   Rebellion in Catalonia (not finally quelled till 1659)
          Portugal recovers independence under new Braganza dynasty
1643   Spanish defeat at Rocroi, land counterpart of rout of Armada
1655   Capture of Jamaica from Spain gives England key to Caribbean
1655–63   Loss of Ceylon and Malabar to Dutch spells eclipse of Portuguese empire in Far East
1659   Peace of the Pyrenees ends 24 years of war with France
1661   Tangier and Bombay ceded by Portugal to England as part of marriage dowry of Catherine of Braganza
1665   Battle of Montesclaros confirms Portuguese independence, leaving Spain Ceuta as solitary reminder of her sixty years' domination
1699   First consignment of Brazilian gold reaches Lisbon
1700   Charles II wills Spanish crown to a Bourbon, grandson of Louis XIV
1702–13   Spain a battlefield for international War of Spanish Succession

1703	Portugal signs Methuen Treaty with Great Britain
1704	Gibraltar passes under British sovereignty
1713	By Treaty of Utrecht Spain forfeits Flanders and Milan, last relics of Habsburg imperial connexion, and Naples
1714	Philip V suppresses Catalan fueros
1733	First 'Family Compact' between France and Spain (second in 1743, third in 1761)
1749	Pope confers title of 'Most Faithful' on Portuguese monarch
1755	Lisbon earthquake, bringing Pombal to power
1759	Jesuits expelled from Portugal (from Spain in 1767)
1805	Spanish naval power all but destroyed at Trafalgar
1807	Portuguese regent and court sail for Brazil as Napoleon's troops enter Lisbon
1808	Charles IV of Spain abdicates to Ferdinand VII and both are lured to France
	Madrid rising of *dos de mayo* against French occupation forces marks beginning of Peninsular War (over for Portugal in 1811, for Spain in 1814)
1810	Overthrow of Spanish authority in Buenos Aires, signal for wars of emancipation that by 1826 had triumphed everywhere on mainland of Spanish America
1812	Constitution of Cadiz, marking birth of liberalism and anti-clericalism in Peninsula
1814	Ferdinand VII returns to Spanish throne and abolishes constitution
1815	Brazil declared a kingdom (in 1822 an independent empire, under Portuguese prince)
1820	First pronunciamiento brings Spanish army into politics
1822	Portuguese constitution proclaimed, closely modelled on that of Cadiz
1823	French army enters Spain to help Ferdinand restore absolutism
	An indirect consequence, enunciation by United States of Monroe doctrine
1833–9	First Carlist War
1846	The 'Spanish Marriages' (costing Louis Philippe the French throne in 1848)
1868	Abdication of Isabella II of Spain (search for a king to replace her leading to Franco-Prussian War)
1871–3	Amadeo of Savoy on Spanish throne
1872–6	Second Carlist War
1873–4	First Spanish republic, coinciding with war in Cuba
1874	Bourbon restoration under Alfonso XII

1877–86 Portugal turns to expansion and 'effective occupation' of her African colonies

1889 Brazil proclaimed republic

1890 British ultimatum to Portugal demanding evacuation of territories linking Angola to Mozambique

1898 Spanish-American War over Cuba marks for Spain, with loss of Cuba, Puerto Rico, and Philippines, the end of empire

1910 Abandonment of throne by Manuel ushers in Portuguese republic

1912 Spanish protectorate established over north-west Morocco

1916 Portugal enters First World War

1923–30 Dictatorship of Primo de Rivera in Spain

1926 Portuguese republic overthrown by army coup

1928 Salazar as finance minister (premier from 1932) assumes direction of Portuguese 'New State'

1931 Fall of Alfonso XIII, followed by second Spanish republic

1936–9 Spanish Civil War, ending with victory of 'Nationalists' under Franco

1942 Spain and Portugal form 'Iberian Bloc'

1945 Falangist Spain branded at Potsdam as unfit to associate with United Nations (admitted to membership in 1955)

1947 Spain declared a kingdom, with Franco as regent

1953 Spain signs agreement with United States, receiving economic aid in return for defence bases

1956 Moroccan independence ends Spanish protectorate

Bibliographical Note

For specialist bibliographical indications the student may consult:

B. Sánchez Alonso. *Fuentes de la historia española e hispano-americana.* 3rd edition. 3 vols. Madrid, 1952

J. Vicens Vives (ed.). *Bibliografía histórica de España e Hispano-américa.* Vol. I (for 1953–4). Barcelona, 1955, and biennially thereafter

R. A. Humphreys. *Latin American History. A Guide to the Literature in English.* London, 1958

and for ready reference:

Diccionario de Historia de España. 2 vols. Madrid, 1952

M. R. Martin and G. H. Lovett. *An Encyclopedia of Latin American History.* New York, 1956

The following brief reading list of authoritative works, most of which have detailed bibliographies, is ordered under (A) general histories in Spanish and Portuguese, (B) general surveys in English, and (C) studies in English on particular themes and periods:

(A)

A. Ballesteros y Beretta. *Historia de España y su influencia en la historia universal.* 2nd edition. 12 vols. Barcelona, 1943–8

R. Menéndez Pidal (ed.). *Historia de España.* In progress. Madrid, 1935–

J. Petit (ed.). *Historia de la cultura española.* 7 vols. Barcelona, 1951–7

P. Aguado Bleyde. *Manual de historia de España.* 6th edition. 3 vols. Madrid, 1954–6

J. Vicens Vives (ed.). *Historia social y económica de España y América.* In progress. Barcelona, 1957–

A. Ballesteros (ed.). *Historia de América y de los pueblos americanos.* In progress. Barcelona, 1940–

F. de Almeida. *História de Portugal.* 6 vols. Coimbra, 1922–7

D. Peres (ed.). *História de Portugal.* 8 vols. Barcelos, 1928–38

J. Ameal. *História de Portugal.* 2nd edition. Oporto, 1942

História da expansão portuguesa no mundo. 2 vols. Lisbon, 1937–42

C. Malheiro Dias (ed.). *História da colonização portuguesa do Brasil.* 3 vols. Oporto, 1921–4

(B)

R. Altamira. *A History of Spanish Civilization*. London, 1930

R. Altamira. *A History of Spain*. New York, 1949

J. P. de Oliveira Martins. *A History of Iberian Civilization*. London, 1930.

L. Bertrand and C. Petrie. *The History of Spain*. 2nd edition. London, 1952

S. de Madariaga. *Spain. A Modern History*. 3rd edition. New York, 1958

E. A. Peers (ed.). *Spain. A Companion to Spanish Studies*. 3rd edition. London, 1956

E. A. Peers. *Catalonia Infelix*. London, 1937

H. J. Chaytor. *A History of Aragon and Catalonia*. London, 1933

H. V. Livermore. *A History of Portugal*. Cambridge, 1947

H. V. Livermore (ed.). *Portugal and Brazil*. Oxford, 1953

H. Herring. *A History of Latin America*. London, 1956

(C)

A. Castro. *The Structure of Spanish History*. Princeton, 1954

R. Menéndez Pidal. *The Cid and His Spain*. London, 1934

A. S. Turberville. *The Spanish Inquisition*. London, 1932

R. Trevor Davies. *The Golden Century of Spain, 1501–1621*. 2nd impression. London, 1954

M. A. S. Hume. *Spain: Its Greatness and Decay (1479–1788)*. 3rd edition. Cambridge, 1913

F. A. Kirkpatrick. *The Spanish Conquistadores*. 2nd edition. London, 1947

R. B. Merriman. *The Rise of the Spanish Empire in the Old World and the New*. 3 vols. New York, 1918–25

S. de Madariaga. *The Rise and Fall of the Spanish American Empire*. 2 vols. London, 1947

R. Herr. *The Eighteenth-Century Revolution in Spain*. London, 1958

H. B. Clarke. *Modern Spain, 1815–1898*. Cambridge, 1906

A. Ramos Oliveira. *Politics, Economics and Men of Modern Spain, 1808–1946.* London, 1946

G. Brenan. *The Spanish Labyrinth*. 2nd edition. Cambridge, 1950

E. A. Peers. *The Spanish Tragedy, 1930–1936*. London, 1936

E. Prestage. *The Portuguese Pioneers*. London, 1933

M. Cheke. *Dictator of Portugal. A Life of Pombal*. London, 1938

V. de Bragança-Cunha. *Revolutionary Portugal, 1910–1936*. London, 1937

Index

PENGUINEWS *AND* PENGUINS IN PRINT

Every month we issue an illustrated magazine, *Penguinews*. It's a lively guide to all the latest Penguins, Pelicans and Puffins, and always contains an article on a major Penguin author, plus other features of contemporary interest.

Penguinews is supplemented by *Penguins in Print*, a complete list of all the available Penguin titles – there are now over four thousand!

The cost is no more than the postage; so why not write for a free copy of this month's *Penguinews*? And if you'd like both publications sent for a year, just send us a cheque or a postal order for 30p (if you live in the United Kingdom) or 60p (if you live elsewhere), and we'll put you on our mailing list.

Dept EP, Penguin Books Ltd,
Harmondsworth, Middlesex

Note: *Penguinews* and *Penguins in Print* are not available in the U.S.A. or Canada *a Penguin Classic*

CAMOENS

THE LUSIADS

Translated by William C. Atkinson

The Lusiads is the national epic of Portugal. Employing *The Aeneid* for a model and the whole divine machinery of Olympus, Camoens (*c.* 1524–80) celebrates in the poem the ten-month voyage by which Vasco da Gama opened the seaway to India. In passing he recites the heroic history of the Portuguese nation and its feats against Spain and the Moors. Certainly the fifteenth and sixteenth centuries were a time for pride: a country of little more than a million inhabitants had carried its flag and its faith across the world from Brazil to Japan to establish the first European seaborne empire.